BRITAIN IN WORLD AFFAIRS

BRITAIN IN
WORLD AFFAIRS

*The Fluctuation in Power and
Influence from Henry VIII to Elizabeth II*

by

Lord William Strang

FREDERICK A. PRAEGER, *Publisher*

New York

BOOKS THAT MATTER

Published in the United States of America in 1961
by Frederick A. Praeger, Inc., Publisher
64 University Place, New York 3, N.Y.

Library of Congress Catalog Card Number: 61-10747

BRITAIN IN WORLD AFFAIRS
is published in two editions:

A Praeger Paperback (PPS-49)
A clothbound edition

Manufactured in the United States of America

To
JEAN
COLIN, BARBARA
and
CAROLINE JANE

Contents

Acknowledgements

IN the writing of this book I have been heavily indebted to Sir Llewellyn Woodward for constant encouragement as the work went on, for early advice on sources, and for his kindly office in reading and annotating my draft and discussing it with me. Sir John Wheeler-Bennett also read the draft and gave me the benefit of his ripe judgment upon it. To him and to Sir John Neale, who looked at the earlier chapters for me, I offer best thanks. At a later stage Professor W. N. Medlicott most generously undertook the task of reading the script in its revised form. I am deeply in his debt for a wealth of illuminating comment of which I have been happy to take advantage. Among the many calls upon him, Alan Bullock kindly found time to read the proofs. I make acknowledgement to these historians, so eminent in their profession, out of a profound sense of gratitude for friendly support so unstintingly afforded, and in no way to impute any shadow of responsibility, which remains mine alone.

To my daughter Jean I am much beholden for the long patience and skill with which she made the first typed copies from my heavily corrected hand-written draft. Thanks are also due to Mrs. K. M. Richardson and to Mrs. K. G. Gowing for their care in putting the revised version into well-typed order.

PREFACE

THE theme of this book—our country's place in the world—is one which has exercised my mind from my youth up. I have used some of the leisure afforded by recent years of retirement in trying to answer for the benefit of the general reader some of the questions which I have put to myself. This is a temerarious enterprise on the part of one who is not a professional historian. It may, however, be some compensation for this that, in its later chapters, the book deals with events of which I have personal knowledge and in which I played some professional part; and that, in general, it is illustrated by judgments which are sometimes coloured by personal observation of the shifts by which statesmen reach their major decisions in the handling of foreign affairs.

Of course, I have relied chiefly on secondary and little on original sources. Some of the works which I have consulted are mentioned in the footnotes. Many others to which I am no less indebted have not been quoted and therefore pass unnoted. I could wish that I had read more—the books that are still on my list unread, and the sources that still remain unconsulted, would take years to absorb. But as time passes, the moment comes to take the plunge and to deliver oneself for better or for worse.

A word may be said about the subtitle of the book. This suggests that there is a distinction between power and influence. It would hardly be profitable for present purposes to try to define and to distinguish them very closely. Broadly speaking, power is here taken to mean the capacity to coerce, based largely upon the possession of material strength, military or economic. Influence is the capacity to persuade, based in some measure, sometimes in great measure, but certainly not necessarily, upon the possession of power. Together, they mean the capacity of a government to get its own way in international affairs. Power, whether immediately available or latent, can beget influence but cannot ensure it. Influence need not be proportionate to power. Political sagacity and the exercise of diplomacy, the skill of manœuvre, have a great part to play. Here there is no

13

regular progress, no steady evolution to record. Clearly, our power and influence today are not of the same order as they were, say, in the generation after Waterloo. If our influence in the present era is not so pre-eminent as it was when Castlereagh and Canning and Palmerston held the office of Foreign Secretary, the reason must be sought not only in the surpassing skill of these three practitioners of diplomacy, or in developments in the character of armaments, or in the decline in our position in the hierarchy of power, but also in the circumstance, common to other governments as well as to ourselves, that the liberty of action of sovereign states is today more circumscribed by the rules and obligations of regional and world-wide international communities.

As the subtitle again suggests, I have been more interested in the fluctuation in our power and influence over the centuries, and in the predicaments which have successively faced our statesmen, than in an attempt to identify and measure the forces which may or may not have determined the course of history. As between the deliberate acts of governments and the supposedly inevitable procession of events as decisive factors in the unfolding story, I cannot dismiss the former as readily as some historians have tended to do, or discount the effect of the exercise of human will, the interaction of human beings and the play of accident.

Even in assessing the considerations which have governed the decisions of ministers, one must have a doubt. If I may speak from experience, I would say that, as a professional adviser, one may know in some measure what information and arguments and advice a Foreign Secretary has before him; one may guess with some confidence some of the grounds, political or personal, which will have weighed with him in reaching his decision. Yet, however well one knows him, the last conclusive factor in the decision may still elude one. There may be the unrecorded and undisclosed conversation, or the well-concealed liking or antipathy. In this respect, with the wealth of information which in these days eventually comes to light, the historian may indeed be in a better position than was the contemporary adviser to follow the mental processes of statesmen. But even so, it is in the power of the reconstructive imagination that the genius of a historian will lie.

But there is more than this. We know from experience that most of the more important decisions in foreign policy represent a choice from among two or more conceivable courses, not one of which is

Preface

perfect, and each of which offers a balance of advantage and disadvantage. In making their choices, statesmen have frequently to come to as wise a judgment as they can upon imperfect information and with too little time to think—a skill which is often akin to guesswork and which is not to be taught by experience alone. The problem is to choose the most advantageous course according to the criterion which is held to be valid for the occasion. When we contemplate a past decision, we cannot judge or evaluate it with any near approach to accuracy unless we can reconstruct the various alternative courses from among which it was the favoured choice, and unless we can identify the factual basis and the political criterion in virtue of which the choice was made. This is usually difficult and often impossible to do. I make no claim in this book to have pursued my themes so far. But this reflection may stand as a warning against confidently asserting, as we are so often tempted to do, that if only such and such a course had been followed on such and such an occasion, instead of the course which was actually chosen, then such and such a problem would have been solved in such and such a way. We really cannot know. The consequences, immediate or remote, of decisions that are taken are, thanks to the crowding in of events, not to be surely or even approximately predicted: how much less so the consequences of decisions which, for lack of sufficient grounds to commend them, were not thought worthy to be taken.

One of my general conclusions is that it was in the generation or so after Waterloo that our influence in the world was at its height; that is to say, it was during that period that we most successfully made our views prevail in the field of international affairs. Other conclusions are that the measure of our pre-eminence in the second half of the nineteenth century has been much over-estimated, and that the degree of our so-called isolationism in the same period, except in the last few years of the century, has usually been over-stated. I also think that too gloomy a view has too often been taken of our international standing in the years since 1945.

As period has followed period, I have tried to assess our relative standing among the nations. This is a tricky business, and historians who have sought to come to this kind of judgment about ourselves and about others have reached an astonishing variety of opinions. As an admonition to observe due caution, and indeed as an injunction to preserve a proper sense of humility, I venture to quote some of them.

15

Preface

Thus, Dr Toynbee says: 'Britain had, indeed, been the arbiter of Europe from before the close of the War of the Spanish Succession till after the close of the Napoleonic Wars. But, in the course of the hundred years, 1815–1914, the balance of power in Europe and in the world had been turned against Britain by the industrialization of Germany and the United States.'[1]

There are two points here. First, if Toynbee means by the word 'arbiter' one who can dictate, or one who has sole control, and not merely the power holding the balance, it seems to me to be hardly true to say that Britain had been the arbiter of Europe from somewhat before 1713 to somewhat after 1815. It would be more correct to say that she had held that position intermittently for short periods; during part of the War of the Spanish Succession and a little after, during part of the Seven Years War and a little after, and during the latter part of the Napoleonic War and after. This period, and especially from 1741 onwards, was the period of the duel between Great Britain and France, either for overseas Empire or for the future of Europe. Sometimes one had the upper hand, sometimes the other. It would surely be misleading to suggest that Great Britain was the arbiter of Europe, in almost any sense of the word, in, say, the time of Walpole or in the time of Bute or of Lord North or even of the Younger Pitt—the Napoleonic War did not begin to turn decisively in our favour until after Pitt was dead; indeed, within a year or two of his death, after Tilsit, we touched our lowest depth.

Secondly, to date the beginning of the shift in the balance of power and of the decline in our position from as early as 1815 is to anticipate the course of events. Indeed, it was rather in the period from 1815 till about the middle of the century that we reached our most commanding position in Europe. The decline did not set in until the 1850s or 1860s and it did not become marked until the 1870s, with the Prussian victory over France, the growing industrialization of Germany and the massive industrial revolution in the United States dating from about 1880. Far more just, I would think, is the verdict of David Thomson: 'The years around the middle of the nineteenth century mark the climax of British power, prestige, and prosperity.'[2]

Contrast with this the directly conflicting judgment of R. C. K.

[1] *The Eve of War, 1939*, Royal Institute of International Affairs, Oxford University Press, 1958, p. 47.
[2] *England in the Nineteenth Century*, Penguin Books, Harmondsworth, 1950, p. 222.

Preface

Ensor when speaking of the position of France. The war of 1870, he says, 'transferred from France to Germany the political ascendancy over Europe, which the former, with only passing interruptions, had exercised for well beyond two centuries.'[3] This, in a very broad sense, may be true; but the interruptions were considerable. There were times when no single power held the ascendancy in Europe, and times during the two centuries between 1670 and 1870 when Great Britain or Russia or Austria could rival France. It could not be said, for example, that France was the arbiter of Europe during the Regency in the early eighteenth century, or during the period of the Bourbon Restoration or of the Orleanist Monarchy in the nineteenth. However that may be, both judgments cannot be correct. Great Britain could not be the arbiter of Europe and France hold political ascendancy there at the same time.

There is, indeed, a third candidate for that role, namely Austria. David Thomson remarks that 'international order after 1815 had rested formally on the "concert of Europe" and more basically upon the continental hegemony of Austria maintained through the "system" of Metternich.'[4]

Amid such conflict of professional opinion, what is the amateur to say?

One of the threads running through this discourse is a consideration of the purpose, mode of operation and effect of the balance of power and the concert of Europe.

The balance of power and the concert of Europe were not alternative or mutually exclusive conceptions. They could be complementary methods of adjusting international relationships, where the objectives of the balance of power would be served by the operations of the concert of Europe.

The balance of power is not, as some political scientists hold it to be, an automatic, self-operating corrective mechanism, but a relative disposition of forces which statesmen try to establish and to maintain. It could be one of a number of things. First, it could be an equilibrium of satisfied states, each being recognized as having the right to a status in the hierarchy commensurate with its population and other resources, the equilibrium being maintained, in the event of a substantial accretion of strength by one power, through the award of appropriate compensation to each of the others.

[3] *England, 1870–1914*, The Oxford History of England, 1936, p. xix.
[4] *Europe since Napoleon*, Longmans, London, 1957, p. 321.

B

Secondly, it could be a system in which, in the event of an attempt by one power to establish its ascendancy, each of the others, severally or preferably jointly, would have liberty, or preferably the obligation, to re-establish the equilibrium by force; also, it could be a combination of victors to maintain their ascendancy over the vanquished. Thirdly, it could be the building up of confronting accumulations of power by two opposing groups of states, on the basis of formal treaties of mutual assistance, jointly or severally concluded. Here, the objective would not be so much a balance in the sense of an equilibrium of forces as a balance in the sense of a surplus on one side.

The working of the first two systems could be, and was usually, combined with the operation of an international concert. The third could not. The first system was most exactly applied in periods when monarchs conducted their own foreign policies and wars were polite affairs, at any rate for the directing combatants. It was a matter of diplomacy rather than of war. The second system was more often than not called into operation when the balance had, through inertia or negligence, been allowed to be destroyed by an ambitious power, and when only war could effectively restore it. The third system—the creation of what would be hoped by each side to be a superior concentration of power—began to be applied in a rudimentary way towards the end of the nineteenth century, after the conclusion of the Franco-Russian Alliance. It has received its most perfect expression in our own day, when the accumulation of nuclear weapons by the western and eastern powers has created an equilibrium of impotence, an equality of incapacity, a balance of terror, which has, we may hope, removed all-out nuclear war from the future calendar of history.

In seeking to understand and to explain the actions of statesmen, there are some pitfalls to avoid.

One cause of error is to assume that statesmen have a free hand to do as they will, when in truth they so often have to act in compelling situations which they have inherited and under pressure of circumstances which they cannot control. However much they may sometimes seem to be guilty of miscalculation, or of muddle or even of plain folly, it is wiser to start from the assumption that, in spite of appearances, there was some rational basis for their action. Not only so, but statesmen who conduct the affairs of great nations can normally be expected to speak and act with a sense of their responsibilities, upon a consideration of the best advice they can muster, and on the strength of the best judgment they can command, both as to the merits of the course which they are minded to pursue, and as to the extent of the support which it is likely to attract. In international disputes, their differences will for the most part derive from opposing political philosophies or from divergent national interests which it will be the business of the chronicler to elucidate.

A second error is, as Sir Llewellyn Woodward once said, to attribute to actors on the stage of history a capacity to pierce the future which men do not possess, and to condemn them if they do not shape their courses accordingly. 'We, who do not know tomorrow, assume that the men of yesterday knew today and that every sower can foresee every harvest.'[5]

Finally, it is well to recognize the limits of human endeavour; to realize that the business of government is not an academic exercise; to reconcile oneself to the fact that there are no neat and final solutions, that international affairs are a fabric without much of a pattern, and that diplomacy is most often, as von Moltke said of strategy, a succession of expedients; to suspect that bold initiatives, imaginative gestures, stirring leads and elaborate blueprints of policy, so beloved of those who are free of the responsibilities of government, are seldom of the stuff of practical statesmanship in international relations; and to remind oneself that men in the past, strive as they might for consistency, have been apt to muddle through as we may find ourselves doing today, moving at the best from one tacit, unavowed agreement to the next, in face of a range of insoluble problems, under the chastening and saving compulsion of a balance of terror.

In these times it is seldom possible to plan a foreign policy very far ahead except on the broadest lines, and it is not often possible to plan its execution except in the shortest term. Broad decisions of foreign policy for long-term application are usually few in number. During and after the War, perhaps three such were taken by the British government: the decision to join the United Nations, the decision to become a party to the North Atlantic Treaty in recognition of the Soviet menace, and the decision not to join an integrated, supra-national European community. The first of these decisions was taken without question; the second with very little

[5] *Great Britain and the German Navy*, Clarendon Press, Oxford, 1935, p. 17.

question; the third after some question but against no really substantial opposition.[6] But these broad decisions, though they set a general course, do not determine a line of action on each of the problems that press successively upon the Foreign Secretary for decision every day of his life. The foreign situation is in constant flux in which the interests and demands of eighty or so sovereign states contend for satisfaction. Every issue that arises has to be looked at in the light of, at any rate, some part of the universal kaleidoscope as it may at the moment appear to present itself. One is fortunate if one can score minor successes; but the essential is to avoid the greater, perhaps irreparable, errors. This, for most of our history, we have been able to do. Since 1066, we have suffered no major disaster, nothing comparable to what then ensued, namely the 'partition of England among a foreign aristocracy organized for war' (Professor F. M. Stenton). Disasters have repeatedly threatened over the centuries and most recently a bare twenty years ago. It is the first care of our foreign policy to guard against another.

Stonesfield   STRANG.
May 1960.

---

[6] There were also the decisions to grant independence to dependent territories, and to manufacture nuclear weapons; but these are not primarily matters of foreign policy.

Sunt enim Scientiae iustar pyramidum,
quibus Historia et Experientia tanquam
basis unica substernuntur

For knowledges are as pyramids,
whereof history and experience are the
basis
> Bacon, *De Augmentis Scientiarum*

Nous ne pouvons acquérir de connaissance
que par la voie de la comparaison
> Buffon

Without contrast there cannot be understanding
> Peter Laslett

Part I

INTRODUCTORY: THE ROAD TO POWER

CHAPTER I

England, France and the Empire: Henry VIII

Henry VIII, in the earlier golden years of his reign, seems to have taken a simple and straightforward view of the balance of power, that device for the regulation of international relations which was to assume a variety of forms of no little complexity both in doctrine and in practice in the period between his age and our own. His maxim was *Cui adhaereo praeest*: The one whom I support will get the upper hand.[1]

Bacon said of him a century later in a memorandum on 'Considerations Touching a War with Spain' dedicated to Prince Charles in 1624: 'It is so memorable, as it is yet as fresh as if it were done yesterday, how that triumvirate of kings, Henry the eighth of England, Francis the first of France, and Charles the fifth emperor and king of Spain, were in their times so provident, as scarce a palm of ground could be gotten by either of the three, but that the other two would be sure to do their best to set the balance of Europe upright again.' This is perhaps to read the conceptions of the seventeenth century into the practices of the sixteenth.

Henry, in his early years, had to deal with three old men: his father-in-law Ferdinand of Aragon, his brother-in-law Louis XII of France, and the Emperor Maximilian. Later he became one of a triumvirate of youthful monarchs. The other two were the brilliant and ambitious Francis I, from 1515 King of France, and the less engaging Charles V, from 1516 King of Spain, and after 1519 Holy Roman Emperor. Francis and Charles were not unfairly matched, though Charles was potentially the stronger, having inherited the Burgundian domains in the Netherlands; Spain with its dependencies

[1] Quoted in Charles Dupuis, *Le Principe d'Équilibre et le Concert Européen*, Paris, 1909, p. 17.

25

in Italy and the Indies; and the territories of Austria. They were engaged in that rivalry for power in the Low Countries, Italy and Germany, first of Habsburg and Valois, and then of Habsburg and Bourbon, which was to colour continental politics for three centuries.

In manœuvring between Francis and Charles, Henry was much the weakest of the three. Spain alone had twice the population and France five times the population of England and Wales. But Henry thought that he had power enough to turn the scale and to reap a national advantage. In practice he did not base his policy on careful calculations of resources or upon the precepts of the balance of power. He usually took sides against France. France was still the traditional enemy, allied to Scotland, bent on the recapture of Calais, and, because of propinquity, potentially dangerous. England had had a tradition of alliance with Burgundy, whose territory in the Low Countries now formed part of the Spanish domain, including the port of Antwerp, through which by far the greater part of English export trade, chiefly in woollen cloth, was conducted. To make war against Charles would risk disruption of our commerce. The Flemings felt the same, and Charles was not unresponsive to their views. The makers of English policy, then and both earlier and later, could at a pinch tolerate Spain, or more readily, Austria, in the Low Countries, if only because, by virtue of geography, England lay across the sea communications between Spain and her dependency and could sever them if need be, and because, when Austria succeeded to the Spanish Netherlands in 1713, Austria was not, and was not in future to be, a serious danger. She was, in fact, usually our ally. France, possessing the possibility of geographical continuity, was potentially, and in time became in very deed, a grave menace. Down to the time of Palmerston and Gladstone, in fact until after the Franco-Prussian War of 1870, when this danger ceased to trouble us so much, the need to keep France out of the Low Countries continued to be an inescapable objective of British policy.

A sceptical critic might inquire why, if we had perforce to bear with the French at Brest, Cherbourg and Havre, we could not bear with them at Antwerp also. He might speculate whether our assumptions in this matter, which might have been valid in certain historical contexts (and more particularly in earlier times when the great bulk of our foreign trade had been channelled through Antwerp), had not hardened into a dogma, accepted without question or examination by successive framers of British policy.

There are two answers to this doubt. The first rests upon a fact of geography. Between Ushant and the Scheldt there was on the French side of the Channel, in the days of sail, no natural haven affording a secure anchorage for the greater ships of war. With the prevailing westerly winds, a French fleet leaving Brest might risk being driven up channel with no harbour of refuge. Control of the Low Countries would give France an inestimably valuable naval *point d'appui*. Secondly, there is the consideration that, since one of the necessary concomitants of English (and British) foreign policy in Europe over the centuries down to the present day has been the transport of armed men in ships across the narrow seas, it has seemed essential to us to have a secure and friendly shore on which to disembark them. As France was for so long—with very brief intervals until near the close of the nineteenth century—regarded as the national enemy, that shore had to be denied to France. If it was in the hands of Spain, when Spain was the national enemy, this had to be endured. But Spain was preferable to France: we could hamper Spanish communications and send forces to help the Dutch insurgents. If neither France nor Spain was there, it would not matter much to us whether the Low Countries, or part of them, were in the hands of a normally friendly power like Austria, or whether they were made into small independent states like Belgium and Holland, one or both of whom would be in special relations with ourselves.

In his first two wars (1512–14 and 1522–25), Henry was thus, not unexpectedly, allied successively with the Emperors Maximilian and Charles against France, the weaker of the two powers. In 1513, his *annus mirabilis*, he chased the French at Guinegate and took Thérouanne and Tournay, while his army under Surrey overcame the invading Scots at Flodden. Francis himself was captured at Pavia in 1525. In this latter campaign Henry did little to help Charles, and got nothing out of the peace. The time was past when, as in the years 1519–21, Wolsey had been 'the arbiter of Christendom'. If, in his third war (1528–29), Henry allied himself with France against the Emperor, this had little to do with the balance of power and much to do with the personal ambitions of Wolsey. In spite of his boast, Henry's intervention did not give France the upper hand. He could contribute a navy and a small though not negligible expeditionary force, but these could not do anything to affect the issue

27

of the wars among the Italian states where Charles and Francis were at grips. The English, in fact, refused to fight, since fighting would mean interrupting trade with Antwerp. The balance of power was disrupted. Charles was triumphant over France, though he still had the militant Lutherans on his doorstep and the Turks in the Mediterranean and at the approaches to Vienna.

Henry's fourth war (1543–46), this time against France, was also needlessly adventurous. France and the Emperor were again in dispute over Italy. Armed and in a strong diplomatic position, England was for the present secure. The Pope had thundered against Henry, but since the Catholic states still paid little heed, the Pope was impotent. Henry had only to keep quiet in order to be *tertius gaudens*, as his father or his daughter Elizabeth would most probably have done. But having designs on the crown of Scotland and being determined to prevent the marriage of Mary, Queen of Scots, to a French prince, he made war on Scotland and joined Charles in war against France. Charles made peace first and left Henry to face Francis alone. From this time onwards, relations between England and Spain were to become increasingly sour. In the summer of 1545, Francis made an unsuccessful attempt at invasion at Portsmouth. According to J. A. Williamson, we had had to face no such comparable threat since the Norman Conquest, and our deliverance by Henry's navy in 1545 is to be compared with our escapes in 1588, 1805, and 1940.[2]

Out of these wars, on the whole so irresponsibly entered into—irresponsible because England had not been in danger, since both Charles and Francis preferred her help to her destruction, and because she had nothing substantial to fight for that was within her limited means to secure—there came one great evil and, by a side wind, one great benefit. Henry had inherited from his prudent and business-like father a bursting treasury and a flourishing national economy; it was indeed the wealth of the English crown, so long as it lasted, that gave Henry his authority in Europe. He left to his successors a country with desperately straitened finances, a bankrupt treasury, a debased currency and the beginnings of a serious inflation,[3] combined, it should be said, with a booming export trade in cloth.

[2] *The English Channel*, Collins, London, 1959, pp. 175–78.
[3] The inflation in Henry's time was not altogether Henry's fault. It was a universal phenomenon, due to the influx of silver from Spanish America.

England, France and the Empire: Henry VIII

On the other hand, Henry, by his own personal initiative, gave England her first battle-fleet. He was a pioneer in modern naval warfare. It was his ships that in 1545 first fired the English broadside. It is true that Henry's ships—there were ninety of them—were clumsy to handle, that they did not have much fighting to do, that they did not fight very well, and that the broadsides were rather bungled; but they did, as never before, have heavy guns mounted low down on the cargo deck, firing through port-holes opened in the side, designed to strike the enemy hulls and not merely to sweep the enemy decks.

Prices in England, compositely calculated, which were at 100 in the first decade of the fourteenth century, and no more than 127 nearly two hundred years later, had risen to 210 in the 1530s and to 287 in the 1540s. In Mary's and Elizabeth's reigns they rose faster still. In the 1550s they were 464 and in Elizabeth's last years, at the turn of the century, 700. (Sir John Clapham, *A Concise Economic History of Britain from the Earliest Times to 1750*, Cambridge, 1949, pp. 186–87.)

CHAPTER II

The Power of Spain: Elizabeth I

There is a story, judged by historians to be apocryphal, of an interview at Dover in 1601 between Queen Elizabeth I and Sully, the enlightened minister of Henry IV of France, in which, according to Sully's *Memoirs*, the Queen, in harmony with Sully's own 'Grand Design', said that she thought that the best thing to do would be to divide Europe into a number of approximately equal states. If this were indeed Elizabeth's thought, her aspiration for a settled peace in Europe based on the perfect balance would have been born of the bitter experience of a long reign of which the greater part was spent in desperate shifts to defend her country against the active hostility of the Counter-Reformation in Roman Catholic Europe, and in particular against the inordinate power and ambitions of Spain.

By the end of her reign in 1603 her main objective had been achieved. In the cold war between Protestants and Roman Catholics she had manœuvred successfully between her own contumacious and totalitarian-minded but most loyal Puritans, and the dissident section of her own Roman Catholics, owing allegiance outside the realm. She had managed to survive for seventy years and to reign for forty-five, in spite of every threat to her life. She had made a religious settlement for an established church which had gained a greater measure of acceptance among her subjects than any other could have done, and which survives substantially to this day. She had reformed the currency and relieved some of the worst distresses which the great inflation had brought upon the poor, though plague and famine troubled the latest of her years. She had both responded to, and inspired, the growing national consciousness of her subjects, attracting their devoted loyalty to the throne and to her own person, though there were, under the surface, signs of ominous rifts in the relations between sovereign and the Puritan element in Parliament. She had in 1588 warded off the supreme attempt of Spain to conquer her kingdom; and though she was to be at war with Spain for fifteen years from the defeat of the Armada until the end of her reign—a war which she neither lost nor won—the weight of the threat from Spain had by that time been lifted. Finally, by merely surviving, and with a measure of good luck, Elizabeth had been able to secure that, on her death, the crown should pass without disturbance to a Protestant successor, the first of the Stuart line that was to bring great evil upon us and, had it been abler, might have brought greater evil still. In her speech, as a young woman, to her first Parliament in 1559, she had said: 'What credit my assurance may have with you I cannot tell, but what credit it shall deserve to have the sequel shall declare.'

Throughout her life, she venerated the memory and admired the example of her father. She was visibly gratified when, during her coronation procession, a bystander called out: 'Remember old King Henry the Eighth.' For all that, she was as much the granddaughter of Henry VII as Henry VIII's daughter, if not more so. She had her father's habit of command, but combined it with her grandfather's prudence and a political genius which was quite her own. It has been said of Elizabeth that she displayed with a singular perseverance for twenty-six years in the earlier part of her reign the talent for letting things alone, combined with energy when energy is called for, which is perhaps the most indispensable attribute of a statesman. This quality of wise parsimony in action will be found again in William III, who exercised it with equal success in another grave crisis in our international life. Whatever the seamen and the poets may have thought—or those who made fortunes out of the inflation—the spacious days of great Elizabeth are more spacious to us in retrospect than they were to the statesmen and administrators who had the responsibility of living through them. William Cecil, Elizabeth's Secretary, later Lord Burghley, in his 'Short Memorial of the State of the Realm' written in 1569 at a crisis in Elizabeth's affairs, lamented that against the existing combination of dangers, he found England without friends and faced with many internal weaknesses —lack of faith, lack of money, lack of munitions of war and lack of martial spirit.[1]

[1] Conyers Read, *Mr. Secretary Cecil and Queen Elizabeth*, Jonathan Cape, London, 1955, p. 437.

Introductory: The Road to Power

When Elizabeth succeeded to the throne at the age of 25 in 1558, on the death of her sister Mary, she inherited a heavy national debt, a small, decayed and unseaworthy fleet, and an unpopular war with France, forced upon the country by Mary and her husband, Philip II, King of Spain, the son of Charles V, who had married her in order to bring England into the imperialist bloc. Within a few months of her accession, she faced one of the supreme tests of her reign. In 1559, France and Spain made peace at Cateau-Cambrésis. Elizabeth made peace too, having to pledge herself to non-intervention in France and Scotland. With the two great rival powers of Europe for once in amity—like Napoleon and Alexander I at Tilsit in 1807 and like Stalin and Hitler in 1939—their opponents could expect the worst. Since the Pope was determined on the extirpation of heresy, the outlook for Elizabeth's small state would be grim if she repudiated the Papal supremacy. This, as Henry VIII's daughter, she felt in loyalty bound to do. France was the more immediate danger. Mary Stuart, Queen of Scots, had married the Dauphin in 1558; and on the death of Mary Tudor in that year, the King of France, Henry II, had proclaimed Mary Stuart Queen of England. In 1559 Henry II died and Mary became Queen of France as well as of Scotland. Her mother, Mary of Guise, was Regent for her in Edinburgh supported by French troops. With Spain in the Netherlands and France established in Scotland, Elizabeth was encircled. Now came her opportunity. A popular anti-Catholic and anti-French revolt, supported by the Protestant nobles, the Lords of the Congregation, flared up in Scotland. The rebels appealed to Elizabeth for help. As a monarch, she had no love for rebels. As a latitudinarian in religion she had little patience with Calvinists like John Knox. There was her obligation of non-intervention under the treaty. But she could not afford not to act; she dared not let the revolt fail; so she acted, but acted covertly: first with promises, next with money and then with arms. This was not enough. After what to her clear-sighted counsellors appeared to be exasperating and almost fatal hesitations, she did move. She had to send a fleet to the Forth and a military force beyond the border before the French could be forced to withdraw. Their withdrawal was confirmed in the Treaty of Edinburgh. Elizabeth had passed her first crisis. The old Franco-Scottish Alliance was disrupted and, whatever France or Spain might do, Elizabeth was secure on the Scottish border. In 1560, as if to set the seal on this, Francis II died and Mary was now Queen of Scots alone.

The Power of Spain: Elizabeth I

In fact, France and Spain did not act together. French Protestant privateers, who had long preceded their English counterparts, continued to harry Spanish shipping and Spanish settlements in the Caribbean. So long as France had continued to be a menace to England, Philip tended to stretch out a protecting hand. He would rather see England heretic and independent than under the power of France. As France's internal conflicts sharpened; as his own difficulties with his revolting Dutch subjects increased; as the Counter-Reformation gathered momentum (in 1570 Pope Pius V pronounced Elizabeth's excommunication and deposition and absolved her subjects from their allegiance); as his own ambitions grew (in 1580 he annexed Portugal and the vast Portuguese overseas empire and acquired the formidable Portuguese Navy); and as, with the mounting tension and with increasing sense of menace, the English exploits in self-defence against the new national enemy, Spain, whether in the Indies, or in the Netherlands, or on the coasts of Spain itself, became less and less tolerable, Philip at last decided to strike. In Spanish eyes, the English had become an insufferable pest, like Serbia to Austria-Hungary in 1914.

In all the years before the coming of the Armada, Elizabeth used every resource to keep out of overt war. She had to husband her tenuous financial resources and to make every pound pay its way. Even 'at the very moment that Howard and Drake were pouring their broadsides into the Spanish Armada in the Channel, Derby and his colleagues were solemnly discussing terms on the Belgian shore and Crofts was writing home to Burghley that he felt convinced of Philip's sincere desire for peace.' Until the very moment when Howard and Medina Sidonia exchanged the first broadsides off Plymouth Harbour Elizabeth did not accept war as inevitable. It has been said that such preparations as were made to meet the Spanish attack were made more or less in spite of her.[2] Her soldiers, sailors and Puritan advisers might lament her policies of appeasement; but it is likely enough that the average Englishman shared her yearning for peace.

Elizabeth's servants served her well. She chose them carefully and used them to the full. She would play one off against another, or one faction among them against another, as modern statesmen like Franklin Roosevelt have done. There were those who were for peace,

[2] Conyers Read, *Mr. Secretary Walsingham*, Clarendon Press, Oxford, 1925, iii. 276, 285.

C

and those who were for war; those who were for prudence and those who were for throwing down the challenge; those who thought primarily in terms of power as between Habsburg and Valois, and those who thought in terms of religion as between Protestant and Catholic. She tried and tested their counsel almost beyond bearing, as Winston Churchill did with his military advisers. These are the rightful prerogatives of sovereigns and statesmen who bear the life of their country in their hands in times of peril. Like Churchill, she was faithful to her chosen advisers. The charge which she gave to William Cecil when, at the opening of her reign, she appointed him as Secretary, marks the spirit of their relationship: it was 'that without respect to my private will you will give me that counsel which you think best.'

At no time in our history has a government in London been in greater need of accurate and timely information about every twist and turn of European politics, or about the activities of Englishmen abroad, than in the first two-thirds of Elizabeth's reign: information from France and Spain, from the Netherlands and Italy and from the German states. Intelligence was sought from Elizabeth's diplomatic envoys and from the secret intelligence service which Walsingham perfected, rudimentary though it may have been even by contemporary standards. Young men making a continental tour, when licensed to travel, were briefed before their departure as to the places they should visit, the persons whom they should see and the matters on which the government wished to be enlightened. 'Knowledge,' said Walsingham, 'is never too dear.' The shifts resorted to in Paris by Sir Edward Stafford, Elizabeth's sole resident ambassador, to penetrate the secret schemes of English Catholics abroad or the polices of the Spanish and French governments, his adoption, so far as he was allowed by Elizabeth to do so, of the role of 'double agent' on a large scale, have led some historians (but not Sir John Neale)[3] to suspect him of treason.

Sir Geoffrey Fenton, with the confidence of a man of letters, might, in an epistle dedicatory to the Queen, assert in 1579: 'God hath . . . put into your hands the balance of power.' To the politicians it was a balance that was subject to every hazard. At no time, probably, have the problems of foreign policy been more anxiously and exhaustively analysed than by Elizabeth's advisers. It was not

[3] 'The Fame of Sir Edward Stafford,' *English Historical Review* (April 1905), xliv. 203–19.

only that they had an unsparing mistress to serve. The times were times of great danger. When some notable event occurs in the foreign field, the first thing which a Foreign Secretary requires from the Foreign Office is an analysis and appreciation of its significance and probable consequences, and advice how to deal with it. On June 30th 1584 there occurred an event of great and terrible moment for a monarch who was herself under threat to her life from foreign agents and from the Roman Catholic fifth column within her own realm, who looked to see her supplanted by the imprisoned Queen of Scots. William of Orange, the other main pillar of the Protestant cause in Europe, was assassinated in his house at Delft.

There has been preserved in the Public Record Office a paper headed, 'Matters to be Resolved in Council', prepared by Walsingham, which sets out the headings for a review of the situation consequent on the death of William. There are twenty-three items, of which the following are examples:

'Whether Holland and Zealand, the Prince of Orange being now taken away, can with any possibility hold out unless they be protected by some potent prince.

'Whether it be likely that the King of Spain, being possessed of these countries, will attempt somewhat against Her Majesty.

'Whether he shall not be provoked thereunto by Scotland and the ill-affected in this realm . . .

'Whether therefore it be not fit . . . to seek to keep him from the possession of the said countries . . .

'Whether it be not fit that the French King should be moved to concur in the action . . .

'Whether if Her Majesty enter into the matter it will not draw on a war.

'What means Her Majesty shall have to maintain and continue the war . . .

'How far the traffic shall be impeached if any war shall fall out with Spain.

'What commodities has this country need of, which are of necessity to be furnished out of Spain.

'Whether the King of Navarre may not be set a work to attempt somewhat for the recovery of the Kingdom of Navarre . . .

'If it be not meet for Her Majesty to take the protection of the said countries but to suffer them to come into the hands of the King of Spain, then what course is to be taken to withstand his attempts. . . .'[4]

This is the kind of work which Elizabeth exacted from her servants, and it was upon this solid basis of fact and judgment that her own decisions to act or, more often, not to act, were founded. If ministers of the Crown in our own day have neither the time nor the patience to conduct an analysis so comprehensive and so penetrating, it is a loss to our foreign policy. Can we suppose that the projected Suez operation in 1956 was subjected to so unsparing a test as this?

How was it that England was able to survive in 1588? One factor was Sir John Hawkins's ships. Another was Sir Francis Drake's conception of naval warfare. For something under fifteen years before the Armada came, Hawkins had, against some opposition from traditional designers, been supplying the Queen with a new kind of ship. These, like the Hurricanes and Spitfires in 1940, were ready just in time. Henry VIII's ships had been slow and unwieldy craft, designed for coast defence, with guns improvised on the cargo deck. Hawkins's ships were ocean-going vessels, able to keep the sea for longish periods, fast, slender, easy to handle, with a special gun-deck constructed over a lowered cargo-deck, which now lay on the water-line. The famous *Revenge*, which was the only ship that Elizabeth was to lose in the whole of her reign, and which in the fight with the Armada carried Drake himself, was one of the first of these 'galleons', as they were called. The *Triumph*, fought by Martin Frobisher, was larger than anything the Spaniards had to show. With these ships, or with as many of them as he could get out of the Queen to supplement the merchant craft used on his semi-private ventures, Drake was able to seek out the adversary on the high seas or upon his own coasts and not simply wait for him to come. What, however, Elizabeth's seamen found it difficult to do was to disrupt the sometimes efficient and seamanlike convoy arrangements for the Spanish treasure fleets across the Atlantic.

As it happened, when the Armada, after long delays, was finally ready to start from Corunna, Elizabeth did at last consent to a foray to the coast of Spain, earnestly advocated by the Lord Admiral, Lord Howard of Effingham. But Howard and Drake were driven back from the Bay of Biscay by contrary winds and had just enough

---

[4] S. P. Domestic, clxxi, No. 80. Quoted in Conyers Read, *Walsingham*, iii. 73–74.

time to put their ships in order at Plymouth before the Spaniards came up. For all that Drake could say, Elizabeth had hesitated until then to take the risk of denuding her own shores, and she cannot be proved to have been wrong. If her ships had beat about the coasts of Spain for months, neither they nor their crews would at the end have been in a fit state for battle; and if they had encountered the Armada far from their own shores they would probably—as the event indicated—have exhausted their ammunition without doing any serious damage to the superbly well-disciplined enemy formation and have left the Armada with a free run up the Channel to its rendezvous with the Duke of Parma's invasion forces off the Flemish coast.

The story that Drake, apprised during a game of bowls on Plymouth Hoe on July 19th 1588 of the unexpected appearance of the Armada off the Scillies, remarked: 'Play out the game; there's time for that and to beat the Spanish after,' has a brave and authentic ring, but is thought by some historians to be an improbable one. If so, it is one of the characteristic myths which peoples, who know their own business very well in these matters, create and incorporate into a national tradition for the inspiration of posterity. The argument is that Howard's ships were cooped up in Plymouth Harbour by the westerly wind that was carrying the Spaniards up Channel, and that it was only by superb seamanship that the fleet was warped out of harbour in time to escape being immobilized, and was then successfully laid to windward of the enemy. There was, it is said, no time to lose, and Drake was not a man to dally in an emergency.

But against this, there is quite a different alternative interpretation of events.[5]

When Captain Thomas Fleming, the commander of a reconnaissance vessel, reported to the assembled captains about 3 o'clock on the afternoon of July 19th that he had sighted the Spanish ships near the Scilly Isles that morning, Drake and many another would have known at once that, with the existing state of wind and tide, it would not be possible to begin warping the ships out before nightfall. There would have been ample time to finish the game. And though there might be tension, there need have been no sense of emergency: warping the fleet out of Plymouth was a familiar enough

[5] See for example Garrett Mattingly, *The Defeat of the Spanish Armada*, Cape, London, 1959. To his eminence as a historian of sixteenth-century England, Mr Mattingly can add practical experience of naval and amphibious operations with the United States Navy in the Second World War.

operation. In fact, the greater part of the fleet was well out of the trap before the Armada came abreast of Plymouth, and the remaining ships were able to join safely a little later. The skill was in laying both parts of the fleet securely to windward of the enemy.

If—the ifs of history are inscrutable—if the Duke of Medina Sidonia had made speed enough and had turned aside to take the English fleet at a disadvantage at Plymouth, or if he had landed in the Isle of Wight and waited there until he could concert joint invasion operations with Parma's forces in the Netherlands, then, it is sometimes said, the course of history could have been very different. But Philip's instructions were specific—the Armada was to go straight ahead. But even if this had not been so, the facts of the situation would have been against Medina Sidonia. At the best, he could hardly have been bold and quick enough to catch Howard in Plymouth. To land anywhere on the English coast would have been a most hazardous operation, with Howard's fleet poised to attack. But most important of all, whatever Medina Sidonia had done, Parma could not have got his flimsy invasion barges out of Dunkirk or Nieuport. Though Howard did not know it, the Dutch fleet under Justin of Nassau was ready to send in its little, fast, shallow-draught fighting craft at the first sign of a move by Parma and they would be operating among the banks and shoals of coastal waters where the great galleons of the Armada could not reach them, and where Parma himself had nothing effective to put up against them. Parma knew very well that this was the crux of the problem. He had repeatedly warned Philip and had urged that the enterprise be at least deferred until he could seize the deep-water port of Flushing, which was still garrisoned by the English. It is hard to see how the invasion, as planned, could have had any chance of success. When he anchored off Calais, with his fleet almost intact, Medina Sidonia had played his part of the operation (with some luck in the weather) with skill, good judgment and resolution; but apparently all in vain.

This does not detract from the glory of the Lord Admiral and his more famous subordinates, Drake, Hawkins and Frobisher. They could not know all this; they did their utmost, and their best was good enough. Their guns, though of longer range, were lighter than those of the Spaniards; and in the engagements in the run up Channel, having to keep out of range and above all to avoid being boarded, they were unable to do very much damage. Off Gravelines, when the six fire-ships had done their work of disorganization, and our ships, now reinforced by Lord Henry Seymour's squadron from the Thames, could go in rather closer (20 per cent of them with 80 per cent of the hitting power were ships of the Queen's Navy Royal), so much of our shot had been used up rather vainly on the previous days that there was not enough left to finish the job, even though the Spaniards were shorter still. The Spanish ships, helped by a 'Catholic' breeze, were able to draw off from the dangerous shoals just in time and to re-form. In spite of wind and weather on their way home northwards round about, Medina Sidonia brought two-thirds of his battered fleet to port at Santander—no mean feat of command on his part and of seamanship on the part of his captains. Spanish sea-power was temporarily blunted, but no more. Unlike the High Seas Fleet after Jutland, the Spanish Navy lived to fight another day. Though the English were disappointed that the Armada had escaped, the decisive fact was that the great enterprise, which had held Europe fascinated for so long, had failed.

It was characteristic of the spirit of the age that English and Spaniards were at one in attributing the result to the hand, or rather to the breath, of God. 'God breathed and they were scattered,' said one of Elizabeth's Armada medals. The truth was quite other. The English gained their success because they had better ships, better guns and better seamen and because they had home ports from which to draw supplies as the battle went on. The Spaniards on the whole had the better of the weather and it was a sudden and fortunate change of wind which, after the fight off Gravelines, saved them at the last moment from drifting to destruction on the Flemish banks. For the English, the defeat of the great enterprise showed that God was, after all, a Protestant: that was the important point. As for the Spaniards, they had not been overcome by the prowess of the heretics but had been chastened by their own loving God for His own inscrutable purposes.

Together with the opening of a new era in naval warfare, still imperfectly understood by the participants, there was a widening of the field of our foreign trade. Cecil had been conscious of the disadvantage of having too many of our eggs in the one basket of our trade with Antwerp. Before we began our long war with Spain, when Antwerp was denied to us with other Spanish territories, we were already finding alternative markets in Europe, Asia, Africa and America. This escape of England from the bonds and the hazards of a one-commodity trade with monopolistic centres on the Continent, and the spread of English commercial enterprise into most parts of the known world, a process which began to gain momentum in the middle of the sixteenth century, brought England into conflict with states who had moved out before her: first with Spain in the West Indies, where trade was often not distinguishable from war or piracy; then with the Dutch in the former Portuguese territories in the East Indies, and in their capacity as general carriers; and later, in the eighteenth century, with the French in India and in America.

Though the war with Spain petered out in frustration for lack of means to pursue it, the thing that one best finds to say about Elizabeth's actions and inactions in the foreign field, apart from the fact that they turned out to be as a whole singularly successful, is that they usually made sense. The same could not always be said of Elizabeth's father, and still less of the two Stuart Kings who immediately succeeded her. She kept her eyes firmly fixed on the concrete national interest, and was little deflected by considerations of prestige or by dynastic predilections or by the appeal of political or religious doctrine. Henry had been too often headstrong, vain and adventurous. James I was a doctrinaire and a pedant, learned and shrewd enough, but unable to refrain from expounding his ideas, good and bad, in and out of season. Charles I was, politically speaking, a man of narrow views and bad judgment; and it is as politicians that governors must be judged and not as husbands and fathers of families or as patrons of the arts. By comparison, Elizabeth, with her other qualities and for all her failings, was the acme of common sense. We shall not find such prudence and skill again until we come to William III nor so masterful a touch with the public till we come to Chatham.

CHAPTER III

Conflict in Europe and Expansion Overseas:
The Early Stuarts

By 1598, that gallant and politic monarch, Henry IV of France, the first of the Bourbons, with some help from Elizabeth, had won his battles against his internal opponents, the Catholic League and their Spanish allies. He had accepted the Mass and had established himself fairly firmly on the throne. He now made peace with Spain at Vervins, leaving Elizabeth and the United Provinces (the Dutch) to continue the fight. When Elizabeth died, James I also made peace. It was not a good peace, since he failed to gain entry into the markets of Spanish America or of the Portuguese possessions, which was one of the things the war had been about: but in the existing stalemate, and with his unwarlike cast of mind, he could not do better. The Dutch fought on alone. This they were able to do. They had made themselves into a formidable commercial and naval power. They were not to conclude their fight for the recognition of their independence and of their right of entry into the Spanish American market for some forty years more. Meanwhile, they would exploit or occupy the rich Portuguese possessions in the East Indies, the modern Indonesia, which were still an appanage of Spain. The war of independence was for them a prosperous war.

Spain had failed to invade England in 1588 or to shake off her harassing attacks in the fifteen years of war that followed. She had failed to prevent the succession of Henry IV to the throne of France. She had failed to suppress the revolt in the Netherlands or to hinder the Dutch from becoming a powerful factor in European politics. She was now, in the coming years, to be involved in the long drawn-out ordeal of the Thirty Years War (1618–48), which was to leave her gravely crippled and to herald the rise of France into the first

41

Introductory: The Road to Power

place in Europe. It was to be the last of the great wars of religion between Catholic and Protestant, arising from an attempt by the Emperor to catholicize and thus to dominate politically the Protestant German states. It was a war in which, well before it ended, France would be actively associated with the Protestants of Germany, of the United Provinces and of Scandinavia. It was to be another phase of the struggle between Bourbon and Habsburg, France against Austria and, secondarily, against Spain. When France at length intervened, she did so in order to prevent the revival of Austrian power in Germany, and in this she succeeded. There would be a new actor upon this stage. Sweden was to make the first of her two spectacular appearances in the world of European war and politics, in the person of her king, Gustavus Adolphus, 'the Lion of the North'. Finally —and it was this which started the conflict—there would be a manifestation of what we should nowadays call nationalism, a revolt of the Protestant Czechs against their Catholic Austrian overlords. The Bohemians chose as their king, Frederick, the Elector Palatine, husband of Elizabeth Stuart, daughter of James I, known as 'The Winter Queen', and in the words of Sir Henry Wotton, 'Th'eclipse and glory of her kind'. Frederick lost his throne in Prague after his defeat by the Austrians at the battle of the White Mountain in 1620, and was driven by the Spaniards from his domains in the Rhineland Palatinate. This couple are of importance in our history, since they were the parents of Prince Rupert, who was to command so gallantly for the Stuarts against the Roundheads on land and sea, and of that Electress Sophia of Hanover from whom our Royal House of Windsor is descended.

What would be the role of England? James was clear in his mind on one thing. He hated war. He was in his odd way an idealist. He saw no reason why there could not be peaceful coexistence between the religious sects and an end to killing. He would fight with ambassadors rather than with bullets. So far as he was concerned, he would take no part in the Protestant crusade which the Puritans in Parliament were urgently pressing upon him. This crusade, they thought, would mean in the first place a war with Spain, which would pay for itself from the plunder of the treasure fleets. James's policy, on the contrary, was to seek a Spanish marriage for his son, Charles. Behind all this, there may have been the perception that England and Scotland were not, with the new turn of events, in danger from Europe as England had been in Elizabeth's time.

42

Conflict in Europe and Expansion Overseas: Early Stuarts

If it was a good rule that England should not go to war in Europe unless she would otherwise be in grave danger, or unless there was something concrete which she could fight for and which it was within her means to secure, there was a strong case for keeping out of the Thirty Years War, which a present-day historian has called a 'meaningless conflict'. France and Spain were anxiously concerned with what was happening in Germany, and were later to be locked in combat. England was not in danger from either. Spain was no longer a menace, and France had not yet become one, though this might not be so clear to a contemporary as it is to those who have the benefit of hindsight. Nor was Protestantism any longer in such peril as it had been in the sixteenth century. In France the trouble was not that Protestantism was weak but that it was now too strong. In 1598 the Calvinists had extorted from Henry IV, after some hard bargaining, the provisions of the Edict of Nantes. This treaty, for that in effect is what it was, gave the Huguenots not merely toleration for the practice of their religion, but some extraordinary political and territorial privileges, including the right for their communities to govern themselves and to maintain their own armed forces, at the expense of the French treasury, in more than a hundred towns including important centres like La Rochelle, Montauban and Montpellier. The Dutch, too, were now a formidable commercial and naval power. Gustavus Adolphus was a military commander of genius and, so long as he was doing their work for them, Louis XIII and Richelieu saw no cause to intervene. It was only after Gustavus had been killed in battle in 1632, and after the tide began to turn in Austria's favour, that in 1635 France entered the conflict. Protestantism was, with the revocation of the Edict of Nantes in 1685, to suffer cruel persecution in France; an unsuccessful attempt was to be made by France to subjugate the Protestant United Provinces; and abortive endeavours were to be made by the later Stuarts, in concert with France, to break the hold of Protestantism in England. But Protestantism was to survive there and elsewhere. In 1713, in the Peace of Utrecht, it would be the Protestant states that would give the law to Europe.

A king like Henry VIII might have tried to play the part of Gustavus Adolphus, though to what national profit is not clear—our future lay not in territorial ambitions in Europe but in commerce and settlement overseas. Neither James nor Charles was of Henry's cast of mind. Nor, in view of the deadlock with Parliament, had they money enough to start upon great adventures. Charles in 1631, against the advice of his Privy Council, declined a request from Gustavus, then at the height of his power, for assistance by land and sea, assistance which, although the stake was the return of the Palatinate, Charles could not find the money to pay for, unless he called a parliament.

When Elizabeth took her great decisions to send armed assistance to the Calvinist Huguenots in France and to the Calvinist Netherlanders in revolt against Spain, she was not—unlike some of her advisers and many of her subjects—swayed by religious or, as we should say, ideological considerations. She had trouble enough with her own Puritans at home, with their nation-wide agitation cells and active pressure groups, their demands for a drastic reform of religion and for a Protestant crusade in Europe. She intervened at the risk of war because the national security was at stake. If the Huguenots and the Dutch were crushed, her turn would come next.

In the early seventeenth century England was not in that perilous situation. She had neither the resources with which to intervene effectively even if she had wished to do so, nor any positive objective at which to aim. There had earlier been, and was to be again, some feeling that England ought to have a foothold on the Continent through which to make an entry if this should prove necessary. Though the possession of Calais had in the end proved to be an embarrassment, and its loss a blessing in disguise, Elizabeth had made persistent but unavailing efforts to recover it by negotiation. James and Charles had no serious aspirations for territorial gains in Europe. It was to be left to Cromwell to revive almost for the last time the conception of a foothold, when he tried unsuccessfully to obtain Bremen as a port of entry into Protestant Germany, and when, two months before his death, he secured Dunkirk from Spain after a war in which he was, strange as it may seem, allied with Louis XIV of France, and in which the Roundheads fought side by side with the forces of the great Turenne against the Spaniards and the English Royalists at the battle of the Dunes. As John Thurloe, Cromwell's foreign secretary, afterwards put it: 'Cromwell carried the keys of the Continent at his girdle, and was able to make invasions thereupon, and let in armies and forces upon it at his pleasure.'

All this was far from James's mind. He laid up the royal ships and dispersed the crews, many of whom, officers and ratings, went into Dutch or Swedish service or signed on with privateers, who were often no better than pirates.[1] So defenceless were we that the Barbary corsairs cruised the Channel at will, picking up our merchantmen, and on one occasion as late as 1640 roamed the streets of Penzance, abducting women and children. The pirates from Dunkirk blockaded the Thames and blackmailed the merchants of the City. Charles tried to repair this situation. He built a fleet with the proceeds of the 'ship money', building well if extravagantly and not always suitably for the purpose.

James did not manage to keep out of war after all. In the last year of his reign, he went to war with Spain, not in defence of any national interest but out of personal pique, shared by Charles, at the humiliating failure of the Spanish marriage negotiation. Thereupon he at once set about arranging a match for Charles with Henrietta Maria, sister of Louis XIII of France, in the vain hope that somehow or other he would be able to satisfy his dynastic pride by securing the return of his son-in-law to the Palatinate. Charles, by a miracle of ineptitude, drifted into a war with France as well, on a variety of grounds, including quarrels over belligerent rights at sea. Both wars were bungled; the amphibious expeditions to Cadiz and to La Rochelle were mismanaged; and Charles made no good use of the fine ships that he had at his disposal. Neither of these wars made any real sense. Neither James nor Charles seems to have understood what was going on in Europe, any more than they understood what was going on in England. The only English war before the latter part of the century that was to make sense, apart from the Civil War, was the Commonwealth's war with the Dutch in 1652. What mattered to us was trade, and here a real national interest was at stake.

The best that can be said of this lamentable series of events is that for the greater part of the two reigns England was at peace and was spared any part or lot in the cruel devastation by fire, famine and slaughter that fell on the population of Germany as the armies crossed and recrossed their land. Although England's prestige and influence were never lower, Edward Hyde, who was later, as Earl of Clarendon, to be chief minister of Charles II, could write in his memoirs under the year 1639 that 'England enjoyed the greatest measure of felicity it had ever known', lapped in peace and plenty,

---

[1] There was, however, in law a sharp distinction between privateering and piracy. Privateering was carried on upon the strength of a licence or commission from a government and was legitimate. Piracy was a crime.

with strong fleets commanding the seas and the trade of the whole world entering her ports.

This is, almost certainly, an over-rosy picture of an imagined golden age before the catastrophe of the Civil War. It is also in keeping with Clarendon's theory of the origin of the Rebellion, namely that the people had become proud through prosperity and that the government had not been skilful enough to handle them. There is little doubt, however, for example, that the paternalism of the government during the eleven years when Charles was ruling without a parliament did favour the poor as against the rich ('from 1631 to 1640,' wrote a historian of the poor law in 1900, 'we had more poor relief in England than ever before or since') and this may have been a minor grievance in the minds of the moneyed men who were behind the great rebellion. The intriguing question is how much it really mattered that both James and Charles were of such little account in foreign eyes, so long as the country was reasonably secure and reasonably prosperous. They were wise to keep out of the Thirty Years War. They would have been wiser to keep out of war altogether and to place themselves in a posture to defend the day-to-day interests of their subjects abroad. In fact, they did neither. That English prestige was low, in itself mattered little; prestige is not always built upon things that matter. What mattered was the failure adequately to defend interests, and this was one reason for the loss of prestige. This would matter a great deal to the seaman or the merchant who was captured at sea by the Spaniards or by pirates, or to the east coast fisherman who was hustled off his grounds by the Dutch. It might matter to the resident ambassador abroad or to the traveller in foreign lands. The reluctance to go into the great war, which was wise, would matter to those people, whom we have always with us, who have an itch to go to war for some sacred cause or other or to intervene with passion in other people's domestic quarrels. But the best answer to the question is probably that it did matter in general because a great many people in the country thought that it mattered. This induced a loss of confidence in, and of regard for, the monarchy, a factor which was to add its quota to the bitter resentment which was in the end to bring the monarchy down in blood. Charles's foreign policy must be held directly responsible for bringing about some of the major events in the growing quarrel between himself and Parliament. It was the exaction of forced loans to equip the raw and undisciplined soldiers recruited for Buckingham's ill-fated expedition to relieve the Huguenots besieged in La Rochelle, the imprisonment of those who refused to lend, and the imposition of martial law, that provoked the presentation of the Petition of Right in 1628.[2]

It was in order to build the ships for the enforcement of Charles's exorbitant claims to the same dominion over the Narrow Seas as over English soil that the writs of ship money were issued from 1634 onwards. The attempted enforcement by the ship-money fleets of the preposterous principles of *Mare Clausum*, the treatise which Selden wrote in answer to Grotius's *Mare Liberum*, ended in fiasco. It was for the sake of this sterile claim, which the Stuarts were the first to put forward, that Charles ran into the great controversy precipitated by John Hampden which marked another decisive stage in his quarrel with Parliament.[3]

Charles's conduct of foreign affairs was one, and not the least important, of the contributory causes of the Civil War. And there was more to it than that. Behind the Civil War in England was the Thirty Years War in Europe. To Puritan eyes, the latter 'was a cosmic struggle in which all the Powers of Light and Darkness were engaged, and this being so, James I's vacillating foreign policy seemed to be criminal folly. Charles I's home policy appeared to be betrayal. . . . The constitutional struggle between the Stuarts and their Parliaments must be seen against the background of this fear and hatred of Catholicism.'[4]

Although we were cutting so poor a figure in Europe, the country had its eyes on wider horizons. Although the kings were inept in domestic and international affairs, the people were full of vigour and were pushing on towards a new destiny in trade, exploration and settlement overseas. Even the early Stuart kings were to show themselves more enlightened in this sphere of national affairs than in any other. Elizabethan enterprise had been energetic, explosive, but indiscriminate and ill-regulated. There had been trading under

[2] Godfrey Davies, *The Early Stuarts, 1603–1660*, The Oxford History of England, 1937, p. 65.

[3] Ibid., pp. 214–15. James would apparently have been content with a monopoly of fishing within fourteen miles of the coast. Charles went much further. He held that no other nation might maintain fleets in the Narrow Seas to exercise any of the rights of war. Foreign vessels in these waters were to salute the King's ships. This was a Stuart innovation, a typical piece of Stuart nonsense. The Tudors had been advocates of freedom of the seas.

[4] Robert S. Paul, *The Lord Protector*, Lutterworth Press, London, 1955, p. 43.

arms in West Africa, an unofficial trade war in Spanish America, the search for the north-west and north-east passages, travels in Muscovy and in Asia. These activities had few positive or permanent results to show. Raleigh's attempted colonization of Virginia in the 1580s was a failure. The most solid achievement was the exploitation of the route round the Cape of Good Hope to south and south-east Asia which led to the foundation of the East India Company in 1600 and its first expedition under Sir James Lancaster in 1601. This venture was to bring us into clashes with the Portuguese and with their successors in the East Indies, the Dutch. So strong was the Elizabethan tradition that it was long before men realized that the real adversary, the most powerful and determined obstacle to English expansion, was not Spain, but the United Provinces. Driven from the islands by the Dutch, the East India Company thrust aside the Portuguese in the Indian sub-continent and settled there. Building on Elizabethan experience, the men of early Stuart times perfected methods, clarified objectives and laid firm foundations for an English empire overseas.

The motives for emigration were varied—an unfounded fear of over-population and unemployment; the belief that colonization, looked at in terms of trade, would be profitable and of benefit to the population at home; the consideration that the new settlements would be a source of supplies for the Navy and a useful base of operations against the West Indies in the event of war with Spain; and a bitter experience of religious intolerance. The settlements in Virginia (from 1606) and Maryland (1634) and in the West Indies (Bermuda, 1609) were a successful follow-up of abortive Elizabethan experiments. The settlements in New England and particularly at Plymouth (the Pilgrim Fathers, 1620)[5], in Massachusetts (1628) and later in Rhode Island and Connecticut were of a different type, more characteristic of the new age. The prevailing motive for emigration was economic. Many of the settlers were labourers whose emigration had been aided and encouraged by the State. But the religious impulse was also strong. In order (as they would put it) to escape from absolute government and religious tyranny, or (as could also be imputed) being rebels against any authority other than their own, large numbers of Puritans chose to start a new life in America. The emigration began in 1620 and stopped abruptly in 1640, when the Long

[5] This romantic name was not contemporary. It dates from 1799 only. See Williamson, *The English Channel*, p. 232.

Parliament set itself to curb kings and bishops. By 1640, there were 25,000 English settlers in New England. Candour requires it to be said that though many of them had fled from religious intolerance of one type, the people of Massachusetts were themselves no less intolerant in their own way. They instituted a kind of closed-shop; the penalty of dissent was the loss of civil rights, imprisonment, flogging and even banishment; only a charter member of the strictly orthodox kind could be a citizen. There was, in fact, on the whole, more toleration in Stuart England than in the Puritan colonies. This was to be corrected by the new charter issued by William III early in his reign; the liberties in New England were to be established by the royal will; but from the outset the people of Massachusetts displayed an independence of spirit which was an augury for the future.

In oceanic commerce, the characteristics were the institution of monopoly in the hands of chartered companies like the East India Company or the Muscovy Company, justified by the extreme risk of the voyages, and by the need, in the general interest, to supervise the conduct of traders and to facilitate the regulation of trade by the government. These measures were applied not so much in compliance with the prescriptions of the so-called mercantile theory, with its insistence on the accumulation of bullion, as with the more general object, not always achieved, of increasing national strength and of pursuing the ideal of national self-sufficiency. The Empire was a 'self-sufficient and exclusive corporation' developed by private enterprise and defended by the Crown. This so-called 'old colonial system' was to be elaborated and codified in the Navigation Acts, the first of which was passed by the Commonwealth in 1650. It was to be the general basis of our overseas commercial policy for nearly two hundred years, that is, until Great Britain turned to free trade in the early nineteenth century.

In all this, James comes out in a good light. Though he appeased the Dutch, he stood up to the Spaniards as regards the settlement in Virginia and the trade in the east. Of Charles also, it has been said that in both colonization and trade 'he was anxious to promote the common welfare, and his ordinances showed him to be abreast of the advanced economic thought of the time.'[6] The Commonwealth was of like mind, but it would go further. It would challenge the Dutch in their own sphere, that is to say, at sea.

[6] James A. Williamson, *A Short History of British Expansion, The Old Colonial Empire*, Second Edition, Macmillan, London, 1930, i. 167.

D

CHAPTER IV

The Sea-Power of Holland: Protectorate and Later Stuarts

The Civil War (1642–51), the Commonwealth (1649–53), and the Protectorate (1653–60) are unique phenomena in our history, both remote and familiar; remote because we have since had no other experience of a legislature acting as an executive or of rule by a military oligarchy under a dictator acting as the direct instrument of God; familiar, because many of the issues that were debated then are still being debated today. The meaning of this period is still a matter of historical controversy. There is a kind of learned civil war going on among historians today as to the part played by the gentry on one side or the other, and as to the economic and social complexion of the participants in this or that group or sect or persuasion engaged in the struggle.

But this may perhaps be said. Revolutions and rebellions are in essence marked by the determination of one set of people to take the place of another set of people in the seat of power, to replace one 'establishment' by another. *Ote-toi que je m'y mette.* Their determination is so deeply seated that they will kill in order to achieve their object. In so doing, they will dress up their purposes in whatever vestments of political or social or religious doctrine may best answer to the climate of the times.

The great English rebellion of the second quarter of the seventeenth century was, shall we say, a movement of this kind, a revolt of one section of the gentlemen of England—the more moneyed section —which dominated the House of Commons (they could, it was said, buy the House of Lords three times over) against the personal rule of the monarch and his servants. Those who opposed the King and those who supported him were divided by conflicting ideas on politics. In laying the foundation for their action, the parliamentarians cooked up a good deal of bogus constitutional history in support of their claims. This political movement could not escape the infection of the age, which was the age, then drawing to a close, of the great religious wars. The two sides were divided by conflicting ideas on religion also. These religious struggles arose essentially from the attempts by certain of the Christian sects each to impose its particular discipline, whether of doctrine or of church government or of morals, upon the whole of the population or upon the State. Behind this there might be, and usually were, considerations of secular power. Men do not exercise self-denial in the presence of power which is there for the taking. In England, one section of the Puritans, backed by the genius of Cromwell and by the power of the army, won a brief and transient victory and a few years' tenure of the seats of power, and by its excesses, or even merely by the practice of its precepts, provoked a nation-wide revulsion which has left its warning mark on the minds of Englishmen today.

The execution of Charles I profoundly shocked opinion in Europe; but governments, deeply involved in the concerns of power, had to take the new régime into their calculations. Spain recognized it at the end of 1650. In the first few years of the Commonwealth there was an undeclared war of commercial reprisal in the Channel with France, which was then deep in civil strife. France and Spain were still at war. France had made peace with Austria by the peace of Westphalia in 1648, but Spain had fought on, and was not to make peace with France until the Treaty of the Pyrenees in 1659. By these two treaties, France was to extend her frontiers on the Rhine, in Flanders and on the Pyrenees. She was to place her two great rivals, the Empire and Spain, at a serious disadvantage. And in spite of a most dangerous rebellion (the *Fronde* 1648–53) of over-great subjects, including members of the Royal Family, against the Regent, Anne of Austria, and her minister and favourite, the Sicilian Cardinal Mazarin, France was able to establish herself as the strongest power in continental Europe. Under her young King, Louis XIV, there would be no more revolts by over-great subjects: he would himself rule the State with outstandingly able ministers of his own choice, and would bend his energies to its further expansion.

Cromwell was worth cultivating. He had what few, if any, British governments have had in time of peace, namely, a superb army and navy, well trained, well found and flushed with success. The army of the Ironsides, by winning battles, had fulfilled the mission entrusted

51

to it by God, and, by the same token, was now to govern the country. The Navy, by going over in great part to the Parliament, had made it certain that the King's cause was lost, unless the King could win quickly. Both services were cherished by the Commonwealth and Protectorate governments. The Navy was greatly expanded, though at ruinous cost, only to be met by debt and confiscations. It was led by fighting commanders of genius or near genius: George Monk, later Duke of Albemarle, who was a professional soldier and was later, when the time came, to bring back a free parliament and with it Charles II; and Robert Blake, Nelson's nearest rival in our naval history, a full man if ever there was one, Oxford graduate, businessman, soldier and Member of Parliament. The ships they commanded belonged mostly to the State. The fleet that beat the Armada had only 20 per cent of royal ships and 80 per cent of private merchantmen, though the hitting power was in reverse proportion. The navy of the Commonwealth and Protectorate was a predominantly national navy. It was Blake and Monk who first introduced the battle tactics of 'fleet line-ahead'. It took two or three anxious years to hunt down the minority of the navy which was still in the hands of Prince Rupert, and to sever the Royalist hold on parts of the Empire overseas; but after that Cromwell had a free hand at sea.

Cromwell, having first meditated war with France, came down on her side, or rather, his war with Spain involved him in alliance with France.[1] The decision was deliberate. At the Council meeting of April 20th 1654, the alternative courses debated were war with France and alliance with Spain; or war with Spain and alliance with France; 'or to have had friendship with both, supposing we might have had good sums of money from both so to do.'[2]

In this Cromwell was out of date in more ways than one. He was out of date because France, not Spain, was the rising power, and

---

[1] Apart from his traditional Puritan attitude towards Spain, the Protector would tend to have a bias in favour of France. At the crucial stage in Charles's differences with Parliament, France, then at war with Spain in the Thirty Years War, supported Parliament against the King, whose policy was sympathetic towards Spain. It was a member of the French Embassy, Hercule de Langres, who, on the afternoon of January 4th 1642, sped hot-foot by pre-arrangement from Whitehall to the Palace of Westminster to warn Pym that the King was on his way with his guards to arrest the five members, thus giving Pym and his colleagues time to escape. (C. V. Wedgwood, *The King's War, 1641–1647*, Collins, London, 1958, p. 58).

[2] Quoted in Paul, *The Lord Protector*, p. 285.

Sea-Power of Holland: Protectorate and Later Stuarts

Cromwell was not to be very many years dead before this would become plain. This was an age when the balance of power was coming into fashion In theory and in practice: the Peace of Westphalia was founded upon it. Cromwell was out of date in thinking of Spain emotionally, in near-Elizabethan terms, as still the national enemy. He was out of date in aspiring to a territorial foothold on the Continent—this he secured at Dunkirk in 1658. He was out of date in aiming at building up a northern Protestant coalition against the states which maintained the Inquisition. National interests had never accurately coincided with religious interests, as French policy since Francis I had shown, and were to do so decreasingly in the future. What is more, Cromwell's amphibious operation in the West Indies, like so many of such operations before and since, was expensively bungled. We gained Jamaica out of it in 1655, while the war was still an undeclared war of reprisals. This was our first conquest from Spain, but it was a prize which was not then thought by either side to be of great value. Cromwell was consciously imperialistic and deliberately aggressive. There was a strong strain of bustling nationalism in the Puritan make-up. His object in the war with Spain was to gain 'an interest in that part of the West Indies in the possession of the Spaniard', in other words, to turn the Spaniard out. In order to find the forces to sustain this policy, he had to resort to prodigal finance and to methods of extorting money going far beyond those practised by Charles. This was one of the many reasons why the Restoration was so widely and so warmly welcomed. Not until we come to Stanhope and Carteret and Chatham in the eighteenth century, and never again after that, shall we find a British government dominated by a deliberately aggressive purpose.

Where the Commonwealth was right was in its challenge to the United Provinces, Protestant republics though they might be. Englishmen were coming to think that if their future lay not in Europe but overseas, the main obstacle in their path was not Spain nor even, at this stage, France, but the Dutch. The Dutch had created for themselves a near monopoly of the sea-borne carrying trade of Europe, which they were determined to maintain. They had developed a great trade with south and south-east Asia, particularly in the spices (pepper, cloves and nutmeg) indispensable for European tables, and had their own ports of call on the way—in West Africa, at the Cape of Good Hope and in India. They would keep competitors out, by force if necessary. They were set upon the destruction of the trade of their new rival, England. To both governments, international commerce was a kind of open war, a fight for the largest possible share of what was regarded as a fixed quantity of trade, not likely to be capable of great expansion. For this purpose, and in order to convoy their merchantmen to and from their home ports through dangerous waters, the Dutch had built a magnificent navy, led by commanders like Tromp, de Ruyter and de Witt, who could bear comparison with the best.

In this struggle, England had two advantages. The first was the one she had enjoyed against Spain: she lay across her adversary's communications. Dutch merchantmen would, unless diverted round the north of Scotland, have to pass up and down Channel and run the gauntlet of the English fleets. The second was that, unlike the Dutch, the English had a strong and growing domestic industry upon which to base their foreign trade, and were even able, if need be, to exist for a while without foreign trade. This the Dutch could not do. In the long run, the odds were on England: in the short run, the issue was doubtful. In the seventeenth century, we had three wars with the Dutch, of which that of the Commonwealth was the first (1652–54).

The Navigation Acts of 1650 and 1651 were not the direct cause of this first Dutch war: it had in fact little immediate effect on trade. What was in issue was a background of intense trade rivalry in America and in the east. There were some specific questions such as the extreme English doctrine of belligerent rights at sea and the English claim to the salute and the levy of tribute for fishing in the North Sea. But what immediately precipitated the war was a series of incidents provoked by the intense hatred of the seamen of one side for those of the other. When the fleets met, they fought with a will, and both sides suffered great damage. The English ships tended to be larger and more heavily armed than the Dutch. It was war for the command of the Narrow Seas, naval warfare pure and simple. In the end the Dutch acquiesced in the salute and in the Navigation Act. The English freed the fishery in the North Sea. The Dutch paid compensation for the torture and massacre of English merchants thirty years earlier at Amboyna in the East Indies in 1623, which James and Charles had allowed to pass, but which Cromwell revived as an issue.

In the time of James and Charles, the prestige of England in Europe had been at a low ebb. When it was asked how much this really mattered, the answer was not very easy to find. The same question arises, in a converse sense, in relation to the Commonwealth and Protectorate. If there is one achievement for which Cromwell has been almost universally commended, it is that he raised the name of England high and made his country respected and feared. This claim is worth examining. Certainly, he gained advantage for English trade from the Portuguese and in the Baltic, the main source of our naval supplies[3] until the North American colonies came into the picture. In the Baltic the situation was complicated by the rivalry between Sweden and Denmark, and by the anxious concern of both the Dutch and the English for their trade in that area. Certainly again the outcome of the Dutch War was a positive achievement. What was being pursued was a legitimate objective involving a vital national interest. If the Dutch had not been withstood, they would have driven us out of the world's trade. We had rather the better of the fight. The result was a compromise, rather in our favour.

But the Dutch War was made by the Commonwealth, not by the Protectorate, that is to say, by the Parliament rather than by Cromwell, if indeed it was not made by the Commonwealth navy, acting of its own volition. Cromwell himself never fully approved of the war. He would rather have pursued his visionary scheme of an alliance with the United Provinces aiming at a partition of the Spanish and Portuguese Empires: America, less Brazil, for England; Asia for the Dutch, who would buy out the East India Company; and Africa divided. So the credit could hardly go to Cromwell. On the other hand, the Spanish War was of his own making. The balance sheet of this war is worth looking at. Cromwell allied himself with a rising power, France, against a declining power, Spain. He gained a useless port, Dunkirk,[4] expensive to maintain and impossible to defend, which Charles II afterwards sold to France, and the Island of Jamaica. The war struck a heavy blow at our commerce. Though

[3] We were for a long time as much dependent on the Baltic for the requisites of naval warfare as we now are on imported oil.

[4] On the other hand, 'to a policy like that of Cromwell, which contemplated intervention in continental wars as a means of making England safe by making her dangerous, the possession of a permanent landing place between France and the Spanish Netherlands was of incalculable advantage.' (G. N. Clark, *The Later Stuarts, 1660–1714*, The Oxford History of England, 1934, p. 57.) It would be plain a very few years later that to fight on the side of France was not the way to make England safe, Dunkirk or no Dunkirk.

the English captured some prizes at sea, the net cost of the war was ruinous, and at Cromwell's death the State was almost insolvent and the people in great distress. It is fair to ask whether the gain in prestige was worth the price, and whether Cromwell should be praised for thinking it right to pay it; and to question further whether mere prestige unaccompanied by some concrete, solid national benefit, is an objective which is worthy of a prudent statesman's ambition, unless it can be cheaply acquired. Cromwell could have adequately defended English interests and made the English name adequately respected without embarking upon this kind of extravagant adventure. Cromwell's foreign policy was spirited enough, but it was, as one critic says, 'the attempt of a half-starved man to dominate his neighbours when he ought to have been filling his stomach'.[5]

With the Peace of Westphalia (1648) which ended the Thirty Years War, a new theory and practice of the balance of power seems to have established itself. With Henry VIII, as we have seen, the conception, though he did not practise it, was that, given two stronger powers of fluctuating strength, and one weaker power, then the weaker power would throw its weight on one side or the other in order to preserve an equilibrium. The Peace of Westphalia introduced the conception of territorial compensation as the basis of a settlement, together with a guarantee of the settlement, in this case by the so-called mediating powers, France and Sweden. This system, adopted as a means of establishing and maintaining a balance in Germany, became almost a principle of law, a right to be insisted upon. The balance of power as thus defined became a part of the theory of politics. Fénelon, following Grotius and Vattel, wrote a learned disquisition about it for the Duc de Bourgogne. In order to create a balance, territories were partitioned and distributed: and, once the distribution was made and confirmed by treaty, any territorial change to the benefit of any one of the parties would give the other parties the right to claim territorial compensation. In this theory, the conception of the international community also had a place. No one state should be able to dominate the rest, and it would be the interest, right and duty of every power to interfere, even by force of arms, when any of the conditions of the settlement were infringed or assailed by any other member of the community.

But the old idea of the throwing of weight to one side or the other

[5] Miss James, quoted by Sir Charles Petrie, *Earlier Diplomatic History, 1492–1715*, Hollis and Carter, London, 1949, p. 154.

still persisted. The Marquis de Ruvigny, coming to London as French ambassador in 1667 after the Treaty of Breda, which ended the second Dutch War, said that in England men's minds were so imbued with the old idea that the weaker of two powers must always be supported, that it was to be feared that there would be a general disposition in England to assist the Spaniards. He need not have been perturbed. There was, for the present, to be no such consistency in English practice. With the sole exception of Sir William Temple's famous tripartite treaty of 1668 (England, United Provinces, Sweden), which constrained France, now at war with Spain, temporarily to withdraw from her threatening posture in regard to the Spanish Netherlands, there was no exercise by England of the switch of influence which the principle of the balance of power, as understood by Ruvigny, would have enjoined. Charles II returned to, and maintained, his corrupt association with France. Torcy, the minister of Louis XIV, saw the truth more clearly when he pointed to the fickleness of the English, whose lack of serious purpose, he said, was well known and who were always changing their minds. Thurloe, Cromwell's foreign secretary, writing after the Restoration, remarked that although it was commonly said that the interest of England was always the same in reference to other nations and remained unaffected by a change of government, experience proved the contrary. Not until the time of William III was a consistent purpose pursued. Between the Restoration in 1660 and the Revolution of 1688–89, the levity of which Torcy spoke was to be much in evidence.

If it was a saving grace in James I and Charles I that they cared for colonial development, so it is a saving grace in Charles II and James II that they cared for the Navy. Charles knew about ships and James knew how to command them. It was Charles who gave the Royal Navy its name. It was Samuel Pepys, the first to hold the appointment of Secretary of the Admiralty, who at this time gave us our first corps of professional naval officers.

It was a saving grace, too, of Charles II and James II that they encouraged colonial expansion and the development of England as the centre of a trading empire. Further Navigation and other similar Acts were passed which somewhat relaxed conditions of trade with Europe but increased the restrictions upon colonial trade. There is good evidence that the effect of these measures was, in fact, of benefit to English trade. Between 1660 and 1688 the total tonnage of our mercantile marine doubled. In colonial policy, it was the tropical slave-holding colonies rather than those in temperate climates like the always troublesome New England which were most valued and most intensively developed. An exception was the foundation of Pennsylvania by the Quaker, William Penn, in 1680–82. But although the old colonial system helped to launch England upon her imperial career in the reigns of Charles II and James II, and was to lend her strength to sustain the French wars of the eighteenth century, it created friction with some of the colonists which was to burst into flame before that century was over.

Of the conduct of foreign policy by the two royal brothers, there is little good that can be said. It has been urged on Charles's behalf that he had the interests of his country at heart and that, in his position of weakness in relation to France, he used the arts of diplomacy to outwit or double-cross Louis. As to this, it might be said that the double-cross is not a reputable weapon in the hands of responsible statesmen, and that, if it is used, it should be successfully used. Charles got relatively little pecuniary assistance out of Louis in relation to his financial requirements, and at this cheap price Louis bought the neutrality and indeed, on occasion, the alliance of England when these were of great value to him. It was to Louis's interest that England should remain internally divided, since she would thus be unable to play the decisive part in the balance of power in Europe which the French diplomatists conceived to be natural to her.

Parliaments and the public are not always wiser than monarchs or governments. Elizabeth's parliaments, and some of her advisers, would again and again have persuaded her to follow courses which, had she not resisted them, might well have brought her to ruin. 'There are,' said Sir J. R. Seeley, 'emergencies in which a persistent abstinence from action, a kind of resolute irresolution, is the only sound policy.' James I's parliament would have launched him into adventures in Europe which England had not the resources to sustain. But in the time of Charles II, Parliament and the public were wise enough to see that the danger to England came no longer from the United Provinces, for all that the commercial rivalry continued, but from the France of Louis XIV, and that there must be a reversal of the King's persistent policy of association with France in the Roman Catholic interest. Parliament was still violently anti-Papist.

The second Dutch War (1665–67)—it was Charles's first—was, says G. N. Clark, 'the clearest case in history of a purely commercial war.' 'The Dutch,' said George Monk, 'have too much trade, and the English are resolved to take it from them.' The Dutch had some help from the French. There were the usual hard-pounding battles in which both the King's brother, James, Duke of York, and George Monk, Duke of Albemarle, distinguished themselves. But the English grew tired of the war. Peace negotiations were opened. Some of the bigger ships were laid up in the Medway, an imprudent step opposed by Monk but dictated by financial stringency. In June 1667, the great de Ruyter, in a Drake-like operation, his ships piloted by unemployed English seamen, bombarded Sheerness, attacked Chatham and towed away the English flagship, the *Royal Charles.* In the compromise peace, the Navigation Acts were modified in favour of the Dutch, and their primacy in the East Indies was recognized. As an afterthought, as though a thing of little account, the Dutch ceded New Amsterdam, later renamed New York, and other neighbouring areas, which by linking New England with Virginia, gave us a continuous seaboard on the Atlantic coast of North America, a development which, though little regarded at the time, was to be pregnant for the future.

The third Dutch War (1672–74) was a very different matter. In 1670, Charles made two treaties with Louis. By the first, the infamous secret treaty of Dover, known only to an intimate group of his ministers, Charles undertook to declare himself a Roman Catholic at a convenient season, in return for help from Louis in money and arms to enforce the re-conversion of England. The two kings also agreed that, after Charles's declaration, which in fact was never made, they would attack the United Provinces and partition the Dutch possessions. The second treaty (it was, in fact, a sham), concluded later in the year, repeated the agreement for an attack on Holland, a step which was still popular enough in certain quarters at court. In planning to destroy the Dutch power, Louis had two objectives, both of them directly contrary to English interests. The first was to facilitate his acquisition of the Spanish Netherlands. This was part of his secret plan, concluded in 1668, to partition with the Emperor, head of the Habsburg family, the whole Spanish Empire in Europe and America, now about to go begging on the expected death, without direct male successors, of Charles II, Habsburg King of Spain. Louis's second objective was to become the maritime heir not only of Spain but also of Holland, in fulfilment of his great minister Colbert's grandiose plan of mercantile and colonial expansion, an ambition on the part of France which was to keep her at war with Great Britain for a good part of the eighteenth century.

In the war with Holland, there was the usual mutual battering by Dutch and English fleets, the French leaving us to do the fighting and to spend our strength; but in 1674 Charles was forced by anti-French opinion at home to withdraw from the war on terms which made little change in the position. Our trade, however, was to gain richly from our neutrality—an advantage which we have not often enjoyed in our history. We were soon to take the place of the Dutch as the great carriers of Europe. The Dutch, for whom this was primarily a land not a sea war, only saved themselves from the French by opening their dykes. They had in 1672 made a constitutional change which was to be of great importance for our history. Since the time of William the Silent, the House of Orange had held the stadtholderate in Holland, Zealand and Utrecht, three of the seven United Provinces. In 1650, in sympathy with the establishment of the Commonwealth in England, the states-general had excluded the House of Orange from that office. Now, in the national emergency, the populace in fury turned upon the Grand Pensionary, John de Witt, did him to death, and recalled William III of Orange, the nephew of Charles II, once more to the stadtholderate and to the command of the forces. John de Witt, besides neglecting the Dutch military preparation, had, until the last, clung to his belief in the good faith of the French, as Elizabeth had done as regards the possibility of peace with Philip II in 1588 and as Neville Chamberlain was to do as regards Adolf Hitler in 1938. Thanks to William's characteristically successful diplomacy, the Dutch were before long to be the centre of a great European coalition strong enough to hold its own against France. William's difficult relations with his own factious people and their stiff-necked states-general were to prove to have been a valuable training when he came to take over the government of the no less factious and stiff-necked English and Scots at a crisis in their history.

Till the end of his reign, in spite of parliamentary and public opinion, Charles, perpetually short of money, was to continue to make or seek agreements with Louis detrimental to the interests of his country. Thanks in part to this, Louis was able by 1684 to establish himself in a dominating position in Europe. English prestige was again, as under the earlier Stuarts, at its lowest point; but though, as the centre of a trading empire, England was prosperous enough and expansively minded, she was now, as she had not been then, in grave danger. Prosperity, like prestige, can be too dearly bought. Cromwell, enjoying security, sacrificed prosperity for the sake of prestige. The England of Charles II became prosperous, but sacrificed both prestige and security. In the later part of Charles's reign the Royal Navy ceased to be a factor in European affairs and British influence fell to nothing.

CHAPTER V

The Struggle with Louis XIV

With the reign of William and Mary we enter upon a period of rivalry between Great Britain and France which was to continue in full force until 1815 and to linger on, in a minor way, until the end of the nineteenth century, when the Entente Cordiale of 1904 brought in a new relationship which has lasted to this day. At this time the most considerable power on their horizon was the United Provinces. For the Dutch the seventeenth century was a great age in colonial wealth and naval power, in art, philosophy and law, finance and agriculture. But unlike France and England, the Dutch Republic had not sufficient domestic resources to sustain for very long the great position which she had reached. Nevertheless for the present she was a power in Europe, the only power on the Continent which could serve as the core of resistance to France. Spain was in decadence, Austria in conflict with the Turks (they laid siege to Vienna in 1683), Italy and Germany were divided and ineffective, while Sweden under Charles XII again had her eyes on the Baltic.

The question was, on which side would England be? James II was not so subservient to France as Charles II had been; indeed, he had a defensive treaty with the Dutch; but his Roman Catholic policy made it unlikely that he would break with France. It was to make sure that England would join the anti-French coalition that William invaded England on November 5th 1688. His ostensible object was to defend the Protestant religion and to assert the right of his wife, James's daughter, to succeed to the throne. By September, 1689, his passionately pursued objective was achieved. England joined the Dutch and the Emperor in an offensive and defensive alliance against France. William, as it was said, had taken England on his way to France. The assent of Parliament, which William was careful to wait for, was the more readily given in that James, with French military and naval assistance, had appeared in arms in Ireland. Spain, Savoy and an impressive number of German states in due course joined the alliance. In the twenty-four years that were to elapse before the Peace of Utrecht of 1713, England was for the first time in her history, and not without opposition from the Tory isolationists of the maritime school, to play a decisive part in a great continental war, furnishing not only finance (the Bank of England was founded in 1694) and sea power, but sizable military contingents engaging in pitched battles on the Continent and, in Marlborough, a military commander and diplomatist of genius, and one of the supreme figures in our history.

We have now to do with two of the seven wars between Great Britain and France that took place between 1689 and 1815: King William's war or the War of the League of Augsburg (1689–97) and Queen Anne's war or the War of the Spanish Succession (1702–13). They were not wars for trade, although British trading interests were deeply involved. They were not wars for colonial empire, although we added very materially to our overseas possessions. They were not wars of religion, though the persecution of Protestants in France after the revocation of the Edict of Nantes in 1685, and Louis's support of James and his recognition of the Old Pretender after James's death, helped to stiffen the resolution of the English in these conflicts. They were conflicts in which, for Great Britain, national security was the predominant issue. They were wars, in fact, for the re-establishment and maintenance of the balance of power, disturbed by the continental ambitions of France. Indeed, as the French Ministry for Foreign Affairs wryly remarked in the instruction issued to the new French ambassador to Austria in 1750: 'The balance of power . . . has always served as a pretext and motive for the coalitions which, for nearly eighty years past, have been framed and renewed against France.'

And indeed there is substance in the judgment. In a broadsheet published in England in 1692, there is a strong plea for the re-establishment of the House of Austria in a position of equality with France. Such equality would be in the interest of Christendom as a whole; but it would be 'to the special interest of England to establish again this equality, so that she may again hold the scales in her hand and turn them to whichever side she desires; for this is the one possible role for us, not only that we may continue to be mistress of the sea, but also that we may be capable of deciding the event of war and the terms of peace.'

King William's war was fought essentially to prevent the conquest of the Spanish Netherlands (modern Belgium) by France, whose objective now and later was to advance to securely fortifiable frontiers, especially in Flanders, an objective involving the vital interest of both the English and the Dutch, and indeed of Louis himself. Queen Anne's war was fought to prevent the union of the crowns of France and Spain under a Bourbon king, an objective which involved the interests of Europe at large, of Austria as well as of the United Provinces and Great Britain. Louis XIV pursued his objectives consistently, but not without occasional hesitations, for which some French historians have blamed him. The coalitions which fought the French in both wars were of William's making, though he was dead before the War of the Spanish Succession formally opened. He had sent Marlborough to negotiate the second grand alliance against France concluded in September 1701 (England, the United Provinces, Austria, later joined by Savoy and Portugal), and he had already made him commander-in-chief.

William and Marlborough were of one mind as to how these wars should be conducted. They both belonged to the continental as opposed to the maritime school of strategy. In the view of the continental school, commitment of sizable English land-forces[1] to the Continent was an inevitable element in any campaign against a European state aiming at excessive power. Naval operations, however important, whether as supporting or as independent action, were subsidiary. To the maritime school, the Navy was the main arm. The objective would be to reduce the enemy by blockade, by trade destruction and by other measures of economic warfare, and to harass him by launching seaborne raids around the periphery of his dominions, and by seizing his colonies and overseas bases. The controversy between the two schools continued down to the Second World War. In both World Wars, the Americans no less than ourselves were constrained by imperative demands of Allied strategy to commit great forces in the land battles in Europe. At the time of which we are speaking, the continental view was taken generally by the Whigs, the maritime view by the Tories.

William's position on the throne was never very securely based.

[1] These forces were not in fact very great. Only 9,000 of the 45,000 troops engaged on the Allied side at Blenheim were English.

He had only been accepted at all because he was the son and husband of Stuart princesses and because James had made himself intolerable even to many of those best disposed to the Stuart cause. Leading men in the country, Whigs as well as Tories, who had helped to bring William over, maintained contact with the Stuarts in France. He was cold-hearted, imperious, distrustful—in fact, not an agreeable character. His strong Dutch sympathies and his foreign interests irked the English to such an extent that in the Act of Settlement in 1700 (with a backward look at the United Provinces and a forward look at Hanover) it was laid down that no foreign-born monarch should engage in war in defence of his continental territories without the consent of the English Parliament. But for all that, public opinion was strongly behind him in the war which opened in 1689 and in the war for which he was preparing when he died. His statesmanship, energy, courage and resource are beyond question. It has been said of him, as it was said of George Washington, that he 'never appeared to full advantage but in difficulties and in action'.[2]

His expedition to England in 1688, a serious military operation of invasion with English, Scottish and mixed European forces, was a gambler's throw, or, since he was a Calvinist, an enterprise founded on faith in predestination. He weakened his military forces at home while the main French armies were committed to an attack upon the Emperor far away on the upper Rhine. His two hundred transports conveyed by fifty sail risked interception by James's fleet, well found and still loyal, waiting for them in the Thames estuary. For all he knew, he might have encountered some of Louis's fleet also, though, in fact, the French ships were far away at Toulon and not at Brest. By great good fortune, favoured by wind and weather, he eluded his pursuers and made his way to Torbay, the destination which his seamen had chosen. He could not be sure what support awaited him in England, where James still had an army. Even after his bloodless victory, when, jointly with his wife, he mounted the throne, his hold on his new country was precarious. While he was away in Ireland in 1690, where James held almost the whole country, and when he was about to win the decisive battle of the Boyne, a battle which was a microcosm of the European war itself, the French Admiral Tourville took advantage of a dispersal of the English naval

[2] These words were used of William by Voltaire and applied by Tom Paine to Washington.

forces to drive off a combined English and Dutch fleet under Torrington at Beachy Head and to take command of the Channel. Had Louis had a force ready, England could have been defeated. 'Perhaps in the whole long period we have reviewed there has been no moment, not even that of the Armada, so critical for England as the Summer of 1690' (Sir J. R. Seeley). But Louis had his eye fixed on Germany, where his immediate objective lay, and could not seize his chance in England. A projected invasion was again frustrated and our naval position restored in 1692 by the victory over Tourville at Barfleur-La Hogue. After that the French Navy ceased to trouble, and the French seamen took to privateering. It was Jean Bart instead of Tourville. The war of 1689–97 was won, so far as it was won at all, chiefly by sea power. The Allies did poorly on land in a war of trenches and sieges. The indecisive Treaty of Ryswick (1697) was of benefit to William as Dutchman rather than to William as King of England.

In the War of the Spanish Succession (1702–13) our security was again at stake. Louis had the Spanish Empire at his disposal, and had Bavaria as an ally. It was not won by sea battles—there was only one fleet action, off Malaga in 1704—but by the ubiquitous presence of sea power. As in the days of Blake, we made our power felt to decisive purpose in the Mediterranean. Our sea power sustained Marlborough's brilliant practice of the new-style war of movement in Bavaria, and in Flanders. In these battles, with the never-failing help of Prince Eugene of Savoy, the commander of the forces of Austria, now free from the Turkish menace, he had the better of the best marshals of France.[3]

William and Louis had tried to avoid war by concluding two partition treaties (1698 and 1700), disposing of the Spanish Empire among the several claimants to the throne of Spain—Princes of the Houses of Bavaria, Habsburg and Bourbon—the second treaty having been made necessary by the death of one of the prospective beneficiaries of the first. War was brought nearer when Louis repudiated the second partition treaty and accepted the testament of the King of Spain bequeathing the whole of the Spanish domains

[3] He was sometimes hampered by the cautious veto of the Dutch field deputies attached to his headquarters. These might be compared to the Presbyterian divines who moved David Leslie, against his better professional judgment, to leave his position of strength and to march down to disaster at Cromwell's hands at Dunbar. The Dutch were always difficult allies, as Elizabeth I had found.

to Louis's grandson Philip of Anjou, though with the stipulation that the two crowns should not be united. It hardly needed his recognition of James Edward, the Old Pretender, as King, the occupation of the Spanish Netherlands by French troops and the exclusion of English commerce from the Mediterranean to convince the English people at length that there was no alternative to war. They were quicker to see this than was Parliament.

From this time, foreign affairs and war became increasingly the concern of Parliament and people—a fashion which the Protectorate had earlier set when it had pamphlets published explaining its foreign policy. It was in the last resort public opinion that drove James out and brought William in. Public opinion supported William's new conception of the conduct of foreign policy, namely the building of coalitions for resistance to France, a conception which, with successive changes in the master-enemy, has lasted to this day. Public opinion again, when Queen Anne's war dragged on to no obvious good purpose, supported the Tory move in 1711 to make a separate peace in breach of the terms of the Grand Alliance.[4] Nevertheless it was William's bold initiative in landing at Torbay in 1688 that determined England's course of action in the European struggle, a course that was fully justified by results.

The Peace of Utrecht, unlike the Treaty of Ryswick, was of great immediate benefit to England. We gained Hudson Bay, Newfoundland, Nova Scotia, captured by a force including the resolute Massachusetts colonists, and the Island of St Kitts in the West Indies from France, and Gibraltar and Minorca from Spain. There were also valuable trading concessions by Spain in America, including an

---

[4] Some historians have severely condemned the action of Bolingbroke in withdrawing from the fighting, leaving Marlborough's loyal brother in arms, Prince Eugene, to fight alone; in making a separate peace behind the back of his allies, the Austrians and the Dutch; and in sacrificing the Catalans, who had fought with us in Spain, to the Bourbon King Philip. Others had done the same before and were to do so after. Henry IV made peace with Spain at Vervins in 1598, leaving Elizabeth and the Dutch in the war. James made peace a few years later, leaving the Dutch to fight on. Charles II withdrew from the third Dutch War in 1674, in advance of his ally, Louis XIV. George III was to make peace with France in 1763, leaving Frederick the Great of Prussia in the lurch. In 1763, as in 1711, it was the Tories who made peace and the Whigs who wanted to continue the war. It can be said for the Tories that they had public opinion on their side; and indeed, when coming to terms with France before the Treaty of Utrecht, they were careful to secure the concurrence of Parliament at every step: but people and parliaments can be dishonourable, no less than ministers and monarchs.

exclusive contract for supplying African negro slaves to the American colonies. In Europe, the Spanish territories outside Spain had been conquered and were divided up between Austria and Savoy. Louis XIV's grandson, Philip, was allowed to continue to hold the throne of Spain and the Indies. The alternative would have been a Habsburg as King of Spain as well as Emperor and a revival of the Empire of Charles V. It was a condition of the treaty that Philip should solemnly renounce all claim to succeed to the throne of France. Of special importance to England was the transfer of the Spanish Netherlands from Spain to Austria. Austria, unlike Spain in the past, or France then and later, or Germany in a more distant future, was not, from our point of view, a dangerous neighbour. In this way it was hoped that a balance of power would be maintained. The phrases, 'a just balance of power' and 'the balance of the powers of Europe' are used in the treaty itself. France was bankrupt: but at least she kept some of her fortresses in Flanders and had warded off a junction between Austria and Spain. The Dutch were exhausted and, already in decline, had to be satisfied with less than their due share of fortresses in Flanders to serve as a barrier against the French.

Great Britain had done well out of the war, and was strong and prosperous. Commercially and financially she was supreme. The American colonies, from being a factor in mercantilist self-sufficiency and a source of raw materials including naval stores, now, with their fast-rising population, were becoming a valuable exclusive market for manufactured goods, a more purely economic asset which could be exploited for the development of home industry. Great Britain was becoming the centre of a trading empire, and with all this went a new naval supremacy. Admiral Mahan said of Queen Anne's war: 'before that war England was one of the sea powers. After it, she was the sea power, without any second.' France's navy, built up by Colbert, had been a serious menace: it was a menace no longer. England was again secure. Her security was not again to be seriously threatened for over sixty years. She was not to be involved in a serious war again for a generation.

We have seen that the purpose of the settlement of Utrecht was to re-establish and maintain the balance of power in Europe, disrupted by the preponderant power developed and exercised by Louis XIV. But it may be asked how it was that the mechanism of the balance of power was not employed successfully to curb the ambitions of Louis at an early stage. The theory of the balance of power was plain enough. Grotius and Fénelon had stated it, and it could be summarized as follows: 'There, then, are the grand expedients of the balancing system: vigilant inspection to discover, and prompt union to counteract, in their birth, all such projects of encroachment as powerful states will ever, when opportunity offers, be ready to form.'[5] States might, of course, grow strong by prudent government. In that case they should be watched and, if need be, alliances should be formed to balance them. If they attempted to grow strong by violence, intervention against them would be both a right and a duty: this would be a just war. If they grew strong by marriage or inheritance, as for example France did in 1702, this would in itself give no right to take up arms: but, if such states had already shown an encroaching disposition, as France had certainly done, then the balancing system would authorize immediate interference to procure securities or to prevent the aggrandizement.

The problem would therefore be two-fold: to discern the first beginnings of a course of aggression; and to decide to take action to halt it. It did seem that in 1668 this course was being followed. Temple's tripartite treaty (England, United Provinces, Sweden) did, by its very conclusion, throw the balance in favour of Spain and against France. It helped to keep Louis, for the time being, from encroaching further in the Spanish Netherlands, and to constrain him to return Franche-Comté to Spain. But thereafter, although a coalition was made (without England), the situation was allowed to drift. Louis's encroachments in the Netherlands and Germany were not effectively resisted. Louis was helped by Austria's preoccupation with the Turkish danger and by the complaisant policy of England. The French regarded England as the key to the situation, the potentially decisive factor in the balancing system. We have noted the fear of Ruvigny, the French ambassador in London, in 1667 that England would take the side of Spain, the weaker party; this she did once, in 1668, but not again. It was most important for France that England should be allied or neutral or impotent. Pomponne, one of Louis's most sagacious ministers, had said: 'This perpetually agitated state of England is that which suits us best. So long as she is divided within herself she will be little equal to making herself considerable abroad and to holding that balance which seems to lie

[5] Quoted from the article on 'The Balance of Power' in *The Encyclopaedia Britannica*, Eighth Edition, 1854.

naturally in her hands among the contentions of Europe.'[6] Indeed, Louis boasts in his memoirs of having supported both Charles and his opponents at the same time.

From this point of view it is clear enough that Charles II was the wrong kind of king for the European situation which he had to face. The 'ifs' of history do not abide our question: but if Cromwell had been younger and alive and in power in 1670, with his strong army and navy and resolute outlook, it is possible that Louis would not have been permitted to begin to disrupt the European balance as he did and to rise to the great height which he had reached by 1684. It is possible. We cannot tell; there are so many uncertain factors; but in terms of power, it would have been possible, if not in terms of practical politics. On the other hand, some historians have doubted whether the mechanism of the so-called balance of power could be counted on to be effective in cases where one power was determined to prevail over the rest, and was able to develop the necessary resources to make the attempt. The hope that such attempts might be nipped in the bud would usually prove to be illusory. What in fact would happen would be that the threatened powers would not bestir themselves to act individually or jointly until the threat had become patent; and they would then, in desperation, form *ad hoc* coalitions and, in face of the emergency, develop resources and fighting power going far beyond what they could achieve in more normal times. There is much to be said for this view. This is in fact very much what happened in 1689 and 1701. Coalitions were formed against Louis and he was only curbed at great cost after he had reached the zenith of his power. Thereafter, a new balance was established in the peace settlement at Utrecht which was preserved for many years. This pattern has repeated itself more than once since then. *Ad hoc* coalitions were formed against Napoleon, William II and Hitler, but only effectively after the war was in progress. The time to have halted Prussia was during or after the wars of 1864, 1866 and 1870, which, as was recognized at the time, destroyed the European balance established after the Napoleonic Wars. The time to have halted the German Republic was when it first became plain that she was rearming in breach of the Treaty of Versailles. The time to have halted Hitler was in the Rhineland in 1936. The time to have halted the Soviet Union was in 1945, when the Americans had overwhelming

[6] Quoted by G. N. Clark, *The Later Stuarts*, The Oxford History of England, 1934, p. 105.

atomic power: to say, truly enough, that this was politically impossible is an explanation not a rebuttal. 'The object of the balance of power, rightly understood,' it has been said, 'is not to carry on war with success, but to avoid war altogether.' If war breaks out, the system has failed.

CHAPTER VI

The Duel for Empire

In 1713, after the settlement at Utrecht, Louis XIV said that there were two satisfied powers in Europe, France and Austria, and two unsatisfied powers, Great Britain and Prussia. This was broadly speaking true, though as France's forces revived so did her ambitions. Austria came out of the War of the Spanish Succession with the Spanish Netherlands and Spanish territories in Italy, and a continuing feud with Spain which was to be a cause of disturbance in Europe. Spain, under Philip V and Alberoni, and later under Ripperda, was making the pace in Italy and much of European diplomacy until 1729 turned on this. Austria was for a while to be a conservative rather than an acquisitive power, the victim rather than the author of aggression. Louis XIV drew the necessary conclusion from this, and so did his great-grandson and successor, Louis XV, and the latter's minister, Cardinal Fleury. The conclusion was that there was no longer any sense in perpetuating the Bourbon–Habsburg antagonism: nevertheless, Austria remained the enemy of France in Europe as her enemy both in Europe and overseas was Great Britain. France took long to change her course. It was not until 1756, early in the Seven Years War (1756–63), that the switch to alliance with Austria against Prussia could be made, the object being, in part at any rate, to occupy Austria's attention while France settled her account with England. Even then, this new step was widely regarded in France as a national disaster; and it was remembered as a reproach against the monarchist régime by the men of the revolution after 1789.

France's first thought after the settlement of Utrecht was to reconstitute her shattered economy and to repair her military strength. For this purpose she sought an accommodation with her late enemy, Great Britain. The regency in France and the new Hanoverian dynasty in England, with a pretender in the offing, were not firmly seated. Both saw an interest in mutual support, given by the treaty concluded by Stanhope with Cardinal Dubois in 1716.

The diplomatic history of the eighteenth century is more complex than that of the seventeenth because there are more pieces on the board. Russia now makes an appearance; and Prussia, Poland, Sweden, Denmark and Savoy all now play a part in addition to France, Spain, Austria and Great Britain. No one continental power acquires a predominance over the others. There is no Charles V or Philip II; no Louis XIV or Napoleon. There are no wide coalitions of the threatened states against one state. The various powers, in order to maintain their relative positions *vis-à-vis* one another, transform the theory of the balance of power into the doctrine and practice of repartition or sharing out of territories. 'Whatever the variants or shades of meaning, the idea remains the same: ceaselessly balancing by way of constant repartition. But the passion for repartition becomes stronger than the concern for balance; or, more precisely, in the end throws overboard the conditions for preserving the balance.'[1] At first the bargaining for territory goes on in relation to the welter of small states in Germany and Italy: but the passion for sharing out culminates at last in the three partitions of Poland in the last quarter of the century. Indeed, the Emperor Francis II and Catherine II of Russia made a treaty in January 1795 not only for the completion of the partition of Poland, but also for the prospective partition or acquisition of Turkey, Venice and Bavaria.

There is a constant switching of alliances. Austria sometimes against and sometimes with Spain. Spain with, and then against, then again with, France in the Family Compacts. Prussia sometimes with and sometimes against Austria, sometimes against and sometimes with France. Russia, newly arrived on the Gulf of Finland and in the Baltic States and in Poland, manœuvres between France and Austria as she was to do in 1939 between the western powers and Germany. Great Britain sides with France and against Austria and then with Austria and against France. And the great reversal, the French switch from enmity to alliance with Austria in 1756.

After the Peace of Utrecht Great Britain, having let down her allies, Austria and Holland, was isolated. It was Stanhope's great achievement to repair this position by making treaties with Holland

[1] Translated from Charles Dupuis, *Le Principe d'Équilibre et le Concert Européen*, p. 41.

and Austria as well as with France in 1716. He also took strong action to curb Spain in the Mediterranean, and to maintain the balance between Sweden and Russia in the Baltic[2] and to protect our commerce against both. One of the greatest of our foreign ministers, Stanhope had, before his death in 1721, done much to pacify Europe, to establish Great Britain's position on the basis of a good understanding with France, and to pave the way for Walpole's ministry of peace and financial reconstruction, which in its turn prepared Great Britain for the ordeals to come.

In the years that followed, there was in London, as so often before and since, a tug-of-war between those who advocated a forward policy of continental involvement and those who worked for a policy of abstention, between aggressively minded Whigs like Townshend and Carteret on the one hand, acting often in the Hanoverian interest,[3] and that pacific Whig, Walpole, on the other, who was devoted to a policy of peace abroad and retrenchment at home. These divergent policies were framed and pursued in face of a Europe in which the powers engaged in manœuvres of the utmost complexity in a self-contradictory search for national advantage and for the maintenance of the balance. In the circumstances, there can be little doubt that Walpole's policy was in general the one best suited to Great Britain's situation at the time. The ambitions of France had not yet crystallized—Cardinal Fleury, who took office in 1726, was at the outset as much devoted to peace as Walpole himself: if there was a power with which we had difficulties, it was above all Spain, now temporarily revived in strength under Cardinal Alberoni, and these difficulties arose over the still persisting question of trade with Spanish America.

In our relations with Europe, a turning point came in 1731. Walpole, who had already in 1729 come to an accommodation with Spain, now reversed Townshend's adventurous policy of alliance

[2] It will illustrate how active our foreign policy was in this period to note that in 1727 'when Russian support for the Duke of Holstein seemed to threaten a new upheaval in northern Europe, a British squadron once more appeared in the Baltic to protect Sweden against the threats and pressure of her over-mighty neighbour—the tenth time in fourteen years that the British navy had appeared in force in these waters.' (M. S. Anderson, *Britain's Discovery of Russia, 1553–1815*, Macmillan, London, 1958, p. 109.)

[3] At one stage Townshend had plans to partition the Austrian Netherlands with France and Holland and thus give us a foothold on the Continent.

with France and others against Austria and made a treaty with Austria guaranteeing the Pragmatic Sanction by which Maria Theresa, the daughter of the Emperor Charles VI, was to succeed to the Habsburg possessions, and entering into mutual guarantees of the two countries' possessions. The treaty also put an end to interloping by the Austrian Netherlanders in the trade of the British and Dutch East India Companies. This treaty marked the beginning of a cooling-off in our relations with France and a return to William III's old combination with Holland and Austria. It would have been of greater benefit to us in later years had we not, upon a rather flimsy pretext, failed to come to Austria's assistance in fulfilment of an obligation when she was attacked by France, Spain and Savoy in the so-called War of the Polish Succession, a war which, in spite of its name, was in substance an episode in the secular rivalry of France and Austria. The result was a strengthening of France, a weakening of Austria and a general distrust of British policy. Walpole's remark to Queen Caroline in 1734 is well known: 'Madam, there are fifty thousand men slain this year in Europe, and not one Englishman.' This may have been fair enough: but our defection left us without an ally, and when Walpole was forced against his better judgment to go to war with Spain in 1739, we were once more isolated.

The Peace of Utrecht was soon seen not to have given us all the trading facilities in Spanish America to which we aspired. The monopoly of the trade in slaves (the so-called *Asiento*) and the one trading ship a year were not enough. Over the years acute grievances accumulated on both sides and there was a popular clamour for war. Walpole worked hard for peace, but the final word was spoken, not for the first or last time where peace or war are in question, by public opinion. Walpole held the war to be unjust and therefore impolitic and dishonourable. It was a war deliberately made, not for security, but for trade and empire, the so-called War of Jenkins's Ear. It was the result of an outburst of the old anti-Spanish feeling, the urge to tap the riches of the Spanish Empire, that had prompted the expeditions of Drake and the aggression of Cromwell.

In the eighteenth century, there was in British minds none of the uneasiness that often shot through the revived imperialism of the late nineteenth century, no talk of 'the white man's burden', no aching doubts such as inspired 'The Recessional'. Adam Smith had not yet subjected colonialism to cool economic analysis. Burke had not yet proclaimed the principle of trusteeship. Evangelicals had not yet preached the moral basis of the political life. At the most, there were later on to be occasional misgivings lest the overweening power to which Chatham brought us should provoke the formation of a European coalition against us, which indeed it eventually did.

It soon became increasingly plain on both sides of the Channel that it was between France and Great Britain that the struggle for mastery in the world would lie. The war with Spain that began in 1739 soon became a war with France which lasted until 1748. By 1740, France had, as Frederick of Prussia said, become 'the arbiter of Europe': she was both the strongest power and the power that held the balance between Austria and her adversaries. She still had ambitions in what was now the Austrian Netherlands and it was here that Great Britain was vulnerable. At one point in the War of the Austrian Succession (1740–48), Louis XV was able to advance into Belgium and for a time to occupy Antwerp. This was likely to be more advantageous to France than to campaign against Austria in Central Europe, where the only effect would be to serve the ends of Frederick, or, as the phrase went, *travailler pour le roi de Prusse.* When France was later allied to Austria, she could no longer invade the Austrian Netherlands, and to that extent France's switch of alliance was advantageous to Great Britain. It was advantageous in another way also. So long as France and Prussia were on the same side, as they had been in the war of the Austrian Succession, the Hanoverian domains of the new dynasty were in jeopardy, and it was for the sake of his beloved Electorate that George II fought in person against the French at Dettingen in 1743. Once Great Britain and Prussia were allied, as in the Seven Years War, the protection of Hanover could be made part of the bargain. Unlike the United Provinces in the time of William III, Hanover in the time of the Georges was an entangling embarrassment to Great Britain rather than a source of allied strength; our practice of paying Hanoverian troops with English money had the result, so the Elder Pitt declared in 1742, that England 'was considered only as a province to a despicable electorate.'

It was as a duel for empire overseas, and chiefly in America and India, that the main battle between Great Britain and France in the eighteenth century was fought. British and French statesmen were less conscious of this at the outbreak of the War of the Austrian Succession than they became during that war and after it. It had been touched off by Frederick of Prussia's invasion of Silesia, challenging the rights of Maria Theresa under the Pragmatic Sanction. It was a war which, since there were also Habsburg territories in the Netherlands and in Italy, as well as in Austria and in Hungary, came to involve pretty well the whole of Europe on one side or the other. We and the French were originally involved, not as principals but as auxiliaries of Austria and Prussia respectively. We ourselves were drawn into this war more than anything else through the Hanoverian connection. For us, it was unsuccessful on land, successful at sea. France won land battles, but lost her navy and was financially and economically crippled. As it proceeded, overseas rivalry with France grew, and hostilities continued overseas after the peace in Europe.

In the following Seven Years War, precipitated by Frederick's invasion of Saxony, as the earlier war had been by his invasion of Silesia, there was no doubt on either side of the Channel what the real issue between us was. As has so often happened when we have gone to war, the earlier stages of the Seven Years War were disastrous for us. So much so, that the public, who had clamoured for war in 1739, were now in panic and, as one historian has said, 'roaring for Pitt'. By the end of the war, under Pitt's inspired leadership, the French Navy was again destroyed and the French Empire, including Canada, India and most of the West Indies, almost completely conquered; and, what Pitt thought more important, French trade was disrupted. When Spain later entered the war, much of the Spanish island empire, including Havana and Manila, also came into our possession, though most of it was restored at the peace. The two wars of the mid-eighteenth century brought prosperity to Great Britain, as the two world wars of the first half of the twentieth century did to the United States of America.

This was the most aggressive period in our history, of which the elder Pitt will stand as the symbol. He did not recoil from resort to aggression for the sake of commercial expansion.[4] It was in revenge

---

[4] In the eighteenth century Great Britain was nearly self-sufficient—more completely so than Holland or France. Without their carrying trade and their foreign lending the Dutch could not have lived. We ourselves did not need to export in order to live. Nor had we yet begun to lend abroad. We exported our surplus of grain and textiles in order to buy necessary imports like naval stores and colonial goods and in order to pay interest on our foreign debt and the expenses of our hired foreign mercenary troops. On established mercantilist principles we exported also in order to build up as large as possible a surplus on overseas account, including an accumulation of precious metals, as a source of national strength. For this

for this that, after the partial restitution of the Treaty of Paris in 1763, and profiting from George III's neglect of the Royal Navy and from the revolt of the American colonists, France formed a most dangerous active coalition against our world-wide Empire, a coalition which included France, Spain and later Holland, with the hostile Armed Neutrality of Russia, Sweden, Denmark, Prussia, Portugal and Turkey. This was a new experience in our history. It not only ensured the independence of the United States, but placed our own security in such jeopardy that, but for Rodney's victorious battle off the Islands of the Saints in the West Indies in 1782, our isolation might have proved disastrous.[5]

Both France and Great Britain in the period after the Peace of Utrecht had had difficulty in determining their policy. The French tried without success to pursue both a continental and an overseas imperial policy. It was not till later in the century, in 1758, when French policy came into the hands of the Duc de Choiseul, a statesman of the calibre of Colbert and of Chatham, that France began to restore her fleet, building better ships than we did and manning them better, and to repair her diplomatic position. She was in 1763 to make a peace which saved much from the wreck. Choiseul's successor, Vergennes, timid and cautious though he might be, followed Choiseul's policy, and went near to bringing Great Britain to defeat. The fear and enmity between France and Great Britain was mutual. 'The English,' wrote a French official about the middle of the century, 'will rule the seas through their fleets and the land through their wealth, and America will furnish them with the means of dictating to Europe. . . . France alone is in a position to prevent this catastrophe, and France must do so for her own sake and that of all Europe.' On the other side there was Pitt declaring prophetically in 1763 after the Treaty of Paris: 'France is chiefly, if not solely,

purpose we could use the proceeds not only of exports but also of re-exports (e.g. of West Indian sugar), of the traffic in African slaves and of the profits (to use no harsher word) brought home from India. The picture is totally different from that of Great Britain in the later nineteenth century, no longer self-sufficient and with an economy nourished by massive investments abroad.

[5] France paid dearly for her intervention. Turgot warned Louis XVI in August 1774 that 'the first gunshot would drive the State into bankruptcy'. The consequence was, in fact, a financial and economic crisis of the first magnitude, which was one of the preludes to the revolution. By contrast, England, launched upon the industrial revolution, continued to prosper, and her trade with the lost colonies actually increased.

to be dreaded by us in the light of a maritime and commercial power: and therefore by restoring to her all the valuable West Indian islands, and by our concessions in the Newfoundland fishery, we have given her the means of recovering her prodigious losses and of becoming once more formidable to us at sea.' France saw England as a threat to her imperial self-sufficiency. For Pitt, the commercial prosperity of the British Empire was still precarious: the industrial revolution had not yet gathered momentum.

Two such adversaries were not likely to relax until one or other was subdued. The Peace of Aix-la-Chapelle, which had closed the War of the Austrian Succession in 1748, was an uneasy truce, derided in France: *bête comme la paix*, as the phrase went. Hostilities continued in the interval both in America (where Colonel George Washington took part in General Braddock's disastrous expedition against Fort Duquesne at the forks of the Ohio) and in India (where Clive and Dupleix strove for mastery) until the outbreak of the Seven Years War in 1756. At least four times in the century, the French organized potentially formidable attempts at invasion, once in 1744, again in 1756 and in 1759, and later in combination with Spain in 1779, when the enemy had sixty-six ships to our thirty-nine. All four were either abortive or were averted by a combination of good luck, including the luck of the weather, and of sound and at times superb naval dispositions. But it was touch and go, as it had been in 1588 and in 1690, and as it was again to be in 1797 and 1805, and in 1940. If Choiseul's plan for a surprise invasion out of the blue in time of peace had been tried, there might have been a different story to tell. We have had more good fortune, perhaps, than we have deserved; but the operation of invasion was never likely to be an easy one, and we were helped by the miscalculations, hesitations and sometimes plain ineptitude of the other side.

France's other weapon against us, the *guerre de course*, maritime commerce raiding, though it inflicted heavy losses (we lost 3,000 merchant ships, one-third of our tonnage, in the war of 1778–83), did not in the eighteenth century come anywhere near crippling us. Napoleon's later campaign of economic warfare was a more serious matter and our people suffered great hardship: but Napoleon bungled his scheme. It was not until the two World Wars of the first half of the twentieth century that commerce raiding from the air, from the sea and from under the sea brought us near to capitulation. Again, as so often in our history, it was a near thing. Not until Pitt took over supreme direction of war and foreign affairs in 1756 as Secretary of State and leader of the House of Commons, first nominally under Devonshire and later under Newcastle, did British policy follow a clear and decisive line, and it was an aggressive line, for sea-power, for trade, for empire. 'When trade is at stake,' said Pitt, 'it is your last retrenchment: you must defend it, or perish.'

Before these mid-century wars began, the Navy had been neglected. It was commanded by aged admirals. Operations were under the 'fighting instructions', officially tied to the rigid tactics of line of battle ahead. These, if followed by both sides, ensured a drawn engagement. Only if, often in breach of the rules, a commander went into a *mêlée* or ordered a chase was there likely to be a clear-cut victory. It has been calculated that between La Hogue in 1692 and the Saints in 1782 we engaged in fifteen major drawn battles of this kind in which no ship was lost by either side. Anson at Finisterre, Boscawen at Lagos on the coast of Portugal, and Hawke at Quiberon, were shining exceptions.

Indeed, by that time, a new spirit was alive in the Navy.[6] Hawke's audacious foray against the ships of Conflans at Quiberon in 1759 scotched Choiseul's invasion plan and put the French Navy out of the running for twenty years, until, by neglect, we became vulnerable once more. By contrast, in the numerous engagements between Admiral Hughes and the great French admiral, the Bailli de Suffren, off the coast of India, not a ship was lost on either side. It was the superb co-operation between Admiral Saunders and General Wolfe in 1759, on the basis of James Cook's masterly navigation, which assured the success of the well-planned but most hazardous combined operation for the capture of Quebec.

There has been nobody quite like Chatham in our history, either before or since. Elizabeth I was infinitely various in shifts of policy and knew how to wait. An artist in kingship, she was able to withstand her Parliament and people, and yet to gain their devotion. William III was cool, calculating, implacable, imperturbable, a man who lost battles and won campaigns, and he also knew how to wait, but was without popular appeal. Marlborough had an adamantine, Olympian quality both in war and diplomacy. The younger

---

[6] Admiral Vernon's capture of Porto Bello on the Panama Isthmus in 1739 so impressed George Washington's elder brother, Lawrence, who was serving with him, that he gave the Admiral's name to the plantation at Mount Vernon which was later to be George Washington's home on the Potomac.

Pitt had little of his father's genius, but was well served by what John Ehrman has called his 'peculiar blend of rectitude and political good sense', and by an all round practical adequacy as a statesman and parliamentarian. (The Napoleonic Wars, unlike earlier and later great wars, were won without an outstanding national leader—Pitt died ten years before Waterloo.) David Lloyd George was a statesman of dynamic energy and undaunted resolution and a politician of abounding if questionable resource who, as a statesman, saved his country but, as a politician, could not save himself from inglorious eclipse. Winston Churchill, in the great crisis of his life, drew upon and was sustained by our political and military history in deploying his own indomitable courage, his grasp of global strategy, his capacity to inspire and harness his military advisers and commanders, and the appeal of his sober but heartening and invigorating eloquence to both Parliament and people. Has there been in our history any greater in time of peril since King Alfred? Chatham was something of a manic-depressive, always in bad health and often, especially in later life, out of his mind. He took the conduct of the war in all theatres into his own hands and directed it with demonic energy and unerring skill, through young men of his own choice inspired by his own contagious enthusiasm, using the fervid support of the people to dominate Parliament and to quell opposition. He told the public the truth, whether there was good news or bad, and at first there was much bad news: 'I despise the little policy of concealments, you ought to know the whole of your situation.' When Abercromby met disaster at Ticonderoga in 1758, he at once, as Shelburne said, 'laid the whole detail open to inspection of the nation at large'. In this appreciation of 'the protective value of candour', he was followed by two other great leaders of their people through bad times and good, George Washington[7] and Winston Churchill. In 1761 the 'system' and the court brought him down. He had in a high degree that flamboyance and vaingloriousness which in good measure

---

[7] 'Washington had learned long previously the protective value of candour in dealing with the American people and he knew that one reason for their trust in him was their belief that he would tell them the whole truth.' (Douglas Southall Freeman, *George Washington*, Eyre and Spottiswoode, London, 1948, vi. 339). This is apropos of Major-General St Clair's disastrous expedition against the Indians in the north-west in 1791, when his troops were shot down, as Braddock's red-coats had been, in George Washington's own presence, on the River Monongahela by Fort Duquesne in 1755.

F

was to be found also in Wolfe and Nelson and in Montgomery of Alamein.

The peace of 1783 is commonly said to have marked the end of the first British Empire. We certainly lost the richest part of the Empire and the only part with a large English-speaking population; but we held Canada and most of the West Indian islands, and India was saved by Warren Hastings from the wreck. The loss of the American colonies is usually deplored by historians. Certainly there is much in the conduct of king, ministers and Parliament which reflects little credit on them. But the severance was probably inevitable sooner or later. Almost from the beginning, the colonists had developed a different outlook from people at home. Most of them left our shores, not to plant another Great Britain overseas, but to escape and to plant a new polity. It might perhaps be said of the colonies that we were well rid of them. Until near the end, the colonists were loyal to the King. Speaking to the Virginia Regiment on May 17th 1756, on the outbreak of war with France, Colonel George Washington said of George II: 'Let us show our willing obedience to the best of kings, and . . . demonstrate the love and loyalty we bear his sacred person.'[8] Benjamin Franklin said later of George III: 'I can scarcely conceive a king more truly desirous of promoting the welfare of all his subjects.' Nevertheless they wanted to live their own lives in their own way. This sentiment was at first stronger in New England than in the middle and southern states. The men of Massachusetts from the first showed a strong spirit of independence. They were more ready than those of Pennsylvania or Virginia to act in their own defence against the French. They twice helped to take Louisburg, Vauban's fortress in what is now Cape Breton Island. It was at Lexington in Massachusetts that the first shot in the War of Independence was fired; but the first move for independence came from Virginia on the basis of precedents drawn from the Great Rebellion and Commonwealth in England. Virginia, it was proudly claimed, 'gave the first written constitution to mankind.' It was to a Tirginiaa gentleman, surveyor, soldier, land speculator and slaveholding tobacco planter, George Washington, that the insurgents turned for their commander-in-chief and their first President. The break was long preparing. The causes were multifarious and cumulative. To one contemporary, the prime cause was the old colonial system, exercised not so much as in the past to accumulate bullion

[8] Quoted in Freeman, *George Washington*, ii. 205.

or to acquire raw materials, but for the benefit of the export trade of the home manufacturers. 'It was not,' wrote Arthur Young, 'the Stamp Act nor the repeal of the Stamp Act, it was neither Lord Rockingham nor Lord North, but it was that hateful spirit of commerce that wished to govern great nations on the maxims of the counter.' There is a good deal of exaggeration in this. The British colonial system was much more lenient than that of France or of Spain. There were many exceptions. Some of the provisions of the Acts of Trade were of advantage to the colonists, and those that were disadvantageous were widely evaded, with acquiescence in London.

Grenville's policy of 'thorough' raised the temperature between London and the colonies—his attempt to restore our economy and to build up our strength after the Seven Years War by trying to enforce in some measure the widely violated rules of trade under the colonial system, and by requiring the colonies to defray less than half the cost of their own defence. Time and time again between the enactment of the Stamp Act in 1765 and Cornwallis's capitulation at Yorktown in 1781, the way seemed to be open for a compromise that might perhaps have kept the colonies under the Crown. Tragically, George III and his ministers, unlike Pitt, Burke and Shelburne (the last-named, like Turgot in France, saw little use in colonies), were not alive to the spirit of the times; and Parliament was insistent not only upon its theoretical omnicompetence where the colonies were concerned, but also upon exercising some of its power in practice. The stubbornness was not all on one side. The colonists could have tried for a settlement which maintained a link with the Crown, if they had had a mind to it: but the intransigent minority were determined to force the issue and were no more ready than was London to compromise. The only practicable alternatives for London were to surrender or to fight. There were even then on both sides of the Atlantic those who glimpsed the possibility that the colonies might remain in loyal allegiance to the King and be proud to form part of his empire and yet enjoy complete self-government, as the older members of the Commonwealth do today; but this conception was too much in advance of the times. As George III said in his speech from the throne on November 29th 1774: 'You may depend on my firm and steadfast resolution to withstand every attempt to weaken or impair the supreme authority of this Legislature over all the Dominions of my Crown, the maintenance of which I consider as essential to the dignity, the safety and the welfare of the British Empire. . . .'[9] And indeed, for all the liberalism of their outlook, and their willingness to compromise in practice, neither Pitt nor Burke would dissent from this declaration as a statement of the principle of the supremacy of Parliament.

The conquest of Canada in 1759–60 made the independence of the colonies certain. The colonists were never for the most part more than half-hearted in their co-operation with the home government in resistance to the French and their Indian allies who hemmed them in between the Atlantic and the line of the St Lawrence, Ohio and Mississippi, and they moved more quickly towards independence once the French danger had been removed by Pitt's brilliant campaigns. Though the French seem to have set less store by Canada than by some of their other overseas possessions (Governor Duquesne had, for example, been warned by Paris in 1754 that unless the excessive upkeep of the Canadian colonies was reduced, the government would abandon them), they were bent on revenge upon the bloated British imperial power, and the American revolt gave them their opportunity. Washington's forces were in bad shape and on the edge of disaster, though he himself was indomitable as ever, when providentially Rochambeau by land and de Grasse by sea, profiting by a temporary superiority over the Royal Navy, helped him to bottle up Cornwallis in Yorktown and brought the war to a close. It was the French again, in the person of Napoleon, who, by negotiating the sale of Louisiana [10] to the United States in 1803, opened up the continent to the westward and pointed to the manifest destiny of the great new American and world power.

[9] This was, in fact, to restate the policy of the Commonwealth, enshrined in the Navigation Act of 1650, namely that 'colonies are and ought to be subordinate to and dependent on England—and subject to such laws and orders as shall be made by the Parliament of England.'

[10] The purchase covered not merely the present state of Louisiana but a vast territory stretching north-westward towards what is now the Canadian border.

CHAPTER VII

The French Revolution and Napoleon

In 1712 Great Britain, having deserted her allies, emerged victorious from a great European war. Within twenty years she had lost much of her influence. In 1763, having deserted her chief ally, she was again victorious. In 1763, 'the English race was at the top of golden hours' (G. M. Trevelyan) and 'for the time being . . . we appeared . . . at the peak of our glory' (Basil Williams). By 1781 we had lost the American colonies and stood alone against a powerful European coalition backed by the armed neutrality of most other European powers. In 1918 Great Britain and France, as members of a powerful coalition which included the United States, emerged decisively victorious from a great world war which left the enemy prostrate. Twenty years later they were coerced by their late enemy into sacrificing a small ally and were before long fighting for their existence. For reasons which we shall have to examine, this melancholy result did not follow the peace-making of 1815. The pattern is, however, so familiar that it is comforting to find that after the peace of 1783, which was not so disastrous as we deserved, we did seem to have learnt a lesson. As in 1588, when we met the Armada, so in 1793, when revolutionary France declared war on us, the Navy was in excellent shape. For this, that great sailor and administrator, Charles Middleton, later Lord Barham, must be given much credit. He was to Nelson what Hawkins had been to Howard and Drake, the man who built and equipped the ships and found the men, though unlike Hawkins, who had to suffer from Elizabethan parsimony, he was able as time went on to draw on the substantial resources provided by the younger Pitt's provident financial administration and care for the Navy.[1] From 1778 to 1790 he was Comp-

---

[1] That loyal supporter of the House of Hanover, strong Union man and admirer of the younger Pitt for his father's sake, Robert Burns, had something to say about this. When there was talk of a reduction in the estimates

troller of the Navy; but this was not the sum of his service to the State. Called to be First Lord of the Admiralty in 1805, at the age of 80, he was responsible for the superb naval dispositions, defensive and offensive, as bold as they were imaginative, that finally frustrated the invasion of Napoleon's Grand Army and, after that Army had turned its back on the Straits of Dover and started on its way to smash the third coalition at Ulm and Austerlitz, at Jena and Friedland, led up to the victorious offensive at Trafalgar.

It was not only in naval affairs that the inter-war years were well used. Pitt, Chancellor of the Exchequer at 22 and Prime Minister at 24, died in despair early in 1806 shortly after Austerlitz at the age of 46. A man of the nineteenth rather than of the eighteenth century, the type of Huskisson and Peel, he brought a new spirit into the conduct of political and economic affairs. Had it not been for the obstinacy and rancour of George III, who deserted him, the inertia of Parliament, and the long ordeal of the revolutionary and Napoleonic Wars, the age of reform would not have had to wait until the next century. France, unlike Great Britain, was able to remodel and modernize her state apparatus in the course of the conflict. Pitt did try to introduce parliamentary reform and he would have liked to abolish the slave trade. He reorganized the finances of the country. A disciple of Adam Smith, he believed in freeing trade from the restraints, largely nullified by smuggling, of the old colonial system. In 1786 he concluded a commercial treaty with the late enemy, France, based on the principles of free trade, which he planned to extend to other states. All this was in harmony with the underlying spirit of the times. The static and obsolete political system that still persisted was plainly in contradiction with the industrial revolution which was powerfully and pervasively moving its way into the national life, on the basis of an already rapidly increasing population. English commercial and industrial ascendancy did not take its rise from the industrial revolution. Already in the seventeenth

for the Royal Navy, Burns respectfully protested. Writing in 1786, he said:

> I'm no mistrusting Willie Pitt,
>   When taxes he enlarges,
> (An' Will's a true guid fallow's get,
>   A name not envy spairges),
> That he intends to pay your debt,
>   An' lessen a' your charges;
> But, God sake! let nae saving fit
>   Abridge your bonnie barges
>   An' boats this day.

century England was noted as 'adapted for a mighty trade' and re-nowned for the skill and ingenuity of her manufacturers. Nevertheless, it was this new source of industrial power which was, more than anything else, to sustain us in the long wars that were to come, making good the equipment of our armed forces and providing the means by which the successive European coalitions were to be financed.

Pitt has been set down by historians as a great peace minister, but as one without sureness of touch in foreign policy or strategy. Two of his early essays in diplomacy are worth noting.

The first is the episode of the Nootka Sound in what is now Van-couver Island. There is an interesting north Pacific background to this. The Russians had reached Kamchatka in 1697, well before they were established by Peter the Great on the Baltic and long before Catherine the Great had established Russia on the shore of the Black Sea. Bering (a Dane in Russian service) crossed the Strait that bears his name, in 1728, and the Russians moved into Alaska. The Spaniards, moving northwards, discovered Nootka Sound in 1774. James Cook passed that way in 1778. Nootka Sound became an important intermediate trading post for British ships in the China trade. The Spaniards, like the Dutch in the East Indies in the seven-teenth century, arrested some English traders. In 1790, Pitt threat-ened war. Spain gave way.

The second episode, the so-called 'Ochakov affair', was a rebuff, but no less significant.

During most of the eighteenth century, there had been a general feeling that Great Britain and Russia were natural allies against France. Our various entanglements with Russia had arisen from the interests of our monarchs in Hanover and in northern Europe, from the strong suspicion that Peter the Great was supporting the Jaco-bites, from our interest in the supply of naval stores from the Baltic, often jeopardized by conflicts between Russia and Sweden, and from the creation of a powerful Russian fleet based on the newly acquired ports in the Baltic. The Great Northern War of the early years of the eighteenth century, in which Sweden was in conflict with Russia and others, drew off Swedish and north German forces that might otherwise have been available in a critical phase of Marl-borough's campaign against Louis XIV in the War of the Spanish Succession. British opinion now for the first time became conscious of Russia, in the person of Peter the Great. Russian troops were to appear on the Rhine in 1735 during the so-called War of the Polish

Succession. And we were, towards the end of the War of the Austrian Succession, to seek by treaty the use of Russian troops, to be paid for by subsidy, for the defence of the Low Countries. Now the scene moves for the first time to the Near East and, if perhaps indirectly, ushers in the great eastern question: indirectly, because although wide Russian designs upon Ottoman territory were already causing apprehension[2] what was really here at stake was the balance of power or the *status quo* in Europe as between Russia and other interested powers and in particular, Prussia, who, with the Netherlands, was then our ally. In her war with the Ottoman Empire, Catherine had in 1788 occupied Ochakov, a small fortress on the Black Sea in the region of what was then the village of Odessa. Pitt, by launching an ultimatum which was not actually delivered, and by calling for increases in our naval armament, sought to intimidate her into giving up Ochakov and the strip of territory between the Bug and Dniester on which it stood, and which constituted our trade route with Poland. Catherine stood firm, insisting on her Dniester boundary with Turkey. Pitt, harried by Fox and his group of Whigs in collusion with Vorontsov, the Russian Minister in London, and in face of strong public opposition to such a bellicose stand against Russia, humiliatingly withdrew, though still unrepentant. His Foreign Secretary, the Duke of Leeds, resigned, holding that we were in honour bound under our treaty with Prussia to act against Russia. The public, however, could understand a maritime quarrel of the traditional kind with Spain about Nootka, but not a quarrel with Russia about an obscure Black Sea fortress. 'The point in dispute not being of a nature to exact any general interest, the abstract principle of preserving the balance of power in Europe . . . did not appear to the public sufficient reason for incurring the risk and expenses of war; and Mr. Pitt, perceiving that the armament was every day growing more unpopular, judged it expedient to abandon all idea of hostile interference.'[3]

[2] A cartoon of the day shows Catherine striding from St Petersburg to Constantinople above the gaping heads of the monarchs of Europe. Another depicts her being tempted by the devil to take Warsaw and Constantinople. The Treaty of Kuchuk-Kainardji (1774), concluded after a war in which the Russians had destroyed a Turkish fleet in the Aegean, gave Russia special rights in the principalities of Moldavia and Wallachia and of navigation through the Straits. In 1782, there had been plans for the partition of Turkey in Europe between Russia and Austria.

[3] George Tomline, *Memoirs of the Life of William Pitt*, London, 1821, ii. 407–8.

The French Revolution and Napoleon

This episode is significant, for one thing, in that it is an early example of the way in which pressure of parliamentary and public opinion can sway the actions of ministers in foreign affairs. Parliament, in debating the question, was fully conscious of the constitutional issues involved in the exercise of what Sheridan called the 'preventive wisdom' of Parliament. William III had been wise enough to wait upon the consolidation of public opinion behind his policies before he embarked on them, though it is fair to say that while he had his eyes on France in Europe, many of those who supported him had their eyes overseas. In making the Peace of Utrecht, the Tories had had the public behind them. In going to war against Russia in 1854 and against Germany in 1939, our governments acted under public pressure. Pitt could claim that Russian expansion in the Near East was dangerous; that our trade with Poland by way of the Black Sea and the rivers was jeopardized; and that we were in honour bound to play in with our ally Prussia. But the course he was set upon was an aberration from normal British policy; and the public saw it as such and would have none of it.

The Ochakov affair is significant too in that in the debates upon it in Parliament in March and April 1791, one in the Lords and three in the Commons, there was much discussion on the practice of the balance of power. The opponents of Pitt's policy did not challenge the principle itself, the principle namely that there would be a national right, and even a national duty, to intervene if the balance was seriously threatened. What they asserted was that the measure of the threat in this particular case did not justify our intervention at the risk of war. They protested against what Fox called the 'diabolical principle' that the object of the balance of power was to maintain all states in precisely the same relative positions of power. Its object was rather, he held, to prevent any one state from acquiring an ascendancy dangerous to the rest. Fox said he had supported its operation in the past against the intriguing, restless policy of France. France was, for the present, no longer behaving in that way and no one, and certainly not Russia, had taken her place.[4]

It is interesting to note how prone we were in the eighteenth century, in the relatively brief periods when we were not at war, to dabble in the now almost inexplicable complexities of European politics and to enter into alliances committing us to afford military

[4] Debates summarized in *Parliamentary History*, vol. XXIX.

assistance. There may have been some excuse for this at times when our kings were exercised about Hanover, as George I and George II both were. But George III cared little about Hanover, and it is difficult to see what British interest was served by these continental manœuvres between 1783 and 1793. They were certainly alien to the characteristics of British policy so penetratingly described by Albert Sorel.[5] We had no continental ambitions and, once the Navy was restored to strength, our security was not seriously threatened. These activities derived from the obsession with the compensatory theory of the balance of power, so cherished by continental and particularly Austrian theorists, which was then the real sport of kings, the theory, namely, that in all cases of territorial acquisition the shares of the various courts were to be fixed, as far as possible, in accordance with the proportions already existing between their respective resources. Into this calculation would enter, for example, not only the numbers but also the quality of the 'souls' acquired in the new territories. This practice of the balance of power was exploded by the Napoleonic cataclysm. Thereafter the preoccupation was, first, to build up coalitions against the actual or prospective aggressor, a procedure that has since become familiar to us; and secondly, once the aspiring conqueror had been subdued, to establish a new balance and to seek to maintain it by a concert of the powers either regionally or universally based. This procedure, also, has become familiar to us. They were both adopted, in parallel, in the peace which brought the Napoleonic Wars to an end.

How was it that Great Britain found herself at war with revolutionary France in 1793? Pitt, as a great peace minister, certainly wanted to stay out of war. He did not see France as a military or naval danger. As late as February 1792, in his budget speech, he said that there never was a time when, 'from the situation in Europe, we might more reasonably expect fifteen years of peace than at the present moment.' When war came, he thought that it would be a short war 'and certainly ended in one or two campaigns'. So indeed, it ought to have been: but, with brief intervals, it lasted for over

[5] 'The English only make up their minds to fight when their interests seem absolutely threatened. . . . Their history is full of alternations between an indifference which makes people think them decadent, and a rage which baffles their foes. They are seen, in turn, abandoning and dominating Europe, neglecting the greatest continental matters and claiming to control even the smallest, turning from peace at any price to war to the death.' (*L'Europe et la Révolution Française*, i. 340–41).

twenty-two years. The French offered help to revolutionary movements in Europe. Still, Pitt would not join the Allies in attacking France in 1792. Unlike Burke, he had no bent for an ideological crusade. Our war against revolutionary France was not an antirevolutionary crusade any more than the War of 1939 was a crusading anti-Fascist war (though many people supported it as such), or the North Atlantic Treaty (as we see it, though not perhaps as some Americans see it) a crusading anti-Communist instrument. The French occupied the Austrian Netherlands, opened the Scheldt and invaded Holland. Now it was the old story again. Here certainly was a *casus belli*. We had an obligation to Holland, though not to Austria. The French saved Pitt the trouble of a decision by declaring war themselves in February 1793, as the Japanese and the Germans saved the United States from a decision in 1941. Unlike the wars of the mid-century, this and the Napoleonic War which followed were for us not primarily wars for trade or empire, but rather wars for security, though we added to the empire in the course of them.

Pitt, as so often happens, prepared to fight the last war but one, the Seven Years War which his father had so brilliantly conducted, by concentrating on naval action, on commando raids on the European coast, and on military operation overseas, chiefly in America, only sending forces to continental Europe to sustain his ally Frederick of Prussia. Europe was to Chatham a secondary theatre, though our battalions covered themselves with enduring glory under 'the German chief', Prince Ferdinand of Brunswick, at Minden in 1759. The war against revolutionary France called for a continental rather than for a maritime policy, for a Marlborough rather than for a Chatham, and Pitt was neither. Pitt's eyes were on the wealthy sugar islands in the West Indies, as Chatham's had been on Canada. He sent a large part of our available forces to the Caribbean, and only a few ill-trained and ill-equipped troops to Flanders. In the West Indies, disease killed our troops by thousands. In Europe, Russia and Prussia were more interested in digesting their Polish spoils than in meeting the revolutionary armies. The Austrians and British were driven out of the Low Countries, which were then absorbed by France. Austria was put out of the war by Napoleon in Italy in 1797. Great Britain, as before and since, was left to fight alone. Spain, as well as France, was now an enemy. We were excluded from the Mediterranean. France had the Dutch, and, later, the Danish fleet at her disposal.

Introductory: The Road to Power

Here the Navy, to its lasting glory, saved the situation by four resounding victories. In February 1797, John Jervis beat the Spaniards at Cape St Vincent, a battle in which Nelson, as a captain, first gave signal evidence of his quality. Surviving a mutiny at Spithead and perhaps something worse at the Nore, our fleets then disposed of the remaining enemy fleets one by one. In October 1797, Adam Duncan, a Scots Member of Parliament, who had successfully bamboozled the enemy during the Nore mutiny, now by an attacking manœuvre of what has been called 'outrageous bravery', destroyed the Dutch fleet off Camperdown. In August 1798, Nelson, now for the first time in independent command of a fleet, by a similar manœuvre, as bold as Hawke's at Quiberon or Duncan's at Camperdown, destroyed Napoleon's fleet in Aboukir Bay and left him and his invading army stranded in Egypt. This Battle of the Nile, coming when it did, brought almost as great relief to British hearts as did Trafalgar in 1805 and the Battle of Britain in 1940. This was so, not because of Egypt (though it was already then held that the possession of Egypt by a great European power would be a circumstance fatal to our interest), but because it removed a grave threat to our security. Then, lastly, Nelson in 1801 destroyed the Danish fleet under the guns of the forts at Copenhagen, and gave the quietus to the armed neutrality of the northern powers, formed to resist, by force of arms if necessary, British search of neutral ships for contraband. We were also able to pick up our adversaries' colonial possessions at will. In particular, the Cape of Good Hope and Ceylon were taken from the Dutch to secure the route to India.

As Russia's change of front had saved Frederick the Great in the Seven Years War, so now Great Britain, standing alone, was to be relieved of a great peril by Russia's withdrawal from the armed neutrality in 1801. It was to be so again when the Tsar Alexander withdrew from the continental system and brought upon himself Napoleon's campaign of 1812. It was, indeed, to be so yet once again in 1941, though not by Russia's doing, when Great Britain stood alone against a triumphant coalition and when Hitler, abandoning his invasion plan, thrust his forces into the immense spaces of Russia, and broke them against the strength of the Russian people.

Before the naval victories of 1797 and the following years, Pitt, isolated and conscious of defeat, had tried without success to come to terms, a project thunderously attacked by Burke in his *Letters on a*

The French Revolution and Napoleon

Regicide Peace. After the naval victories and the breach of the armed neutrality, with Great Britain supreme at sea and much of Europe in Napoleon's hands, he accepted an offer and the Treaty of Amiens (like the Treaty of Aix-la-Chapelle in 1748, a mere truce) was concluded in 1802. Malta, and sea-power in the Mediterranean, and the sea-road to Egypt as the way to the east, were in 1803 the immediate cause of our re-entry, with great public enthusiasm, into the war, again alone. But in substance the establishment of France's natural frontiers, her possession of Belgium with the port of Antwerp, her command of a range of satellite republics, and the consequent threat to national security and overseas trade—even these had been accepted at Amiens—made the continuance of peace intolerable. Napoleon was not a man who would fail to press his advantage to the utmost. He could not stand still.

Napoleon tried three plans for the crippling or subjugation of Great Britain. The first, following an earlier project of Choiseul, was, by seizing and holding Egypt and in the process bringing liberty and enlightenment to that benighted land, to open the way to the overland approach to India, through the traditional invasion route across the north-west frontier. Lacking sufficient naval strength, he could not do what Suffren had only just failed to do in 1783, namely command the sea-approaches by which the western powers had themselves entered the sub-continent. This project and much else was shattered by Nelson's first 'crowning mercy', the victory of the Nile in 1798. Napoleon was, as he himself said, bored with the old Europe. He aimed to restore the greater France of the eighteenth century. He was in the end no more successful than Louis XV had been in trying to make France both a continental and an imperial power. The second project was the favourite French plan of invasion, frustrated by Barham and his admirals. The third was economic warfare, an attempt to bring Great Britain to her knees without invasion, since invasion after Trafalgar was no longer possible. This is a form of attack to which Great Britain is peculiarly vulnerable. The continental system came very near to success. Its objective was not to starve us but to cripple our economy by closing foreign markets to our exports. For a year or two it was touch and go. But Napoleon, being a mercantilist, thought exports to be of extreme importance. So, while trying to shut off the import of British goods into Europe, he allowed European exports even to Great Britain, with the result that it was European wheat which helped to ward off

93

the grave danger of starvation in England in the famine years of 1809–1812. Even the ban on British exports became ineffectual: the smuggling of British goods became a form of 'resistance' by the European populations, and Napoleon himself was forced in 1812 to order and pay for military clothing secretly in England for his army in Poland, a consignment duly intercepted in the North Sea by British cruisers.

Nevertheless the period between 1807 and 1810 was for us one of the two low points in the war. (The other was 1797.) It was the apogee of Napoleon's Empire, his new order in Europe, in which, as Metternich said in 1809, there was no element of permanence, and which, in the words of Münster, the sagacious Hanoverian Minister in London, carried the principle of self-destruction within itself. In 1807, Prussia, Austria and Russia were all at war with Great Britain, and Napoleon was allied to, or exercised control over, almost all the rest of Europe outside the Balkans. The defection of Russia from the continental system at length relieved the strain on Great Britain and provoked Napoleon's campaign of 1812: he was again striking at England, this time through Russia. The fundamental objectives of Alexander and Napoleon in eastern Europe were as irreconcilable as those of Hitler and Stalin were later to be.

Napoleon's success in frustrating the formation of European coalitions against him, and of weakening them or breaking them up when once formed, is the measure of his genius as soldier and diplomatist. The direct way was to knock them out by force of arms as he did the second coalition at Marengo, and through Moreau, at Hohenlinden in 1800, and the third coalition at Ulm and Austerlitz in 1805. But he and the revolutionary government before him were able, by the exercise of the ever-skilled French diplomacy, to play on the ambitions and cupidities of the European powers and to stimulate their rivalries and jealousies. 'It was the hunger for territorial aggrandizement which caused the powers who were joined in coalition against the French Revolution to come to terms with the revolutionary government. . . . During the whole course of the revolutionary and imperial epic, it was repartition, distribution, promises, even the simple hope for the spoils of weaker states, which enabled France to divide her enemies, and to dissolve or forestall coalitions.'[6]

In the end it was not the upsurge or the revolt of the captive or

[6] Translated from Dupuis, *Le Principe d'Équilibre*, pp. 41–42.

oppressed peoples which was decisive in bearing him down, but the inexorable pressure of British sea power, its use to nourish the campaign in Spain, and the military prowess of the imperial and royal armies of the European monarchs, for once hammered together in firm alliance and sustained by British subsidies. The peoples buttressed and seconded their armies, and most effectively so in Spain and Russia, but in the end it is armies that win battles. Just as the successes at Valmy and Jemappes were won, not by raw revolutionary levies but by the veterans of Louis XVI's army, so too 'the steadiest of the Prussian troops who fought Napoleon's last generation of conscripts were not volunteers but reservists trained under the short service system which Scharnhorst had kept in operation with various disguises since 1809.'[7] When, in 1815, Napoleon made a dash into Belgium to forestall the junction of the British with the forces of the central European powers, he was brought to a halt and finally crushed by the fortitude of Wellington and his international force (including a scratch British contingent, trained and equipped by the methods introduced by David Dundas, the Duke of York and John Moore), and by the Prussians under that most loyal and co-operative of allies, Prince Blücher.

As an industrial, maritime, imperial, commercial power, we were better fitted than any of the other European belligerents, as we were again to be in 1914, to endure the course of so long a period of warfare. At the end of it Great Britain emerged, as she could no longer do in the same degree in 1918, 'the strongest, richest and most powerful country in the world' (J. H. Plumb),[8] in a position, if she so wished, to dominate the negotiations for a peace settlement. 'Never before or since,' says Professor H. C. Allen, 'has her influence in international affairs been so great or so unchallenged.' We had been able to draw upon what Canning called 'that vital spirit, that germ of strength which had enabled so small a country to make such extraordinary exertions to save itself, and to deal out salvation to the world.'

Such power and influence abroad, real though they might be, and based as they were on the prestige of an outstanding contribution to Allied victory, and on great industrial and commercial strength

[7] E. L. Woodward, *War and Peace in Europe, 1815–1870*, Constable, London, 1931, p. 10.

[8] This might be true of Great Britain as a world power; but in Europe Russia was stronger.

deriving from a rich and extensive colonial empire, were accompanied by grave internal difficulties, financial and social. Napoleon had been able to batten on Europe. There had been no need to raise French taxes substantially until 1813. In 1815, the French public debt stood at 50 francs a head of the population; in Great Britain it was 1,000 francs. Great Britain had had to carry the coalitions upon her back. She was a prey to 'the confusions and social disasters of rapid industrial change' and 'on the edge of bankruptcy and social revolution' (J. H. Plumb). These dangers were surmounted by a combination of immediate repression with a gradual process of political and social redress and rapid economic expansion during the course of the next half century or so, which historians have called the 'Age of Reform' or the 'Age of Improvement'.

Part II

CLIMAX AND CLIMACTERIC:
WATERLOO TO THE DIAMOND JUBILEE

CHAPTER VIII

Castlereagh, Canning, Palmerston

The predominance of Great Britain in relative power and influence in 1815 was more firmly based than it had been in 1713 or in 1763. In course of time, after the War of the Spanish Succession and the Seven Years War, we suffered fluctuations in our fortunes, and at times our power fell into decline, our influence into eclipse and our security into jeopardy. This process did not repeat itself after 1815. Until about 1840, the Royal Navy was strong enough to meet any conceivable combination. This was not so much because the Navy was kept up to strength. Most of it was laid up for a generation after 1815. At the time of the Battle of Navarino in 1827 only seventeen of the ninety-five capital ships of the British Navy were in commission. As in the years after the Peace of Utrecht, the senior admirals were of great age. The position was, rather, that other powers had also laid up even more of their ships. Not until towards mid-century, with the coming in of iron and steam to displace wood and sail, a development in which the French were ahead of us, did we need to look with anxiety on other fleets. We conformed to the new technique with reluctance. In 1828, the Lords Commissioners of the Admiralty still held that 'the introduction of steam is calculated to strike a fatal blow at the naval supremacy of the Empire.'

In manufacture, in merchant marine, in foreign trade, in international finance, we had no rival. Though still adding to our overseas possessions, we were becoming a satisfied power. Our acquisitions at the Vienna peace settlement were mostly aids to sea-power: Heligoland, Malta, Mauritius, Trinidad, St Lucia, Tobago, the Cape of Good Hope and a protectorate in the Ionian Islands. We resisted the pressure of commercial interests for the retention of other conquests, such, for example, as the Dutch East Indies. As

99

we came, by deliberate act of policy, to adopt the practice of free trade and to apply the principle of 'all seas freely open for all', we moved towards the *Pax Britannica*, using the Royal Navy to keep the seas open for the common benefit, to suppress piracy and the slave trade, and to prepare and publish charts of every ocean. No other of our western rivals now had an empire. The French had lost most of their overseas possessions outside the West Indies. They were later to build a new empire and to come into controversy with us once more. The Spanish colonies in Central and South America were cutting loose from the mother-country and opening themselves to our trade. The Dutch and Portuguese were normally friendly to us, and their still extensive empires would be open to our commerce. Having no territorial ambitions in Europe, and no desire to shut the foreign trader out of our empire, we provoked no coalition against us. We had a secure base from which to exercise our influence in the world. We used that influence to preserve the *status quo* and to ward off threats to key points in our communications—the Baltic, the Channel, Gibraltar and the Straits.

The bare recital of the instruments which composed the post-Napoleonic settlement[1] can give no idea of the immense and sustained effort required to achieve their conclusion. It involved the creation and maintenance of a coalition of powers with diverse systems of government and diverse interests and aspirations, through all the alarms and uncertainties of the last campaigns against Napoleon, whose military skill was still formidable and whose name had still not lost its appeal. There could be no certainty that he would be beaten: indeed, again and again Austria pressed for a compromise peace. The four powers had to decide whether to negotiate with Napoleon or to dethrone him, and, if the latter, whether or not to work for the restoration of the Bourbons. They had to settle how best to safeguard themselves and the rest of Europe against a possible recrudescence of French aggressive power. They had to keep the peace among themselves. Above all, they had to provide for the reconstruction and future stability of a Europe which had been shaken to its foundations by the explosion of the French Revolution, and thrown into the political melting-pot by the creation of the

[1] The Treaty of Chaumont (March 1814); the First Treaty of Paris (May 1814); the Treaty of Vienna (June 1815); the Holy Alliance (September 1815); the Second Treaty of Paris and the Quadruple Alliance (November 1815).

Grand Napoleonic Empire which, at its maximum, had established its sway over Europe from Madrid to Warsaw. It is not surprising that Castlereagh wanted Europe to return to peaceful habits.

Talleyrand now raised, for the benefit of the Bourbons, the principle of legitimacy, by which kings and princes dispossessed by the revolution or by Napoleon claimed to regain their seats. But it meant more than this. It stood for legality and due process of law as against such things as mob rule or Napoleon's rule of force. It did not stand in the way of constitutional advance—Louis XVIII himself granted a constitution in 1814. It was unsuccessfully invoked later by the despots in order to inhibit all change. If it was to be more successfully challenged by popular movements in Europe, it was at any rate more respectable than the principle of kingship by conquest and loot as applied by the House of Bonaparte.

Here a new factor enters into the history of Europe. For the first time, the two peripheral powers, Great Britain and Russia, play a major part in the remodelling of the Continent, and for the first time Russia plays an active part in the current politics of western Europe, particularly in France, in Italy and in Spain. The role of Great Britain in the reconstruction was the greater of the two. This could be so because Great Britain, alone of the great powers, had never been constrained to ally herself with the conqueror; because her naval power ensured for her a wide freedom of action; because in the campaign in the Peninsula she had administered the first real check to the armies of Napoleon; and because she was the dispenser of the subsidies without which the continental powers would have been unable to fight. Along with this was the fact that she had a government the members of which were united and steadfast to continue the struggle; and the further fact that, for the conduct of her foreign relations, she could call on two men of outstanding distinction, Viscount Castlereagh,[2] the Foreign Secretary, and the Duke of Wellington, the victor in Spain, for a time ambassador in Paris, in due course to be the victor of Waterloo, the commander-in-chief of the Allied forces of occupation in France and a minister of the Crown. Castlereagh and Wellington knew each other well, were usually of one mind and could work together in the fullest confidence.

[2] Robert Stewart, Viscount Castlereagh, held a courtesy title as heir to the earldom (later the marquessate) of Londonderry. He sat in the House of Commons until he succeeded his father in 1821.

Nevertheless, the ascendancy which Castlereagh was able to exercise so often during the ten years of his Foreign Secretaryship (1812–22) over the deliberations of the sovereigns and ministers of the powers before, during and after the Congress of Vienna, owed most of all to his own qualities of mind and character. The power of Great Britain counted for much; but if a Foreign Secretary can speak with knowledge and act with courage and composure, if his appraisements are habitually cool and realistic, if he is frank, patient and conciliatory in approach and exposition, if he is skilful in diagnosis and in manœuvre and shows a concern for the general interest as well as for the interest of his own country, if he has no claims of his own to put forward which conflict with the territorial aspirations of his interlocutors, and if he has no desire for personal glory and is content to reap his successes quietly and unobtrusively, confining them to essentials and leaving something over for the other parties to the negotiation to put to their credit, then his influence will grow. His foreign colleagues will turn to him in difficulties, and will allow him to mediate in their controversies, and will rely on him to act with decision in emergencies. Castlereagh had all these qualities. Thiers, no friendly critic, said of him: '*Personne n'eût voulu sans lui prendre un parti ou donner une réponse.*'

Thanks to this, no one did more than Castlereagh to marshal the forces that brought about the downfall of Napoleon, to secure Europe against a feared renewal of French aggression and to re-create and confirm a new European balance of power. He must sometimes share the credit with the Tsar Alexander, as when, with Wellington, they protected France from Prussian spoliation and revenge; and sometimes with Metternich, who was to help him to resist some of Alexander's later plans for intervention against popular movements; but without his strong guidance it is unlikely that the coalition would have stood to the end against Napoleon, or that so durable a settlement would have been devised, or that the alliance which was designed to bind the four powers together after the settlement would have been concluded.

Castlereagh was absent from London continuously for nearly sixteen months from December 1813, when he joined the conclave of Allied representatives at Basle, until, after a peripatetic course from headquarters to headquarters, he handed over to the Duke of Wellington at the Congress of Vienna in February 1815, to return via Paris to London, on the eve of Napoleon's return from Elba.

Later in 1815 he was away in Paris for several months. To our modern ideas, it is extraordinary that his colleagues in the Cabinet should have allowed him such wide discretion to take decisions in their name on the gravest matters of peace or war. He went to the Congress of Vienna without first returning home for instructions, and seems to have carried no special instructions with him, though he knew the mind of the Cabinet from letters received from the Prime Minister, Liverpool, and from Bathurst, the Secretary of State for War and the Colonies. His colleagues usually endorsed what he did, though sometimes with misgivings. On occasions when they had other ideas than his, he felt sure enough of his own judgment and of his powers of persuasion after the event to secure their approval. Liverpool, who had himself twice been Foreign Secretary, was kept in touch through an active correspondence with Edward Cooke, Castlereagh's under-secretary, who conducted himself with impeccable loyalty. Neither the Cabinet nor orthodox public opinion was much interested, except by fits and starts, in anything but the overthrow and dethronement of Napoleon and the achievement of security against France: as to this the public felt very strongly indeed, especially after the second overthrow of Napoleon. The Whig and Radical opposition was weak and divided, unskilful in debate, and seldom gave serious trouble. It is again astonishing, to our ideas, that Liverpool did not think it necessary to seek Cabinet approval before ratification either of the secret treaty with Austria and France of January 3rd 1815 or of the Second Treaty of Paris, or before approving the terms of the Quadruple Alliance.

Castlereagh's staff, both in the Foreign Office at home and at his conferences abroad, was extremely small.[3] There was no regular diplomatic service, and Castlereagh did nothing to create one. After so long a breach of relations with so many countries in Europe, staffs for missions in foreign capitals had to be found in haste. In spite of this, he was well enough served. Both in London and at European conferences, though no doubt partly by preference, he had to write his drafts in his own hand. He did not open his full mind even to his most trusted subordinates, but he could be assured of their complete devotion. By his own practice, by general precept and by individual admonition, he brought a new spirit into the practice of British diplomacy. Missions in foreign countries were to

[3] In 1821, the Foreign Office had a staff of twenty-eight persons. Canning increased it to thirty-six.

act in a spirit of trust and goodwill, to discourage any spirit of petty intrigue or perpetual propagation of alarm upon slight evidence, and to inspire so far as possible a temper of morality and confidence. Since his day, his precept and example have not been forgotten and have left their mark on the outlook of the Foreign Office and its agents abroad.

The statesmen who made the post-Napoleonic settlement were still attached to the principles and practice of the balance of power. Gentz, the busy, volatile Jewish secretary of Metternich and of the Congress of Vienna itself, and unofficial assistant to Castlereagh, wrote a treatise on the subject. Metternich himself thought it was chimerical to suppose that there could be repose without equilibrium. Castlereagh spoke again and again of the need for a 'just equilibrium'. Gentz cynically remarked that the real object of the congress was the partition among the victors of the spoils seized from the vanquished; but there was more than this in the minds of the participants. Territories were certainly distributed without regard for the wishes of the population, but there was a desire for stability. Castlereagh's idea of a balance was, first, to contain France. He was as adamant on keeping the French out of the Low Countries as he was in declining to discuss British maritime rights at the Congress. France was to be held in the north, by bringing the Austrian Netherlands (the future Belgium) together with Holland into a new, enlarged kingdom of the Netherlands, and—in order to strengthen this as a barrier—by ceding the Rhineland to Prussia; in the south, by restoring Piedmont to the kingdom of Sardinia, adding Savoy and Genoa, and, again to strengthen the barrier, by allotting Lombardy and Venetia to Austria. France would be back within her frontiers of 1790 and contained by barrier states north and south. In the centre, the independence and neutrality of Switzerland would be guaranteed. These precautions—the barring of the customary French invasion routes—were necessary, though France after 1815 never again became a serious menace to Europe as Germany was allowed to do after 1918.

The next problem was to strengthen central Europe as a buffer between France and Russia. For this purpose, the German states, which had been reduced in number by Napoleon from three hundred to thirty-nine, were formed into a loose confederation centred in Frankfurt. As a corporate body it proved to be impotent, being dominated by Austria and Prussia, who were members of it in respect of part of their territories. In addition to this, there was to be a grandiose combination, one element of which would be the incorporation of the kingdom of Saxony in Prussia. Prussia and Austria would thus be in contact, and both would be strengthened. The second element would be the elevation of the Napoleonic Grand Duchy of Warsaw (carved chiefly out of the Prussian share of the partitions), or some portion of it, into an independent state, or, failing this, a limited annexation of Polish territory by Russia, against whom this would provide a second barrier. Russia would retain Finland, which she had conquered from Sweden, and Sweden would take Norway from Denmark, who would receive compensation elsewhere.

The combination completely broke down. This was the first of Castlereagh's two great failures. The Tsar held to his plan for Poland. He would create from his conquests in the Grand Duchy a kingdom to which he would give a constitution, and of which he himself would be sovereign. He ranged Prussia on his side. Austria withdrew her always reluctant consent to the incorporation of Saxony into Prussia. It needed a bold step by Castlereagh, namely the drafting and signing on January 3rd 1815, without reference to London, of an alliance between Great Britain, Austria and France against Russia and Prussia,[4] and some war alarms, before a solution could be found. The Tsar had his way, conceding some former Polish territory to Prussia. The King of Saxony kept his throne, but lost some territory to Prussia.

Poland here provided the basis for a *rapprochement* between Russia and Prussia which was, down to the Congress of Berlin in 1878, to be one of the fixed points in the European political scene. In 1831 and 1863, Great Britain and France were powerless to help the Poles, in face of a stand by Russia with Prussian (and in 1831 also Austrian) support. In 1919, when Russia and Germany had both gone down in defeat, Poland at last regained her independence. In 1939, whereas the existence of an independent Poland lying between Russia and Germany prevented Great Britain and France from forming a coalition with Russia against Germany, these two

---

[4] Castlereagh had been warned by London not to take any step that would involve war, so that he was here acting against the spirit of his instructions. His hand was strengthened by the receipt on January 1st of news of the signature at Ghent of the treaty of peace with the United States. But he knew that he was not taking a serious risk.

latter powers themselves came to an agreement on the basis of a new partition of Poland. In 1945, not all the power of the United States and Great Britain could prevent Russia, now standing alone, from bringing Poland within her exclusive sphere of influence. As in Alexander's day, a Polish state, shorn of the Russian share of the eighteenth-century partitions,[5] has again been established under Russian control. Again this situation is supported by Prussia, which is itself, in the guise of the so-called German Democratic Republic, also under Russian control.

Castlereagh was not the first or the last British minister to discover that eastern Europe is not a sphere where British diplomacy can work with much hope of success. Pitt had certainly found this to be so in his encounter with Catherine the Great in 1791. Perhaps from having continued so long in the realm of diplomatic combinations, Castlereagh had allowed his habitual sense of realities to desert him. Certainly, the Government in London, though less well informed, took a more detached and probably a juster view than he did of the international situation and its possibilities. Experience suggests that Foreign Secretaries who become deeply immersed in the intricacies of foreign relations can sometimes profit from the broader, less professional outlook of their Cabinet colleagues.

Castlereagh's second great failure was the ill-success of a project which was very near his heart. His experience of the Allied meetings at headquarters and elsewhere during the war had taught him to believe that joint meetings of persons in authority—monarchs or their ministers—were a better method of removing international misunderstandings and of reaching international agreements than the cumbersome, slow, chancy machinery of traditional diplomacy. Article VI of the Second Treaty of Paris had accordingly laid it down that the powers would hold periodic meetings 'for the purpose of consulting upon their common interest and for the consideration of measures most salutary for the maintenance of the peace of Europe'. Within a few years, the diversity of interpretation given to so loosely defined an objective was to disrupt the European concert which it had been hoped to create. The new method seemed to justify itself at the first post-war conference of Aix-la-Chapelle (1818), called to settle the affairs of France. But at the later conferences of Troppau (1820) and Laibach (1821), which dealt chiefly with Italy

[5] It is worth noting that the Polish territories then acquired by Russia were for the most part ethnically non-Polish.

and which Castlereagh declined to attend in person, the split between the constitutional and the despotic governments which formed the alliance became manifest, though Metternich sometimes did his best to bridge the gap. Castlereagh liked revolutionary movements no more than did the three despotic monarchs, but, unlike those monarchs, he did not believe that it was the business of the alliance as such to suppress them when they appeared in Spain or in Naples or elsewhere. Unlike them, he could not, as the representative of a constitutional régime, regard the mere voting of a constitution as akin to revolution. The alliance could not, he protested, be made into a union for the government of the world, an armed guardian of all thrones or a general European police for the superintendence of the internal affairs of other states. He would only contemplate intervention against a revolutionary movement if it threatened the security of neighbouring states and the balance of Europe. Had Castlereagh lived, he might have kept the conference system working for a while longer than in the event it did; but it was his own personal creation and it could not be expected very long to survive him, even had it not been that his successor, Canning, would have nothing to do with it.

Castlereagh, Tory though he was, was in this in advance of his time. He was still more so in an earlier project, which he had inherited from Pitt but which he soon abandoned, for a general guarantee by all the powers of Europe in one comprehensive treaty of the whole of the European settlement. He became much more cautious: he would only consider armed intervention if the territorial balance of Europe was disturbed, or if actual danger menaced the European system. He could not and would not act upon abstract and speculative principles of precaution.

He may be thought to have been looking ahead when he proposed the independence of Poland, or when he suggested that Turkey in Europe should be brought into the Vienna settlement (a suggestion which would have deeply divided the powers and which the Tsar and the Sultan both rejected); or when he contemplated recognizing the belligerency or even a possible government of the Greek insurgents; or when he did not recoil from the possibility of recognizing the independence of the Spanish American colonies. But the truth is that he was not looking forward to the coming phase in human development of which Canning was to have so keen a sense. He was seeking for ways to hold the existing order together by the operation of the traditional mechanics of power, under the mediating hand of Great Britain.

Canning, the new man who both preceded and succeeded the patrician Castlereagh as Foreign Secretary, was, like the latter, an avowed disciple of the younger Pitt, who, unlike his father, left a living political heritage behind him. Nevertheless, the differences between the two men, in their persons, in their policies and in their methods, have been more emphasized than have their resemblances. Castlereagh, it was said, never made a speech without making a friend, nor Canning without making an enemy.

It could, of course, be said that the objectives of their foreign policies, broadly considered, were the same, and that they would have defined the vital interests of Great Britain in the same way. It could be said further that in some respects they took a common view of some of the main considerations governing the conduct of British foreign policy. They both held that the maintenance of the balance of power was essential to the peace of Europe. They were both faithful to the Quadruple Alliance and were defenders of the territorial settlement of Vienna. Canning was a member of Liverpool's administration when Castlereagh's classic definition of the policy of non-interference in his paper of May 20th 1820, was fully discussed by the Cabinet, and there is some reason to think that its tone was influenced by Canning among others. They both believed that if, nevertheless, Great Britain felt called upon to intervene in arms, she should only do so, as Canning put it, 'in great emergencies and then with commanding force.' They are both on record as declining to base policy or action upon considerations of an abstract character.

When so much has been said, however, it remains true that the differences are more striking than the resemblances. The conduct of foreign relations consists not merely in the formulation of general lines of action. It involves the application of general policies to the problems that present themselves from day to day. Indeed the substance and colour of a foreign policy are determined as much, if not more so, by the details of its application as by the direction of its general drift. Canning held strongly that, especially in times of difficulty and danger, it was men, not measures, that mattered. And certainly, in the diplomacy of Castlereagh and of Canning, it is the men that confer the characteristic quality.

Castlereagh, as Wellington said, could neither talk nor write;

Castlereagh, Canning, Palmerston

Canning was brilliant as orator and writer. Castlereagh liked to work unobtrusively; Canning trumpeted his successes to the world. Castlereagh disdained to score off a diplomatic opponent; Canning took pleasure in using the force of his intellect and his command of words to discomfit an adversary and to be clever at his expense. Castlereagh told the House of Commons as little as he could and had no gift for public relations; Canning laid papers liberally and promptly before Parliament and used the House and the public platform as a sounding board in order to attract the support of the Press and of public opinion at home and abroad for his policies. Castlereagh was essentially a conservative; Canning, Tory though he was—he opposed parliamentary reform and the repeal of the Test Acts for dissenters—saw that the world was changing and did not recoil from the prospect. Germany, he had declared in 1814, was 'no longer a name, but a nation.' Castlereagh had looked for what he once called the 'European Commonwealth' though it eluded his search, and Metternich had spoken of a 'society of states'; Canning's slogan was 'every nation for itself and God for us all.' His policy was to destroy the congress system of 'summit conferences'—though he did agree to an ambassadors' conference at Petersburg in 1824— and to break up the alliance of the despotic powers lest they should combine against Great Britain or threaten the independence of other states. This he was able to do over the Greek question when, by a diplomatic revolution, he drew Russia and France together with Great Britain in opposition to Austria and Prussia. Castlereagh was one of the most European of our Foreign Ministers; Canning conducted his policy in a nationalistic spirit—Great Britain was to be the impartial umpire, not a member of a team. Castlereagh left the Foreign Office and the diplomatic, consular and messenger services much as they were; Canning, without greatly increasing their size, introduced reforms in organization, methods and conditions of service, and stimulated them by his peremptory bluntness of language[6] and by his own gigantic powers of work.

Castlereagh's diplomatic method could be safely applied to the policy of Great Britain no matter what her international situation might be. Of Canning's method, one might judge that it would only be appropriate in a situation where Great Britain could rely

[6] To Lord Strangford, ambassador in Petersburg, he wrote in December 1825: 'The instructions which I have now to give Your Excellency are comprised in a few short words, *to be quiet*.'

confidently upon her power and prestige and need not be too fearful of war. To crush by force and brilliance of argument like Canning, to use the hectoring tone of Palmerston, to deliver severe lectures like Lord John Russell, or to glory in bold manœuvres, would hardly be in keeping with Great Britain's outlook or with her position after the close of Palmerston's ministry in 1865. Foreign Secretaries would no longer boast of 'capital hits'. There might be a residue of vainglory in Disraeli; but henceforward the quieter ways of Castlereagh would prevail. Salisbury was the first of our later statesmen to understand the true purpose and achievement of Castlereagh and to take him as a model.[7] So also in Grey, in Eden and in Bevin, to name no others, it is the tradition of Castlereagh rather than of Canning that informs the handling of affairs. In the United States, a new country and one still growing in strength, the era of 'big-stick' diplomacy persisted longer and has not yet entirely passed.

Canning's methods were suited to his time, and they brought him some brilliant successes. Though he was unable to prevent the French from marching into Spain in 1823 and restoring the despotic régime,[8] he intimated that an advance into Portugal or an attempt upon the Spanish colonies in America would mean war. At this moment of peril, when Great Britain was isolated in face of France and the eastern despotic powers, Canning was at least able to avert the major threat to British interests. Since the late seventeenth century, it had been one of the consistent objects of our policy to prevent French control over the Spanish empire in America. Since the breakdown of the Spanish monopoly, our trade with Spanish America had greatly increased, and our exports of cotton textiles to that market were an important interest. Canning succeeded in persuading the French ambassador, the Prince de Polignac, in October 1823 to agree to a memorandum in which France abjured any design

[7] See, for example, the article on Castlereagh contributed to the *Quarterly Review* in January 1862.

[8] We should not have had the necessary land forces available; and Canning had small chance to use the weapon of diplomacy. George IV and some members of the Cabinet openly took the French side. About this time the King was in dangerously intimate and indiscreet relations, behind Canning's back and in opposition to his policies, with the so-called 'coterie' of legitimist foreign ambassadors in London—the Russian, Lieven (and his wife, the arch-busybody of Europe), the Austrian, Esterhazy, and the French, Polignac. George also had his Hanoverian foreign service, through which he could make his views known, independently of his British ministers. Canning's popularity at home defeated all foreign attempts to bring about his fall, and the King became reconciled to him.

of acting against the Spanish colonies by force of arms, and disclaimed any intention to appropriate to herself any of the Spanish possessions in America. This was an outstanding achievement. When, in his famous speech of December 12th 1826, he was concerned to defend his decision not to intervene against the French invasion of Spain in 1823, and when he looked back upon these events and upon his recognition of the new Latin American states in December 1824, reluctantly agreed upon by the King and the Cabinet[9] but demanded by the merchant community and supported by the public, he was able to parade his famous boast: 'If France occupied Spain, was it necessary, in order to avoid the consequences of that occupation, that we should blockade Cadiz? No. I looked another way—I sought materials of compensation in another hemisphere. Contemplating Spain, such as our ancestors had known her, I resolved that, if France had Spain, it should not be Spain "with the Indies". I called the New World into existence, to redress the balance of the Old.'[10]

This magnificent piece of rhetoric had in truth a number of real meanings. It meant not only that he had frustrated any intention the French might have had of upsetting the balance of the Old World by acquiring or exploiting Spanish possession in the New. It meant also that he had brought the new Latin American states into the balance of the Old World to the extent that their sense of obligation

[9] Liverpool and Canning pushed this through under threat of resignation.

[10] These, it seems, may not have been the words which Canning actually used in the debate. Speeches in the House of Commons were corrected, revised and sometimes almost rewritten for later publication in the Press. The text quoted above is drawn from the corrected or so-called authentic version of the speech, and not from the first report of the speech, as actually delivered, as it appeared in the Press next day. In places, this first report follows almost identically the text of the later corrected version, but in other places it differs substantially, and this is one of them. The first newspaper report of this passage read as follows: 'I look at the possessions of Spain on the other side of the Atlantic; I look at the Indies and I call in the New World to redress the balance of the Old (great cheering).' It is worth noting that the passages about Spain do not occur in the speech in which Canning opened the debate on the Address—this was about Portugal—but in his speech in reply to the debate, in the course of which the events of 1823 were raised. His famous words were not, in fact, his peroration. (See Harold Temperley, *The Foreign Policy of Canning, 1822–1827*, Bell, London, 1925, pp. 307, 383, 579–85.)

Foreign Secretaries today have not such liberty to revise their speeches, and may therefore be excused if they hold somewhat closely to a prepared text.

to Great Britain would strengthen Great Britain's position in Europe. He had, in fact, made them a part of the European system. And in so doing, he had, he held, prevented the formation of a general transatlantic league of republics under the leadership of the United States which might, he perhaps wrongly surmised, have been raised up in opposition to a European league of monarchies and have had the effect of erecting a barrier between the continents. The act of recognition aroused the angry dismay of the despotic courts, whose appeal to the principle of legitimacy Canning treated with sardonic contempt. The best monument to his policy is that his name is still remembered in Latin American countries as their most effective supporter and protector in their time of need. If neither the danger from France nor the importance of Latin America in world politics was as great as he thought them to be, this does not detract from the merit of his achievement.

As for the Monroe Doctrine (December 1823), which was largely the work of that formidable figure, John Quincy Adams, United States Secretary of State, former minister in London and future President, it was, as its name indicates, a statement of principle, a declaration of hemispheric interest, not a programme of action. The United States had no intention of fighting for it. Nor was it officially communicated to foreign governments. It was only in later years, when the United States had gained strength, that it acquired significance as one of the fixed points of United States policy. Canning did not inspire it, except in so far as it was devised as a means of evading his somewhat embarrassing proposal for a joint Anglo-American declaration which, in addition to warning off the European powers, and in particular Russia and France, would have bound both Great Britain and the United States not to acquire for themselves any portion of the Spanish American colonies. To the hard, suspicious mind of Adams, this looked like an attempt by Canning to compromise the freedom of action of the United States in the Americas, and, while still postponing recognition of the new Latin American states, to gain influence for Great Britain at the expense of the United States, as well as to bar possible United States aspirations in Cuba or to hamper what Canning called her 'pushing policy' in Mexico. Adams thought it best for the United States to act on her own. Though Adams could not be sure of this (he seems not to have known of the Polignac memorandum until after Monroe's message had been delivered), the immediate need for action was passing. France had given assurances of non-intervention which Great Britain was ready if necessary to enforce, while Russia was about to make treaties with both the United States and Great Britain defining the southern limit of her Alaskan territory. As a republican manifesto against the propaganda of the despotic powers the message could, however, serve a purpose. There remained what Canning, perhaps wrongly, suspected to be its possible application to Great Britain if, on behalf of Canada, she prosecuted her claim to still unallotted territory in Oregon. It was for this reason that Canning said that he could not yield obedience to it and must reject it: how could America be closed to future British colonization when America's geographical limits were still unknown? The controversy about the Oregon boundary was soon to open.

This was not one of Canning's more dexterous exploits. He was, it is true, the first British minister to recognize expressly the leading position of the United States on the American continent; and for both economic and political reasons he thought that, in the special circumstances of the time, America was 'out of all proportion more important than Europe'. Nevertheless, in the handling of relations with the United States, Castlereagh had a happier touch. It is pleasant to record that both Castlereagh and Canning had in Richard Rush a United States minister in London who was direct and comprehending in his approach and entirely free from that peculiar harshness of tone which Castlereagh had found to be characteristic of United States diplomacy. On Castlereagh's death, Rush paid a just and moving tribute to him. Already Anglo-American relations were being conducted in a different world from that of the Alexanders and Metternichs, the Lievens and Esterhazys.

Another exploit of which Canning was inordinately proud was his armed intervention in Portugal at the end of 1826. He was, he claimed, not intervening in support of a constitutional régime which was under attack—this would have been in conflict with his own and Castlereagh's doctrine of non-interference—but in defence of the integrity of Portugal, which was under threat from Spain. Dom Pedro, constitutional Emperor of Brazil and later, upon the death of his father, King of Portugal, rather unwisely, Canning thought, decided to give Portugal a constitution when yielding the throne to his eight-year-old daughter, Donna Maria. She was married by proxy to her uncle, Dom Miguel, Pedro's younger brother, who most unwillingly took the oath to the constitution. The French armies were still in Spain, having overturned the constitutional régime there. Canning, with great skill, secured a formal promise from France not to send troops into Portugal. But the supporters of Dom Miguel, with intent to restore the despotic régime in Portugal, gathered in Spain and, with the help of arms and equipment locally supplied with the complicity of the Spanish government, made incursions into Portugal against the constitutional party. Portugal, under the Regent, the Infanta Isabella, Dom Pedro's sister, appealed to Great Britain for assistance under her ancient treaty. This was at once given. Canning despatched a fleet and 4,000 men to Lisbon. The Spaniards desisted. Miguel's party was broken up, and the constitution, for better or worse, was preserved.

In the famous debate of December 12th 1826 in which Canning spoke of calling in the New World, he took credit for his action in Portugal; indeed, the debate was occasioned by these events. 'We go to Portugal,' he declared, 'not to rule, not to dictate, not to prescribe constitutions, but to defend and preserve the independence of an ally.' This was all very well, but in the eyes of the despotic monarchies, the affair had a different colour. A constitution had been brought from the New World into the Old. It had been preserved by the armed intervention of Great Britain, whose Foreign Secretary, for all his disclaimers, had in fact, in his speech, taken up a position in defence of the constitution. 'May God,' he had cried in words that rang through Europe, 'prosper this attempt at the establishment of constitutional liberty in Portugal!' This was in line with what he had said over five years earlier when out of office after the popular outbreaks in Turin, Naples, Lisbon and Madrid: 'I see the principles of liberty in operation, and shall be one of the last to attempt to restrain them.' It was an unexceptionable sentiment to be expressed by the minister of a constitutional monarch, and the more so in that the Portuguese constitution was the gift of the sovereign: but to the absolutist régimes it carried a note of menace. The Austrians had restored absolutism in Naples and the French in Madrid. Was the tide now on the turn and was liberalism to be sustained in Europe by the arms of Great Britain? The answer to this question would be of great moment to the despotic powers since 'the British Minister had raised his country to a position such as she had never surpassed, and had seldom equalled, in her history.'[11]

[11] Harold Temperley, *Cambridge History of British Foreign Policy, 1783–1919*, Cambridge, 1923, ii. 83. This language is perhaps excessive.

'The man,' said Metternich, 'was a whole revolution in himself alone.' In fact, Canning's influence would be exerted by force of opinion, not by force of arms; and he was far from being a crusader for liberal constitutions. He held that it was 'not . . . a British interest to have free States established on the Continent,' and he confessed that 'the general acquisition of free institutions is not necessarily a security for general peace.' What he preferred was the British type of constitutional monarchy, the *via media* between despotism and democracy.

Another of Canning's acts in the foreign field was to prove of notable advantage to British imperial interests. During the Napoleonic War, the Moluccas and Java had been captured from the Dutch, the latter upon the urgent plea of Stamford Raffles, then a subordinate official in Penang. Against the protest of Raffles, now lieutenant-governor of Java, Castlereagh, whose policy was to concentrate on India and, in pursuance of his European policy, to leave the commerce of the East Indies to the Dutch, returned Java with the Moluccas to the Netherlands at the peace. Great Britain was left with Penang and Bencoolen, a small, decayed trading post in Sumatra, of which Raffles became governor. In 1819, Raffles, with the support of trading interests in London and of Canning at the Board of Control, secured a reversal of Castlereagh's policy and the purchase from the Sultan of Johore of the almost uninhabited island of Singapore, at the tip of the Malay Peninsula, a step which was deeply resented by the Dutch. By Canning's treaty of 1824 with the Netherlands, Great Britain ceded Bencoolen and all claims on Sumatra, constrained the Dutch to recognize her possession of Singapore and received Malacca. The acquisition of Singapore as a potential trading and naval outpost at the crossing of the sea-ways set the stage for a rapid expansion of commerce with the East Indian archipelago and for a further development of trade with South China which, at the time of Palmerston and later, was to become so important a factor in our foreign policy.[12]

Palmerston,[13] in his first two and most successful periods of office

The Portuguese operation was a diplomatic success, but its results were ephemeral.

[12] Raffles said of Singapore that it 'completely outflanks the Straits of Malacca, and secures a passage for our China ships at all times and in all circumstances.' Canning called it 'the *unum necessarium* for making the British Empire in India complete.'

[13] Henry John Temple, 3rd Viscount Palmerston, in the peerage of

115

(Foreign Secretary, 1830–41, with a short interruption, and 1846–51), though he was later to profess to have had no system of policy other than the defence of British interests, did lay down certain lines for himself. Like his predecessors, he held that the general tendency of British policy should be to watch attentively and guard with care the maintenance of the balance of power. There should be full liberty to resist, on the principle of self-defence, attempts to seize territory, as deranging that balance. There should be no formal engagements with reference to cases which had not actually arisen or which were not immediately in prospect. There should be no interference by force of arms with changes in internal government in foreign countries. These were estimable principles, but he interpreted them under the impress of two characteristic convictions. The first was that he was 'generally desirous to keep England on the side of liberal opinion', that is, to support constitutional monarchies against despotisms, and to assert the freedom of peoples to determine their own conditions of political existence.[14] The second was a bent in favour of intervention by diplomatic action backed up by threat of force. Even in his best and most fruitful period, he brought upon himself the charge of 'restless meddling activity'.

Influence in international affairs, the capacity of a government to constrain or to persuade other governments to conform to its will in act or in policy, will be most effectively exercised if that government can deploy immediately effective armed force in support of its will, and if it can be confidently expected to employ such force in case of need. But such influence can be, and is indeed often, exercised on the strength of what is called prestige. Influence can be powerful, even in the absence of strong and immediately available armed forces, if there has been recent successful assembling, deployment and use of such forces in war. Influence can persist if the required resources in manpower and finance are present, and if there is a manifest national will to recreate and use those forces if occasion

Ireland, was eligible for a seat in the House of Commons, to which he was first elected in 1807. Castlereagh died at 53 and Canning at 57, both from overstrain, the former by his own hand. Palmerston, also a very hard worker, was a minister of the Crown for over fifty years and lived to 81.

[14] He began as a Tory of the school of Pitt and Canning. He ended as the head of our first Liberal government, of which one member was Gladstone, an ex-Tory of the school of Peel. Though not an advocate of parliamentary reform, Palmerston was an early Free Trader and fervent for the abolition of slavery.

should arise. Great Britain enjoyed such prestige during Palmerston's several periods of office between 1830 and 1851. Though her immediately effective force was small, her material resources were there for all to see. Her will was expressed in robust terms through the mouth of her Foreign Secretary. The conditions of warfare in Europe were such that, if war broke out, time would be given to her to bring her forces up to the requisite strength. We were never again to exercise such decisive influence so easily, nor to do so at such small expense. As Palmerston said in the House of Commons on July 11th 1831: 'No country on the face of the globe is likely to suffer less than England from war,' a claim which echoed Canning's earlier boast: 'England is strong enough to brave consequences.' Small wonder that Palmerston was so ready to threaten war: war against France in 1831 unless the French withdrew from Belgium; war against France in 1840 over the Near East; war against the United States in 1841 if a British subject, Alexander McLeod, were condemned and executed for killing a man in 1837 in a raid into United States' territory to destroy an American steamer which had been helping the Canadian rebels. In each case he achieved his purpose.

But prestige is a wasting asset. It is the product of expectation about future conduct based upon present or remembered performance. It has to be constantly renewed. As the years passed, our military renown faded and it was little revived by the effort of improvisation forced upon us by the Crimean War, though somewhat more by our handling of the Indian Mutiny. The day of large conscript armies was soon to arrive, and the raising and transport of such forces were believed to be outside both our capacity and our intention. Naval supremacy was irresistible within its sphere, but its sphere was limited.

Great as our influence was in the period after 1815, it was not even then all-powerful. Castlereagh could not keep Russia from maintaining control over Poland. Canning could not prevent the French from invading Spain. Wellington's government could not in 1828–29 save the Turks from Russian attack. Aberdeen confessed in 1829: 'We are at the mercy of the Emperor [of Russia] and he can insult us if he pleases.' Even where we were most successful, and where our interests were most closely involved, we usually made it our policy to try to work with the power whose independent action seemed to us most to be feared: as Canning did with Russia in Greece in 1826–27, and as Palmerston did with France in Belgium in 1830–31, with France in Spain and Portugal in 1834, and with Russia in the Near East in 1839–41.

Palmerston's conduct of affairs in the crises about Belgium and the Near East shows his quality. Seldom, if ever, has a British Foreign Secretary found himself in a position to manœuvre in the foreign field with such superb confidence and with such easy mastery in conditions so well attuned to his method and his temperament.

In the Belgian crisis, Palmerston averted war, perhaps a European war, and kept the French out of Belgium. The issue was a popular revolt against the post-war territorial settlement in the Low Countries, which had been designed to ensure the containment of France. Its importance for Great Britain was manifest. The Belgians would no longer tolerate their integration in the kingdom of the Netherlands. Would the French now again press a claim to Belgium which the Emperor Napoleon, even at his blackest moment, had refused to abandon?

The settlement ultimately reached—separation from Holland and a guaranteed neutrality under a Coburg, not an Orleanist, monarch —was a solid and long-lasting contribution to the peace of Europe, reached by a European concert led by Palmerston.[15] The enlarged kingdom of the Netherlands, which included both Holland and Belgium, had been constructed as a barrier to French access to the north European plain. After the separation, the guarantee of the neutrality of Belgium was designed to the same end, in much the same way as, further south, the neutrality of Switzerland had been guaranteed in 1815. By this means, although the settlement of 1815 was amended, the balance would be preserved. 'There never was a period,' said Palmerston in the House of Commons on March 26th 1832, with pardonable pride, 'when England was more respected than at present in her foreign relations, in consequence of her good faith, moderation and firmness.' Certainly, as has been said, during the long-drawn-out Belgian crisis, 'the proceedings of Palmerston and Grey in their conduct of Foreign Policy, formed an unbroken record of patience and wisdom.'

The Near Eastern settlement was almost too successful. Palmerston's over-confidence caused much apprehensive head-shaking, even among the well-disposed. His forthrightness for a while damaged our relations with France, with whom in 1840 we came

---

[15] He attended seventy meetings of the conference in London and was concerned in the drafting of its seventy-eight protocols.

near to war. The king of the French, Louis Philippe, called him 'the enemy of my House'. France, as Palmerston guessed, had not recovered from the Revolution and the Napoleonic Wars and was no longer so great a power as she had been in the seventeenth and eighteenth centuries. The advantage of greater population and a more fertile soil did not compensate for the lack of the overseas markets and the industrial strength based on coal and iron which gave Great Britain pre-eminence. Her foreign policy was also, under Louis Philippe, too often ineptly conducted.

Russia was becoming our main adversary, the power which could, by partitioning or controlling Turkey, bar our road by land through the Levant, or by sea through the Mediterranean to India; the power which could, by advancing in central Asia, threaten the northwest frontier. From the policy of partition, the thought of which had caused anxiety in London in the crisis of 1791, Russia had switched about 1830 to the policy of maintaining the integrity of a weak Turkey under her own control, a policy of 'sap' rather than of 'storm'. Her reward for helping Sultan Mahmud against his vassal, Mehemet Ali,[16] Pasha of Egypt, the imperially-minded disciple of Napoleon, was the Treaty of Unkiar Skelessi of 1833. This treaty made Turkey almost a protectorate of Russia. As Palmerston said: 'The Russian Ambassador becomes chief Cabinet Minister of the Sultan.' Russia showed moderation and did not push her advantage. When, once again, Mehemet Ali threatened to disrupt the Ottoman Empire by advancing far into Asia Minor, with encouragement from France, the four powers (Great Britain, Russia, Austria, Prussia), led by Palmerston, coerced Mehemet Ali and made a settlement in 1841 without France. Mehemet Ali was confined to his Egyptian dominions. Once again the Ottoman Empire was preserved. The treaty of Unkiar Skelessi was tacitly dropped. The 'ancient Ottoman rule' that the Sultan, if at peace, would close the Straits to the warships of all other powers, a rule which was stated in the Anglo-Turkish Treaty of 1809 and was thought by many, though not by Palmerston, to have been breached at Unkiar Skelessi, was for the first time embodied in an international convention. France thought it well to accede to the settlement.

Palmerston had secured his objects. He had prevented the

[16] Mehemet was probably of Albanian origin. He came from the north Aegean coast, like the Ptolemies and Kemal Atatürk. He had been born in the same year as Napoleon.

disruption of the Ottoman Empire by Mehemet Ali. He had secured the dropping of the treaty of Unkiar Skelessi and the conclusion, for the first time, of a Straits convention based on an agreement among all the powers concerned. He had avoided a combination between France and Russia, which had been mooted in the early stages of the crisis. He had separated Russia from Austria. He had averted a war with Russia over Unkiar Skelessi, and a war with France over Mehemet's possession of Syria. He had removed the danger to the road to India which would have been presented by the permanent establishment in Syria of Mehemet Ali in alliance with France, and this at a time when we had serious differences with Russia in Central Asia. He had done this in concert with Russia, who was only too relieved to see a breach between the two liberal powers, Great Britain and France.

Russia, baulked in the protective policy enshrined in the Treaty of Unkiar Skelessi, now reverted to the idea of partition. In 1844 and again in 1853, Nicholas I, preoccupied by the dangers that would ensue upon a Turkish collapse which he thought to be imminent, hinted at a deal with Great Britain to the exclusion of France, by which, in that event, the territorial spoils would be ear-marked: Egypt and Crete to Great Britain, the Danubian principalities under Russian protection, Constantinople a free city. The British response was evasive and discouraging. In 1845 he even told Metternich that he would be willing to agree to an Austrian control of Constantinople in the event of a Turkish collapse. Metternich, too, was unresponsive. Nicholas's main objective in all this was to see that, whatever happened, Great Britain did not get Constantinople. It has been argued that a chance to solve the Eastern question was here allowed to go by default. But to try to make such a comprehensive agreement without France would have been highly dangerous to European peace. As statesmen and diplomatists well know, complex and deep-seated international controversies involving what are, rightly or wrongly, held to be vital interests are not to be solved by bold strokes, cutting Gordian knots. The Turkish problem was not yet ripe for solution.

For all but five of the years between 1830 and 1851, the latent strength of Great Britain was exploited by a statesman with the skill and self-confidence to make the most of it. Great Britain's prestige and inner resource were still unimpaired, and Palmerston rode high upon them. In the years between 1841 and 1846, when the upright

but indecisive Lord Aberdeen was Foreign Secretary ('A good man,'
as Kinglake said, 'in the worst sense of the term', a man whose
'*innocence politique*' had been remarked upon by foreign colleagues
in earlier years), the latent potentiality was still there: but no longer
were there leaders with the capacity to make it good. If we have any
doubt about the decisive role which personality can play, in the
short run at any rate, in determining events in foreign affairs, we
have only to consider the fumbling conduct of our foreign policy by
Wellington, Dudley and Aberdeen in the years 1828–30 as compared
with the confident handling of affairs by Canning before, and by
Palmerston after, those years.[17] We may fairly ask ourselves what
Aberdeen would have done with the Belgian crisis if he, and not
Palmerston, had had to deal with it; and whether, if Palmerston had
been not merely one of the more strong-handed members of a
divided Cabinet, but Prime Minister instead of Derby and Aberdeen, or Foreign Secretary instead of Granville, Malmesbury, Russell
and Clarendon in the years after 1851, we should have stumbled into
the Crimean War in 1854. Palmerston was rumbustious; but he
knew every inch of his ground and he kept out of European war.
His prime concern was to preserve the peace of Europe. He was
strongly anti-Russian, and was temperamentally responsive to the
public clamour for war in 1854: but his skill and resolution might
have avoided the conflict.[18]

Palmerston owed his success, in some measure, to his superb
technical equipment. He spoke and wrote French easily and had a
good knowledge of Spanish, Italian and Portuguese. He attended
personally to the concordance of the four texts—English, French,
Spanish and Portuguese—of the Quadruple Alliance of 1834 and
did much of the drafting of the treaty himself. The staff of the Foreign
Office was still small, in contrast to its counterparts in Paris and
Vienna, and he had to rely on his own resources. 'He read everything,' said one of his subordinates, 'and wrote an immense quantity.'

[17] The correspondence between the capacity and personality of a Foreign
Secretary and the character and effectiveness of his policy was closer
when subordinate staffs were very small and when the minister had to do
a great deal of the work himself than it can be in modern conditions where
the minister presides over a great professional machine. The machine may
hamper his self-expression, but it can also cover his shortcomings.

[18] On the other hand, the dispute with France over the Spanish marriages might have been quietly resolved if Palmerston had not replaced
Aberdeen in 1846 at a critical point in the affair. Aberdeen and Guizot
had confidence in each other.

'He comes to any conference,' said a foreign diplomatist, 'fully and completely master of the subject of it in all the minutest details.' He kept always under his hand, for immediate reference, manuscript books containing a detailed running digest of correspondence received and despatched. He was never at a loss. If, as Sir Charles Webster once sagely remarked: 'The conduct of foreign policy depends largely on the mastery of a mass of detailed information,' then the basis of Palmerston's achievement becomes plain. On this sure foundation, he could operate with freedom, with apparent unconcern, with disregard for the feelings and opinions of others and with what might appear to be rashness: so much so that he was in constant difficulty with his Cabinet colleagues and with the Court. His delight in taking calculated risks laid him open to the charge of what we should now call 'brinkmanship'. His championship of liberalism, combined with a masterful and truculent manner, made him anathema to most of the monarchs and statesmen of Europe. 'If,' it was said in Germany, 'the devil had a son, his name would be Palmerston.' On the other hand, though Whig and Tory wiseacres might often shake their heads, he enjoyed wide approval among the public, which he was careful to nourish by assiduous attention to the Press. In particular, he could usually count on support from the Radicals in his opposition to Russia and Austria, in his defence of Turkey against Russia, in his cultivation of good relations with France, and in his protection of liberal movements in Europe. This support would continue until, under the impact of Cobden's teaching in the years after the Crimean War, some part of radical opinion would veer towards what Gladstone called 'calm and peace' as opposed to 'brusqueness and war'.

It is a fair test of the British position in the world to inquire how Great Britain fared in her encounters with the United States. We may take two of the demarcation disputes on the northern United States border which had been left over from the peace treaties, and were still unsettled—the Maine and the Oregon boundaries.

The chief point about the Maine border was that the northern salient of the state of Maine claimed by the Americans cut across the route of the military road and of the projected railway required to connect Quebec with Halifax across the Appalachian Barrier. Relations were disturbed by local incidents which occurred during and after the Canadian rebellion in 1837. The crisis was at times acute, with clashes between the authorities of Maine and New Brunswick. There was the further complication that nine of the American states were repudiating or defaulting on their loans from Great Britain. Nevertheless, the matter was handled with coolness by both governments. On the one side was a conciliatory Foreign Secretary, Aberdeen, and, as special plenipotentiary, Alexander Baring, Lord Ashburton, a great power in the world of overseas finance,[19] a banker of pro-United States sentiments married into a distinguished Philadelphia family, and a negotiator with a preference for informal personal discussion. On the other was the sagacious Secretary of State, Daniel Webster, who had declared on taking office: 'No difference shall be permitted seriously to endanger the maintenance of peace with England.' The Ashburton–Webster Treaty of August 1842 was, on the main issue of the Maine boundary—it dealt with other matters also—more favourable to the British than to the Americans. Later research has suggested that the Americans probably had the better claim. The settlement was attacked in both countries: but what may be called 'the comedy of the maps' helped to gain acceptance for it. Webster, unknown to Ashburton, had a map from the French archives and a second from another source which both supported the interpretation of the treaty of 1783 upon which the British based their claim, and he used these to overcome objections to the settlement from the state of Maine and from the Senate. The Foreign Office, for their part, had a map which supported the American thesis, and Aberdeen used this with good effect to meet Palmerston's criticism of the treaty.

In the Oregon dispute, the Americans succeeded better than their claim warranted. This was a more serious matter than the Maine boundary and caused much excitement in public opinion on both sides of the Atlantic. The independent state of Texas, about which there had been difficulties between Great Britain and the United States in relation to their respective positions in the Caribbean area, was annexed in 1846. This was followed by the war between the United States and Mexico, as a result of which the United States acquired a vast western territory, including California, running up to the 42nd parallel, which had been the northern boundary of former Spanish territory agreed upon in 1819. (It is now the southern

[19] The French Prime Minister, the Duc de Richelieu, is reported to have said: 'There are six Powers in Europe, Great Britain, France, Russia, Austria, Prussia and Baring Brothers.'

boundary of the states of Oregon and Idaho.) The area, loosely called Oregon, lying between the 42nd parallel and the parallel of 54° 40′, which was the latitude of the southern tip of Russian-held Alaska fixed by treaty between the United States and Russia in 1824, had, since the Anglo-American Treaty of 1818, been under 'a kind of unorganized condominium'. The question of the future disposition of the area had been quiescent for some years; but with the turning of eyes to the Pacific coast, and with the coming war with Mexico, it now became a critical issue between the two countries. Where was the boundary between British and American territory to run? The extreme American claim ('fifty-four forty or fight') would have given the United States a common frontier with Alaska and would then have cut Canada off from the Pacific. The extreme British claim, the line of the Columbia River, would have bitten deeply into the present state of Washington. The more moderate American claim, the line of the 49th parallel, would have partitioned Vancouver Island. There was some aggressive language by the new Democratic President, James K. Polk (in this a precursor of Grover Cleveland and Theodore Roosevelt), when he said in his Inaugural Address in March 1845 that the American title to the Oregon country was clear and unquestionable and would be maintained by every means. There were some extensive naval preparations in Great Britain and a statement by Peel in the House of Commons in April 1845 in which he said: 'Having exhausted every effort to effect that settlement, if our rights shall be invaded, we are resolved, and we are prepared, to maintain them.' There were also strong influences on both sides in favour of a compromise, including Peel and, once again, Aberdeen. There was a friendly *Times* leader of January 3rd 1846 ('We are two peoples, but we are of one family. We have fought, but we have been reconciled') which, as Professor H. C. Allen has said, 'might lay claim to constitute the most important turning point in Anglo-American relations.' Polk, too, whatever he might say, was disposed to reach an accommodation, since he was about to have the Mexican war on his hands, and since he thought it well to close with Aberdeen, who was likely soon to go out of office. By the agreement, which was embodied in a draft presented from the British side, the boundary followed the 49th parallel westward to the coast and then dipped south to leave the whole of Vancouver Island to Great Britain.[20]

---

[20] This, however, was not the end of the story. The agreement was

Castlereagh, Canning, Palmerston

These two agreements with the United States suggest that, when Great Britain is strong, a firm but conciliatory policy can bring a settlement that is fair and just. They also raise the question whether, in these transactions with the United States, the rougher methods of Palmerston, suitable enough in his day for Europe, would have brought such good results as did the gentler hand of Aberdeen. Palmerston himself was to recognize in later years that there would always be some disadvantage for us in negotiating with the United States on an American question: 'We are far away, weak from Distance, controlled by the indifference of the Nation . . . and by its Strong commercial Interest in maintaining Peace with the United States. The result of this State of Things has been that we have given away step by step to the North Americans on almost every disputed matter.' The Maine and Oregon agreements will stand in contrast with later and less favourable settlements with the United States, negotiated when British influence was no longer so powerful.

We may have had our finest hours in 1588 and in 1940, but we do not so often remember that the period of our most decisive influence abroad falls within the undistinguished reigns of George IV and William IV and the not so apparently glorious early years of the young Victoria. Men were conscious of this at the time. Lord Granville, George IV's ambassador in Paris, remarked to the King's physician in January 1826 that it was impossible that His Majesty 'could not be proud of the commanding station which his Kingdom occupied among the nations of the World, far beyond that of any former reign in the History of England.'

The first forty years of the nineteenth century, in spite of the domestic strain set up by the Napoleonic War and by the darker features of the industrial revolution, were for Great Britain a period which saw the flowering of a humane and generous spirit which yet lost nothing of its robustness. It was the age of the abolition of the slave trade, of the enactment of Catholic Emancipation, and of a mitigation of the horrors of the criminal law. In South Africa in 1828, black and white were made equal before the law; in India there was still little British social exclusiveness based on colour—this was a later nineteenth-century development. It was thanks largely to the British Government and to Castlereagh and Wellington in particular that at the peace settlement France was saved from

vague about the boundary in the channel between Vancouver Island and the mainland. This was later submitted to arbitration.

dismemberment and ruin. Thanks to Castlereagh again, our relations with France and the United States, with both of whom we had been at war, were placed upon a basis of enduring peace. From now on, in sharp contrast to the age of Chatham, British foreign policy, for all that it will bend itself, sometimes ruthlessly, to protect and to promote British interests, will display an element of altruism, a care for European and world concerns as well as for the national cause. It will gain a new sense of responsibility which will derive from the possession of power and from a new climate of public opinion.

A spot-light is thrown upon the outlook of the people at large in a remark by Byron. During the campaign in the Peninsula, Byron, no friend of the Portuguese and no supporter of the war against Napoleon (When the news of Waterloo came through, he said, 'I am damned sorry for it.'), could still bear this generous witness: 'When the Portuguese suffered under the retreat of the French, every arm in Britain was stretched out, every hand was opened, from the rich man's largess to the widow's mite, all was bestowed, to enable them to rebuild their villages and replenish their granaries.' In this full-hearted way, so far removed from the coarser spirit of the earlier part of the preceding century, England had saved herself by her exertions and Europe by her example.

The common people were to respond nobly to challenges again and again in the years to come: when, during the American Civil War, the textile workers of Lancashire cheerfully endured the effects of the cotton famine in 1862 in firm adherence to the cause of the North; when the unemployed men and women of Blackburn, thrown out of work by the Indian boycott of British cotton goods which had closed their factories, cheered Mahatma Gandhi on his visit to their town in 1931;[21] and when, in the Second World War, as Lord Birkett once said: 'humble folk everywhere put on courage like a mantle.' So also, after the Second World War, our people gave succour to homeless refugees from troubled regions abroad: 'The need has been met . . . to a most staggering degree by the ordinary men and women of Great Britain, who have not only opened their hearts, but have opened their hands and minds and have visualized

---

[21] Perhaps, however, they owed India, vicariously, some amends. In the 1830s the machine-made Lancashire cotton cloth undercut Indian handloom weavers to such an extent that, in the words of the Governor-General: 'the bones of the cotton-weavers are bleaching the plains of India.' (John Strachey, *The End of Empire*, Gollancz, London, 1959, p. 52.)

for the first time, perhaps, what it must mean to have lost everything.[22]

Together with humanity, there was no lack of moral robustness in these early years of the century. In 1830, when Ruskin was twelve, his pious Tory parents included Byron's *Don Juan* among the works to be read aloud with the dessert at dinner. By the age of fifteen Ruskin knew his Byron 'pretty well all through'. Compare this with the prim and arid liberalism of John Morley who, writing in 1870, said of *Don Juan* that 'the wit and colour and power served to make an anti-social and licentious sentiment attractive to puny creatures, who were thankful to have their lasciviousness so gaily adorned.' Among such 'puny creatures' had been Mr John James Ruskin, wine merchant of London, residing at Herne Hill, and his wife and young son.[23]

We may note, as an epilogue to the review of this period, two developments which, of marginal importance in our own history, have come, over the ensuing century, to stand as inaugurating and symbolizing dark and humiliating periods in the history of other peoples. The first concerns Egypt. Mehemet Ali founded a dynasty in Egypt and his successors opened a new age which is marked in modern Egyptian eyes by ruthless financial exploitation and political subservience at the hands of the western peoples and their governments. Against this, the benefit of Anglo-French control as a check to colossal Khedivial financial profligacy, the contribution of French culture and the British achievement in bringing good government, administrative order and sound finances to Egypt stand for little. It was the purpose of the present revolutionary movement in Egypt to put an end for ever, at whatever the cost, to what was proclaimed to be a century-old era of foreign exploitation and domination.

Then again, by the Treaty of Nanking in 1842, after the so-called but ill-named Opium War[24] in which the British had bombarded Canton, taken Shanghai and penetrated the Yangtse valley, the Chinese were constrained to recede in practice from their immemorial

[22] Stella, Marchioness of Reading, Baroness Swanborough, speech in the House of Lords, March 4th 1959.

[23] See R. W. Chambers, *Ruskin (and Others) on Byron*, English Association Pamphlet, No. 62, November 1925.

[24] The war was not fought to force opium on China. It was caused by the harsh conditions imposed on foreign merchants by the overbearing attitude of the Chinese government and its local officials at Canton. The British government made no demand after the war for the right to import opium.

pretensions to superior and contemptuous exclusiveness. They were forced to open Shanghai and Canton and other towns as treaty ports for the free conduct of trade; to cede the then uninhabited island of Hong Kong; and to pay claims of merchants, including claims for opium seized by the Chinese authorities. Later, by the Treaty of Tientsin in 1858, more ports were opened and extra-territorial rights were granted to British and French subjects. Other powers also enjoyed the benefit of such concessions. The way was open for the progressive European and Japanese spoliation of China in pursuit of what has been called 'the chimera of inexhaustible trade'. These impositions, in modern Chinese eyes, mark the opening of a century of intolerable foreign oppression by which the age-old Chinese civilization, hitherto inviolate, was subjected to the bondage of the 'unequal treaties'. From this unforgivable humiliation, by the Communist revolution of 1949, China has liberated herself, gathering her military and economic strength, restoring her ancient dignity and independence, moving at last into the common forward-moving stream of modern world-development, technological and industrial, while still asserting once more the bland conviction of her superiority over the rest of mankind. Some aspects of our dealings with China in the 1840s and later typify a less pleasing, reverse side of the beneficent *Pax Britannica*. The seas were indeed to be free and open for the commerce of all under a law which Great Britain herself would prescribe: but the lands were also to be free and open for trade, and were to be prised open by force if this should prove to be necessary. But there is something to be said on the other side. There was every reason to think that the Chinese did want foreign trade. The British government were anxious to observe the treaty guarantees that worked in favour of China as well as those provided for British and other foreign merchants, to such an extent that the less scrupulous merchants complained that the local British representatives were more Chinese than the Chinese. And as a coping stone they promoted the establishment, largely under British consular control, of the efficient and incorruptible Chinese maritime customs service.

CHAPTER IX

Early Victorian Climax

In February 1852, Palmerston, who had been bundled out of office in the previous December after a series of indiscretions which, though not disapproved by public opinion, had incensed his colleagues and the Queen, offered some welcome advice to Lord Malmesbury, who had just succeeded Lord Granville as Foreign Secretary. He said to him, among other things: 'You have no idea till you know more of your office what a power of prestige England possesses abroad, and it will be your first duty to see that it does not wane.' Palmerston also advised him, in view of the uncertainty as to the Prince President Louis Napoleon's policy towards England after his *coup d'état* against the Second Republic in December 1851, that the Government should strengthen the national defences both by building fortifications and by increasing armaments. Malmesbury then adds the comment: 'This is also the ruling feeling at Court and throughout the country, as the long rule of the Whigs has let down all the defensive power of Great Britain. If in 1840 Thiers had had his way, and France had gone to war with us, we should have been totally unprepared, even in our navy.' This is the judgment of a political opponent which need not be accepted *in toto*. But it suggests upon what a narrow basis of effective strength, as distinct from latent power and prestige, Palmerston's vigorous and successful policies had at times been founded. The day was coming when such conjuring tricks would no longer be possible. 'Between 1817 and 1850 there was extraordinary military or naval expenditure only in nine years: from 1851 to 1870 there were only four years without this expenditure.'[1]

It was the French who gave the stimulus. In the change over in propulsion from sail to steam, in construction from wood to iron,

[1] E. L. Woodward, *The Age of Reform, 1815–1870*, p. 160.

and in the provision of armour for protection, the French were ahead of us. From the late 'forties, at the time of Palmerston's breach with the French towards the end of the reign of Louis Philippe, we felt our security to be threatened for the first time since the Napoleonic Wars. The French had lined up with Russia, Prussia and Austria, and were said to be planning invasion. The Duke of Wellington wrote to Sir J. Burgoyne on January 9th 1847 that steam propulsion had rendered England assailable at all times from the sea. As a result, a militia force of 150,000 men was raised. By the late 'fifties our fear of Napoleon III's designs for a time amounted to panic.

In November 1859 the French launched *La Gloire*, the first of four screw-driven, wooden-hull, armoured battleships, herself of 5,600 tons. There was now a widespread fear of invasion by the incalculable Emperor of the French in addition to apprehensions aroused by his acquisition of Nice and Savoy and by the construction of the Suez Canal, which Palmerston had said would set 'a French colony in the desert of Egypt'. On land, coast defences and fortifications were built, and a great, new, enthusiastic volunteer movement was started, celebrated by Tennyson in 'Riflemen, form!'[2] At sea, we gave the answer in the *Warrior*, launched in 1860, a line-of-battle ship as revolutionary in her way as the *Dreadnought* half a century later. Earlier ships became obsolete. Our lead in effective capital

[2] The last of the four stanzas reads as follows:

> Form, be ready to do or die!
> Form, in Freedom's name and the Queen's!
> True we have got—*such* a faithful ally
> That only the Devil can tell what he means.
> Form, Form, Riflemen Form!
> Ready, be ready to meet the storm!
> Riflemen, Riflemen, Riflemen Form!
>   (*The Times*, May 9th 1859)

It is illustrative of the equivocal state of our relations with France—the two countries were estranged by mutual antipathy and thrown together by common interest—that it was during this period of anti-French agitation in England that in 1860 the back-bench Radical, Cobden, having won over the Chancellor of the Exchequer, Gladstone, to his view, negotiated a commercial treaty with France. By this treaty, one of the landmarks in the economic history of Europe, Great Britain abandoned protection for herself and lowered her revenue duties, while France started on a new course away from protectionism, making similar treaties with other countries, based on the principle of the most favoured nation, every concession to each being enjoyed by all. As Cobden said: 'It is God's method of producing an *entente cordiale* and no other plan is worth a farthing.'

ships was narrowed. As, later, after the introduction of the *Dread-nought*, we had to rebuild our naval supremacy over again and at much greater cost.

Prince Albert's Great Exhibition in Hyde Park in 1851 will stand as a symbol of the soaring self-confidence, indeed of the over-confidence, of the rulers and people of the United Kingdom at mid-century, before the foreign anxieties of the later 1850s came upon them. It has been said that the period between 1815 and 1850, as a whole, can show a development of domestic resources swifter than at any time in our history before or since, though it was punctuated by booms and slumps, the worst of them in 1847–48.[3]

The discovery of gold in California in 1849 and in Australia in 1851 was one factor working strongly in favour of further expansion. Thanks to this fortuitous gift of fortune, the era of free trade, confirmed by the beginning of the repeal of the Corn Laws in 1846 and by the disappearance of the last remaining Navigation Acts in 1849, got away to a flying start, unimpeded by the exchange difficulties which had made the expansive British economy vulnerable in earlier decades. There was a feeling, which was to be justified by events, that a period of bounding prosperity, agricultural as well as industrial, was about to open. The 1840s were the great decade of railway building. In 1843, there were about 2,000 miles of line in operation; in 1849 there were 6,031. To lay these tracks, with their cuttings and embankments, their tunnels and their viaducts, was a colossal achievement, performed without the help of public finance or modern earth-moving machinery.[4] The Great Exhibition was a demonstration

[3] In the period 1815–47, the percentage annual increase in industrial output was 3·5. Between 1847 and 1873 it was slightly less, namely 3·2 per cent. Over the last quarter of the nineteenth century and the early years of the twentieth it was not more than about 1·7 per cent, and in the latter part of the period it was much less. The rate of growth of population over the whole period was a little above or below 1 per cent per annum. Not until the years after the Second World War would figures comparable to the highest of those quoted above again be reached.

[4] Isambard Kingdom Brunel (1806–59) may stand as a type of the Early Victorian age. He built the Great Western Railway, with its great bridge over the Tamar at Saltash, in a way that first enabled railway trains to run at speed. He designed the *Great Western*, the first successful transatlantic steamer; the *Great Britain*, the first large steamer to combine an iron hull with screw propulsion; and the *Great Eastern*, six times the size of any ship afloat. It was said of him in 1910: 'Brunel had no contemporary, no predecessor. If he has no successor, let it be remembered that . . . the conditions which call such men into being no longer have any existence.'

to the British people and to the world of our soaring energies and industrial supremacy. The year 1851 'was a year of national festival, the climax of early Victorian England, the turning-point of the century.'[5] Emerson, visiting England in 1847–48, said: 'A nation . . . has . . . obtained the ascendant, and has stamped the knowledge, activity, and power of mankind with its impress.' 'Of all the decades of our history,' said G. M. Young, 'a wise man would choose the eighteen-fifties to be young in.'[6]

In its review of the year 1850, *The Times* of January 1st 1851 said: 'In commercial history there has never been a year that could be reviewed with more satisfaction than 1850. . . . It is impossible to consider its course without a sense of the seal which it has set upon England's enlarged and courageous policy.' In its review a year later, it said of the year 1851: 'To the mass of the people it has been the most prosperous on record,' adding in a leading article: 'We believe we may say with literal truth that the year 1851 has been unexampled for national prosperity.'

Of the foreign scene, it spoke with less confidence: 'We are not among those who expect that the triumphs of peace are likely in our time to extinguish the passions of peoples and the ambitions of adventurers; but we nevertheless think we may dwell with satisfaction and hope on the memory of an event the direct and natural tendency of which is pacific and profitable.' The revolutions of 1848 had been suppressed and the forces of order in Europe were reasserting themselves. Nevertheless, in 1850, there had still been 'troops . . . in movement on the Continent more numerous than at the downfall of Napoleon' and the only comfort was 'the certainty that England could not be compromised.' Speaking of the international situation of Great Britain at the end of 1851, *The Times* said: 'Insulated in position, with a mixed political constitution, the asylum for refugees from all nations, showing her flag on every sea, and thrusting her manufactures into every market, unable to sympathize entirely with either monarchs against peoples or

(See L. T. C. Rolt, 'The Man Who Spanned the Tamar', *The Times*, May 2nd 1959.)

The railway contractor, Thomas Brassey, at one time employed 80,000 men. Apart from work at home, he was at one period constructing railways and docks in five continents.

[5] Asa Briggs, *1851*, Historical Association Pamphlet, London, 1951, p. 3.

[6] *Victorian England, Portrait of an Age*, Oxford University Press, London, 1936, p. 77.

peoples against monarchs, she commands the respect, the fear, and even the admiration of mankind, but not their love or free co-opera tion.'

Nothing clouded the optimism with which the material future was regarded. 'The creation of wealth, power and comfort upon a scale altogether new, the justifiable pride of achievement in directing minds, during the years between the Great Exhibition of 1851 and the Franco-Prussian War of 1870–71, became the foundation of a new and often boastful optimism. That optimism later came to seem too slender a foundation for the hopes and expectations which had been based upon it.'[7] Already there were clouds on the horizon. Professor Lyon (later Lord) Playfair published a pamphlet in 1853 on *Industrial Education on the Continent* in which he pointed to the superiority of technical education in Germany. No action was taken on this pamphlet. After mid-century, the industrialization of western continental Europe, much of it promoted by British skill and enterprise, began to take shape. At international exhibitions after that of 1851, Belgian, French, German and American industries were seen to be improving their techniques and organization. Even so, the external trade of the United Kingdom in 1870 was greater than that of France, Germany and Italy combined, and over three times that of the United States. Such was Great Britain's initial advantage, and so solid-seeming her own growing prosperity, that the threat of competition in this field, where she had so long held a near-monopoly, was for long not consciously recognized. It was not until the report of the Royal Commission on the Depression of Industry and Trade in 1886 that international competition was seen to be henceforward a continuing condition to be faced in domestic and overseas trade.

Two international controversies which both fell in the year 1850 will testify to the extent and character of the power and influence of the United Kingdom in the world at mid-century. They will also point a contrast between the handling of foreign relations by Palmerston in Europe and in North America. These are the affair of Don Pacifico in Greece and the affair of the Mosquito Coast in the Caribbean.

The Don Pacifico incident raised two main issues in international

---

[7] W. H. B. Court, *A Concise Economic History of Britain from 1750 to Recent Times*, Cambridge University Press, 1954, p. 256.

comity. How far is a government entitled to go in enforcing upon a foreign government the claims of its nationals for compensation for losses suffered in a foreign country as a result of public disorder? And how far is a government entitled to act independently in bringing pressure to bear on a foreign government in respect of which it has common obligations of guarantee undertaken in company with other interested powers?

The main facts were simple enough. Don Pacifico, a Portuguese Jewish moneylender, resident in Athens (where he acted as Portuguese Consul-General), a British subject in virtue of his birth at Gibraltar, had his house pillaged and burnt by an anti-Semitic mob in April 1847. He put in a claim including £8,000 in respect of furniture and £27,000 in respect of Portuguese bonds, all allegedly destroyed by fire. Normally such a claim would be carefully scrutinized and assessed before being put forward officially. Palmerston swallowed it whole. It was undoubtedly grossly inflated: in respect of the bonds, a later arbitration board reduced the figure of the claim by five-sixths. The Greek Government as usual prevaricated. For Palmerston this was the last straw; he had for years been exasperated by a series of evasions of responsibility by the Greek authorities. He sent a fleet (equal to that commanded by Nelson at the Battle of the Nile) under Admiral Parker to the Piraeus to concert with Mr (later Sir Thomas) Wyse to enforce payment. In January 1850 they issued an ultimatum, and on its expiry proclaimed a general blockade of Greece. The Admiral then seized a Greek vessel of war, the *Otho*, at Piraeus and some merchant ships at Salamis.

The affair now moved into the wider field of international politics. By agreements concluded in 1830, 1831 and 1832, Great Britain, France and Russia had established and guaranteed Greece as an independent state under a hereditary monarch in the person of Otho of Bavaria. Greece appealed to the other two guarantors. Both France and Russia protested. France offered good offices, reluctantly accepted by Palmerston. Russia complained in scathing terms of Palmerston's single-handed action, embarked upon without consultation with the two co-guarantors. Palmerston was unrepentant and unperturbed. France and Russia, he said, were furious that their client, Greece, whom they had for years been encouraging 'to insult and defy England, should at last have received a chastisement from which they are unable to protect him.' He had, as usual, correctly taken their measure.

Early Victorian Climax

Agreement was at length reached in London between the British and French governments, but Palmerston failed to inform Wyse of this. The latter insisted on his earlier stiffer terms and reinforced the blockade. The Greeks paid up. The Russians renewed their protest. The French ambassador was for a time withdrawn from London, his further residence there being 'no longer compatible with the dignity of the Republic'.

This was only one of a series of characteristically high-handed, independent acts of Palmerston in the years 1847–51, which led to his dismissal in the latter year.[8] But it should be noted, first, that in most of these exploits, he had the strongly vocal support of the British public; and secondly, that the fact that he could so blatantly disregard the susceptibilities of foreign governments without serious damage testifies to the strong position still held by Great Britain at mid-century.

Palmerston's courses were widely and strongly criticized in the Press, in Parliament, in the political world, and by the Queen and the Prince Consort. A hostile motion was carried in the House of Lords, whereupon Palmerston reverted to the settlement agreed upon with the French in London. In the House of Commons, on the other hand, Mr Roebuck's motion in support of Palmerston was

[8] Palmerston was no doubt at fault in expressing to the French ambassador a personal opinion in favour of Louis Napoleon's *coup d'état* against the Second Republic in December 1851, an opinion which was not in keeping with those of either the Court or the Cabinet as a whole. Yet it was a fair enough opinion. We might well be better off with a Bonaparte than we should have been with another Jacobin revolution or with an Orleanist restoration: Lord John Russell and Clarendon thought the same. Furthermore, the Queen's requirement that draft notes to foreign ambassadors and of despatches to H.M. representatives abroad on important matters should always be sent by the Foreign Secretary to the Prime Minister and submitted by the latter for approval by Her Majesty was burdensome to ministers. In practice it would mean that the drafts were subject to scrutiny by one German, if not by two, Prince Albert and his mentor, Stockmar. However well-informed and sagacious these advisers might be, the procedure was hardly consistent either with the expeditious conduct of public business when, as Palmerston said, 'events are going at a hand-gallop', or with the very proper sentiments of a British Foreign Secretary. The royal pretension was already becoming out of date. The Queen was sensible enough not to press it too hard, and her ministers were prudent enough not to raise the constitutional issue which it involved. In later years, as the Queen aged, the practice was relaxed and despatches submitted to her continued to be headed 'draft' even though they had already gone off, it being understood that they could be amended by telegram.

passed by 310 to 261, after a debate spread over five days. In the debate on the Ochakov affair in 1791, one recurrent theme had been the question whether Parliament should have unquestioning confidence in the Crown's handling of foreign policy, or whether it should be entitled to ask for a full explanation of the Government's policy, and thereafter to warn or restrain. In the event, Pitt had been curbed by force of parliamentary and public opinion. Not so Palmerston. He won a resounding triumph, riding high upon a comprehensive defence of his policy over twenty years, and upon his well-known peroration, as magnificent a piece of rhetoric as that of Canning about calling the New World into existence to redress the balance of the Old. 'We have shown,' he declared, 'that liberty is compatible with order, that individual freedom is reconcilable with obedience to the law' (he is here contrasting Great Britain with the post-revolutionary despotisms of the Continent); and he 'therefore fearlessly challenged the verdict' of the House, 'as representing a political, a commercial, a constitutional country' (such as he consistently aimed to support in Europe), 'whether the principles on which foreign policy . . . has been conducted and the sense of duty which has led us to think ourselves bound to afford protection to our fellow-subjects abroad are proper and fitting guides for those charged with the government of England; and whether as the Roman in days of old held himself free from indignity when he could say "Civis Romanus sum", so also a British subject, in whatever land he may be, shall feel confident that the watchful eye and the strong arm of England will protect him against injustice and wrong.'

Seldom, if ever, can there have been a more notable debate on the principles which ought to govern the conduct of foreign policy. Some of the greatest voices of the nineteenth century were heard in opposition to Palmerston, voices more characteristic of the nineteenth century than was Palmerston's own, voices which were sufficient indeed for their own secure times but were never required to ring out for the nation as, in times of peril, those of Elizabeth, of Chatham and of Winston Churchill have done.

Gladstone proclaimed that the intervention had infringed 'the general principles of the law of nations'. He expounded 'the principle of non-intervention in the domestic affairs of other countries' and laid it down that 'interference in foreign countries should be rare, deliberate, decisive in character and effectual for its end.' It was no part of the Englishman to claim the standing of a Roman citizen, who was a member of a privileged caste, a conquering race. What mattered was that he should stand well in 'the general sentiment of the civilized world' and enjoy 'the moral supports which the general . . . convictions of mankind afford.'

Richard Cobden also urged 'non-intervention in the domestic affairs of other nations'. 'With what face could you get up and denounce the Tsar for invading Hungary after the doctrine advocated tonight?' He did not believe in Palmerston's policy of championing liberalism abroad: 'I believe the progress of freedom depends more upon the maintenance of peace, the spread of commerce and the diffusion of education than upon the labour of cabinets and foreign offices.'

Peel, in his last public speech (he died a few days later), impartially condemning Palmerston's action and disapproving of the Greek Government's attitude, said that the dispute could have been settled quietly. That is what diplomacy is for. 'Diplomacy is a costly engine for maintaining peace . . . if your application of diplomacy be to fester every wound, to provoke instead of soothing resentments . . . promoting what is supposed to be an English interest by keeping up conflicts with the representatives of other Powers. . . . Constitutional liberty will be best worked out by those who aspire to freedom by their own efforts. You will only overload it by your help, by your principle of interference.'

Palmerston was to win the day; but in the course of the next generation, when Palmerston's last term of office was over, the policy of non-interference would for a while prevail.

In his relations with the United States Palmerston was much more circumspect.

The war with Mexico had brought California and the Pacific coast into the United States. The settlement of the boundaries of Maine and Oregon had determined the northern frontier with Canada. But thoughts of what the founding fathers had seen as a rising American Empire were still active in American minds. John Quincy Adams, President Monroe's Secretary of State, had written to the United States minister in Spain in April 1823, apropos of erroneously suspected British aspirations in the Caribbean: 'There are laws of political as well as of physical gravitation, and if an apple, severed by the tempest from its native tree, cannot choose but to fall to the ground, Cuba, forcibly disjoined from its unnatural connection with Spain, and incapable of self-support, can gravitate only toward the North American Union.' And, with a sweep of wider ambition, he added: 'Looking forward to the probable course of events for the short period of half a century, it is scarcely possible to resist the conviction that the annexation of Cuba to our Federal Republic will be indispensable to the continuance and integrity of the Union itself.'

Along this same line, President Polk, in his Annual Message on December 2nd 1845, had, in view of British and French opposition to United States designs in Texas and Mexico, given an extended interpretation to the Monroe Doctrine. 'We must,' he said, 'ever maintain the principle that the people of this continent alone have the right to decide their own destiny. Should any portion of them, constituting an independent state, propose to unite themselves with our Confederacy, this will be a question for them and us to determine without any foreign interposition.' And he completed his warning by adding: 'It should be distinctly announced to the world as our settled policy that no future European colony or dominion shall with our consent be planted or established on any part of the North American continent.'

The Southern states had a dream of a great slave empire in the Caribbean, and British action against the slave trade aroused deep hostility. The Northern states looked confidently for the annexation of Canada. Had it not been for the growing cleavage between North and South on the subject of slavery which was within a few years to burst into a war between the states, the aspirations of both might have been realized. Anti-colonial sentiment and Little Englandism were prevalent in the United Kingdom. In the last resort, London would not have resisted the acquisition of Central America by the United States. As the *Economist* was to say in 1856: 'We could not hinder the ultimate absorption by the Anglo-Saxon republicans of the whole of Central America if we would—and we are by no means certain that we would if we could.' The Tory Foreign Secretary himself, Lord Malmesbury, went so far as to say in 1858 that 'he was one of that class of statesmen who believed that all the southern part of North America must ultimately come under the government of the United States.' Even in regard to Canada, which became self-governing in 1848, opposition in the United Kingdom and in some Canadian quarters to annexation to the United States was, at this period, unlikely to have been very strong or very long-lasting. But the growing rift between North and South was decisive in inducing moderation on the American side. North and South were bitterly divided on the question whether the new middle western states should be slave or free. The South could not abide the prospect of the accession of the great free territories of Canada, while the North set their face against the acquisition of new slave states in the Caribbean, disliking the extension of slavery more than they desired to see the expansion of the United States.

As for the British Government, what might have been acceptable to them in Central America in the last resort was not necessarily acceptable to them in the short run, especially in view of existing American difficulties. On the other hand, their own growing embarrassments in Europe induced in them also a mood of moderation. So, while Palmerston, who was in office as Foreign Secretary from 1846 to 1851, was no imperialist and thought that we already had more colonies than we could handle, he held nevertheless that we ought to delay the probable United States expansion southwards as long as possible. As he said later, in 1857: 'Propitiating the Yankees by countenancing their schemes of annexation . . . would be like propitiating an animal of prey by giving him one of one's travelling companions.' At the same time, both governmental and public opinion in London had become conscious of the need to maintain good relations with the growing power of the United States, and to handle their relations with Washington cautiously, the more so in that this was 'a feverish period in American history' and, as Sir Henry Lytton Bulwer, British minister in Washington, said in 1851, 'the people who live under this government are of a wild, adventurous and conquering character.'

Within this framework, we may look at the main facts.

The expansion of the United States to the Pacific coast after the Mexican war, and the discovery of gold in California in 1849, made the construction of a canal across the Central American isthmus increasingly desirable as an object of American policy, quite apart from the Southern aspiration for an empire in the tropics. There were four main routes, one across Mexican territory, one across the Panamanian territory of New Granada (now Colombia), one through Honduras and one through Nicaragua, the two latter both debouching on the Gulf of Fonseca on the Pacific coast. The two latter were at this time preferred over the two former. Great

Britain had a settlement but as yet no sovereignty at Belize in what is now British Honduras. She had claims to the Bay Islands as an off-shoot thereof, and a protectorate over the Indians of the Mosquito Coast, along the Caribbean shore of Nicaragua. These would give control over the Caribbean ends of the two most favoured canal routes (Honduras and Nicaragua), including, in particular, the terminus of the Nicaragua canal near Greytown, occupied by Mosquito forces in 1848. During the administration of the Democratic President, James K. Polk, and after the advent of the Whig régime of President Zachary Taylor in 1849, there were unauthorized acts by emissaries of both sides. Both sides made competitive treaties with central American states in pursuance of their claims, and a serious state of tension arose.

However, the new Secretary of State, John M. Clayton, fearing an Anglo-American rupture, came to an understanding with Nicaragua by which neither the United States nor any other power could claim exclusive control of any canal that might be constructed. He also told the British minister in Washington that he did not hold to the non-colonization principle of the Monroe Doctrine. Palmerston, for his part, disclaimed any idea of our wishing for exclusive possession of the mouth of the river on which Greytown stood. On this basis, Clayton and Bulwer, after a long and difficult negotiation, concluded in April 1850 the Treaty which bears their names. Under the Treaty it was provided that neither party would ever 'obtain or maintain for itself any exclusive control' over any ship canal through any part of Central America. The canal would be neutralized, with a free port at either end, and with equal rights in commerce and navigation for the nationals of both parties; and any other communication across the isthmus, whether by canal or by sail, would be protected by the two powers. So far, so good. But there was a crucial clause, the terms of which had, for the sake of agreement, been left, or made, deliberately ambiguous—a most tempting but most undesirable procedure in diplomacy. Neither party was to occupy, or fortify, or colonize, or assume, or exercise any dominion over Nicaragua, Costa Rica, the Mosquito Coast, or any part of Central America. What was left in doubt was whether this left existing British claims, e.g. the protectorate over the Mosquito Coast, still standing, or whether it extinguished them. The British held to the former interpretation, the Americans to the latter, and the dispute was not resolved for ten years. Nor was this all. Arising out of this ambiguity, there was a clarifying declaration by Bulwer, a counter-declaration by Clayton, and a counter-counter declaration by Bulwer, the last of which seems never to have reached Clayton's hands, being dated a few days before his retirement. These made it clear that Belize was excluded from the Treaty, but left the position of the Bay Islands still obscure. The supplementary statements were not known to members of the Senate, indeed they had not been made, when the Senate approved the Treaty by a large majority on the understanding that it nullified the Mosquito protectorate. Bulwer held that the Treaty 'was intended to apply to future and not to present possessions in Central America.'

Though Palmerston did not at first press his claims, action by local representatives generated a state of tension. A British proclamation of the Bay Islands as a colony, with an eye to a commercial station when the canal was built, brought the issue again into official channels. With the advent of the more bellicose Democratic administration of President Franklin Pierce in 1853, tension again grew. By a liberal interpretation of his instructions, in the face of local disorders, the commander of the United States sloop *Cyane*, by an American variant of 'gun-boat diplomacy', bombarded and destroyed the settlement of Greytown. In spite of strong disapproval among the American public, the United States government assumed official responsibility for what the Foreign Secretary, Clarendon, called an outrage 'without a parallel in the annals of modern times'. For all that, with the Crimean War in progress, the British Government and people took this quietly and the Government contented itself with a protest. At one point, the American Secretary of State broke off relations with the British minister, but although the Crimean War was now out of the way, Palmerston's Government maintained a calm and conciliatory attitude. They realized that their largest claims were not well-founded, and they had no wish to jeopardize the very large and growing Anglo-American trade. For his part, President James Buchanan, who took office in 1857, was to say: 'The English and American peoples owe it to their own dearest principles and interests to cultivate the most friendly relations with each other.'

After a long-continuing deadlock, during which both sides maintained their positions, but both made it plain that they desired to avoid a rupture, a face-saving solution was reached in 1860. This was certainly promoted by the shadow of civil war in the United States.

The British kept the Clayton–Bulwer Treaty, but made direct agreements with Honduras and Nicaragua which interpreted it broadly in the American sense. The Mosquito protectorate was relinquished; the Bay Islands were ceded to Honduras; Great Britain retained Belize with the boundaries claimed by her; Greytown was made a free port; while the Isthmus remained neutralized, as the Clayton–Bulwer Treaty provided. This was a compromise, but one in which the more substantial concessions were made by Great Britain and, on the whole, justly so. Clayton has been harshly judged by some American historians for making with Palmerston a treaty so disadvantageous to the United States.

This episode provokes certain reflections. It marks a turning point in Anglo-American relations. Great Britain had come to recognize the growing power of the United States, especially in a local issue. The United States was also a commercial rival. We do not often remember that in 1850 the merchant tonnage under the American flag was beginning to rival that of Great Britain, and that within ten years it was very near to equality with it, an equality which did not survive the growing use of iron for ship-building and the destruction wrought during the Civil War. In view of the increasing complexity and uncertainty of European affairs, the British Government saw that it would be more prudent to have the United States as a friend than as an enemy. As Disraeli was to say in the House of Commons on June 16th 1856: 'It would be wise if England would at last recognize that the United States, like all the great countries of Europe, have a policy, and that they have a right to have a policy . . . it is the business of a statesman to recognize the necessity of an increase in their power.' The liberal tendencies of British governments at home and in the empire made it easier for the United States to respond, though they were slower to do so than were the British to make advances. George III and the traditional view of colonialism died hard. They are not dead even yet. It is significant, too, that the British government and people could take so calmly the experience of being at the receiving end of an exercise in gun-boat diplomacy. On the other side, it is illustrative of Great Britain's position in the world, based on preponderant sea-power, that the United States should still recognize her right to a say in the affairs of Central America, and in particular in the conditions in which a canal would be constructed across the Isthmus. Before the century was out, British concern with a South American state would bring her near to war with the United States. In the affairs of the Mosquito Coast, war was never in sight.[9]

The conception of the balance of power at mid-century in orthodox British minds remained very much what it had been as Burke defined it in the Ochakov debate in 1791. There is an interesting exposition of this view in the article on 'The Balance of Power' in the *Encyclopaedia Britannica*, Eighth Edition, 1854, mentioned on p. 69 above. The writer explains that the balancing situation is not grounded upon an equality among states in respect of power, but upon a union of powers to repress the enterprises of the strong and ambitious, and to counteract the effects of necessary individual inequalities by aggregate strength. There should be vigilant inspection to discover, and prompt union to counteract, in their birth, all such projects of encroachment as powerful states will, when opportunity offers, be ready to form.

There is nothing here of the continental theory—or what Burke called the 'diabolical principle'—that, by constant interference on the basis of an elaborate search for mathematically calculated territorial compensation, all states should be maintained in their existing relative positions of power. This is natural enough, since alone of the European powers, we had no territorial ambitions in Europe. The system here described is something more rough-and-ready: and it hardly needed in this period to be applied in any spectacular way since, as yet, no one power in Europe threatened clearly to over-top the rest. The complex diplomatic manœuvres of the European powers, a process that might sometimes go by the name of the concert of Europe, were sufficient to maintain a kind of equilibrium, such as had been established by the Vienna Settlement. In 1854, however, it appeared to France and Great Britain that Russia was overstepping the mark and threatening the continuance of the equilibrium by action in regard to the Ottoman Empire, which had not come within the range of the Vienna Settlement. In the course of the second half of the century, we shall find the mechanism of the balance of power operating by the formation of formal or less formal understandings or alliances designed to correct or restore a threatened balance, and, in the end, a drift of the powers into two opposing

[9] In preparing the foregoing outline of the complex isthmian controversy, the author has relied mainly on H. C. Allen, *Great Britain and the United States*, Odhams Press, London, 1954, and (from the American side) on Samuel F. Bemis, *A Diplomatic History of the United States*, Henry Holt, New York, 1955.

rival camps in a vain attempt to avert the clash arising from aggressive ambition.

Meanwhile, looking at the position of Great Britain at the date of writing, the author of the article concludes that even with a navy well capable of preventing the invasion of the homeland, it is better for us to have friends and confederates in Europe. As a colonial power, our need is greater. Our commerce and our colonies, which are the support of that navy, render it indispensably necessary, he holds, that we should more particularly observe some nations and ally ourselves with others.

There is thus no thought yet, in the mind of an orthodox writer at mid-century, of 'splendid isolation'. But there was an influential school of thought that expressed total dissent from orthodox views and from the orthodox conduct of foreign policy. For Cobden, the balance of power was 'an undescribed, indescribable nothing; mere words'. For Bright, it was 'a mischievous delusion which has come down to us from past times; we ought to drive it from our minds.' These ideas were to grow in favour in the public mind, especially after the Crimean War: but they had not yet made an impact on public policy.

A present-day historian, in a passing reference to the shock administered to English susceptibilities by the outbreak of the Crimean War in 1854 after forty years of peace, noted that there had also been 'twenty-five years of virtually isolationist policies'.[10] Another has spoken of Great Britain's 'effective detachment from Continental and American affairs, which marked her foreign policy between Canning's day and the Civil War in the United States.'[11] These statements, as the foregoing recital will have suggested, are hardly borne out by the facts. Isolation or isolationism has a variety of meanings, but, whatever may have been the position in the later years of the nineteenth century, and this will have to be examined, none of them could be properly applied to the years between 1830 and 1851, which cover the sixteen years of Palmerston's successive periods of office as Foreign Secretary. It is curious how persistently the belief in British isolationism in early and mid-nineteenth century continues to survive. Isolationism, by an extreme definition, may mean the attempt to seal off a country from all or almost all contact with the world overseas, as it came to be practised by China and

[10] H. C. Allen, *Great Britain and the United States*, p. 425.
[11] Court, *Concise Economic History*, p. 314.

Japan until they were prised open by force by western peoples in the nineteenth century. It may mean what Cobden meant by 'no foreign politics'; no intervention by force for the weak against the strong or for the right against the wrong; no diplomatic meddling; 'as little intercourse as possible between governments, as much connection as possible between the nations of the world'. Peoples are to talk freely to peoples, but as between governments international relations are to be regulated mainly by commercial treaties, arbitration and agreed limitation of armaments. By such criteria, Cobden judged us to have been 'the most combative and aggressive community that has existed since the days of the Roman Dominion'. Isolationism, again, may mean what the United States meant by their neutrality legislation of the 1930s, that is to say, abstention by governments, and abstention enforced by law upon nationals, from activities likely to involve the nation in international complications leading to danger of involvement in war. It may, by contrast, mean merely the more normal late nineteenth-century United States policy of the free hand: liberty to act, if need be by force, in one's own interest, but the assumption of no obligation to intervene in arms in other people's quarrels or for the maintenance of international law or morality.

None of these definitions will meet our position in the second quarter of the nineteenth century. Our policy in the years in question was, certainly, the policy of the free hand. We were in a position to meddle, and we freely meddled. We were ready to intervene by force, and time and again we threatened to do so. The affairs of Europe were our intimate concern. While we kept free of diplomacy by regular conferences, we played our part in the concert of Europe, indeed we often led it. Where our interests were directly and substantially affected, as in Belgium in 1830 and in the Near East in 1840–41, we intervened with all our diplomatic strength, and would have gone to war had this been necessary. Palmerston, defending his intervention in Portugal, said in June 1833 that 'the principle of embarking in the contests of other countries had prevailed, and had been acted upon, in the brightest periods of our history.' At the same time and in addition to this, we were ready, if need be, to accept obligations. But here we made a distinction. We no longer made the kind of treaty we had entered into in the eighteenth century when, for example, we had in 1731, together with the Netherlands, given a guarantee to the Emperor Charles VI for the integrity of all his possessions and the secure succession to them of his daughter, Maria

Theresa. Our new policy had been clearly laid down by Palmerston to Talleyrand in 1833: 'We have no objection to treaties for specific and immediate objects but we do not much fancy treaties which are formed in contemplation of indefinite and indistinctly foreseen cases. We like to be free to judge of each occasion as it arises, and with all its concomitant circumstances.' Thus, we were still bound, with the other great powers, to uphold the post-Napoleonic settlement against France. Jointly with Russia and France, we guaranteed the independence of Greece in 1832. When, in respect of Belgium, the Vienna settlement had to be varied as a result of the Belgian revolt, we entered into a new obligation in 1839 to uphold the new settlement and, in order to preserve the equilibrium, guaranteed the neutrality of Belgium. This was an obligation of which we never ceased to be conscious throughout the remainder of the nineteenth century, however we might try to reinterpret it. It was an obligation which we were called upon to make good, and did make good, in the twentieth century. If we kept out of war in the forty years after 1815, this was not from any doctrine or practice of isolation, but because we were usually strong and influential enough and diplomatically successful enough to get what we wanted, if we wanted it badly enough, without war. 'Save for a brief interval at the close of the nineteenth century, Britain has never been able to pursue a policy of deliberate isolation—though the appetite for intervention has varied very considerably.'[12]

In a period of national security such as we usually possessed at the time we are discussing, there is something to be said for a policy of isolation, or at least for a policy of rather strictly defined non-interference, such as was advocated by Cobden and Bright. This judgment rests, in some degree, on hindsight. We were, as it proved, secure enough; but responsible ministers at the time were not able to be secure in their minds in face of a turbulent continent. They could not contract out of international life. If only because of her world-wide trading interests, Great Britain was in no position to wash her hands of foreign complications. Every important foreign event called for consideration and might call for action. Every step would need to be reflected upon like a move on the chessboard, and even more than in chess it would be a step in the dark. They could never be sure that there might not be formed some combination or coalition

[12] R. W. Seton-Watson, *Britain in Europe, 1789–1914*, Cambridge University Press, 1937, p. 36.

dangerous to our own safety, or capable of treating one of our vital interests in Europe in a manner detrimental to our security. They could not ignore what was, at any rate, a possible risk. Guizot, shortly before he was, with Louis Philippe, driven from power by the revolution of 1848, was, it seems, trying to bring France into a coalition with Russia, Prussia and Austria directed against Great Britain. This was at a time when we were beginning to be worried by the appearance of steam and iron in the French Navy. The fact that no such combination was ever effectively formed, either then or at any other later time, is not to say that, had our foreign policy been less judicious or less active or less alert or less interfering, a dangerous hostile coalition might not have been formed. More than this, mere habit and tradition required that there should be, in Cobden's phrase, 'foreign politics'. Had ministers been remiss in this, there were always their colleagues, or Parliament, or the Press, or the Queen, to require them to show a due, though not an excessive, activity. It is hard for Foreign Secretaries to be quiet and to wait: they must always be doing something, if only for the sake of doing something, in order to be able to show, when their conduct is questioned, as it may be day by day, that they are not being idle.

It is the commonly accepted view that, after the American War of Independence, having lost one Empire we sat down and built another. It was neither, on the one hand, as catastrophic, nor, on the other, as deliberate as that. In the first place, we did not entirely lose an empire, though we certainly lost the most populous, profitable and dynamic part of it. After the loss of the American colonies we still held, in the Americas, Upper and Lower Canada (though these were at that time mere truncated remnants of a wide territory, with small population and frontiers grossly favourable to the Americans), New Brunswick, Nova Scotia, Newfoundland and the Hudson Bay trading stations, Bermuda, the Bahamas, Jamaica, Barbados and other Windward and Leeward Islands, Honduras and the Falkland Islands. In Africa we had company trading posts in West Africa and at St Helena. In Asia, there were the province of Bengal and the presidencies at Bombay and Madras under the East India Company, as well as Penang. In Europe, we held Gibraltar. After a few years in Australia (in 1788 and 1803), we established penal settlements in what are now New South Wales and Tasmania. This was quite a substantial empire still.

In the second place, we did not deliberately plan to build another empire, except perhaps in so far as the blanket annexation of the eastern half of Australia at the time of the foundation of Sydney in 1788 was seen as a somewhat empty set-off in the Pacific against what had been lost in the Atlantic. At the settlements of 1814 and 1815, we could have had the pick of the Spanish and Dutch island empires and of what was left of the French. (The Portuguese empire was not in question because Portugal was an ancient ally and, unlike Spain and Holland, had not been drawn into alliance with Napoleon.) In fact, we took relatively little. What we kept, we kept mainly for strategic reasons, for use as naval stations or the like: in the Americas, Trinidad (from Spain), St Lucia and Tobago (from France), Demerara in Guiana (from Holland); in and about Africa, the Cape of Good Hope (from Holland) and Mauritius and the Seychelles (from France); in Asia, Ceylon (from Holland); in Europe, Heligoland, Malta and, as a protectorate, the Ionian Islands. It is noteworthy that we paid the Dutch £6,000,000 for what we took from them. We returned Martinique, Guadeloupe, Cayenne, Réunion and Pondicherry to France; and Surinam, the Moluccas and the great island of Java, and in 1824 our settlement in Sumatra, to Holland.

It is true that by 1850 we had largely extended the territories already under our rule or control. In the Americas, company trading posts on the Pacific Coast; in and about Africa, Natal (1843) the Orange River Territory (1848 but independent in 1854); in Asia, most of India proper, taken over in part during the Napoleonic War and in part later, e.g. Sind (1843) and the Punjab (1849), Assam and the coast of Burma (1826), Singapore (purchased in 1819); in Australasia, New South Wales (1823), Tasmania (1825), South Australia (1836), New Zealand (1839), Victoria (1850). But in South Africa and Australasia, territories were taken over, albeit reluctantly, either, as in South Africa and New Zealand, in order to regulate the relations of the settlers with the Bantu and Maori natives, or, in general, to provide an administration for the growing body of emigrant settlers in territories opened by pioneer explorers. These things were not done, either of set purpose or, as was afterwards alleged, in a fit of absence of mind, but under the almost inescapable pressure of events. More often than not, the hand of London was forced by men on the spot, including the missionaries, or by zealots at home.

Early Victorian Climax

In India, the East India Company tried in vain to set a limit to the expansion of its territories; but as a political power it came into conflict with bellicose native rulers who had no mind to co-exist peacefully with it. When, after the India Act of 1784, the Secretary of State and the Governor-General took effective control, the Government at home became more directly involved, however much ministers and the directors of the Company might yearn after a policy of non-intervention. Marquis Wellesley, Governor-General from 1798 to 1805, decided that the only way to meet armed opposition, fomented by the French, was to crush it, and that the only way to get rid of tyranny and anarchy was to suppress them by force. In seven years, until forced to resign by opposition in London to his independent forward policy, he had, with the help of his brother, that brilliant field-commander, Sir Arthur Wellesley, the future Duke of Wellington, changed the face of India. The power of the great Maratha kingdom was crushed at Assaye in 1803. Later Governor-Generals were led to follow the policy of expansion. In the 1840s, Lord Ellenborough, a Governor-General as bellicose as Wellesley, violating treaty engagements, attacked and annexed Sind (1843), a course of action that was condemned by the Company and disapproved by the Cabinet. He was recalled. His action had closed one of the gaps in our north-west frontier. His successor, Sir Henry Hardinge, though pacific by temperament and conscious that London had no desire to extend British territory in India, was forced to react to a challenge by the Sikhs, the last remaining powerful state in India, beat them in battle and made a moderate settlement (1846). In the time of his successor, Lord Dalhousie, the Sikhs again attacked, were defeated though with heavy loss, and the remainder of the Punjab was annexed (1849), an act for which the Governor-General had no authority from London. Again the hand of the Government was forced. Again, another gap in the north-west frontier was closed. The frontier now lay among the mountains.

As the fear of the French had, in part, stimulated our war-time action against their protégés in the south of the peninsula, so now fear of Russia drew us, in 1839–42, into a disastrous, aggressive and probably unnecessary campaign in Afghanistan.

The empire in India thus grew not by design but by necessity. Our mere presence in the sub-continent for purposes of trade had led, step by step, ineluctably, to the conquest of three-fifths of the whole country. The possession of India laid the basis of our expanding power in Asia. Our position was confirmed by the suppression of the Great Mutiny in 1857–58. We gave unity under law to a subcontinent that had fallen into political chaos. With unity, came an economic transformation: India's overseas trade increased threefold between 1834 and 1856, from about £12,000,000 to about £36,000,000. Conquest made possible, as nothing else could have done, the India which we see today. When we came to India, many Indians were as much strangers and foreigners to each other as we were to them. When we left India, they had a fully developed national consciousness, but one which was not yet universal enough to exorcize the spirit of separation, a heritage of the unhappy past, which imposed partition on a communal basis.

Sir Thomas Munro, one of the most enlightened servants of the Company, who was Governor of Madras between 1820 and 1827, looking forward, even a long time forward, with hope, wrote in 1824 that India should be maintained as a possession 'until the natives shall in some future age have . . . become sufficiently enlightened to frame a regular government for themselves, and to conduct and preserve it. When such a time shall arrive, it will probably be best for both countries that the British control should be withdrawn.' Macaulay thought that, when this happened, it would be 'the proudest day in British history'.

Munro was thinking like the radical imperialists and not like the Manchester school. In the minds of the latter, colonies, whether settled or conquered, were coming to be regarded as a costly burden, adjuncts of a mercantilist system that was becoming out of date. The advocates of the rising doctrine of free trade had no use for them. There were on the other hand radical imperialists, like the Earl of Durham ('radical Jack') who was responsible for the report of 1837 which laid the foundation for the self-government of Canada. He believed, with men like Charles Buller and Edward Gibbon Wakefield, in systematic colonization and economic development and in the political emancipation of the colonies under representative government as free daughter communities. Like Burke, they held that there were bonds of sentiment and enlightened self-interest which would hold the settled colonies to the Motherland. These men had personal failings which lessened their achievements, but their influence persisted in enlightened administrators like Lord Elgin in Canada and Sir George Grey in Australia, New Zealand and South Africa. Men like these were able to mitigate the harsh materialist doctrines of the *laissez-faire* Manchester school which were triumphant by 1850, even in minds that had little in common with the Cobdenites. What mattered was peace and profits. We were no longer able wholly to feed ourselves; in order to survive, we needed peaceful markets for our world-wide trade. Colonies were apt to be the cause of war, and in any event were not a profitable investment. Let them cut adrift if they would, to sink or swim.

In 1839, the number of British subjects living overseas was a mere 1,200,000. The great days of migration were yet to come. In 1854, less than a quarter of our overseas trade was done with the colonies: wool from Australia and New Zealand and timber from Canada in return for cotton and woollen textiles, iron, tin and hardware. As Great Britain became a world-trader, colonial trade had become less important. In 1853, a large part of the system of colonial preferences was abolished. Even Palmerston thought in 1850 that we already had more colonies than we could manage. Sir James Stephen, the Under-Secretary for the Colonies, wrote in 1849: 'It remains for the Canadians to cut the last cable which anchors them to us . . . The same process is in progress in the Australian colonies.' Of the smaller colonies, including apparently New Zealand, he said that 'these detached islands with heterogeneous populations' were 'wretched burdens which in an evil hour we assumed'. He thought that dissolution was inevitable, willed by the colonists themselves. As regards Africa, Earl Grey, Secretary of State for War and the Colonies, urged in 1846 that the acquisition of African land would be 'not merely worthless, but pernicious—the source not of increasing strength but of weakness'. In 1850, little Englandism in colonial affairs was the creed of men of all parties, of Tories like Disraeli and Peel as well as of Whigs like Palmerston and Russell. Not till the last quarter of the century would the creed of deliberate imperialism revive. With it and, indeed, in advance of it, the constructive ideas of the radical imperialists of earlier years would come into their own.

If, as it is here suggested, the period of greatest British influence in foreign affairs fell between Waterloo and mid-century, it may be asked upon the strength of what factors, and in what relative degree, that influence may be judged to have been developed. To the extent that the British Government made its will prevail, and determined the acts and opinions of other governments, how is this to be explained? A few generalizations may be attempted. They apply, obviously, to international conditions in the nineteenth century when states were not inhibited by international law from using force as an instrument of national policy. Clearly, effective and immediately available military power can be an asset of over-riding importance. But some qualifications suggest themselves. There must not only be the possession of military power: there must also be the will to use it, and the conviction in the mind of the adversary that the will exists. Then, the military power must be of a character appropriate to the task which it has to fulfil. A navy alone cannot strike at a land-locked state, or strike effectively at a large state with continental rather than maritime interests. An army cannot strike unless it can be transported overland or overseas to the scene of the projected action. Mere distance may be an effective obstacle to military action: a weak state on its own ground may stand up successfully to a strong state with its base of operations across the ocean. Then again, there are some problems which are not susceptible of solution by military action: a dependent people in revolt may be coerced into submission, but its loyalty and willing collaboration cannot be re-created by force.

Even if sufficient and immediately effective military power is not available, influence may still be successfully exercised, though its range and scope will be less extensive and subject to greater limitation. It can be effective if it rests on recent and remembered military prowess; and if there is the conviction in the mind of the potential adversary that there is the necessary economic and financial strength and political will to re-create the requisite forces in good time if the need arises, and that there is the resolution to use them. The greater the distance, and the less favourable the geographical and strategic conditions, the less will be the probability that mere prestige will prevail. On the other hand, the more accessible, and the more vulnerable to limited military action, e.g. blockade, the adversary is, the greater the play of prestige in diplomatic action. There is also, in every case, the relative importance which the two parties attach to the particular issue in question. The United States has usually been more intimately interested than ourselves in the matters of trans-atlantic concern which have arisen between us. That, together with the factor of distance, and our reluctance, since the early nineteenth century, to land ourselves in hostilities with what is held to be a kindred though completely foreign nation, has usually weighed the scales of negotiation down on the American side.

Early Victorian Climax

Apart altogether from effective military power or the prestige that rests on military potential, there are factors which can weigh substantially in the diplomatic scales. One of them is sheer diplomatic skill. Power of exposition, choice of timing, the appeal to reason or to good faith or to international comity and morality, or to personal relationship, or to self-interest; the canvassing of support, the judicious threat, the dangled inducement, the hint of support or opposition on other issues, the sagacious estimate of the other minister's standing with colleagues or with his sovereign, or with his public, or of the strength and standing of the other government: as between well-matched adversaries, these skills can play a substantial part. So can a well-founded reputation for fair dealing, for truth-telling, and for a liberal regard for the common interest.[13]

To represent a nation which enjoys stability, unity, prosperity and good repute is an asset in negotiation. A Foreign Minister or an ambassador can speak the more persuasively when it is the whole nation and what it stands for that lend force to his words. Great Britain enjoyed singular advantages in this respect in the decades between the Napoleonic Wars and the middle years of the century, the high period of the *Pax Britannica*. Her foreign and domestic policies were well attuned to the new political, economic and social aspirations of Europe and the world. At most times secure herself from attack, she threatened no one. In foreign affairs she played a consistently mediatory role. At home, she found a new way to prosperity. She showed how to introduce political and constitutional change without revolution and by process of discussion. Trade was progressively freed from tariffs and from the restrictions of the Navigation Acts. Colonial commerce was thrown open to all, and the first steps were taken towards colonial self-government and fiscal autonomy. Once again, as in the days of the younger Pitt, Great Britain was saving Europe by her example.[14]

Palmerston, in his periods as Foreign Secretary between 1830 and

[13] As Castlereagh said in his instructions for the negotiations at Châtillon early in 1814: 'The power of Great Britain to do good depends not merely on its resources but upon a sense of its impartiality and the reconciling character of its influence . . . a steady and temperate application of honest principles is her best source of authority.'
[14] There is a penetrating essay on this theme, and one gratifying to British readers, in Albert H. Imlah, *Economic Elements in the Pax Britannica*, Harvard University Press, Cambridge, Massachusetts, 1958, Chap. I.

1851, could count on an effective naval force, sufficient to confer security on the United Kingdom and her overseas possessions, except perhaps Canada, and usually adequate to support his diplomacy in Europe. It could, if need be, transport military forces at will, and it could establish a blockade. He could bank on a great, though gradually diminishing, national prestige resting on a recognized naval and military renown and on a still undoubted military potential. Great Britain having, unlike the other powers, no territorial ambitions in Europe, his policies could in that respect incur no suspicion in the minds of his continental associates in the European concert. He also possessed unrivalled knowledge, superb diplomatic skill of the rougher kind and a fine political judgment. But the supremacy of Great Britain in Europe in his day, such as it was, lay not so much in the power to gain her own ends by her own authority. She was seldom able to intervene successfully in a European crisis except in association with some continental power. It lay rather in the power and skill to tip the balance in her favour in every issue that arose which was of substantial interest to her.

Palmerston manipulated the balance of power within the concert of Europe in the interest of Great Britain. Great Britain still, as Vattel had said in the middle of the eighteenth century, had 'the honour to hold in her hands the balance of power, and she is careful to keep it in equilibrium.' An equilibrium certainly, but an equilibrium that was, if this could be achieved, positively and not merely negatively in the British interest. Palmerston went one better than Henry VIII's maxim. It was not merely: 'The one whom I support will get the upper hand,' but: 'With such support as I choose, I get the upper hand.' He did not necessarily seek the support of the weaker against the stronger, as the classic doctrine of the balance of power would normally suggest. On the contrary, his tactic was often to work with, and so seek to control, the power which, for geographical or strategic reasons, was in the strongest position and, on grounds of national interest, was most deeply concerned in the issue. Some of his most triumphant successes were achieved in this way. In the Belgian crisis of 1830 and following years, he worked at critical moments with France rather than with the three autocratic powers, Prussia, Austria and Russia. In 1834 he achieved his 'capital hit', the Quadruple Alliance, in association with France and the constitutional governments of Spain and Portugal against the autocratic powers and their clients in the Iberian peninsula. In 1840, on the contrary, he worked with the three autocratic governments, in disregard of French susceptibilities, in the settlement of the Near East.

When he returned to office in 1846, there was a break with France over the Spanish marriages, for which the French must bear most of the blame. Palmerston, like William III, Chatham and Canning before him, was still disturbed at possible French control over Spain, even though Spain had by now lost her empire in South America. This breach was to persist until the Orleanist régime was swept away by the revolution of 1848, and Louis Philippe and his Prime Minister, Guizot, found refuge in England. Meanwhile, Guizot set himself to frustrate Palmerston's policies in Europe, sometimes in concert with the despotic monarchs of Austria, Russia and Prussia. One consequence of this was that neither Great Britain nor France, standing alone, could prevent the violation of the Vienna Settlement of 1815 by the autocratic powers, when they extinguished the Republic of Cracow and arranged for its absorption into the Habsburg empire. Even had Great Britain and France been able to act together, it is unlikely that they could have restrained the eastern powers from acting on their own ground. It is rare in history to find the western powers able to do anything effective to help Poland, except in special circumstances, like those of 1919, when Germany, Russia and Austria were all prostrate. The Poles, for their part, have sometimes, if unconsciously, served the West. Had the attention of the eastern powers not been concentrated on Poland and diverted from western Europe in 1789 and in 1830, the French Revolution might have been crushed and Belgian independence denied.

Against Palmerston himself, Guizot had singularly little success. In Spain, in Portugal and in Switzerland, he was, as the *Cambridge History of British Foreign Policy* has it, 'out-manœuvred, outwitted and outfought by the superior knowledge, higher principle, and stronger will of the British Minister'. What is more, in the case of Switzerland in 1847, Palmerston saw his cause prevail, not against France alone but against a combination of France, Austria, Prussia and Russia. Nothing daunted by his sole efforts in diplomatic support of the well-led Federal forces, and facing the alternatives of diplomatic humiliation or the hazards of single-handed war, he succeeded in restoring the integrity of the Swiss Federation against the seceding Catholic cantons of the *Sonderbund* and the dismembering ambitions of the other powers. None of his achievements shines more brightly than this. It was an exercise in pure diplomacy, unsupported by overt threat of force. Not often has our diplomacy prevailed against such odds. When the revolutionary storm struck continental Europe in 1848, it was Palmerston's calm mastery and common sense which, more than any other factor, saved Europe from going down in general war. For his manners, for his methods, even for his policies, then and later, he was widely condemned or reviled by people of position, at home and abroad, and not without excuse, though he kept the enthusiastic support of the British people. In 1851, not without justification, he was dismissed. He was now 67. He had thoroughly enjoyed himself. He was almost immediately to return as Home Secretary, and in 1855 as Prime Minister, with Lord John Russell as Foreign Secretary from 1859. The roles of these two 'dreadful old men', as Queen Victoria called them, were thus reversed. But the world Palmerston was returning to was by now rather a different place, where he would not always enjoy himself quite so much.

These early Victorians may, as *The Times* observed, have been respected abroad, but they were certainly not loved. Tocqueville, explaining why the British of his day were so much disliked by others, said that this derived from 'the conviction in the minds of every people in the world that England never looks upon them except from the point of view of her own greatness; that, more than any other modern nation, she lacks any feeling of sympathy for anything which is foreign to herself.' Metternich said, with sour misunderstanding: 'These people haven't either the will or the power to fire a gun. Their game is completely Machiavellian, and anybody who gets involved with them won't be very long before he repents of it.' Talleyrand, while serving as French ambassador in London, unburdened himself about the people of the capital when he said that in London 'there are today fifteen hundred thousand souls, if the egoists who inhabit it can be called such.'[15] Tennyson spoke for the orthodox opinion of the age when, in a white heat of patriotic passion against Napoleon III, he wrote in 1852:

> 'No little German state are we,
> But the one voice in Europe: we *must* speak;'

adding:

[15] These three quotations are translated from E. L. Woodward, *War and Peace in Europe, 1815–1870*, Constable, London, 1931, pp. 260, 270, 281.

Early Victorian Climax

'Tho' niggard throats of Manchester may bawl,
What England was, shall her true sons forget?
We are not cotton-spinners all,
But some love England and her honour yet.'

CHAPTER X

Mid-Victorian Climacteric

It is one of the arguments of the present study that the influence of Great Britain in international affairs has never been greater than it was in the period between 1815 and 1850, when her foreign policy was in the hands of Castlereagh, Canning and Palmerston. In no comparable period before or since has she been able so often to settle international controversies in her own favour. She owed that influence mainly to her effective naval strength; to the military potential which, thanks to her military renown, she was believed to be capable of developing and using; to her outstanding commercial, financial and industrial strength; to the relative weakness of the other great powers of Europe, and of France in particular; and to the high capacity of those who framed and conducted her foreign policy. Even so, her predominance was not absolute. She was a leading rather than a dominating power, whose object was to maintain an equipoise and to keep the peace. She could not usually intervene successfully in Europe unless she was associated with some continental power, but this she was often able to do. She was content to negotiate on something like a basis of equality with the United States. But the homeland and the overseas possessions—except conceivably Canada and India—were safe from invasion, and the sea-ways of the world were kept open for the commerce of all nations. The suppression of the trade in African slaves was still her active concern, and her outlook on the 'non-white' empire was marked by idealism and a sense of responsibility. Without deliberately setting out to do so, she rounded off the territories of what has been called 'the second British Empire'. Moving, at the turn of the half-century, into a period of domestic and general world prosperity which ushered in 'the long secular boom' between the late 'forties and the middle 'sixties, she could face the future with high confidence.

Mid-Victorian Climacteric

We were still the only fully developed industrial country in the world. But we were, by our exports of material, of credit and of skill, promoting the rise of industrial rivals in Europe and America; and there were some who sensed the coming threat to our economic predominance. In 1870, W. E. Forster, who was in charge of education in Gladstone's government, said in the House of Commons: 'If we are to hold our position among men of our own race or among the nations of the world, we must make up for the smallness of our numbers by increasing the intellectual force of the individual.'

But certainly, there was a high level of general prosperity. All classes benefited from the boom. Agriculture, as well as commerce and industry, was making money. Prices rose, but wages more than kept up with them. Most working-class families were 10 per cent better off in 1870 than in 1850. There was an absence of industrial unrest. The submerged sections of the population, living in poverty and destitution, were not within the range of public consciousness. Visible imports and exports increased three-fold between 1850 and 1870. By the latter date exports were for the first time acquiring their modern character as the root of our economic existence. They were now increasingly required in order to pay for food. In 1868, we still produced at home four-fifths in value of the grain, meat and dairy produce which we consumed. By 1878, only ten years later, we were producing less than half. Here was a second prospective threat to our economic security. But the most remarkable development in our economic history in this quarter-century, and one which was to exercise in later years an influence on our foreign policy, was the mushroom growth of overseas investment. This was at its maximum for the century during the years between 1850 and 1875. In 1850, our total lending abroad was £300 million: by 1870, the total had risen to £800 million. Whereas, until the early 1850s, most of our investment had gone to Europe (railway finance was a strong link between London and the régime of Louis Napoleon), after about 1857, the main flow was to more distant lands—India (particularly for railways between 1856 and 1869), Australia and Canada. More and more, investment was in the form of foreign or colonial government loans, and the cosmopolitan financier became a familiar figure on the international scene. The impact upon our foreign policy was still small. Until the financial crises in Turkey and Egypt at the end of this period, of which something will be said later, governments did not think it right or expedient to intervene officially with other governments on behalf of their bondholders. The policy of non-intervention usually applied here also. If investors took a risk for the sake of a high return, that was their own look-out. Person or property was one thing—something to be resolutely defended: investment was another. Nor did the British Government as a rule, unlike other governments, officially use its influence to direct the flow of investment towards politically desirable, and away from politically undesirable, destinations.[1] What influence there was, and it might well be effective, would arise from personal relationships existing between the City and Whitehall.

But industrial, commercial and financial supremacy does not of itself bring political power and influence; and it will be less likely to do so where, under a system of *laissez-faire*, economic strength is not exploited as an instrument of national policy. Failure to recognize this has contributed to an over-estimate of Great Britain's position of power in Victorian times.

It has become a commonplace, which almost attains the quality of myth, to attribute to the power and influence of Great Britain in the nineteenth century an all-embracing predominance which they did not in sober fact possess. When we look back nostalgically upon those reputedly happy and glorious days, it is the mid-Victorian period which we most often have in mind. A happy age indeed, marked by what G. M. Young called 'the proud and sober confidence which irradiates the mid-Victorian landscape'.[2] Yet it was, in truth, an age when we were to find ourselves moving in a decreasingly congenial world and one less responsive than before to the assertion of our claims and interests; when our foreign policy, in the hands of men divided in mind, would hesitate and falter; and when Palmerston himself would sometimes lose his happy touch.

Two examples of this common misjudgment, taken at random, may be quoted.

Writing in 1937, an eminent American publicist, who later became the doyen of political commentators, said: 'The invisible, the unexamined and unrecognized premise of American isolation has always been an international system in which naval power in British

---

[1] To such a point did the Government carry its policy of non-intervention that it declined to interfere with the flotation of a loan for Russia in the London money market during the Crimean War, the purpose of which was to pay interest on existing loans. This, said Clarendon, the Foreign Secretary, was in 'the ordinary way of business'.

[2] *Victorian England*, p. 148.

hands is predominant over all other military power. . . . Such an international system existed in the century between Waterloo and the Marne, and all our preconceptions about world politics implicitly assume the continuation of some such system.'[3] As a general diagnosis of the position of the United States in the world, this is just, and in 1937 it needed saying: but can it be true that 'naval power in British hands' was 'predominant over all other military power'? All military power, of every kind, everywhere?

Then again, a distinguished American jurist, writing in 1940, said: 'The inconsistency of neutrality with an effective international law was obscured during the nineteenth century because Great Britain had so firm a devotion to law and liberty that British control of the world, facilitated by the doctrine of neutrality, did not wholly destroy the rule of law. Neutrality lasted because it facilitated the *Pax Britannica*. Its influence in weakening the law of nations was not observed because the law of England was substituted.'[4] Again, the tribute is just and may be gratefully acknowledged. But what are we to make of this postulated 'British control of the world'? The whole world? Europe, America and all?

These phrases were no doubt casually thrown off, as mere commonplaces, universally accepted: but it is the unmeditated phrase that reveals the mind. It will be well to test the validity of these confident and sweeping assertions from the record as it unfolds.

A pointer to the outlook of orthodox opinion upon the state of international affairs in the mid-Victorian period is to be found in the article on 'The Balance of Power' in the *Encyclopaedia Britannica*, Ninth Edition, published in 1875.[5] Its purport is in striking contrast to that of the article on the subject in the Eighth Edition (1854) which has been noticed on page 143. Whereas the writer of the earlier essay was content with the functioning of the international mechanism as being in the interest of Great Britain and of the rest of Europe, the later writer looked on developments in the intervening years with the gravest misgiving.

His general argument was that the current policy of non-inter-

[3] Walter Lippmann, *Fore gn Affairs*, New York, July 1937.

[4] Professor Quincy Wright in *American Journal of International Law*, 1940, p. 410. Both quotations are from J. L. Brierly, *The Outlook for International Law*, Clarendon Press, Oxford, 1945, pp. 31–32.

[5] The author was Henry Reeve, for forty-four years Registrar to the Judicial Committee of the Privy Council, for fifteen years on the staff of *The Times*, for forty years editor of the *Edinburgh Review*, the intimate of statesmen and diplomatists at home and abroad—an eminent Victorian.

vention, in the absence of some such European concert as was established at the Vienna Settlement, or even of any system of alliances, was responsible for the existing international anarchy and for the breakdown in international law. 'Peace can never be secure unless it is protected by the concurrence of the leading nations of the world' (i.e. a concert of Europe), 'and by their determination to oppose a combined resistance to those who have no object but their own aggrandizement and ambition' (i.e. a balance of power). The Prussian campaigns against Austria in 1866 and against France in 1870 totally destroyed the balance of power, as established and maintained under the settlements of Westphalia, Utrecht and Vienna. The key to that balance was always the extent of the power held in German lands and its division among the various holders. (This is a situation, with a Germany again divided and the powers in balance, with which we of this generation are again familiar.) 'For the last two centuries there has not been a time at which all confidence in public engagements and common principles of international law has been so grievously shaken.' Non-intervention meant limited war and individual settlements. In the Franco-Prussian War of 1870 'no third state was drawn by political considerations into the conflict. The terms of peace were settled between the vanquished and the conquerors without reference to the general interests of other nations; and no attempt has been made to place these arrangements under the sanction of the public law of Europe.' The conclusion which the writer drew was that if the practice of common consultation and action by the great powers of Europe could not be restored then the best course would be to create relations of positive law among the nations, by the conclusion of treaties, as a basis for the balance of power.

Further contemporary testimony as to the outlook in 1875 will be found in *The Times*.

On January 1st 1876, *The Times*, departing from custom, published a review of the history of the preceding twenty-five years instead of the usual review of the past year alone. The arbitrary sub-division of centuries into half and quarter centuries for purpose of historical treatment can provide a convenient framework upon which the memory may rely, but it is seldom significant and is often misleading. In the nineteenth century, however, the third and fourth quarters of the century do mark significant periods. Many things changed round about the years 1850, 1875 and 1900, which may fairly be said to mark important turning points. The terms 'mid-Victorian' (say 1850–75) and 'late Victorian' (say 1875 1900) are not mere names or labels. In the position and fortunes of Great Britain, each marks a real and profound shift.

Looking back on the past quarter-century, *The Times* judges this period never to have been surpassed in importance, in interest or in the surprising character of its events. For Englishmen, it had been 'one continued triumph of progress, though not always in the way that had been expected.' Manufactures, trade and commerce had been extended beyond all anticipation. The colonies had risen to the rank of free states and valuable allies, strengthened by the discovery of gold and the flow of emigrants. The electric wire had been carried to every post-office and station in the country.

Contemplating the year 1875 just passed, *The Times* had a different story to tell. The year had not been prosperous. Industry and trade were showing no sign of improvement. Exports were down, and the elasticity in revenue had not been maintained. It was extremely difficult to find employment for money. The 'Turkish financial catastrophe' and the repudiation of debts by South American states had hit the City hard.

Looking overseas, Englishmen were conscious that in building an army it was now 'impossible to compete in numbers with the vast establishments of foreign powers'. Nevertheless the new model army created by Edward Cardwell, Gladstone's Secretary for War (eight army corps, of which one was wholly of regulars, amounting on paper to 288,000 men, of whom 40,000 would be available for foreign service) would be adequate for our purposes 'in the remote contingency of threatened invasion'.

There are some points to be noted about the years between 1850 and 1875. There had been no war involving European great powers in the forty years between 1815 and 1854. There were in the sixteen years between 1854 and 1870 no less than five. In only one of these five wars (the Crimean War) was Great Britain involved. Only one of these wars (again the Crimean War) was followed by a peace settlement evolved by a congress or conference, including powers other than the belligerents. The period was for Great Britain one of great domestic prosperity and wide commercial and financial expansion overseas; but by 1875, that phase of general prosperity had come to an end. British policy after the Crimean War was in general a policy of non-interference or non-intervention; and it was held by some that this British policy had been in good measure responsible for the deterioration in international relations, for the decay of the concert of Europe and for the disturbance of the balance of power.

The validity of this latter thesis will be examined as the argument proceeds; but it may be suggested at the outset that the immediate impact and aftermath of the continental revolutions of 1848 were factors which would affect the potency of anything that might be said or done in London; and that among the circumstances making for deterioration in the international order were the rise of such disturbing personalities as Napoleon III and Bismarck with great armies at their disposal and a readiness to use them, and the initiatives which they took, the former unsuccessfully and the latter successfully, to exploit a fluid situation in Europe and to tear up the Vienna Settlement to the national advantage. This was a new situation which Her Majesty's ministers had not themselves done anything to create, but rather one to which, for better or for worse, they now had to adjust themselves. In this new turbulent Europe, where Liberals, in order to attain their ends, allied themselves with aggressive nationalism, the unregulated pursuit of individual national objectives developed at the expense of joint consultation for common purposes and without concern for the balance.[6]

For another thing, our position was weakened by the advent, from the 1860s onwards, of large conscript armies on the Continent. When in 1856, near the end of the Crimean War, we had a great fleet and a strong well-equipped army and resources still intact, and when the British public, unlike the French, was anxious for a fresh campaign to make victory complete, the judgment of Clarendon, the Foreign Secretary, was: 'Whatever Palmerston in his jaunty mood may say, we could not have made war alone, for we should have had all Europe against us at once, and the United States would have followed in the train.'[7]

---

[6] The accepted doctrine, to which Liberals also subscribed, was that any national war by which the political unification of a nation was brought about was a just war. German Liberals supported Bismarck's policy of 'blood and iron' as applied to foreign affairs. Indeed some of them went further. These ultra-nationalist and pan-German forerunners of Hitler were, unlike the cautious and politic Bismarck, strong for the Greater Germany. To Bismarck, Greater Germany was abhorrent, since it would mean the submergence of the Prussian Junker régime and the road to conflict with Russia.

[7] Clarendon was four times Foreign Secretary, under Aberdeen, Palmerston and Gladstone. He had high professional skill. He had in early life

This fear of a European coalition is never to be far from the minds of our statesmen for the rest of the century. This is true even of Palmerston in the 1860s. Professor Max Beloff has observed that fear of war with one or more European powers was the dominant anxiety in Palmerston's mind during his last premiership. After the Prussian victory over France in 1870–71, our position was even more disturbing: 'Britain, entirely isolated, though enjoying the safe shelter of her powerful fleet, was almost irresistible overseas, but on the Continent was faced by the powerful combination of the three Imperial Powers of Eastern Europe.' There was now, as Disraeli said: 'no balance.'[8]

The omnipotence, even the predominance, so often attributed to us in the later nineteenth century is a myth. Not in Europe alone do our limitations appear. The *New York Herald* wrote during the Civil War: 'Four hundred thousand thoroughly disciplined troops will ask no better occupation than to destroy the last vestiges of British rule on the American continent, and annex Canada to the United States.' Queen Victoria wrote in her diary on February 12th 1865: 'Talked of America and the danger, which seems approaching, of our having a war with her as soon as she makes peace; of the impossibility of our being able to hold Canada, but we must struggle for it; and far the best would be to let it go as an independent

served as minister at Madrid. He was competent and universally well-liked; but he had not Palmerston's zest or robustness in action or the touch of generous idealism which irradiated his massive common sense. In the eastern crisis in 1840, he wanted to appease Mehemet Ali, and thought that war with France 'would almost amount to national ruin'. Palmerston, who had taken the measure of Mehemet and of Louis Philippe and his ministers, was confident that the pasha would yield and that France would not go to war. Unlike the Queen and Palmerston, Clarendon did not think we should be able to reconquer India at the time of the Mutiny. It is to his credit that he foresaw as early as 1840 that, for the safeguarding of the road to India, Egypt was more important than the Straits. Like Castlereagh, Canning and Palmerston, he was a tremendous worker. His letters are full of wails about the mountains of boxes that followed him everywhere: to Paris (with the Queen), to Windsor, to Holyrood and to Balmoral. On one day in December 1856, he had six and a half hours of interviews without a moment's interruption, all of which had to be recorded by himself. Fourteen hours a day had, he said, been his average run of work for nearly four years; he was not able to delegate responsibility, and therefore had to look into everything himself. It was during his period of office that, in an attempt to relieve the strain, a Parliamentary Under-Secretary, to work side by side with the Permanent Under-Secretary, was appointed.

[8] R. W. Seton-Watson, *Britain in Europe*, p. 506.

kingdom under an English prince.' The Canadian Prime Minister, Sir John A. Macdonald, was to say in 1871 after the conclusion of the Treaty of Washington which he had helped to negotiate: 'England has got the supremacy on the sea—she is impregnable in every point but one, and that point is Canada.' So much for the present: but then with a flash of vision he went on to say, for the future: 'I hope to live to see the day, and if I do not that my son may be spared to see Canada the right arm of England, to see Canada a powerful auxiliary to the Empire, and not a cause of anxiety and a source of danger.' Macdonald pierced the future more surely than Lincoln's Secretary of State, William H. Seward, had done when in 1865 he had declared: 'I know that Nature designs that this whole continent, not merely these thirty-six States, shall be sooner or later, within the magic circle of the American Union.'

It is a mistake in foreign affairs to frame a policy closely upon a distant prognosis or, in time of trouble, to throw up the sponge too soon, as Foreign Secretaries are so often urged to do by people to whom future trends in the international situation can present themselves with a certainty and a clarity which may be belied by the wayward, accidental or recalcitrant course of events themselves. The apparently inevitable does not always occur. If not accepted, it sometimes does not happen. It may well be a good maxim in politics to guess what is going to happen, and back it. But the possibility or even the probability that a thing may happen some time is no good reason for behaving as though it is certain to happen tomorrow. The better course is to bide your time and be ready for it, if it does happen. Salisbury in 1892 recognized the Egyptian aspiration for freedom; but he saw it as 'some distance off; much too far to enter into a calculation for the conduct of present diplomacy.' 'It is,' thought Cromer, 'generally bad diplomacy to force on a conflict even when it seems inevitable.' At intervals during the nineteenth century and even earlier, it was declared to be inevitable that, with the collapse of the Ottoman Empire, Constantinople must fall to Russia. Later, it was even promised to her by treaty. The Ottoman Empire has since been demolished. Turkey has lost her Balkan, North African and Arab territories. But, founded upon the hard, national core of Anatolia, Turkey still bestrides the Straits and holds Istanbul, as a solid member of the Western defensive coalition against the successors of the Tsars. Again, for much of the nineteenth century it was widely assumed, and not in the United States only, that sooner or later Central America, the West Indies and Canada would be absorbed within the authority of the American Union. Why should 'manifest destiny' stop short at the Rio Grande and the 49th parallel? Today, Mexico, the Central American and South American states are still independent. Canada has long been, and the Federated British West Indian islands are on the way to become a free and independent member of the British Commonwealth. France and Holland retain their Caribbean possessions. Cuba, Haiti and the Dominican Republic are independent. The only accessions of territory to the United States in all this vast region are the island of Puerto Rico, the 'perpetual use, occupation and control' of the Panama Canal Zone, the lease of a base in Cuba, and the bases held on lease from Great Britain in the Caribbean and Western Atlantic.

On both these topics Palmerston spoke with characteristic good sense. Of Turkey he said that 'no empire is likely to fall to pieces if left to itself, and if no kind neighbours forcibly tear it to pieces.' And because he was sure that any partition of the Ottoman Empire would precipitate a European war, his policy was to hold it together as long as he could. Of the United States, he said that while he 'felt inwardly convinced that the Anglo-Saxon Race will in Process of Time become Masters of the whole American Continent North and South . . .' yet 'whatever may be the effects of such a Result upon the interests of England, it is not for us to assert such a consummation, but on the contrary we ought to delay it as long as possible.' The forces making for stability and equilibrium in the world should not be underrated or too easily discounted. In a time of rapid change like our own, we should not despair too soon. The human animal has a deep-seated capacity for resistance, survival and recovery.

In the mid-Victorian period, the policy of non-interference or non-intervention[9] came to have a wider meaning than it had possessed when it was revived and defined by Castlereagh and Canning. For them, it was not so much a policy in itself as a counter-policy. It stood in opposition to the policy of the Holy Alliance, the policy, that is to say, of joint action, armed or diplomatic, by a group of powers in the internal affairs of other states, and of the institution

[9] 'Non-interference' was the term commonly used by Castlereagh and Canning and preferred by Palmerston. 'Non-intervention' was the French equivalent, reimported into English.

of a general European police for the safeguarding of thrones against revolutionary or even constitutional movements. As Guizot saw it, it was the policy of resistance to the subjection of Europe to one dominating system or to one ruling idea: it was in fact identical with the principle of a nation's liberty. In its classical form, it required a state 'not only to refrain from acts of intervention, but also to frustrate attempts at such acts on the part of others.'[10]

It has been noted above how the policy of non-interference was interpreted by Castlereagh, Canning and Palmerston. Castlereagh acquiesced in the suppression by Austria of the revolutionary movement in Naples, on the ground that Austria had some sort of treaty right to do so, and was acting in her own interest and not on behalf of the Holy Alliance. Canning himself intervened by force in support of the constitutional government in Portugal, but claimed to do so in virtue of a treaty which bound us to defend Portugal against foreign attack. He did not regard himself as under any obligation to turn the French out of Spain. Both Castlereagh and Canning would admit as an exception to the policy the case where our own security or the peace of Europe was threatened by internal disturbances in another state. In that event we should be free to intervene by force or by diplomatic action backed by threat of force.

The doctrine of non-intervention was taken up by Talleyrand in 1830 as an instrument for the protection of the Belgian insurgents; but the obscurity of its real purport in practice is emphasized by the witticism commonly attributed to him, that non-intervention was a metaphysical and political phrase meaning almost the same thing as intervention.

Palmerston, for one, allowed himself much latitude in his interpretation of it, drawing a distinction between intervention by deed and intervention by word. Even in intervention by deed, he permitted himself some liberties. During the civil war against the Carlists in Spain, he allowed the fleet and its marines to defend the northern ports against the insurgents, and issued an Order in Council to permit the formation and despatch of a volunteer British Legion to help the government forces. In his later career, it was his avowed policy to support and safeguard liberal movements in foreign countries by diplomatic action. But he did not regard the proclamation of the doctrine, or his practical interpretation of its scope, as obliging him in any way to act if he did not consider it in the interest

[10] Ruggiero, *The History of European Liberalism*, Oxford, 1927, p. 412.

of Great Britain to do so. There was no obligation to intervene in arms against armed intervention.

By about mid-century, however, the doctrine had begun, in one school of thought in Great Britain at any rate, to change its character. It was no longer advocated as a counter-policy but as a policy in itself. The objective was not now to keep the despots from suppressing the liberties of Europe but to restrain the British Government from entangling itself in continental affairs, whether by war or by diplomacy. The Manchester doctrine of *laissez faire* in economics was matched by the Manchester doctrine of non-intervention in international politics. Bright declared in 1855: 'It is not my duty to make this country the knight-errant of the human race.' 'The sacred treasure of the bravery, resolution and unfaltering courage of the people of England' was not to be 'squandered in a contest for the preservation of the independence of Germany, and of the integrity, civilization, and something else of all Europe.' Cobden held that we had not the material strength to protect the weak against the strong. 'There is a right and a wrong in every case, and if we are always to choose one side or the other because it is thought to be right, how is it possible we can ever enjoy any peace or quietness in this country?' Bright, in his equivocal way, would have made an exception to this doctrine of non-intervention in a question affecting 'the honour and interest of England' and involving 'those great principles of justice and moderation which are necessary to the transactions of great Powers if the peace of Europe is to be preserved'; but he would have been hard to persuade that an exception had arisen.

The mood of the British public during the third quarter of the century was non-interventionist in this broader sense. Between the earlier Jingoism (not yet so called) which inspired the anti-French volunteer movements around 1850 and 1860 or the anti-Russian fever which contributed to drive the Aberdeen Government into the Crimean War, and the later Jingoism (properly so-called) which brought us near to war with Russia in the late 1870s, there was a period of withdrawal when the public wanted to have as little as possible to do with European quarrels and when armed intervention in Europe was out of the question. There was in the public mind, as a writer in *The Spectator* said in October 1864, 'a weariness of the line of action called "a spirited foreign policy".' The three wars in Europe between 1864 and 1870 (Prussia and Austria against Denmark, Prussia against Austria, and Prussia against France) aroused little or no bellicose sentiment in Great Britain. Although the face of Europe was being transformed to our disadvantage before our eyes, we kept our minds on other things—upon the enjoyment of our prosperity in domestic manufacture and foreign trade and upon the improvement of our own institutions. Whereas the suppression of the Hungarian rising by the Russians in 1849 had aroused strong indignation in England and had made Kossuth a national hero, the Polish insurrection of 1863, no less brutally put down by the Tsar, provoked no similar reaction.

This mood of withdrawal was a revulsion from the disillusioning experiences of the Crimean War. The public had wanted the war, but this sentiment did not long survive the war itself. For the first time, the public were enabled to read in their newspapers first-hand accounts of conditions of warfare and to see photographs of the camps and trenches. The death and misery of war were brought home to them, and the more so as a result of the blunders of commanders and of the inefficiency of the obsolete supply and medical services. Opinion was whipped up by a powerful campaign in *The Times* against the Government and high command based on despatches from their correspondent at the front. The lesson was driven home by those who, like Cobden and Bright, had always opposed the war. Better in future stay out. Bright, no less a master of rhetoric than Canning or Palmerston, delivered himself at Birmingham in October 1858 of his famous judgment and even more famous gibe, so resounding and yet so ill-founded: 'The more you examine this matter the more you will come to the conclusion which I arrived at, that this foreign policy, this regard for "the liberties of Europe", this care at one time for "the Protestant interest", this excessive love for the "balance of power" is neither more nor less than a gigantic system of outdoor relief for the aristocracy of Great Britain.' The views of the Manchester School, the middle-class business men who governed opinion, were to colour the public outlook until Disraeli, basing himself upon a wider franchise, introduced a new interventionist and imperialist note from 1874 onwards. Meanwhile British foreign policy, under the predominantly Whig or Liberal governments of the twenty years from 1855 to 1874, and even under the intermittent Tory régimes,[11] was to take some impress from the

[11] Of this way of thinking, Lord Stanley, a Tory, was, among ministers, the most extreme exponent. He became Foreign Secretary in 1866 in the third Cabinet of his father, the Earl of Derby. He himself, as Earl

prevailing climate of opinion. This did not mean that our governments no longer had any interest in Europe. On the contrary, they were perhaps more deeply concerned than ever in the rapidly changing Continent, and were actively involved in the diplomatic field. What it did mean was that, since their influence was impaired by the state of public opinion, and by the unfavourable shift in their relations of power with continental states, they were less often able to intervene with success than in early Victorian days.

Side by side with non-interventionist opinion in the third quarter of the century, there went also non-imperialist opinion, though here also there were signs of a change. Charles Dilke gave the title of *Greater Britain* to his book of travels in 1868, and by 'Greater Britain' he meant the colonies of European settlement; but the new line of thought which this foreshadowed was not to become evident until a few years later, when Disraeli struck a more definite note. Disraeli was at an earlier date still of the old persuasion. 'These wretched colonies,' he had said in 1852, 'will all be independent in a few years, and they are a millstone round our necks.' In 1862, the House of Commons passed a resolution that self-governing colonies ought to undertake their own defence against internal and local enemies, and that they should assist in their external defence in wars arising out of general imperial policy. Imperial garrisons were accordingly greatly reduced or entirely withdrawn.[12] Official opinion in Great Britain was preparing for 'eventual parting company on good terms' or for 'a friendly relaxation' of relations. Gladstone was still saying that the Empire was too great a burden to be borne. But events were moving the other way. Expressions of disinterest in London led on to local movements for self-government. This created, as the radical imperialists of the 1830s had argued that it would, new and firmer bonds of family relationship than the old colonial system had provided. The Commonwealth was creating itself in spite of London. The Manchester School had built better than it knew.

The record for these years shows few acquisitions of territory and

of Derby, was again Foreign Secretary in Disraeli's second Cabinet in 1874.
    [12] This did not, of course, apply to non-self-governing territories like India. After the Mutiny, the number of British troops maintained in India was substantially increased. In the early 'sixties our military establishment in India is said to have cost more than the armed forces of any European monarchy. See L. H. Jenks, *The Migration of British Capital to 1875*, Cape, London, 1938, p. 223.

a steady growth of self-government. The initiative for the establishment of the Canadian Federation under the British North America Act of 1867 came from Canada. It involved the dissociation of British Upper Canada from French Lower Canada and the inclusion of both as units in the Federation. The Canadians would have liked to call themselves a 'Kingdom', but the name 'Dominion' was chosen as being thought to be less offensive to United States susceptibilities. British Columbia (1871) and Prince Edward Island (1873) joined the Federation. In Australia, Queensland was established in 1859. New Zealand received responsible government by Act of Parliament passed in 1852. In South Africa, the Transvaal (1852) and the Orange Free State (1854) became independent, and Cape Colony attained responsible government in 1872. In this latter year, Disraeli made one of his first protests against the Gladstonian policy of lukewarmness to the imperial connection, arguing for 'a great policy of imperial consolidation' and for a mechanism 'which would have brought the colonies into constant and continuous relations with the home government.'

In order to illustrate the measure of British influence during the mid-Victorian era, when non-interventionism was strong, at any rate after the Crimean War, it will be instructive to review some of the international episodes of the time.

There are a few guiding trends to bear in mind. For Great Britain the more likely enemies were France and Russia. France, because she was traditionally so; because she alone of the European powers could threaten us with invasion; because our Mediterranean communications were vulnerable to her; because under Napoleon III her policy was ambitious and restless; because her objective was to upset the settlement of 1815, and this meant Belgium; because, as a colonial power, she was again, though in a more limited way than in the eighteenth century, our rival overseas. Russia, because she appeared to be the most formidable power in Europe, pursuing oppressive and reactionary policies, and threatening the balance of power; because, having a sense of mission in the Balkans and being bent on controlling if not acquiring territories of the decaying Ottoman Empire, she threatened our road to India; because, by her conquests in Central Asia, she was moving towards the north-west frontier of India, where, if she chose to affront us, we should, in contrast to Europe, have no allies to help us to withstand her.

With Austria and Prussia, on the other hand, we had no clear conflict of interest. With Austria, we had a common objective in checking Russia in the Balkans and France in Italy. With Prussia, which until the advent of Bismarck in 1862 was the weakest of the European great powers, we had a common interest in checking France on the Rhine.

Cutting across these conflicts and communities of interest, there was another grouping of the powers, the three and the two, the relic of the opposition of the three eastern autocracies of the Holy Alliance to the two liberal powers, Great Britain and France. In spite of their mutual antipathy, there were factors which brought France and Great Britain together. France had rivals everywhere. She was the rival of Russia in the Near East (where she had recently secured from the Sultan, much to the anger of the Russian government, the restoration of privileges in the Holy Places for the Latin Christians whom she supported against the Greeks) and, generally, as the aspirant to the leadership in Europe. She was the rival of Austria in Italy and of Prussia on the Rhine. Almost against their will the two western powers sometimes found themselves working together.

The Crimean War broke out because the concert of Europe had ceased to function. It was primarily a Turkish, secondarily a French, and only on the last count a British war against Russia. Austria, who did not enter the war, played an important part in bringing it to an end. The main causes of the war were first Russia's forward policy in Turkey, her determination to reassert her influence, which had declined since the settlement of 1841, and in particular her claim to protect the Greek Orthodox Christian subjects of the Sultan and so to exercise a kind of suzerainty over Turkey; secondly, Turkey's stiff resistance to these claims, based on the confident expectation of European support; and thirdly the split among the four other powers at crucial moments, Austria and Prussia tending to the Russian side and Great Britain and France to the Turkish.

In face of the aggressive violence of the Russians; of the intransigence of the Turks; of the determination of Napoleon III to seize the opportunity to challenge Nicholas I (who still declined to accept him fully as a fellow sovereign) and to wipe out the memory of 1812; and of the indecision of the British government which was brought to action in the end by the anger of the British people, the peace of Europe was broken. Nicholas had thought that Cobdenism, if not Aberdeen's friendly feelings towards himself, would keep Great

Britain out of the war; and that France would not fight alone, especially if restrained by Austria and Prussia. He seems to have thought that he could get his way by threats alone, as Palmerston had so often done. Not for the first or last time was the national temper of Great Britain gravely misapprehended on the Continent.

The shortcomings of the military leadership in the Crimean War and the insufficiency of the supply, sanitary and medical services, which are our most vivid memories of the campaign, should not blind us to the military merits of the operation. The joint Anglo-French sea-borne descent upon the new naval base at Sevastopol, the symbol of Russia's aggressive intentions in the Near East, 'the eye-tooth of the Bear', was an enterprise which, like the British attack on the Gallipoli peninsula in 1915, came very near to early and complete success. It had been ordered from London and Paris, against professional advice, and was not favoured by the local commanders. The Russians had full warning of it from the London Press. The French had more men in the field than the British and their fighting men came out of the war with equal credit.[13] Though they had had less hard fighting in the campaign, it was to them that in the end the fortress of Sevastopol fell. By this time, Napoleon's ministers, some of them for personal financial reasons, were anxious to make peace. French public opinion, unlike the British, was tired of the war. It was chiefly thanks to Napoleon himself that the two governments were kept in line until the end.

Historians have argued that the Crimean War need not have occurred, and that if one of a great number of things had happened instead of what did in fact happen, peace could have been preserved. It was indeed an unnecessary war in that, unlike some other wars, it was not deliberately made by any one or more of the participants. Nicholas, by threatening war in the Palmerstonian manner, landed himself in a war which he did not really want. Paris and London, perhaps rather too readily, took up the challenge. It might well have been one of the many wars that were successfully averted, as a war between Great Britain and France over the Orsini affair was averted in 1858, or a second Franco-German War in 1875, or a second war with Russia over Turkey in 1877, or a war between Great Britain

---

[13] Incidentally, it is of interest to note that, according to a French historian, the epithet applied by General Bosquet to the Charge of the Light Brigdae was 'superb', not 'magnificent': '*C'est superbe, mais ce n'est pas la guerre.*' Octave Aurby, *Le Second Empire*, Arthème Fayard, Paris, 1938, p. 144.

and the United States over Venezuela in 1895, or between Great Britain and France over Fashoda in 1898. But there were solid grounds for war. Throughout its course, the war was popularly supported in Great Britain; and a man so high-minded as Gladstone thought that it was justified. If it was in the general European interest that Russia should not dominate Turkey in Europe, or control the mouths of the Danube, or command the Straits and debouch if she could into the Mediterranean—and it was not unreasonable to fear that these were Russia's aims—then the Crimean War served a useful purpose. It was, as Clarendon once said, not simply a war 'for such a cause as two sets of Barbarians quarrelling over a form of words'. The Russians were kept out of the Balkans and shut up in a neutralized Black Sea. The question would be whether, if this was to be the objective, it would be better to try to achieve it by bolstering up Turkey, or by promoting the full independence of the Balkan Christian peoples in the hope that they would maintain their independence against Russia no less than against Turkey. In that choice lay the heart of the great Eastern question that was to agitate Europe for years to come.

The Congress of Paris, where peace was negotiated in 1856, was not limited to the participants in the war. Austria was represented from the beginning and joined in negotiation with British, French, Turkish, Sardinian and Russian delegates. Prussia was admitted at a later stage. To this extent the concert of Europe was revived, and Turkey was now for the first time admitted to it. Turkish independence and territory were guaranteed by the signatory powers, who renounced all right of joint or several interference in Turkey's internal affairs. Russia thus admitted that not merely the Straits, as in 1841, but all Ottoman affairs were henceforward of international concern. The principalities of Moldavia and Wallachia (the modern Roumania) and Serbia were guaranteed a kind of semi-independence under the suzerainty of Turkey, the powers renouncing any individual right of protection or interference. Those who think that British policy in this period was strictly isolationist should recall that, at the Congress of Paris, Great Britain and Austria, joined reluctantly by France (now cultivating good relations with Russia), bound themselves by secret agreement to treat as a *casus belli* any future infraction of Turkish integrity and independence. As regards the Straits, the Treaty of Paris confirmed on an international basis what had been, for the first time, settled on an international basis in

1841, namely the closing of the Straits, Turkey being at peace, to all foreign, i.e. non-Turkish, warships. But there was this signal difference that the Black Sea was now to be neutralized. Neither Russia nor Turkey was to maintain naval bases, arsenals or fleets there, though Turkey would be free to station warships in the Sea of Marmora or in the Mediterranean. This is the measure of the check to Russia's liberty of action in an area which was vital to her. It was a situation that could not, and did not, endure. When France was struck down in 1870 and Great Britain isolated, Russia freed herself from the restrictions imposed upon her in the Black Sea.

In the crisis that led to the formation of the Kingdom of Italy in 1859–60, Palmerston and his Foreign Secretary, Lord John Russell, had a last fling in the old Palmerstonian manner. Not until the Congress of Berlin in 1878, when Disraeli was in power, was there any comparable stroke of British policy.

In the two Austrian provinces of Lombardy and Venetia, in the absolutist princely states like Parma, Modena and Tuscany and in the states of the Church, there was a double aspiration in the minds of the people, an aspiration for free institutions and an aspiration for a united Italy under the constitutional House of Savoy, now ruling in Piedmont and Sardinia. In both France and England, statesmen found themselves in a dilemma. As a liberal, Napoleon III could not but favour the claim for free institutions. As a French statesman, he could not but work for the weakening of Austria. As a Bonaparte, he could cherish visions of military glory at Austria's expense, particularly if it would reverse the settlement of 1815. While he could contemplate a moderate accretion of strength for the House of Savoy, he had no desire to see a united Italy under King Victor Emmanuel, which, unless he could control it, would be a second Prussia upon his frontier, a new disturbing element in the European balance of power, and not least in the Mediterranean. In Great Britain, popular and literary opinion was for the Italians, the Court and the conservatives for Austria. In London, distinguished Italian exiles were held in high regard and carried on political agitation. The Government, whether of Derby or of Palmerston, had no intention of intervening by force. There was no important British interest at stake as there had been in the Crimean War. But three powerful men in Palmerston's government—Palmerston himself, Lord John Russell and Gladstone—were fervent supporters of the principle of 'Italy for the Italians'. By Italy they meant, at the outset,

North and Central Italy only. As in Paris, there was no desire in London to see Naples and Sicily brought into a united Italy.

If statesmen in London and Paris were divided in mind, there was single-mindedness of purpose in Italy, at least upon the main objective, which was to bring the whole of Italy under the crown of Savoy, starting with the north. For this, Victor Emmanuel and Cavour worked without scruple. It is not necessary that those who work for a good cause should be good men; and if the cause is good, much will be forgiven them.[14]

Napoleon made an advance apportionment of the spoil with Cavour in hugger-mugger[15] at Plombières in July 1858; won two costly victories over the Austrians at Magenta and Solferino in June 1859, in a war provoked by the Austrians; then, fearing an attack by Prussia, lost his nerve and hastened to come to provisional terms with Austria behind Cavour's back at Villafranca in July 1859. This abortive arrangement incensed Cavour in that Lombardy alone and not Venetia would go to Victor Emmanuel. It shocked the political sense of the British Italophile triumvirate in that Austria would still control the new Italian Confederation, and outraged their liberal consciences in that the despotic rulers of the Duchies of Tuscany and Modena would be restored, if need be by force.

The situation now passed beyond Napoleon's and indeed Russell's control, though Napoleon was able, against Russell's lone but violent protest, to secure Savoy and Nice for himself, in compensation for the accession of the duchies to the Italian kingdom. Sicily revolted against the Bourbon, Francis II. Garibaldi brought both Sicily and Naples to Victor Emmanuel, after Russell had declined a proposal by Napoleon to prevent his crossing to the mainland.

In this situation, Russell wrote his famous despatch of October 27th 1860 to Sir James Hudson, the British minister at the Sardinian court at Turin, a representative who had been said by Malmesbury to be 'more Italian than the Italians themselves'.[16] This despatch

[14] That bluff, free-living, coarse-fibred monarch, Victor Emmanuel, because he fell foul of the Pope, was seen by many good souls almost in the guise of a Protestant hero. The British and Foreign Bible Society sent him a copy of the Protestant version of the Old and New Testaments.
Cavour's confession to Azeglio is well known: 'If we were to do for ourselves what we are doing for Italy, we should be great rogues.'
[15] He did not tell his Foreign Minister what he was doing, and he denied in public that any agreement had been made.
[16] An ambassador should have a sympathetic understanding of the motives and purposes of the government to which he is accredited; but

was made public and created a scandal in Europe. Brunnow, the Russian representative in London, said: '*Ce n'est pas de la diplomatie, c'est de la polissonnerie.*' The Cabinet had not been consulted and were indignant, the Queen even more so. And yet, in substance, there was not very much in the despatch which Palmerston and Russell had not said in public before. Russell had over a year earlier, in July 1859, proclaimed the right of peoples to choose their sovereign, as had been done by the English when they brought William III to the throne in 1688 (as a Whig of the first water, Russell would always go back to the Glorious Revolution), and as had been done also in Belgium, Holland, Sweden and France. This was good nationalist, liberal doctrine as stated by Locke when he asserted the right of rebellion against 'inconstant, uncertain, unknown, and arbitrary government'. Palmerston, later in the same year, had propounded the principle of self-determination when he said that the Italian people, particularly in north and central Italy, 'should be left free to determine their own condition of political existence.' The difference was first, that what Russell was now defending was not the right of self-determination but the intervention of Victor Emmanuel; secondly, that he had changed his mind about the accession of Naples and Sicily to the Italian kingdom, an event which he had previously discountenanced lest it should lead to further French territorial demands in compensation; and thirdly that his views were formally embodied in an official diplomatic despatch.

In protest against the action of Victor Emmanuel, other powers had withdrawn their ministers from Turin. Russell, on the contrary,

he should be able to combine this with a cool and detached judgment of the bearing of its policies upon the policy and interests of his own government, which it is his first duty to promote. Violent partisanship, strong personal policies and the crusading spirit are less frequently found in a highly professionalized Foreign Service such as we have today than they were in earlier times; and it may be that we have lost something. But the lot of Victorian Foreign Secretaries, with ambassadors like Hudson and Stratford de Redcliffe pursuing their own policies, and the Queen and her 'good German' consort deep in correspondence with foreign monarchs and statesmen behind the backs of Her Majesty's ministers and diplomatic representatives, and often in opposition to them, was sometimes barely tolerable. Clarendon called Stratford 'a pest', and on one occasion wrote to him saying that he had marked Stratford's 'general disregard of whatever had the appearance of instructions'. Palmerston once went so far as to ask the Queen whether she was not 'requiring that I should be Minister, not indeed for Austria, Russia, or France, but for the Germanic Confederation.'

left Hudson at his post and delivered himself of his views. The Italians, he said, were the best judges of their own interests. Since 1848, there had been a conviction that the only way to secure independence from foreign control was by the establishment of a strong government for the whole of Italy. So wise a jurist as Vattel had justified the assistance afforded by the States-General of the United Provinces when William of Orange had invaded England. The test was whether or not peoples had good reason to take up arms against an oppressor. He could not say that the peoples of southern Italy had not good reason to throw off their allegiance, and he could not blame Victor Emmanuel for assisting them or join in the censures upon him. He preferred to turn his eyes to 'the gratifying prospect of a people building up the edifice of their liberties'.

Palmerston's and Russell's liberal manifesto was widely applauded at home. It gained us the friendship of Italy for seventy-five years; but it was costly in its effect upon our general influence in Europe for some years to come. It can be defended not merely as a gesture of generous liberalism but also on grounds of hard policy. It can be argued that the only alternative to the annexation of Naples and Sicily to the crown of Savoy would have been either social revolution and anarchy, or armed intervention by France and the establishment of French influence in south Italy, both of which would have been contrary to British interests and to the maintenance of a just balance of power. Neither in 1859–61 nor later was the Italian question made the subject of concern at a congress of the powers. The concert of Europe was in abeyance, and it would be only intermittently revived. The settlement of 1815 was, on this occasion, revised by independent action. Gone were the days when there was something like a concert of Europe with Palmerston to lead it.

In the 1860s, British influence in this new Europe was to fall to depths not experienced since the 1770s and 1780s. This was made plain by the course of our diplomacy in the Polish insurrection of 1863 and the crisis over the duchies of Schleswig and Holstein in 1864.

The Polish insurgents, unlike the Italians, had no co-national power like Sardinia to help them. Unlike the Italians, they had not one oppressor (Austria) but three (Russia, Prussia, Austria). Napoleon III, the supporter of movements for liberation, was not, as in the Italian case, near at hand, eager to get to grips on familiar ground with the secular enemy, Austria, but far distant, less inclined now for adventure, and for broad political reasons not anxious to impair the *entente* with Russia against Austria. The Polish cause was popular in France and in Great Britain; and anti-Russian feeling was still strong in Great Britain; but the personal sympathies of British ministers were not engaged for Poland, as they had been for Italy, and Poland meant very little to the masses who, swayed by Bright, were all for peace and quiet. Not only was there 'the predominance of the Quaker interest in our councils', but the Navy had again been neglected. During the years of the American Civil War (1861–65), our attention was drawn across the Atlantic and our forces concentrated, as a measure of precaution, in Canada. The coasts of Italy had been open to the Navy; our ships could not act in Poland.

In its handling by the powers of Europe, the Polish crisis was submerged in the cross-currents of rival interests which dominated the policies and diplomatic acts of the Chancelleries. One of its consequences was a rift in the *ententes* of France with Russia and with Great Britain, and the near-isolation of both France and Great Britain in Europe.

The action taken by Russell was meddlesome and ineffective. It did nothing to help the Poles and much to confuse the situation in Europe. There was first a despatch by Russell to St Petersburg in March in which, basing himself upon the treaty of 1815 as entitling Great Britain to express her opinion on events in Poland, he suggested the proclamation of a general amnesty and the restoration to Poland of the privileges granted to her under that treaty. He even went so far as to suggest, in a talk with the Russian ambassador in London, that the Russians might well give representative institutions to themselves as well as to the Poles. Later, in April, notes were presented in St Petersburg by Great Britain, France and Austria. Prussia, since 1862 guided by Bismarck, took the Russian side. In his note of April 10th and in a conversation with the Russian ambassador, Russell used language which could only be interpreted as a threat of war, but whether this was to be war by Great Britain or by other powers was less clear. What he said was that the condition of things in Poland was 'a source of danger, not to Russia alone, but also to the general peace of Europe', and that the disturbances 'might under possible circumstances produce complications of the most serious nature'. To the ambassador he said that if the emperor were not to take conciliatory steps, 'dangers and complications might arise not at present in contemplation.'

In May, Lord Napier, British ambassador to Russia, told Russell:

'The revolt is spreading in the hope of foreign intervention. If the English Government do not mean to fight, let them say so, and stop the loss of life and the suffering attendant on a rising which, unaided, cannot succeed.' Russell persisted and persuaded the French and Austrian governments to present yet another note in June. The reply of Gorchakov was to set aside the intervention of Great Britain and France and to propose discussions with Austria and Prussia alone, the two other powers directly interested. This was the end of the matter. Poland was not to be any longer a matter of European concern, as she had been in 1815. The three eastern powers had drawn together. The Poles, fighting amongst themselves as well as against the Russians, were left to their fate. France and Great Britain were divided. Russell had brusquely rejected Napoleon's proposal in November 1863 for a European congress to deal not only with Poland and Schleswig Holstein, but also with the whole territorial structure of Europe, based as it was on the settlement of 1815, which was, Napoleon held, in decay. The way was open for Bismarck to exploit the new disposition of forces to his advantage. Russia and Prussia were to be associated together and France and Russia were to be estranged for a good number of years. The reputation of Great Britain, said Lord Robert Cecil,[17] had received its first deadly blow.

The affair of the Elbe duchies, Schleswig and Holstein, in 1864, was to drive this lesson home. British statesmen, even men as experienced as Palmerston and Russell, had lost the measure of Europe. Neglect of the armed forces and a policy of non-intervention which were imposed upon the Government by the current climate of opinion were no basis for an active and effective foreign policy. This was even more evident in the case of Denmark than it had been in Poland. Here was a prime British interest at stake in a region accessible to the Navy, where the country concerned was one with which we had long-standing relations of friendship and recent dynastic connections. In face of the German powers, Prussia and Austria, we beat an even more humiliating retreat than we had done over Poland. In 1849, with continental support, we had prevented German acquisition of the duchies. Alone we could not now do so.

The dynastic and legal complications of this problem were extreme; but in essence it was a conflict between two opposing nationalisms, Danish and German, exploited by Bismarck in order

[17] Later the third Marquess of Salisbury, Foreign Secretary and Prime Minister.

to extend the power of Prussia. In February 1864, a joint Prussian and Austrian expedition entered Schleswig, and in March passed into Danish territory proper. Denmark appealed to Great Britain.

Queen Victoria, following the view of her late husband, had always favoured the Prussian side. Her 'heart and sympathies' were 'all German'. Her ministers and the British public strongly supported the Danes. Palmerston had said in the House of Commons as far back as July 1863: 'We are convinced, I am convinced at least, that if any violent attempt were made to overthrow [the rights] and to interfere with [the] independence of Denmark, those who made the attempt would find in the result that it would not be Denmark alone with which they would have to contend.' To speak so was to threaten Prussia and Austria with European intervention, since it was manifest to Europe that Great Britain could not intervene effectively alone, even if she would. But the concert of Europe, which had acted in this question in 1852, was in no position to act in 1864. Russia, weakened by the Crimean War and by the Polish insurrection, and supported by Prussia in the Polish affair, would not act against Prussia now. Napoleon could not, with his nationalist record, object in principle to a nationalist solution of the problem of the duchies, by which German populations would come into the German fold. What he hoped for was a liberal, national Prussia, friendly to France and hostile to Russia. He would not go to war unless he could get something substantial for himself out of it, and the combination of Prussia and Austria was too much for him. If Great Britain were to act, she would have to act alone; and this, reasonably enough, she decided not to do. Even Palmerston in his best times had felt the need of an understanding with at least one continental power if he was to secure his ends in Europe. Russell, more bellicose, would have liked to resort to arms, and he had a minority of the Cabinet with him, including Palmerston; but as Palmerston said, acquiescing in the view of the majority and in the verdict of public opinion: 'We could not for many weeks to come send a squadron to the Baltic, and . . . such a step would not have much effect upon the Germans unless it were understood to be a first step towards something more; and I doubt whether the Cabinet or the country are as yet prepared for active interference. The truth is, that to enter into a military conflict with all Germany on continental ground would be a serious undertaking.' It would indeed, and the more so in that the bulk of our effective military forces were in Canada, guarding the long open frontier against a possible attack by the formidable northern armies of the Civil War. Cobden hailed this conclusion as a decisive defeat for the mischievous policy of incessant intervention. But another judgment is possible. The failure of Great Britain and France to prevent the rape of Schleswig by Prussia in 1864 might be compared with their failure to eject Hitler from the Rhineland in 1936, though the latter was a much easier problem. Could they only have known it, this was the moment to call a halt.

Bismarck had conducted his first great European operation with complete success. Intervening ostensibly in defence of the treaty of 1852, and with the support of the German liberals, he had in the end wrenched both duchies from Denmark's grasp and incorporated them in Germany, Prussia taking Schleswig (Danes, Germans and all) with its port of Kiel, and Austria being given Holstein, a useless and embarrassing gift, soon to pass also into the hands of Prussia.

Writing in the *Quarterly Review* in April 1864, Lord Robert Cecil said that England now occupied 'a position in the eyes of foreign Powers which she has never occupied before during the memory of any man now living.' Her influence in the councils of Europe had passed away. We had been left in Europe 'without a single ally, and without a shred of influence', as a result of a policy which 'delights in parading valour without danger and power without expense'. This is an attack by a coming young Tory upon the policies of two aged members of a liberal administration. His own advice would be: 'The policy of honour is also the policy of peace . . . let Germany see distinctly that war with Denmark means war with England.' But given the mood of the country, the level of our armaments, and the state of our relations in Europe and the United States, this would not have been a possible policy.

The fault of Palmerston's government was not that they did not go to war. They could only have done so with prospect of success if they had secured the alliance of France or of Russia or of both; and such alliances could only have been bought, if at all, at the cost of concessions on the Rhine and in the Black Sea which might have outweighed our interests in the Baltic. Their fault was to treat words, unbacked by a reasonable prospect of deeds, as being good international currency in a Europe where, in the prevailing state of international anarchy, force alone, either actual or plainly foreshadowed, could count effectively.

Our pusillanimity in Europe was not matched, however, in our dealings with weak and vulnerable states elsewhere, provided that they were well within the reach of the Navy. The beneficence and moderation of the *Pax Britannica* are not to be under-rated. The benefits conferred upon colonial territories are not to be lightly dismissed. The genuine humanitarianism of our approach to world problems, and the admirable devotion shown by countless workers in the foreign and colonial field, are things which can be remembered with pride. No people and no government has a better record to show at the bar of history. Yet candour requires it to be confessed that there were acts of our authorities which can today only be contemplated in retrospect with astonishment and indeed with horror. The record of the exercise of British power in the mid-Victorian era would not be complete without one example to illustrate this less estimable side of our policy.

Peacefully, but under hardly concealed threat of force, Japan was opened to foreign commerce by Commodore Matthew C. Perry of the United States Navy in 1853. By 1858, other western powers had secured treaties permitting commercial intercourse. British traders resorted there and resided in conditions of some peril. The central government, before the days of the Meiji Restoration, was weak. The great feudal lords, the daimios, maintained large retinues of armed retainers who were both warlike and anti-foreign, regarding the slaughter of the intruders as a religious duty. On days when the daimios and their suites performed their ritual processions along certain roads leading towards the capital, foreigners were given warning and asked to keep away. In 1862 a certain Mr Richardson and his friends were riding along one of these roads between the treaty port of Yokohama and Yeddo, the capital, when they met a procession of which no warning had reached them. Mr Richardson was struck and mortally wounded.

The instructions which Russell, Foreign Secretary in a Liberal government of which Gladstone was a member, sent to H.M. Consul and Chargé d'Affaires in Japan can only be described as ferocious. The Japanese Government were to apologize and pay a penalty of £100,000. The daimio Prince of Satsuma was to bring to trial, and to execute in the presence of the Royal Navy, those who had perpetrated the murder. He was to pay £25,000 for distribution among the relatives of the victim. If the Japanese Government were to refuse redress, the Consul was to call on the Admiral or Senior Naval

Officer 'to adopt such measures of reprisal or blockade, or both, as he may judge to be best calculated to attain the end proposed.' If the daimio did not immediately comply with the demands made upon him, the Admiral was to take or send a sufficient force to the territory of the Prince. 'The Admiral or Senior Naval Officer will be better able to judge than Her Majesty's Government can be, whether it will be most expedient to blockade this port, or whether it will be possible or advisable to shell the residence of the Prince.' The Prince's European ships might also be seized or detained.

The daimio was given twenty-four hours to comply. His representative replied that if the offenders could be detected and were found guilty, they would be executed in the presence of British witnesses. This was not enough for the Admiral and the Consul. The Admiral said there could be no delay. 'Kagosima is at my mercy; hostilities once commenced, the town would be destroyed'; adding: 'You must remember that we are one of the first nations in the world, who, instead of meeting civilized people, as you think yourselves, in reality encounter barbarians.' The Admiral attempted to seize some ships. The Japanese guns opened fire. The Admiral bombarded Kagosima. Two days later the Consul, Lieut.-Colonel Neale, reported: 'The operations were attended with complete success . . . the fire, which is still raging, affords reasonable ground for believing that the entire town of Kagosima is now a mass of ruins.' The action of the Admiral and the Consul was approved from London. The murderers were never found. Incidents like this could be matched in the annals of other European governments.[18]

It is a relief to pass from the unhappy experiences of Palmerston and Russell in Europe and their bullying of weak governments and peoples to their statesmanlike handling of relations with the United States of America during the American Civil War of 1861–65. Here Great Britain conducted herself like a great power in her transactions with another power which was showing itself to be mighty in energy, in economic strength and in political and military resource, and whose accession to the ranks of the great powers could not now be gainsaid.

[18] '. . . the principle that the doctrines of international law did not apply outside Europe, that what would be barbarism in London or Paris is civilized conduct in Peking . . . and that European nations had no moral obligations in dealing with Asian peoples . . . was part of the accepted creed of Europe's relations with Asia.' (K. M. Panikkar, *Asia and Western Dominance*, Allen and Unwin, London, 1953, pp. 42–43.)

Climax and Climacteric

The war between the States in America or the war of the Rebellion was one of the greatest events of the nineteenth century, as the American Revolution was one of the greatest events of the eighteenth, and as the rivalry between the United States and the Soviet Union has proved to be one of the greatest events of the twentieth. The issue for Americans in and after 1765 was independence. In 1861, it was union. Today it is survival. The Civil War had its seamy side; but it has become in the American mind a proud agony, the centre of United States folk mythology, and the more so now as its centenary approaches.

When, at Gettysburg near the end of 1863, after a long oration by Edward Everett, Abraham Lincoln rose to speak his few immortal words, he posed the question whether any nation 'conceived in liberty, and dedicated to the proposition that all men are created equal' could 'long survive'. That question is one which comes to American minds in their ordeal of the mid-twentieth century. 'Only a few of us know,' wrote William Faulkner, 'that only from homogeneity comes anything of a people or for a people of durable and lasting value—the literature, the art, the science, that minimum of government and police which is the meaning of freedom and liberty, and perhaps most valuable of all a national character worth anything in a crisis—that crisis we shall face some day when we meet an enemy with as many men as we have and as much material as we have and—who knows?—who can even brag and boast as we brag and boast.'[19]

Lincoln concluded by enunciating the high resolve 'that government of the people, by the people, for the people,' should not 'perish from the earth'. To southern ears this assertion would have an equivocal ring. As that great liberal historian, A. F. Pollard, once suggested: 'The south believed that under this specious phrase Lincoln was asserting a claim to the government of the people of the south by the people of the north for purposes of which the north alone approved . . . his essential principle was the right of the majorities to coerce minorities.' Or again: 'To the thirteen colonies in 1776 as to the southern states in 1861, the part was greater than the whole; and to many an individual his single soul is more than all the world.'[20] The passionate tenacity with which the northerners

[19] *Intruder in the Dust*, Chatto and Windus, London, 1949, p. 154.
[20] *The Evolution of Parliament*, Longmans, London, 1934, pp. 343, 344, 345.

and westerners (Lincoln, Grant and Sherman were all—by formation if not by origin—from the Middle West) fought to save the union was matched by the knightly devotion with which, under Lee's inspired leadership, the armies of the south, rightly (as they felt) struggling to be free, fought for self-determination. Lord Acton could say to Lee in 1866: 'I saw in State Rights the only availing check upon the absolutism of the sovereign will, and secession filled me with hope, not as the destruction but as the redemption of Democracy.'

From the number of men engaged, from the equipment and supplies furnished to them, from the strategy and tactics of the campaign, and from its duration, the war between the States marks a stage in the history of warfare. It revealed a quality in the American people which was too soon forgotten. When Pickett's division on July 3rd 1863, charged up the slopes of Cemetery Ridge at Gettysburg in a vain attempt to pierce the northern lines, or when, at the Battle of Chattanooga on November 24th of the same year, the northern army of the Cumberland, under General George H. Thomas, himself a Virginian, of its own volition, in spite of an order to halt, assaulted and carried the apparently impregnable southern position on Missionary Ridge (Who, Grant angrily asked, ordered this suicidal charge?), they were the forerunners of many an exploit in the War of 1941–45 on land and sea and in the air, when a welcome truth about the United States became evident to all the world.

Opinion in Great Britain was deeply divided about the war, the Conservatives being generally for the South and the Liberals for the North. But personal sentiment could cut across party or social lines. Sympathy for the North could be tempered by distaste for the domination of 'a tyrannical sectional majority'. Sympathy for the South could be tempered by revulsion from the 'peculiar institution' of slavery, an evil heritage which, as the best minds of the South well recognized, must be purged, but in their own time and in their own way, and not under dictation. A demagogue like Bright could see little in the war but a fight between what he called democracy and what he called privilege. He used it to conduct a campaign for parliamentary reform at home. His oratory did much to create enthusiasm for the Northern cause among the masses. A more subtle mind like Gladstone's could see more clearly into the real issues. He and Russell, both members of the Government throughout the war, could find in the Confederate cause some echo of the causes which they had supported in Italy and in Poland. It has been made a reproach to the British Government that they were slow to perceive the inevitability of the Northern victory and to shape their course accordingly by giving up all thought of recognizing the Confederate government. Hindsight is a powerful but unscrupulous advocate. It was pretty plain after Antietam (September 1862) and plainer still after Gettysburg (July 1863) that the South, in spite of their superiority as soldiers, could not beat the North; but it was never plain until very near the end that the North, for all their immensely greater resources, would be able to hold on long enough to beat the South. Gladstone said at Newcastle in October 1862, in words which he later repented as having been 'a mistake . . . of incredible grossness': 'There is no doubt that Jefferson Davis and other leaders of the South . . . have made a nation.' 'There is all but unanimous belief,' wrote Cobden to Senator Sumner in July 1862, 'that you *cannot* subject the South to the Union.' And if the North had not beaten the South, if the result had been stalemate, the South would have prevailed; they would have succeeded in resisting the enforcement of the Union upon them. They were only ground down in the end by the unconquerable tenacity and resolution of Lincoln and Grant.[21]

With opinion divided at home and the military prospect in the war uncertain, it was natural enough for the Government in London to be cautious. They had to think of the national interest of Great Britain both as a neutral in the war, and as a state which would have to maintain relations after the war with whatever state or states should issue from it, one republic or two. They lost little time in proclaiming their neutrality and in recognizing the Confederate states as belligerents. They were bitterly reproached for this in the North, but the government in Washington soon, in effect, followed in their wake by declaring a blockade of the South, an act which in itself involved recognition of the belligerency and the granting of belligerent rights. What Palmerston's government did not at any time do was to convey formal *de jure* recognition to the Confederate authorities at Richmond as an independent government. They were

[21] Lincoln had as deep a sense of right and justice as Gladstone or Woodrow Wilson, but he was less prodigal than they were in professing it. He was singularly uncorrupted by power and could question and test his own moral rectitude. Being at the same time an adroit practitioner of the political art, he was more successful than they were in living the good political life in action. It is this that makes him so outstanding a figure in history.

pressed hard to do this by the South, by some European governments and by a strong trend of opinion at home both among the public and in the Government itself. They were strongly tempted to do so as the prospect of a Northern victory seemed to wane. Wisely, as it turned out, they refrained. Had they committed themselves to the act of recognition, there might well have been war with the North, with the fate of Canada thrown into the balance.

As between London and Washington, the position that had led to the war of 1812 was reversed. Great Britain was now the neutral and the United States the belligerent, the neutral desiring to protect trade to the maximum, the belligerent to make the blockade as effective as possible. When the law of the sea had been defined in the Declaration of Paris after the Crimean War, the United States had declined to accept this code because it did not sufficiently protect neutral rights: they thought that the enemy flag should cover not only neutral goods (other than contraband of war) but also privately owned non-contraband enemy goods. With the outbreak of the Civil War, the United States Government, as belligerent, was content to apply the Paris rules. When the North set up a long-distance blockade of the Southern ports, the Royal Navy did not interfere, partly because the Admiralty saw that this would be a useful precedent for themselves —as indeed it proved to be in the period of United States neutrality in both World Wars.

While there was continued tension between London and Washington as a result of the mere fact of the British declaration of neutrality and of the possibility of British recognition of the South, the two main specific controversies that arose between the two Governments were precipitated by episodes which threw a spotlight on their conflicting views of the rights and duties of belligerents and neutrals at sea. These were the *Trent* case and the *Alabama* case.

In the *Trent* case, the Americans were undoubtedly at fault. A zealous United States naval officer, Captain Charles Wilkes, commanding the *San Jacinto*, seized in November 1861 from the British merchant ship *Trent* on the high seas the persons of two 'Special Commissioners of the Confederate States of America', James M. Mason and John Slidell, proceeding as representatives of the South to London and Paris. The British view was that though the ship could be made a prize, the seizure of the men was illegal. Russell demanded the return of the men and an apology. Thanks to a softening of the terms of the note by the Prince Consort (almost his last act before his death), to the conciliatory skill of Lord Lyons, Her Majesty's Minister in Washington, and to the candid, if reluctant, recognition by Lincoln's Cabinet that there was a fault on the American side, the crisis, which had aroused intense public feeling in both countries, was peacefully surmounted. But many had thought that war was inevitable, and the Secretary of State for War, Sir G. Cornewall Lewis, had said: 'We are making all our preparations on the assumption that there is to be war.' The Americans made no explicit apology, but, while claiming that Mason and Slidell were contraband of war which could properly be seized, they admitted that Captain Wilkes had erred in not bringing the *Trent* into port for trial before an American prize court. The prisoners were returned.

In the *Alabama* case, a much more serious one, where *per contra* the complaint was by the United States against Great Britain, the point at issue was whether a neutral government was bound to prevent, within its jurisdiction, the construction, arming and departure of any vessel which it had reasonable ground to believe was intended to carry on war against a power with which it was at peace. The United States held that a neutral had such a duty—and we can measure from this the significance of the step which the United States took when, as a neutral, in return for the lease of bases in the Western Atlantic and Caribbean, she supplied Great Britain with fifty destroyers in the Second World War for use in the war against Germany. The British view was less clear-cut. The Foreign Enlistment Act seemed to prohibit the arming, if not the construction of such a ship, but provided no means of enforcement.

The war-steamer *Alabama*, as she was afterwards called, a small screw vessel of a thousand tons, was built at Liverpool, was manned by a crew of British volunteers, and sailed in July 1862 to rendezvous with a British ship at sea in order to take on her armament and war material, thus, it was thought, circumventing the Foreign Enlistment Act. Thereafter, as a unit in the Confederate navy, she raided Northern commerce most destructively, putting out of action no less than 250 ships. The United States Government had called on the British authorities to prevent her departure. Through hesitation, delay, inefficiency and legal doubts, they failed to do so. What was worse, they delayed until the very last the necessary preventive action in later cases of a similar kind, in one of which two ironclads were in question. The repercussions of this affair were not to die down for ten years, for it was not until September 1872, during

190

Gladstone's first government, that the international arbitration tribunal at Geneva set up by the Treaty of Washington of May 1871, gave its award. Great Britain was adjudged to pay fifteen and a half million dollars to the United States for her lack of 'due diligence' in the *Alabama* case.[22]

The settlement which led up to this award was an example of that kind of face-saving—one of the stock devices of diplomacy—which has often been the basis upon which the United States and Great Britain have patched up their family-like quarrels. Great Britain expressed regret for the escape and depredations of the *Alabama* and agreed to arbitration on the American claims. She admitted that a neutral was bound to use 'due diligence' in a case of this kind, and agreed that the arbitrators should be governed accordingly. But, while she agreed to observe this rule in future, she denied that the rule had been in force as a principle of international law at the time when the claim first arose. She yielded, in fact, as an act of grace, in the interest of Anglo-American relations, and in so doing she established a rule of law which seemed to her at the time to be rather to her advantage than otherwise. The Americans, for their part, acquiesced in the exclusion from the proceedings of their inflated claim for compensation for the allegedly premature British recognition of the belligerency of the South. (Some Americans thought that the only way for Great Britain to settle these enormous claims was to surrender Canada.) It was the American arbitrator, Charles Francis Adams, the minister to Great Britain, who, by an act of great courage, ensured that these indirect claims should not be proceeded with.

The handling of the *Trent* and *Alabama* affairs reflects some credit on both Governments. In spite of intense public feeling, they were able, by skilful and sensitive diplomacy, to resolve their differences. The settlement of these two disputes confirmed and reinforced a tradition which had already given Anglo-American relations a character of their own. However deep the differences dividing the two Governments and however heavily charged the conflicts between them might be, again and again a peaceful settlement by compromise was eventually reached on a basis of mutual respect and fair dealing. The two Governments had thus established a standard in international relationships which contrasted sharply with the

---

[22] The cheque for the *Alabama* claims, when cleared and cancelled, was framed and hung in the Foreign Secretary's room in the Foreign Office.

deterioration in method and behaviour which was to be the mark of European diplomacy in the age of Bismarck. This deplorable retrogression in 'the moral areopagus of Europe' is to be seen in Bismarck's double-dealing in the events leading up to his wars for the expansion of Prussia, in his double-crossing of his ally Austria in the Reinsurance Treaty with Russia in June 1887, and in Napoleon III's persistent manœuvres to secure compensation, in agreement with Prussia, on the Rhine, in Belgium and in Luxembourg—by what Bismarck contemptuously called 'the policy of pickings'—and his anti-Prussian intrigues with Austria and the south German states. It will be illustrated in particular by the conduct of both Napoleon and Bismarck on the eve of the outbreak of the Franco-Prussian War of 1870–71.

The Franco-Prussian War, though it had long been foreseen upon some cause or other, came out of the blue. In February 1870, Bismarck had written: 'The political horizon seen from Berlin appears at present so unclouded that there is nothing of interest to report.' The Tsar Alexander II had met King William I of Prussia and Bismarck at Ems between June 1st and June 4th 1870. There had been no hint between them of trouble with France. On June 30th the French Prime Minister, Émile Ollivier, declared in Parliament: 'At no period has the maintenance of peace appeared to be more assured.' It was only on July 2nd that news came to Paris that the Spanish Government had sent a deputation to Germany to offer the crown to Prince Leopold of Hohenzollern. It was shortly after this, but before the news of the offer and of its acceptance was known in London, that Hammond, the Permanent Under-Secretary in the Foreign Office, told his new minister, Granville, not unreasonably, that he had never known 'so great a lull in foreign affairs'. The war may have been inevitable in the end, but it need not have happened when it did. It would not have happened if Napoleon, swayed by the Empress and a bellicose Paris, having won a diplomatic victory and secured from William I as ample an assurance as he could reasonably ask for about the withdrawal of the Hohenzollern candidature, had not gone on to press that easy-going monarch for a guarantee for the future which he could not be expected to give. It would not have happened if Bismarck, who, it is now thought, had from the beginning laid a trap for the French, and who was now in his turn more than ready, as were the French themselves, to face war, had not issued as an official communiqué for the Press a tendentiously shortened version of the telegraphic report from the King at Ems, giving an account of his interview with the French ambassador, Benedetti, at which his refusal of the French demand had been conveyed. This was, as Bismarck had calculated, a 'red rag' to the French, and a declaration of war from Paris had followed.

We may note three incidental consequences and one decisive result of the Franco-Prussian War.

The first was the impact upon Great Britain. She was powerless to intervene on the Continent, even if she had wished to do so. Prussia and her associates were at the outset able to mobilize 457,000 men with adequate reserves. Within a month of the oubreak of war, ten battles were decided and 300,000 men were killed, wounded or made prisoners. A British expeditionary force could number at most 10,000. What she did do was to try to safeguard the neutrality of Belgium. In 1852 Napoleon had intended to annex Belgium, but had been successfully deterred. In August 1866, in the discussions about compensation for France after the Austro-Prussian War, a treaty with the same object had been drafted, at Bismarck's sugges-tion, in Benedetti's handwriting. This was now made public by Bis-marck. Gladstone thereupon pressed the French and Prussian Governments to reaffirm by treaty the guarantee of the neutrality of Belgium given by the three states and by Austria and Russia in 1839. The treaty would also provide for British armed co-operation with the other of the two parties in defence of Belgium if one of them were to violate Belgian neutrality. Prussia agreed at once, France after some delay. No steps were however taken to make it possible for Great Britain to give effect to her promise of armed assistance. When Cardwell urged that something should be done, Gladstone brushed him aside.

Gladstone strongly disapproved of the transfer of Alsace and Lorraine to Germany without consultation with the inhabitants. With his concern for 'the public law of Europe' and his reliance on 'the general judgment of civilized mankind' he wished to arouse 'the conscience of Europe' against it. He was dissuaded by the Foreign Secretary, Granville, who saw no use in 'laying down general prin-ciples when nobody will attend to them, and when in all probability they will be disregarded.' There was also the consideration that if we were to try to get Russia or Austria to act, this would only be at a price commensurate with their own special interests, which might well be contrary to our own. In general, British opinion was not at first perturbed by the Prussian victory. Belgium, it was thought, would now be safer. Germany might well be a 'natural ally' as Austria had been in the past, and a more congenial one, being predominantly Protestant not Catholic. Great Britain was slow to realize what was happening on the Continent. Her thoughts were concentrated on improvement at home and on trade overseas. But Disraeli, for one, saw that the balance of power had been destroyed, and that England would suffer more than the other powers from the change. He watched with anxiety the growing power and influence of Germany under Bismarck. Not until he came to power in 1874 would there be a turn away from non-intervention to renewed concern in Europe, and from anti-colonialism to the new imperialism.

The second incidental consequence of the Franco-Prussian War was the abrogation by Russia in October 1870, at Prussian instigation, of the provisions for the neutralization of the Black Sea imposed on her in 1856, an act which was of deep concern to Great Britain as well as to Turkey. Without any other ally in Europe, we could not withstand Russia, so we had to save face. Granville, this time agreeing with Gladstone on the enunciation of a principle of political morality, asserted that a party to a multilateral treaty cannot free itself from its stipulations without the consent of the other signatories, since otherwise the essence of treaties would be destroyed. Having said this—and Odo Russell, Her Majesty's ambassador in Berlin, having, by a Palmerstonian touch and without instructions, told Bismarck that we should, failing a solution, be compelled, with or without allies, to go to war with Russia—Granville was ready for a bargain. At an international conference which met in London in January 1871, this principle was accepted. But with it came an agreement to abrogate the Black Sea clauses, which Gladstone had never liked. This was a reasonable settlement. The neutralization of an area so vital to Russia as the Black Sea could not have been permanently maintained. The British public, traditionally anti-Russian, took it badly; and their passions were to be aroused a few years later when the Eastern question again became acute in 1876–78. There was also the galling consciousness that England, so great in the realm of commerce, finance and industry, so secure in the art of government, so supreme in world-trade, had so weak a voice in the councils of Europe.

Gladstone, like Palmerston, was more successful in foreign affairs in his earlier than in his later periods of office. During his first government from 1868 to 1874 he and Granville could put to their credit Belgium, the Black Sea and the *Alabama* settlement. Such successes, modest as they were, were not readily to fall to him again. They were certainly modest. In Belgium we guarded against a danger which did not in fact materialize. In the Black Sea we gained the form but not the substance. In the *Alabama* case we confessed our error and paid up, a step which many thought to have been a deplorable surrender.

The third incidental consequence was the completion of the unity of Italy by the entry of Victor Emmanuel's forces into the city of Rome in September 1870.

The decisive result of the war was to make clear the displacement of France by Germany as the leading power on the Continent. In future, the threat to the balance of power, if it were to come, would come from the new German Empire and not, as had formerly, perhaps wrongly, been supposed, from France. In fact, it would be Bismarck's care, so long as he was in power, to keep the balance, and he would do so with superb skill. His successors were to mar his work and to bring Europe to the holocaust of 1914. The late Victorian era, to which we shall now come, was in Europe the age of Bismarck.

France, though she had made the round of the capitals of Europe for allies, had been left to fight alone. Like most of Europe, she had over-estimated the efficiency and fighting quality of her army, as Europe was again to do at the outbreak of the Second World War. She was left to make peace alone. As Thiers discovered, 'Europe was not to be found.' The concert of Europe, which had dealt with Luxembourg and Crete in 1867 and 1869, and would deal with the Black Sea in 1871, could do nothing to influence this decisive shift in the balance of power which was to govern events in Europe for over forty years. In vain had Gorchakov said to Bismarck in August 1870: 'It is impossible that the other Great Powers be excluded from the future negotiations for peace, even if they do not take part in the war.' Eight years later Gorchakov himself would be constrained, at the Congress of Berlin, to submit for the scrutiny of the powers the terms of his treaty with Turkey.

It has been said, and it was believed by that acute diplomatist, Robert Morier, at the time, that Great Britain could by energetic intervention have prevented war in 1870.[23] This presupposes the

[23] Bismarck professed to think the same: 'If . . . the English had said to Napoleon, "There must be no war", there would have been none.' He

possession of power and the will to use it. We had neither. Nor would the ground for threatening armed intervention have been clear, other than the respectable and valid ground that peace in Europe is a British interest. If the interest had been the preservation of the balance of power, it would not at that time have been evident to which side the predominance would be likely to shift and on whose side the intervention should be. Who could have said with certainty in 1866 whether Austria or Prussia was the stronger, or in 1870, France or Prussia? In 1866, Prussia had a population of 18 million as against Austria's 33 million, and Austria had the better artillery. In 1870, France had some superiority in the number of professional soldiers, in iron and steel production, and in the quality of her rifles (*chassepots*). Bismarck's wars of 1864, 1866 and 1870 were not so calculated or so deliberate as he afterwards made out, and it was not until they were all over that it was manifest to the more clear-sighted that a great change had occurred. At this crisis in the affairs of Europe, Great Britain had no predominance and not even any effective part to play. Clarendon, out of office, wrote from Florence in March 1868: 'Belief in the selfishness that dictates our present system of isolation has reduced our importance, and therefore our influence, on the Continent to zero.' All that Great Britain could fairly claim was that she herself was still reasonably safe from invasion, though indeed the Navy itself was becoming antiquated. Her naval power was not 'predominant over all other military power'. There was no such thing as 'British control of the world'.

If it be admitted that British influence was strong in the generation or so after Waterloo and weak in the third quarter of the nineteenth century, the question may still be asked, what did we gain by our earlier success or lose by our later failure? To this complex question a short if partial answer may be given. After 1815, thanks in large measure to the strength of British influence, founded upon military renown and diplomatic skill, peace among the great powers of Europe was preserved during the turbulent post-war period, even during the revolutions of 1848, and the spread of liberal institutions in Europe was promoted. In both respects, British interests were well served. In the later period, the inability or the failure (whichever it might be) of Great Britain to exercise such beneficent, though by

also once said, whether seriously or not, that if Clarendon had not died and had been in office in the summer of 1870, he would have prevented war.

no means decisive, influence in continental affairs as she had formerly often done was accompanied by a series of wars in Europe and, at the end of the period, by the disruption of the balance. Whether the inability or the failure was attributable to lack of material power, or to lack of will, or to lack of diplomatic skill, or to a fundamental change in the situation in Europe, might be argued.

In neither period was the military, as distinct from the naval, power of Great Britain other than modest. Certainly there was a failure of skill. Palmerston had been clever enough before 1850 to find occasions for intervention when the combination of European rivalries offered a good chance of intervening cheaply and with effect. Disraeli was to show after 1874 that, as in Palmerston's earlier years, this could be done again without very much in the way of military strength to back it up. Certainly again there was a change in Europe. The post-Napoleonic generation had had no stomach for a general war. Now there were leaders like Napoleon III, Cavour and Bismarck who had better nerves and no such inhibitions. There was a change in England also. Non-intervention and retrenchment were the slogans of the time. But with them there was the contrary trend in public opinion, against which Cobden and Bright were to protest, the assertion of a duty to defend small nations and to right the wrongs of humanity. We were to disarm, but we were to be expected to intervene indiscriminately in arms. We shall find this (so to speak) aggressive pacifism again in the 1930s. In these conditions, the later Palmerston and Gladstone, except on rare occasions, lacked effective influence in Europe.

In the short term, this may not have seemed to damage British interests very much, if at all. The minimum of commitment in Europe, the minimum of preparation even for imperial defence, neglect of agriculture and growing reliance on overseas food supplies may have served well enough so long as Great Britain was secure at home; but they were ill-suited to the dangerous world which was soon to grow up around her. In the longer term, by her inability or failure to play her due part in the ordering of Europe in the third quarter of the century, Great Britain not only forfeited her own security later in the century; she must also bear a share of responsibility for the increasing international tension in Europe, and consequently for the ultimate catastrophe which descended upon the Continent and upon herself in 1914. It may well be that nationalism, anti-nationalism and national ambitions had, in the crucial formative period, created a situation too complex and too explosive for us to handle alone: but at least we might have tried, as Disraeli did with some success after 1874. Cobdenite doctrine and Gladstonian finance[24] have much to answer for. In a few pregnant years, the face of Europe had been changed to our detriment.

[24] Gladstone, as retiring and again prospective Chancellor of the Exchequer, had written to Russell in October 1865: 'I am bound by conviction . . . to the principle of progressive reduction in our military and naval establishments and in the charges for them, under the favourable circumstances which we appear to enjoy.' The allegedly favourable circumstances in which we found ourselves were that in the preceding year we had been unable, for lack of armed forces, to protect Denmark against Prussia, a decision which Gladstone himself (facing both ways) had called 'a tolerable, not the best conclusion'. Presumably the best conclusion, to his mind, would have been joint Anglo-French action, in which France would have borne the main burden in view of our military weakness.

CHAPTER XI

Late Victorian Afterglow

Historians, reflecting on the course of human affairs which it is their purpose to trace and to interpret, are often drawn to mark what seem to them to be turning-points in the procession of events, to note a particular year or short period of years after which, in some respect or other, the colour or flavour of life or the balance of forces or the character of institutions was seen in retrospect to have undergone a significant change. E. L. Woodward, in his volume in the Oxford History of England (*The Age of Reform, 1815–1870*), finds such a turning point round about the year 1850. R. C. K. Ensor, in the companion volume (*England, 1870–1914*), sees in the years round about 1870 the beginning of a new epoch in the history of England and of Europe. In our own history, 1868 is the important date: it marks the opening of the Gladstonian era in domestic and foreign policy. David Thomson, both in *Europe Since Napoleon* and in *England in the Nineteenth Century, 1815–1914*, chooses the same years 1850 and 1871 (or 1874) to mark the dividing lines in his treatment of the century between Waterloo and the outbreak of the First World War. In Europe, according to his analysis, the period after 1871 is the period of democracy and socialism, of colonial expansion and imperial rivalries, and of confronting systems of alliances. At home it marks the growth of the modern state, the demand for social security and the appearance of the new imperialism.

To illustrate the character of the late Victorian period (1875–1900), and the changes which it brought in the British position, we may note some of these turning points. Abroad, the most notable event was the Franco-Prussian War which transferred the reputed primacy on the Continent from France to Germany. It ushered in an era of great conscript armies and of an armed peace, with each of the

199

powers of Europe trying to establish a favourable balance and to prevent the formation of hostile coalitions, and coming in the end to a system of alliances or understandings which split Europe in two. The balance of power was no longer an 'equilibrium of satisfied states', but the confronting accumulations of armed force. In 1871, for the first time, the British public began to fear a German, not a French, invasion, made vivid for them by a widely-read pamphlet on *The Battle of Dorking*. It was not in the armed forces alone that the menace lay. In the factories, schools and universities the rival was reinforcing his strength.

At home, the years round about 1870 mark the onset of both advance and retreat. On the positive side were the extension of the franchise by Disraeli's Conservative government in 1867 and a long series of political and administrative reforms instituted by Gladstone's first government of 1868, and of social reforms introduced by Disraeli's second government of 1874. Great Britain was becoming a modern state.

On the negative side were developments which could not but weaken Great Britain's international position. The years 1876–77 marked the end of the long period of prosperity and of rapid economic expansion. For the first time, English manufacturing industry began to experience serious foreign competition at home and abroad, first from Germany and then from the United States: our near-monopoly had gone. Side by side with this, our agriculture suffered disaster. In August 1879, Disraeli confessed: 'It is difficult to carry through a commanding policy with a failing exchequer.' Financiers turned increasingly away from Europe and towards the less developed countries as an outlet for capital investment. European rivalries translated themselves into a competition for colonial territories. The 'scramble for Africa' began.

The change in Great Britain's economic position in the last quarter of the nineteenth century was fundamental. It is true that at the end of the nineteenth century Great Britain was again by far the greatest naval power; and, thanks to the introduction of steam and steel, she was again pre-eminent as a builder, owner and operator of merchant shipping. She was still well ahead as a producer of cotton textiles. But in most aspects of her economic life, she suffered a decline. Great Britain was no longer in the same degree the workshop of the world. British goods had to meet competition and tariffs abroad.[1] Industrial output, although increasing somewhat more than the slackening growth of population, was rising slowly as compared with the rapid expansion during the fifty years after Waterloo. Before the end of the century the United States and Germany both overtook and passed us in the production of steel (of which we became importers), and the United States in coal. The rate of increase of national wealth became progressively more sluggish. Foreign trade also increased, but that of our new rivals, the United States and Germany, grew faster. Already by mid-century we had begun to depend increasingly on our exports for our livelihood. With the advent of competition, foreign trade became a struggle for existence. We became dependent for most of our wheat and meat on sea-borne imports, which had to be paid for by exports. The United States and Germany were also drawing ahead of us in industrial techniques. Their exports tended more and more to include new products requiring high manufacturing skill, while ours were too often drawn from the traditional coal, iron and steel groups. Between 1880 and 1910, exports of coal increased from £8,373,000 to £36,620,000 and exports of machinery from £9,264,000 to £19,620,000. We were selling our raw material instead of using it ourselves, and were equipping our rivals with the ships and machinery with which to compete with us. Not until well on in the twentieth century did we diversify our manufactures and make the most of our inventiveness and technical skill. It would not be too gross a caricature of our national economy in late Victorian times to say that it was one in which agriculture was in distress, when most of our food had to be imported, and when our imports were paid for in large measure by the export of increasing quantities of coal and by the proceeds of shipping freights and overseas investment.

In one other respect there was a decline. In the period between 1874 and 1904 there was a marked lull in the progress of British long-term investment abroad. In the years 1870–74 the average annual investment had been £61 million. It fell to £1·7 million in the years 1875–79 after the world-wide panic of 1873. In 1890–94 it was £45·6 million and in 1900–1904 it was £21·3 million. The recovery came in the new century when, in the years 1904–1909, it

---

[1] And even in the Empire. As early as 1859, the year before Cobden's free-trade treaty with France, Canada had put a protective tariff on cotton goods, iron and steel to foster her own manufactures, a truly shocking event to liberal-minded British industrialists.

jumped to £109·5 million and in the next four years to £185 million. But there was this difference from earlier times. From about 1877, the funds lent abroad were found, not from new capital accumulations but from the interest on money already invested.

Subject to this limitation, British money and British skill and enterprise gave a powerful impulse to the opening up of undeveloped lands in distant parts of the world. Whereas Paris and Berlin catered for foreign governments, and more often than not for unstable and improvident governments in eastern and south-eastern Europe, London turned its eyes to other continents, where there was pioneering to be done. British contractors took up chances in India, South America, Canada and Australia, the United States and Africa, anywhere that there were railways to be built, lands to be settled, mines to be worked or construction to be done. In Great Britain there were 'half a thousand groups whose experience and financial venturesomeness no strangeness or difficulty could appal, who knew how to work mines at any height or climate, and hew plantations out of jungles, who for a century had been opening up hidden resources of distant interiors.'[2]

The change in our foreign policy which dates from Disraeli's advent to power in 1874 was deliberately made. The objective was now a 'commanding policy' instead of a policy of non-interference. Disraeli saw Great Britain as 'an imperial country'. Salisbury said of him that 'zeal for the greatness of England was the passion of his life'. In Europe, there was to be 'a policy of determination', a 'determination, in the event of European complications, not to be neutral and un-interfering, but to act, and to act with allies.' That patriotic Radical and former opponent of Disraeli, J. A. Roebuck, said on the eve of the Congress of Berlin in 1878: 'England now holds as proud a position as she ever held; and that is due to the sagacity, and power, and conduct of the despised person once called Benjamin Disraeli, but now Lord Beaconsfield.' That opinion was endorsed by Her Majesty's ambassadors reporting from Berlin and from Vienna. The policy itself had the wholehearted support of the Queen. No longer having her work prepared for her by the Prince Consort, and being no longer subjected to his methodical and circumspect guidance, the Queen had come to give rein to her own impetuous temperament. 'Oh,' she wrote to Disraeli in January 1878,

[2] Herbert Feis, *Europe the World's Banker, 1870–1914*, Oxford University Press, London, 1930, p. 183.

'if the Queen were a man, she would like to go and give those Russians, whose word one cannot believe, such a beating!' Disraeli had difficulties within his own Cabinet over his forward policy of resistance to Russia. 'In a Cabinet of twelve members,' he wrote to the Queen in November 1877, 'there are seven parties, or policies, as to the course which should be pursued.' With Salisbury, he reached an accommodation which led to close co-operation. With Derby, his arch-non-interventionist Foreign Secretary, it came to a breach and to the latter's resignation. Gladstone, with implacable personal and party rancour, looked upon Disraeli as the 'great corruptor' and as 'the worst and most immoral Minister since Castlereagh'.

An early opportunity to use our influence in Europe came in 1875, when there were fears of a German attack upon France. In concert with Russia, Disraeli's government put in a strong word of caution in Berlin which convinced Bismarck that Great Britain had again become a power to be reckoned with. But it was in the great Eastern question of 1876–78 that Disraeli attained the commanding position in Europe to which he aspired.

Conditions in Europe were, as it happened, propitious for the exercise of British initiative. There were three kinds of initiative at three successive stages of the crisis—before, during and after Russo-Turkish hostilities.

The crisis arose out of a rebellion by Turkey's Slav Christian subjects in Bosnia and Hercegovina and later in Bulgaria, whom the Tsar, swayed by powerful Slavophile influences, felt it a duty to defend. The powers of Europe—in contrast to the attitude of some of them before the outbreak of the Crimean War—were anxious to avoid a general war: France, because she was still weakened by the war of 1870–71; Great Britain, because it was still felt that she could not act effectively against a land-power in Europe without a continental ally; Austria, because she had already promised Russia benevolent neutrality in return for the promise of the occupation of Bosnia and Hercegovina; Germany, because Bismarck, though he was not averse from fishing in troubled Russo-Turkish waters, had established a balance in Europe favourable to himself which might be upset by a European war. Disraeli's government were clear on two points: they would not countenance or participate in any joint forceful coercion of Turkey, although they were strongly pressed by Gladstone and some other members of the opposition to do so; nor would they acquiesce in the occupation of Constantinople by Russia. In the early stages of the crisis, therefore, they stood out against the so-called Berlin memorandum, which was a plan of reform for Turkey devised by the three imperial courts of Russia, Austria and Prussia with a hint as to the possibility of coercion. They proposed and brought about a meeting of the powers at Constantinople at which revised proposals were prepared for presentation to Turkey. As a measure of precaution for the protection of British subjects and interests, and of the subject Christian populations, they sent a fleet to lie off Besika Bay outside the Straits. They helped to secure an armistice between Serbia and Turkey. And they promoted the opening of negotiations between Russia and Turkey.

When, owing largely to Turkish obstinacy, war broke out, the policy of London was one of conditional neutrality, that is to say, neutrality provided that Russia would respect British interests in Turkey, such as Constantinople, the Straits, Egypt and the Suez Canal. Plans were made to meet the possible threat of a Russian seizure of Constantinople; one was for the despatch of a fleet to Constantinople protected by the occupation of Gallipoli by an expeditionary force from England for which Disraeli was told that the requisite forces could be made available; another was for the seizure of Cyprus and Alexandretta as footholds for possible further action on the mainland. Whether we really had the necessary forces for these operations must be a matter of doubt. It was only at a late stage in the war, after the crushing of the long and heroic Turkish resistance at Plevna in December 1877 and the Russian approach to Constantinople, that the British public became fully roused and the Jingo war-fever broke out. The Turk was no longer remembered as the author of the Bulgarian atrocities so passionately denounced by Gladstone and others but seen as the victim of the brutal Russian. The fleet of five ironclads with other craft steamed into the Sea of Marmora and anchored off Constantinople. The Russians after Plevna had not the strength to pursue a mid-winter campaign; they stopped short of Constantinople and agreed to an armistice at Adrianople in January.

The next stage was opened by the negotiation between the Russians and Turks of a treaty at San Stefano by which a 'Big Bulgaria' was to be carved out of Turkish territory stretching to the Black Sea, the Aegean and westwards to the Albanian mountains, over-riding the claims of other Balkan nationalities and threatening to establish

Russian predominance in the Balkans. Again Great Britain acted. As a measure of precaution, and as a deliberate demonstration of imperial strength, a contingent of 7,000 Indian troops was sent to Malta, to be ready to seize Cyprus or Alexandretta if necessary.[3] Disraeli also insisted that, as the Treaty of San Stefano dealt with matters which were of common concern to the powers who were parties to the treaties of 1856 and 1871, the whole of its articles should be submitted for approval to a conference. To this re-constitution of the concert of Europe, Russia was constrained to agree.

The Congress of Berlin of 1878 is noteworthy for a number of reasons. It was the last peace congress actually so called to be held in Europe. The great meeting held in Paris after the First World War was called a peace conference, not a congress. The Congress of Berlin, unlike the Congress of Vienna but like the Paris peace con-ference, was attended by the British Prime Minister in person. For Disraeli, British policy in the eastern question was all-important and he had continued to direct it himself. At the congress, his in-fluence was decisive. As Bismarck respectfully remarked: 'The old Jew, that is the man.' It was successful because Salisbury had taken the precaution to prepare for it by making advance agreements with Russia, Austria and Turkey; and because Bismarck, for once playing the part of 'honest broker', wanted a peaceful solution which would, if possible, preserve the Three Emperors' League and, in particular, leave his good relations with Russia intact. In this latter aspiration, he was to be disappointed.

Under Salisbury's agreement with Russia in May 1878, the Rus-sians consented to give up 'Big Bulgaria' and to draw the southern frontier of the principality to run east and west along the Balkan mountains, restoring Macedonia to Turkey. Under the agreement with Austria in June, Great Britain supported the Austrian occupa-tion of Bosnia and Hercegovina in return for Austrian support for the plan for the smaller Bulgaria. By the agreement with Turkey, also in June, Salisbury offered a guarantee of Asiatic Turkey against Russia in return for a British occupation and administration of Cyprus.

These agreements substantially determined the shape of the

[3] Indian troops were used on at least thirteen missions outside the bor-ders of India between 1854 and 1899. See A. P. Thornton, *The Imperial Idea and its Enemies*, Macmillan, London, 1959, p. 97.

settlement which emerged from the congress, not without a threat by Disraeli to break it up if he could not get his way with Gorchakov.

Disraeli claimed with justice that he had brought back 'peace with honour'. He had in combination with Salisbury, by sheer exercise of active diplomacy, for a brief period recalled and rivalled the exploits of Palmerston. His diplomacy had been backed from time to time by overt or covert threats of armed action which no one quite dared to disbelieve. Gladstone thundered that Disraeli had 'taken the side of servitude', had 'sounded the tones of Metternich' and had made an 'insane covenant' with Turkey. It may be answered that Gladstone himself had done nothing for the amelioration of the lot of the Turkish Christians from 1868 to 1874, and had demanded no more than self-government under Turkish suzerainty for Bosnia and Bulgaria; that if Gladstone's objective was to meet the aspirations of the Balkan nationalities who were 'rightly struggling to be free'— the phrase was Gladstone's own—the creation of a 'Big Bulgaria' over-riding the interests of Serbs and Greeks and exacerbating the deadly internecine rivalries of the Balkan Christians was not the right way to do it; that under the Berlin settlement, about eleven million of the subject races were liberated from the Turkish yoke, though not all were given self-government, some coming under Russian, some under Austrian and some under British administration; that if, as sagacious statesmen thought, the time was not ripe for the complete dissolution of Turkey in Europe to be effected without grave danger of war among the great powers, then at any rate the Berlin Congress took a peaceful first step towards this end, imperfect though it might be. There would be no great war in Europe for thirty-six years. As for the agreement about Cyprus—the 'Convention of Defensive Alliance', to give it its correct title—it was a rational proceeding, given the premises that underlay it. The Russians had taken Batum, Kars and Ardahan from the Turks, thus, as we saw it, opening up a possible overland way for them to threaten the Suez Canal and the Persian Gulf. They gave way about Bulgaria, but they would not yield about their conquests in Armenia and could not be coerced or dislodged. To guard against the threat, Great Britain undertook to join Turkey in defending her territory in Asia against any further Russian advance—she assumed that Austria would do the same in the Balkans. In view of the state of the Army, this may have been a rash undertaking, but since it never had to be fulfilled, it may have served. In any event, we did not engage ourselves to take on the Russians single-handed, but to help the Turks to defend themselves: and what Turkish resistance might be worth, the defence of Plevna had just shown. In return, Great Britain obtained two promises. The first was an undertaking to introduce agreed reforms for the protection of Christian and other subjects of Turkey in Asia Minor, to supervise which, military consuls (Major H. H. Kitchener among them) were later sent out. The second was consent to the occupation and administration of Cyprus, by which means alone (it was held) would Great Britain be in a position to fulfil her engagement to help to defend Turkish territory. For this purpose Great Britain required a base in the vicinity of the Turkish coast: Malta was too far distant to be an adequate starting point for operations in Asia Minor. We needed, as the Chancellor of the Exchequer, Sir Stafford Northcote, said: 'a place of arms in the Levant, where our ships could be in bad weather, and troops and stores could be held ready for action.' Cyprus was, as Disraeli advised the Queen, 'the key of Western Asia'. If, in the event, Cyprus was not so used, the reason is simple: four years later Gladstone himself occupied Egypt, and with Egypt in our hands the need for Cyprus had passed. With our withdrawal at last from Egypt nearly three-quarters of a century later, the need for Cyprus as a base has again revived, and its inadequacy for purposes of sea-going operations has been made manifest.

The Congress of Berlin had one incidental result in the wider European field which was to be pregnant for the future. Although Bismarck did everything he could to help Russia at the congress, he could not keep the Three Emperors' League in existence, since Austria, having convinced herself of British friendship, declined to resume her earlier co-operation with Russia. This had become clear by the end of 1878, and Bismarck was forced to make a choice between his two imperial neighbours, or suffer the dangers of isolation. In this series of events it is the British Prime Minister who calls the tune. In the end Germany chose Austria as a partner. The German-Austrian Alliance of 1879 set the pattern of European politics until the denouement in 1914.

As for the part which Disraeli had played, we may quote the judgment of an Austrian historian: 'What is certain is that, ably supported by Salisbury . . . Beaconsfield gained his end without involving England in a war. This achievement of Beaconsfield and

Salisbury will be looked upon as a masterpiece of diplomacy for all time.'[4]

Disraeli's methods could be highly individual. In agreement with the Queen, and without authority from the Cabinet, he once sent an emissary to St Petersburg with a minatory message for the Tsar, threatening intervention if Russia resumed the war against Turkey. Knowledge of this step was deliberately withheld from his own Foreign Secretary (Derby) and from the Foreign Office. He had a poor opinion of the Foreign Office and of ambassadors: of the latter he said: 'I wish we could get rid of the whole lot. They seem to me to be quite useless.' The Foreign Office was certainly not very efficient under Derby, perhaps because it was understaffed and over-worked, perhaps because, as a minister, he was not alert. It was a relief to Disraeli when, in Salisbury, he had a Foreign Secretary who 'acted for himself' and was not too much swayed by the counsels or committed by the action of the permanent officials. He also rejoiced, in a letter to the Queen, that Salisbury, when he became Foreign Secretary in 1878, had, like Canning and Palmerston, taken to writing important despatches himself, thus taking their composition 'out of the manufactory of the Hammonds and Tenterdens [these were successive Permanent Under-Secretaries], who have written every-thing, in their F.O. jargon, during these last ten years.'

Salisbury was to say in 1897 that Great Britain had 'put all her money on the wrong horse', when she had declined to follow up Tsar Nicholas's proposals for the partition of the Turkish Empire, and when she had continued to support Turkey as a barrier against Russia's southward expansion. This was not a particularly just ob-servation. If so many European statesmen—and not British states-men only—thought that the dissolution of the Turkish Empire in Europe could hardly be achieved without provoking a European war, there was much to be said for keeping it together, so far as possible, until the time should be ripe for change. In 1897, in spite of all vicissitudes, Constantinople was still, as it is still now, in Turkish hands. The régime of the Straits has continued to subsist. Turkey was still, and is still now, a buffer against Russian southward expan-sion. And if these things are so, they were Salisbury's own doing as much as anyone's. Had Russia not been halted in 1878, the history

[4] A. F. Pribram, *England and the International Policy of the European Great Powers (1871–1914)*, The Ford Lectures, Clarendon Press, Oxford, 1931, p. 13.

of the world would have been very different. But as to this, speculation is vain. Had Russia not remained bottled up in the Black Sea in the First World War and not been deprived of Allied assistance, the revolution of 1917 might not have occurred, or might not have taken the course it did. Had Russia taken Constantinople and become master of the Straits in 1878, she would almost certainly have been a more powerful state in the late nineteenth and early twentieth century than she in fact became. The First World War, even had it occurred, would have been a different kind of war. And no one can say whether a resurgent Russia, even under a constitutional Tsarist régime, would or would not have been any less dangerous to the stability of the world than Soviet Russia has become.

With the return of Gladstone to power in 1880, there was another shift in our foreign policy. Gladstone thought Disraeli's foreign policy 'the most selfish and least worthy' he had ever known. The mainsprings of his own policy had been indicated while in opposition, first in his pamphlet on the Bulgarian atrocities and secondly in the course of his speeches in the Midlothian election campaign. These he looked upon as a 'battle of justice, humanity, freedom, love . . . all on a gigantic scale' which was 'a great and high election of God'. But apart from its violent anti-Turkish bias, there was not much that was concrete in his exposition. What he advocated was good government at home, as a reserve of strength for worthy occasions abroad; a policy of peace; cultivation of the concert of Europe and common action for common objects; the avoidance of needless engagements; equal rights for all nations; and a policy inspired by love of freedom. On this basis he was able to condemn Disraeli's conduct of the Berlin negotiations and to ride back to power on a wave of moral fervour.

It is useful for a statesman to declare the general objectives of his policy in concrete terms. It settles the lines within which he will work, though it does not relieve him of the need to examine afresh every issue that arises even within these general lines. It is much less useful if general policies are laid down not in concrete form but in terms of moral concepts. This Gladstone was prone to do, as was his disciple Woodrow Wilson after him. For both of them the compulsions of international life too often ran counter to moral aspirations. As a practical statesman Gladstone took account of this, but he did so with a divided mind that made for uncertainty in the handling of foreign affairs. His pacific professions consorted ill with his repeated resort to threat and violence in action. In our own day, Pandit Nehru's assertions of high moral principle in international affairs have won him a well-deserved international standing and have in general been translated into wise policies. But they have not concealed from the world that his dealings with Pakistan over Kashmir have been like those of any normally unregenerate government. Nor have they shielded him from the need to contemplate the normally conventional means of resistance to the aggressive encroachments of his Chinese neighbours.

It has been said above that there has been no one quite like Chatham in our national life. The same may be said of Gladstone. His mind and character were of a complexity that defies definition; an ex-Tory Liberal High Churchman, a deeply religious man and a rancorous party politician, a political crusader with his eye always on the ballot-box or the division lobby, a great statesman and a demagogue, a man, as Walter Bagehot said, who had 'the soul of a martyr with the intellect of an advocate', an opponent of a meddling diplomacy who had an urge to uphold the public law of the world, an anti-imperialist who was driven by inner contradictions into imperialist courses, an orator with a taste for staying at great houses after making crowd-compelling radical speeches, a man of high moral principle and a master of equivocation, a man of noble mind with an obsession with self that would so often strike the false note, a man of flaming sincerity who could at times give an impression of colossal humbug. Disraeli called him 'a vindictive fiend'. A colleague, W. E. Forster, said that he could 'persuade himself of almost anything'. Yet Benjamin Jowett spoke of his 'great simplicity' and the historian, J. R. Green, remarked on his 'unaffected modesty'.

Gladstone's administration of 1880–85, with Granville as Foreign Secretary, has usually been set down as one of the low-water marks of our foreign policy in the nineteenth century. Bismarck wrote in October 1880: 'I do not believe that the direction of English policy has ever been in such incompetent hands since the American War of Independence.' One of Gladstone's enterprises, already foreshadowed in the Midlothian campaign, was a fleeting attempt in 1880 and 1881 to revive the concert of Europe as an instrument of European and British policy for keeping the peace among the great powers. He defined this policy as 'the bringing about the "common accord" of Europe, embodying in one organ the voice of civilized mankind in the actings and fostering care of England.' It aimed at the relaxation of the tension in Europe resulting from the Berlin settlement through a joint coercion of Turkey. In contradistinction to the right of the duty of individual action, which he repudiated, it implied the definition of a common objective, the establishment of a programme of action by diplomatic discussion or by conference, and the execution of the programme by concerted diplomatic operations or by a mandatory state acting in the name of all. It was not taken very seriously either at home or abroad, where it was looked on as 'a phase of British activity'. The powers usually preferred peace by mediation or concession to the risk of hostilities through enforcement by common action. But the policy failed chiefly because it cut across the new course of closed alliances upon which Bismarck had now embarked, first by the Austro-German Alliance of 1879 and then by a new Three Emperors' League of 1881, one effect of which was to warn Great Britain off the Balkans. In opposition to agreement by concert, Bismarck promoted a system of 'balanced antagonisms' based on military power. He did not want the pot to boil over and so spoil his handiwork in Europe, but it suited his peculiar methods, his restless exercise of tortuous diplomacy, to keep the pot near the boil.

Gladstone tried, for example, in the autumn of 1880, to use the concert in order to coerce the Turks, who had been quite unmoved by the united voice of Europe, about the Montenegrin frontier. His successive objectives were a naval demonstration off Dulcigno and a threat to seize Smyrna. His intention was to show that if Disraeli had invoked the concert in 1876 the Turks would have been brought to heel and the war of 1877 prevented. But the concert could not be brought to act as one. France, Austria and Germany declined to play a fully active part, and it was left in the main to Great Britain and Russia to apply the pressure. As it happened, this was enough to make the Sultan give way in the end. But the concert fell apart and was not to be effectively revived.

One of the counts in the criticism of Gladstone's foreign policy has been his handling of the affairs of Egypt and the Sudan. In brief outline, the course of events in Egypt was as follows.

Since 1798, when Nelson, at the Battle of the Nile, had dashed Napoleon's hopes of ruling in Egypt, France and Great Britain had been rivals for influence and advantage. In 1875, Disraeli acquired about 44 per cent of the shares in the Suez Canal, constructed under French auspices and opened in 1869. This did not, as some have said, foreshadow our occupation of Egypt: Disraeli continued to hold that Constantinople, and not Egypt and the Suez Canal, was the key to India. In 1876, the Khedive suspended payment of his huge debt which had grown from £3 million in 1863 to £91 million in 1876. An Anglo-French control was set up in the interest of the bondholders, who were chiefly French. This was one of the first steps in European economic imperialism, namely the practice of governmental intervention in support of bondholders leading to the establishment of foreign control. In January 1882, there was a military *coup d'état* under Colonel Arabi Pasha, nationalist, anti-European and anti-Turkish in character, against the non-Egyptian Khedivial régime. Under the impact of internal disorder, the dual control broke down. In June there were nationalist riots in Alexandria in which fifty Europeans were killed and over sixty wounded. In July, the British fleet (the French having sailed away) bombarded and silenced the forts, the guns of which threatened its security. It was then decided in London that the overthrow of Arabi—Gladstone thought him 'a bad man'—was an indispensable condition for the restoration of any kind of good order. A military expedition, in which the French, with apprehensive eyes on the Rhine, declined to participate, was with some difficulty mounted in England. The force was despatched and, under Wolseley, destroyed Arabi's army at Tel-el-Kebir. This was no inconsiderable test for Cardwell's new model army, so small by continental standards. Gladstone had the church-bells rung for the victory. Gladstone, against his principles as an advocate of peace and retrenchment, had intervened out of a no less deep-rooted concern for the suppression of a régime of violence and for the establishment of law and order and the restoration of financial orthodoxy. Debt enforcement for him was part of the public law. He intervened at Alexandria in 1882 in much the same spirit as he had intervened against the Turks in 1880. There was, too, his passionate reaction against the massacre of Europeans by Moslem fanaticism about which he had roused the country a few years before. He was afterwards bitterly to regret his action and to regard later humiliations as divine retribution for the crime he had committed.[5]

[5] The obloquy that was heaped upon Gladstone and his government for the death of Gordon at Khartoum was not wholly merited, except perhaps in so far as it may be true to say that, while egocentrics or eccentrics like Gordon (and James Wolfe and T. E. Lawrence and Orde Wingate), whom the public are prone to idolize, can maybe render unique services, Govern-

Late Victorian Afterglow

The intention was to withdraw again from Egypt almost at once, and this intention was repeatedly affirmed. But to do so was not possible. Having destroyed the Government, we could not quit and leave chaos behind us. To come out might also lead to a re-establishment of French dominance and thus to loss of control of the Canal. Gladstone and his colleagues would neither accept this nor draw the conclusion that the best course would be to annex or to declare a protectorate. Instead, Egypt remained nominally a part of the Sultan's dominions and became the sport of international diplomacy. Egypt was governed, not directly by a British governor but indirectly by a British agent and consul-general in the person of Sir Evelyn Baring, later Lord Cromer, who held this post for over twenty-three years.

The French, owing to domestic broils and to a natural preoccupation with the danger on the Rhine, had missed the chance to go in with us. They could not turn us out, but did everything in their power by diplomatic pressure to constrain us to come to a settlement that would be more to their advantage, in fact, to come out ourselves, as we had repeatedly said we would do. We not only antagonized Turkey, who now increasingly turned to Germany. We were also estranged from our partner in the liberal alliance, which, in spite of temporary coolnesses, had subsisted since the reign of Louis Philippe. This was, most unfortunately, happening in the formative period of the alliances which were to set the stage in Europe for the rest of the century. In order to out-vote France and Russia on the six-power international commission which was set up to administer the loan issued under the guarantee of all the powers in 1885 (a loan which, in spite of Baring's advice, we had declined to guarantee on our own), we needed the support of the Triple Alliance, that is to say, of Germany. Since Egypt could not in practice be governed without the consent of the international commission, we could not carry on in Egypt without Germany's vote; and for that vote, Germany made us pay elsewhere. This bondage to Germany, added to our breach with France, was gravely to embarrass the con-

ments who take the risk of employing them on public affairs deserve the embarrassments which they may bring upon themselves by so doing. In this case, the Government were unlucky in the man whom, under pressure, they chose for the job. On a vast scale, Gladstone (and Chatham) were themselves men of no less abnormal constitution. Bismarck was inclined to think that Gladstone was insane, and as did Palmerston, he believed that he would end in a madhouse.

duct of our foreign policy for many years. Small wonder that Baring was at pains to observe to Rosebery, when the latter became Foreign Secretary in February 1886, that 'Berlin and not Cairo is the real centre of gravity of Egyptian affairs'.

Bright, who resigned from the Cabinet, called the Egyptian expedition 'a manifest violation of International Law and of the moral law'. The policy has also been criticized on grounds of conception and execution. The real fault, said R. C. K. Ensor, 'was that when [Gladstone] went into Egypt he went half-heartedly and without forethought, and consequently did so on the wrong terms.'[6] No doubt, if Disraeli had acted as Gladstone did, Gladstone's condemnation would have known no bounds, but this would be common form in the unmeasured party controversy of those days. Looked at dispassionately today, with some understanding of the circumstances in which statesmen have to take their decisions, Gladstone's own defence of the act of force at Alexandria in a letter to Bright[7] can attract one's sympathy, though some of the arguments which he used at other times were less convincing. It could be said in his favour that all legitimate authority had been put down and that there was a situation of force which only force could deal with. Europeans had been massacred. Every effort had been made to secure joint action—European, Anglo-French, Anglo-Turkish—but in vain. In the last resort we acted alone, first to destroy the forts threatening the fleet which was going about its legitimate business; secondly, to substitute peace and order for anarchy and conflict in a country through which our vital communications passed, and where it had already been thought right to establish an international (Anglo-French) financial control in the interests of the population and of the bondholders alike. Had we proceeded to annexation or to the declaration of a protectorate, there would have been grave international disturbance. When Salisbury succeeded Gladstone in 1885 he did not reverse Gladstone's policy; there was to be no annexation; there would be control, with the minimum of interference; we should be free to determine the date and terms of our withdrawal; if we were to withdraw, we should reserve certain rights of re-entry for ourselves; meanwhile the policy of economic restoration would continue. The attempt which Salisbury made in 1887 to settle with Turkey the terms

[6] *England, 1870–1914*, p. 86.
[7] Morley, *Life of William Ewart Gladstone*, Macmillan, London, 1903, iii. 84–85.

of a conditional withdrawal on these lines was frustrated by France and Russia, and he was to express the heartfelt wish that we had never gone into Egypt.

Gladstone had acted out of character; but that was perhaps no great matter. The public interest often requires that doctrinaires, when they come to power, should put their doctrines temporarily away. What was important was that he had acted as Disraeli might have done, such was the compulsion of events. If it was better to act than not to act; and if the action taken conformed to the limitations held to be imposed by the existing situation and by force of circumstances, then the action was defensible. Statesmen, any more than other men, cannot be expected to foresee all the consequences of their acts or to know of a surety today what will happen tomorrow. Gladstone did not foresee the long years of embarrassment into which his action would bring us; nor, on the other hand, could he foresee what great benefit our presence in Egypt would be to us in the two World Wars of the twentieth century.

At the end of his *Life of Gladstone*, John Morley asked: 'When was Britain stronger, richer, more honoured among the nations—I do not say always among the diplomatic chancelleries and governments— than in the years when Mr Gladstone was at the zenith of his authority among us?' This question, it will be noted, embodies a qualification of truly Gladstonian amplitude in the distinction which it draws between popular and governmental opinion. It would indeed be hard to contend that we stood high in the estimation of foreign governments during the period of Gladstone's administrations of 1868–74 and 1880–85. That we stood high in popular esteem abroad is perhaps more probable. But, though this might be agreeable, it would by itself be of limited value as a contribution to our international standing in terms of practical politics. Our Italian policy in 1859–61 won the acclaim of liberal opinion, but it created a scandal among foreign governments that for a while undermined our influence in their councils. Our policy in the eastern question and particularly at the Congress of Berlin was condemned by liberal opinion, but it brought us for a short time to a high point of our influence in Europe.

From that point we certainly descended in the years between 1880 and 1885. It was Salisbury's care, when he came to power, to substitute a policy of active and concrete initiative in Europe for a policy which, like Gladstone's, lacked coherent direction, and to have regard to British political interests rather than for British political sympathies in his transactions with foreign governments. By his handling of the Bulgarian crisis in 1885–86, 'in seven months he had raised England from a position of impotent isolation to one of acknowledged leadership in Europe,'[8] and he had achieved what the Queen called a 'triumphant success'. But diplomatic triumphs (for which Salisbury had small taste) are short-lived. Before long the Queen was reproaching him unjustly for what she held to be a diplomatic triumph by Russia over Great Britain, also in connection with Bulgaria.

For over ten years between 1887 and 1900, Salisbury combined the office of Foreign Secretary with that of Prime Minister. For much of that time, his freedom of manœuvre in a most active phase in the development of European politics was restricted by the leverage placed in Germany's hands by our occupation of Egypt and by the international financial arrangements which followed it. Disraeli and Salisbury had weakened the dangerous Three Emperors' League by promoting a cooling of relations between Germany and Russia; but Bismarck in his turn, while doing his best to patch up the league, had worked successfully for the estrangement of Great Britain and France. To make the best of this disagreeable posture of affairs, Salisbury deployed all the resources of his diplomatic skill. One of our greater Foreign Secretaries, he stands out among the statesmen of his time.

No one could have been more unlike Gladstone in his approach to international affairs. He engaged in no crusades: the only cause that moved him was the suppression of the slave-trade.[9] Again, while Gladstone had little understanding of, and no patience with, the intricate manœuvres of the European chancelleries, Salisbury had an 'easy familiarity with the hidden courses of international happenings', and could take initiatives and move with confidence in the field of diplomacy. He had no patience with 'that spirit of haughty and sullen isolation which,' he said, 'has been dignified by the name of "non-intervention" '. His policy was the policy of 'neighbourliness'. 'We are,' he said in 1888, 'part of the community of Europe and we must do our duty as such.'

[8] Lady Gwendolen Cecil, *Life of Robert, Marquis of Salisbury*, Hodder and Stoughton, London, 1932, iii. 289.
[9] In this, if in not much else, he was at one with Palmerston. Towards the end of his life, Palmerston said that nothing in his record had given him greater pleasure than forcing the Brazilians to abolish the slave-trade.

By his responsive understanding, his detached judgment and his sense of justice and moderation he acquired, like Castlereagh, an outstanding position of influence in the councils of Europe. Like Castlereagh, he preferred to work unobtrusively and not to trumpet his successes. 'A diplomatist's glory,' he said, 'is the most ephemeral of all forms of that transient reward . . . There is nothing dramatic in the successes of a diplomatist. His victories are made up of a series of microscopic advantages; of a judicious suggestion here, of an opportune civility there, of a wise concession at one moment and a farsighted persistence at another: of sleepless tact, immovable calmness, and patience that no folly, no provocation, no blunders can shake.'[10] In his methods of work, he was peculiar. He had a small inner junior official secretariat with whom he sometimes worked in isolation from the Foreign Office as a whole and through whom he would conduct policies of which his Under-Secretaries might be kept in ignorance. Important communications from foreign governments were sometimes kept secret from his department. He would sometimes omit to make records of even important conversations with foreign ambassadors. He worked much away from the Foreign Office and did much business, even to the extent of conveying instructions, by way of personal letter.[11]

Unlike Gladstone, he had little sympathy with, or much belief in the virtue of, the self-determination of peoples. But he saw clearly enough that the independence of the Balkan peoples could erect a barrier against Russia; and though he looked on Egyptian nationalism as a 'fashion or moral epidemic of the day', he foresaw the time when Egypt would 'insist on being free from Turkey, or England, or anybody else.' A Tory of the older fashion, he was not an imperialist in the same sense as were the Tory democrat, Disraeli, or the Radical, Chamberlain, or the Whig, Rosebery. Unlike Disraeli and Chamberlain, he was moved by no imperial mission. Unlike Rosebery, he had no desire to place an Anglo-Saxon impress upon the world. Yet during his premiership the Empire received vast accessions of territory and population.

He was far from being the conventional type of English nobleman. He had no love of field sports. He liked nothing better than to slip

[10] These words were applied to Castlereagh in a study of his career contributed to the *Quarterly Review* in January 1862.
[11] It was Salisbury who inaugurated the system of printing Foreign Office telegrams for circulation to the Cabinet. He was also the first to bring a typist into the Office.

away to his villa at Dieppe. He was once refused admission to the Casino at Monte Carlo because of the unconventionality of his attire. He stood alone with Melbourne and Disraeli in the affection and confidence of the Queen. Disraeli said of him that he was the only man of real courage that it had ever been his lot to work with.

The problem which faced Salisbury may now be examined. In his article in the *Encyclopaedia Britannica* on 'The Balance of Power', published in 1875 (p. 161), Henry Reeve had argued that, in the absence of a concert of Europe operating a balance of power, and in substitution (so far as Great Britain was concerned) for a policy of non-intervention, there was need of a positive basis for international relationships, a restoration of the balance of power stabilized by a series of international treaties. It was this course which the governments of continental Europe now adopted. The first momentous and ill-fated step along this road was Bismarck's treaty with Austria-Hungary of 1879.

In this new phase of international politics, Great Britain was placed at a disadvantage by three circumstances.

The first was her reluctance to enter into binding commitments to act in circumstances which could not be foreseen. As Lord Salisbury put it to the Austrian ambassador on January 20th 1897: 'The institutions under which we lived entirely prevented Her Majesty's Government from making any engagements with respect to the military or naval action of England upon contingencies which had not yet arisen': but this meant retaining 'full liberty of action'. There was hardly a statesman from Castlereagh onwards who had not enunciated this principle. Interventionists and non-interventionists held to it alike. Alike, they cherished the policy of the free hand. Where they differed would be in the extent to which the free hand should be practised, whether in threat or in action. The only commitments into which they would enter—and these some of them were inclined to whittle away—were those involved in an area such as the Low Countries, held to be vital to the security of the homeland, or an area like the Near East, held to be vital to our communications with India, Australasia and the Far East. These, as Philip Currie,[12] Assistant Under-Secretary in the Foreign Office, said in 1885, were the two questions on which Great Britain would fight—if she had an ally.

[12] Later Sir Philip (and Lord) Currie, Permanent Under-Secretary and ambassador at Constantinople and Rome.

A second disadvantage was one which reduced our standing and reliability as a possible ally in the eyes of continental statesmen, namely the constitutional procedures which required the major steps in our foreign policy to be disclosed to and debated in Parliament. Bismarck said: 'It is difficult to embark upon and conclude reliable agreements with England otherwise than in full publicity before all Europe. But such public negotiations, at the instant of their inception, and before anything has been achieved, exercise a detrimental influence upon the majority of our other European relationships.' This need for publicity was clear in the minds of British ministers. Clarendon had written to Lord A. Loftus, H.M. Ambassador in Berlin, on March 9th 1870: 'The people everywhere are claiming and must obtain a larger share in the administration of their own affairs.' But, forgetting the public clamour for war in England in 1853, and not foreseeing the war-fever in France and Germany later in 1870 and again in England in 1878, he added, optimistically: 'In proportion as they do the chances of causeless wars will diminish.'[13]

The third disadvantage arose from Great Britain's preoccupation with her world-wide overseas interests. For a continental power to ally itself with Great Britain might be, as Germany was to realize, to risk involvement in overseas conflicts in which it would have no desire and no interest to engage itself.

In the course of European treaty-making which now opened, Great Britain took little part.

Bismarck's settled aim was to perpetuate the association of the despotic courts in its later form of the League of Three Emperors of 1873. But the rise of Balkan nationalism which Russia, for Slavophile reasons, could hardly fail to support, and which Austria, in view of her own Slav populations, could hardly fail to resist, had for the moment divided Russia and Austria in a region which, in Russian eyes, was perhaps at this period second only to Poland in importance, and which to Austria, owing to her retreats in Italy and in Germany, was now all-important. By failing to afford Russia all the support she needed in 1878, Bismarck had caused some estrangement with St Petersburg. His great decision was now to choose Austria-Hungary as an ally. Once the alliance was made, he would

[13] Salisbury characteristically took the contrary view. He thought that the increasing destructiveness of weapons of war would make war less rather than more likely to break out; and that if war came, it would be more likely to be caused by popular clamour than by the acts of Governments.

hope to reconcile Austria and Russia. The treaty provided for a defensive alliance between Germany and Austria against Russia, and for benevolent neutrality in case of war with any other power. No such treaty between the great powers had been made in peace-time since the eighteenth century.

Bismarck was linking his own national state with an Empire which could not continue to exist if the principle of nationality should prevail. He was allying himself to a state whose vital interest was in the Balkans and the Black Sea, where Germany at this time had no direct interest and no desire to play a part. It was conflict between Austria and Russia over the Balkans involving Germany as Austria's ally which precipitated the First World War. Bismarck was thus taking a first, inadvertent step towards the catastrophe of 1914.

The treaties by which Bismarck contrived to build up his system of stability in Europe were achieved, it has been said, by a series of conjuring tricks. The German-Austrian Alliance of 1879 was followed by two feats of sleight of hand—the revival of the League of Three Emperors in 1881 and the conclusion of the Triple Alliance of 1882. The first was secured by offering Russia what, since 1878, she had most needed, namely a measure of security against Great Britain in the Straits and the Black Sea, where she still had no fleet. The second conferred on Italy a much desired status in Europe and gave Austria the assurance of Italian neutrality in case of war with Russia.

Historians have pointed to the inconsistency of Bismarck's operations, one with another. In his search for stability in Europe, he allied himself with two restless powers which had European ambitions: Austria, with her civilizing mission (*Drang nach Osten*) in the Balkans, and Italy with her eyes on Trieste and North Africa. The ambitions of France (apart from Alsace-Lorraine, not to be forgotten but not yet to be spoken of) and of Russia lay increasingly outside Europe. While the League of Three Emperors was designed to promote co-operation between Austria and Russia, the Triple Alliance was framed to meet the case of a war between them. Its immediate purpose seems to have been to bring Italy into friendship with the central powers so that she would not side with Russia. This was in practice immaterial. So long as the strongest power in Europe was bent on lending stability to a disposition of forces favourable to itself, peace in Europe could be preserved. So long as that power did not challenge the ambitions outside Europe of the peripheral powers, Great Britain and Russia, these would have the less call to intervene. In attending to her affairs in the wider world, Great Britain would expect to find in her path either France or Russia, but not Germany or Austria-Hungary or Italy.

Or so one might have thought. But Bismarck, in order to keep France and Russia apart, began courting France. In order to lend verisimilitude to his approaches, he gave them an anti-British turn by embarking deliberately upon a colonial policy. It also suited him in his internal policies to turn domestic opinion away from expansion in Europe towards expansion abroad, and to set up a measure of international tension. His acquisition of territory in South-west Africa in 1884, though provocatively staged, failed to disturb British opinion. He tried to pick quarrels in New Guinea and in East Africa. His suggestions to the French for a maritime league against Great Britain in 1884 and 1885 were coolly received. This had one good result. It roused the British out of their torpor about the Navy. From the naval scares of 1888 and 1893 dates the beginning of the creation of a great new navy which was to reach the peak of its ascendancy before the end of the century. The naval estimates, which amounted to £10·2 million in 1880 and to £13·8 million in 1890, had by 1900 risen to £29·2 million.

We now come to one of the more curious episodes in our late nineteenth-century history, and one which is not much remembered, the so-called Mediterranean agreements of 1887. It was Salisbury, the reputed exponent of what he himself ironically called 'splendid isolation', who entered into those commitments, the first of which, the agreement with Italy, was, in his own words, 'as close an alliance as the Parliamentary character of our institutions will permit'. These agreements, the first with Italy, of February 1887 (extended to Austria in March), and the second, with Italy and Austria of December of the same year, were symptomatic of British weakness in a Europe which seemed, though perhaps delusively, to be on the brink of war. It is true that Salisbury scored a success over Russia about Bulgaria in 1885, and that Gladstone had, a little earlier, by well-judged resolution, halted a Russian advance on the borders of Afghanistan. But our position in Europe was not strong. In 1885, under Bismarck's leadership, the great powers of Europe combined to issue a successful warning to the Turks not to accede to the British request for a passage through the Straits. We were also forced in 1887, under pressure from France and Russia, to give up our agreement with Turkey about withdrawal from Egypt. We were particularly

221

conscious of weakness at sea. The Mediterranean agreements would not have been made a few years later, when British naval predominance had again been assured. They derived from the continuing state of tension with France over Egypt and, more particularly, from the new and serious crisis that had arisen in the Near East over the declaration of union of the two Bulgarias, which had been separated at the Congress of Berlin. They may be explained by the preoccupation with the eastern Mediterranean and the Aegean and the Straits which haunted British minds at this period, and by the consciousness of the need for diplomatic support against France and Russia in Egypt. For Salisbury, isolation—'the abyss of isolation', as he called it—was at this juncture not at all splendid but distinctly disagreeable. Britain, he told the Queen in January 1887, 'cannot in the present state of public opinion interfere with any decisive action abroad . . . We have absolutely no power to restrain either France or Germany, while all the power . . . we have will be needed to defend our influence in the South-east of Europe.' 'If,' he wrote to her in the following month, 'in the present grouping of nations . . . England was left out in isolation, it might well happen that the adversaries who are coming against each other on the Continent, might treat the English empire as divisible booty, by which their differences might be adjusted,' and, though England could defend herself, it would be at fearful risk and cost.

It is a commonly stated view that British policy in Europe at this time was coloured by the confidence felt by all in the capacity of the Royal Navy to protect the coasts from invasion and to safeguard trade routes and overseas interests. It may be admitted that, in the light of history, Great Britain did enjoy something like complete security for most of the second half of the nineteenth century. But this is not to say that her statesmen were without anxiety. They did not have the advantage of piercing the future. They could only contemplate, and do their best to guard against, the perils which the future might bring. It was not Bismarck alone who was perturbed by the spectre of hostile coalitions. The minds of British statesmen could never entirely relax their anxious scanning of the continental scene and, as the years passed on towards the end of the century, their anxiety grew.

The Mediterranean agreements were supported, even promoted, by Bismarck, who wanted to see Great Britain linked to the Triple Alliance and committed (so far as she could be committed to anything) to Italy, the power which, rather than Germany, would be the prime support of Austria should the latter run into war with Russia over the Balkans. Like most of the treaties or understandings, formal or informal, contracted at this period among the powers of Europe, these agreements betrayed a desire on the part of each of the parties to get the other party or parties to pull his particular chestnuts out of the fire for him.

What the Italians asked for in the first agreement was the maintenance of the *status quo* in the Mediterranean, Adriatic, Aegean and Black Sea. They offered support for Great Britain in Egypt in return for British support in Tripoli and Cyrenaica against invasion by a third power. The weight of this support would thus be primarily against France. In reply to this, all that Salisbury could offer was the same kind of help in Tripoli as the Italians would give in Egypt. For the rest, he could only promise support 'in general and to the extent that circumstances shall permit'. Salisbury's subsequent exchange of notes with Austria gave a vague assurance in regard to Russia, namely the maintenance of the *status quo*, particularly in the Aegean and Black Seas, though not in the Balkans. Salisbury had gained his main objective, which was diplomatic support in the Egyptian question, and he had secured it without giving any pledge of action.

Between the first and second Mediterranean agreements, Bismarck renewed the Triple Alliance and, in June 1887, performed another of his conjuring tricks, namely the secret conclusion of the so-called Reinsurance Treaty with Russia. Bismarck's settled policy, in spite of his complex of alliances, was never to break with Russia, and never to support Austria, except defensively, against Russia. The second Mediterranean agreement, which had in fact little to do with the Mediterranean, was more specific than the first. It was directed against Russia rather than against France. The three powers agreed to maintain the *status quo* in the Near East, that is to say, the freedom of the Straits, the Turkish position in Asia Minor (this was new, and inserted at Salisbury's suggestion) and her suzerainty in Bulgaria. The Italian fleet would still be of some value as a counter to France in the Mediterranean. For a government which, traditionally, declined to enter into commitments to take action in circumstances that could not be foreseen, and which was reputed to follow a policy of isolation, this was going very far. This agreement, like the first, was kept secret, and remained so until 1920.

The crowning act in the late nineteenth-century drama of treaty-making was the conclusion, after many vicissitudes of negotiation, of an alliance between the Autocrat of All the Russias and the President of the Third French Republic in January 1894. An impulse towards this was given by an Anglo-German *rapprochement*, which reached its high-water mark in 1890 with an agreement by which Germany, in return for the cession of Heligoland, surrendered her rights in Zanzibar and set limits to her claims in East Africa, as well as by French fears of rumoured new links between Great Britain and the Triple Alliance. In its early stages, the Franco-Russian understanding was a diplomatic *entente* which was anti-British rather than anti-German. But the alliance, when it came, would operate in restraint of Germany, and would ultimately bring Bismarck's system in Europe to an end. Meanwhile, whereas Great Britain had welcomed the German-Austrian alliance, since she hoped it would strengthen Austria against Russia, she disliked the Franco-Russian alliance because it associated the two powers with whom she was most at odds in the field of empire. Germany, now over-estimating the significance of these peripheral differences, assumed wrongly that Great Britain had no alternative but to come into the Triple Alliance on German terms. Great Britain had, however, at last one new element of security, namely a fleet of two-power standard. Nevertheless she was to become unpleasantly conscious of her isolation, especially at the time of the Boer War (1899-1902) when there was again talk of a continental league against Great Britain.

G. M. Young noted 'that passionate jealousy of England which for a generation was the most widely diffused emotion in Europe, a generation when it seemed at times not wholly out of reckoning that a second League of Cambrai might be formed for the spoliation of a greater Venice.'[14] The German historian, Max Lenz, had in 1900 propounded a slogan about a future war of the English Succession. The opportunity for this might well have appeared more propitious than ever. Great Britain was engaged, in a distant theatre, in a troublesome and costly war which was violently reprobated by European opinion. But in order that a compact of this kind may become effective, two things are necessary. There must first be a strong enough common interest among the participants to make it worth their while to face the responsibilities and to run the risks which it will entail. The fact was, however, that the conflict of

[14] *Victorian England*, p. 138.

interest among the three great powers, Germany, France and Russia, in European questions, their need to stand well with Great Britain on some issue or other, and their need also to have Great Britain in the background as an element in the balance, were more potent than any common interest which they might have in restraining or coercing Great Britain. There was at this time, as Bülow noted later, 'only a seeming community of interest against England in Europe.' As with France and the Empire in the time of Henry VIII, what the continental powers really wanted was our assistance rather than our destruction. Had Germany not annexed Alsace-Lorraine in 1871, there could have been a different story to tell. Russia at one time and Germany at another might propose joint action, but at no time would the others take the responsibility of assenting. The second requisite for the formation of a league is that, if action is contemplated, it can be carried into effect. If action meant naval action, the Royal Navy was still supreme. If it meant transporting contingents from among the European conscript millions, the Navy commanded all the seas and could bar the way. One possibility would have been for Russia to reopen the threat to India in Central Asia, and the Tsar did at one moment debate this possibility. But Russia held back: her interests were now more particularly directed to the Far East. Even if the league had been concluded, it could have done little.

Nevertheless the misgivings in the minds of British statesmen were not unjustified. They could not be sure that the league would not be formed. The fog of diplomacy is no less dense than the fog of war. They could not be confident that the policy of isolation would continue to serve. Grey, looking back in 1928, thought that the danger of complete isolation in the later years of the century had been greater than we knew at the time. However that might be, the realization of the hazards of isolation was sufficient to bring about a fundamental change of course in the new century. If the danger did not mature, the credit should go in part to the skill of our diplomacy, and in part to the stability, continuity and homogeneity of our national institutions. But it is attributable too, in some degree, to the general recognition of the services which Great Britain was rendering to the world, in the common interest as well as in her own, in setting herself to reduce international tension and to preserve the peace, in policing the seas, in providing a sure financial and commercial mechanism for the conduct of world trade, services which

P

were indispensable for the maintenance of the fabric of international life and which could be provided by no other power. We were to reap the rewards of our solid serviceability in the time of our greatest peril. Speaking of 1940, Sir Roy Harrod has said: 'What is remarkable is how neutrals and others continued to sell us their goods against sterling of restricted negotiability. That showed a notable confidence in us British, since our final victory was not so palpably obvious in the early years of the war; those living outside these islands backed our victory to the extent of giving us credit for thousands of millions of pounds, a fact insufficiently advertised. They did so in the confidence that sterling would become negotiable again after the war.'[15] The wheel had come full circle. The country that had so often subsidized coalitions against tyranny, was now herself being buttressed by financial aid from abroad.

Both at Fashoda in 1898 and in South Africa in 1899–1902 Great Britain pursued her own courses without interference from the Continent, winning a diplomatic victory over France on the Upper Nile and a hard-won military victory over the Boers. The Navy, if it was strong enough, was still sufficient to allow us to act alone: but this would never be so again. British naval supremacy and the *Pax Britannica* which it established upon the seas might be a convenient and comforting thing for the United Kingdom. Continental opinion, while acknowledging the benefits which it conferred and the moderation with which it was exercised, might feel that its embrace was too close, its containment too constricting, its encirclement too complete. The need to break out became imperative, especially in the German mind, when, in the late 1890s, German interest moved beyond the confines of the European balance of power into the realm of world politics. 'If there is anything certain in the history of the world,' said Friedrich Naumann in 1900, 'it is the future outbreak of a world war, i.e. a war fought by those who seek to deliver themselves from England.' The great German historian Meinecke, writing in 1916, said: 'Universal maritime supremacy is only another form of universal monarchy, which cannot be tolerated and must, sooner or later, fail.'[16] But Germany had not been designated by the iron laws of history, as German historians too confidently predicted, to be the agent for the liberation of the Continent from the bondage of

---

[15] *The Listener*, February 12th 1959, p. 271.
[16] Quotations from Ludwig Dehio, *Germany and World Politics in the Twentieth Century*, Chatto and Windus, London, 1959, pp. 82, 58.

British naval power. The coalition, when it came, would be with, not against, England, and against, not with, Germany. But this is to anticipate. In the closing years of the century it was to Germany that Great Britain first vainly turned, through Chamberlain and through Lansdowne, when in search of support for the containment of Russian expansion in the Far East, which threatened the seemingly all-important British political and commercial interests in China, particularly in the Yangtse valley. The price demanded by Germany was full British accession to the Triple Alliance, a price which a still isolationist government could not pay.

The meaning of the 'splendid isolation' (the phrase seems to have been coined by G. E. Foster, a member of the Canadian Parliament) in which Great Britain found herself in the last years of the nineteenth century is not easy to define, and its period is not easy to date. Substantially, it meant a growing aloofness from European concerns and from the balance of power as a European mechanism. There was as yet no single European power which seemed likely to secure a decisive mastery on the Continent. The one European question which had dominated British policy for most of the century, the question of the Straits, had become of less moment now that Russia had fixed her ambitions on the Far East. We were strong enough to hold Egypt, and this was sufficient to safeguard our position in the Eastern Mediterranean. The real problem was now the Far East, and here, so far from wishing to isolate ourselves, we earnestly sought allies, before, during and after the Boer War. The difficulty was that we could not find an ally in Europe without paying a price in Europe. Germany was not willing to support us against Russia in the Far East unless we would support Austria-Hungary against Russia in Europe. We were isolated because we would not pay the price of alliance.

It may be worth noting some of the landmarks in this period of isolation. In 1891, Salisbury could lay it down that the policy should be 'to keep absolutely clear of engagements and to leave the country free to take any action which it might think fit in the event of a war.' But he still held to the Mediterranean agreements. In 1895, Great Britain was elbowed out of the revision of the settlement after the Sino-Japanese War by Russia, France and Germany. In the same year, Salisbury disinterested himself in the Straits, turned his thoughts to the partition of Turkey and was ready to let Russia have Constantinople. He seems to have come to the view that the independence

227

of Turkey was no longer a British interest. In 1896, Great Britain decided to stay on in Egypt (the occupation of which was still temporary and provisional) and to reconquer the Sudan for Egypt (which Kitchener did in 1898), the naval advice being that the way to check Russia was not in the Dardanelles but 'by holding Egypt against all comers and making Alexandria a naval base'. We no longer needed Austria and Italy. In January 1897, Salisbury declined to renew the second Mediterranean agreement, since the defence of Constantinople was 'an antiquated standpoint'. In the year of the Diamond Jubilee, British isolation seemed to be complete.

Whatever date one chooses for the inauguration of the period of 'splendid isolation', and whether one dates its close from the Anglo-Japanese Alliance of 1902 or from the Anglo-French Entente of 1904, it was of brief duration, a mere ten years or less, a fleeting and uncharacteristic episode in our history.[17] During most of the period, our attempts to reach an alliance with Germany against Russia and France in the Far East (as distinct from accession to the Triple Alliance in Europe) were persistent and unavailing. Germany's interests in China were not substantial enough to make it worth her while to run risks with Russia and France in Europe unless Great Britain would give a guarantee in Europe. Germany, as the Kaiser said, would not 'go to war with Russia for the purpose of driving her out of China'. In 1899, Chamberlain offered British support (against Russia) for the German project for a Baghdad railway, and (against France) for an Anglo-German partition of Morocco. In 1900, Lansdowne tried to persuade the Germans to join Great Britain in preventing French participation in any future war between Russia and Japan. In 1901, Lansdowne tried more than once for a defensive alliance between Great Britain and Germany. This the Germans evaded, as usual, by repeating that Great Britain should instead join the Triple Alliance. France and Russia began to talk of a convention for joint military and naval action against Great Britain. It was at this point that Japan intervened to offer Great Britain the alliance which she required. With Japan, as had not been possible with Germany, Great Britain could find a common interest substantial enough to form the basis of a treaty.

[17] The determination of the period would depend on the definition of the term 'isolation'. When Joseph Chamberlain said in May 1898: 'Since the Crimean War, nearly fifty years ago, the policy of this country has been a policy of strict isolation', he was either being unhistorical or giving the word a very narrow interpretation.

Late Victorian Afterglow

In order to throw further light on Great Britain's position in the world, it will be well to look at the outcome of her encounters with the United States at the turn of the century. There were four main matters of controversy; the Venezuelan boundary, the Panama Canal, the Venezuelan claims and the Alaskan boundary.

In the dispute between Great Britain and Venezuela about the boundary between Venezuela and British Guiana, the United States Government intervened in order to press a solution by arbitration upon the British Government. In doing so, the Democratic President Grover Cleveland's Secretary of State, Richard Olney, used language of unaccustomed vigour in the relations between the two countries. In a note of July 1895, Olney claimed that the honour and interests of the United States were involved; that by advancing her boundary line against a weaker American state and refusing to arbitrate it, Great Britain was violating the Monroe Doctrine and thus committing 'an act of unfriendliness towards the United States'. He then went on to assert, in words that, as has been said by American historians, 'alarmed Latin America, insulted Canada, and challenged England':[18] 'Today the United States is practically sovereign on this continent, and its fiat is law upon subjects to which it confines its interposition.' After thus stretching the Monroe Doctrine to the limit, Olney then delivered a threat. This was so, he said, because 'in addition to all other grounds, its infinite resources combined with its isolated position render it master of the situation and practically invulnerable as against any or all other powers.' This might be true enough in terms of geography but it was more questionable in terms of available power. Great Britain had at that time forty-four battleships and forty-one first-class cruisers afloat, while the United States could count but two second-class battleships and twelve cruisers. But, on the other hand, Great Britain had preoccupations in Europe; and Canada was vulnerable.

Salisbury's reply to Olney's 'twenty-inch gun', not delivered until November 1895, was cool and cogent. The Monroe Doctrine must be mentioned with respect, but 'no statesman, however eminent, and no nation, however powerful, are competent to insert into a code of international law a novel principle which was never recognized before.' The Venezuela boundary had nothing to do with the Monroe Doctrine. 'It was simply the determination of the frontier of a British

[18] Morison and Commager, *The Growth of the American Republic*, Oxford University Press, 1942, ii. 320.

possession which belonged to the throne of England long before the Republic of Venezuela came into existence.'

Later in the year, in December, in a message to Congress, President Cleveland said that the time had come for the United States, after due investigation, to determine the true line for herself; after which it would, in his opinion, 'be the duty of the United States to resist by every means in its power as a wilful aggression upon its rights and interests the appropriation by Great Britain of any lands or the exercise of governmental jurisdiction over any territory which after investigation we have determined by right belongs to Venezuela.' 'This,' said R. C. K. Ensor, 'was certainly one of the most unexpected, least warranted, and least excusable steps ever taken in modern times by a Great Power.'[19]

A wave of jingoism spread over the United States, now moving into her period of open imperialism; but, as will almost always happen, an opposition began to raise its voice, and there were powerful pleas in favour of moderation. The British public had, on the whole, remained cool. The Kaiser's telegram to President Kruger at the time of the Jameson raid in January 1896 revealed, by a sudden flash, a new trend in German policy and drove Venezuela out of their heads. In any event, there was a widely held view that a war against the United States 'would be a crime against the laws of God and man'. Salisbury publicly recognized that it was as natural for the United States to take an interest in Venezuela as for Great Britain to feel an interest in the Low Countries. After a visit by Joseph Chamberlain to the United States, a compromise was reached. Great Britain accepted arbitration; but it was not the enforced arbitration by the United States which Olney had proposed. Long-held British territory claimed by the Venezuelans was in effect excluded from it, and there was to be arbitration by a tribunal on which both Great Britain and the United States were represented together with a neutral member. The award, rendered in October 1899, confirmed the line long ago put forward by Aberdeen, with one appreciable deviation in favour of Venezuela. The British Government and people, behaving with calm and dignity in face of some irresponsible rodomontade, came well out of this episode. But it was becoming clear that the United States was now a power to be reckoned with, and that Great Britain, in her existing situation in Europe, could not afford to quarrel with her.

[19] *England, 1870–1914*, p. 230.

Late Victorian Afterglow

In the Panama Isthmian controversy, settled by the treaty concluded in November 1901 between John Hay, Secretary of State in the administration of Presidents McKinley and Theodore Roosevelt, and the British ambassador, Sir Julian (later Lord) Pauncefote, Great Britain had much the worst of the deal. Relations between the two countries had been greatly improved by the friendly British attitude during the Spanish-American War of 1898 and by the friendly American attitude during the Boer War. But Great Britain needed good relations more than did the United States, and it was she (and, on occasion, Canada) who had to pay the price for them. With the growth of the imperialist spirit, and the establishment of an American territorial stake in the Far East (i.e. in the Philippines) after the war with Spain, the construction and control of the Panama Canal became, for naval and other reasons, an increasingly vital interest for the United States. What the Hay–Pauncefote Treaty did, in effect, was to abrogate the limitations upon American control of the projected Canal embodied in the Clayton–Bulwer Treaty of 1850. On this, the United States was now strong enough and determined enough to insist, and Great Britain, with the Boer War on her hands, was in no position to maintain what the Americans held to be an obsolete and outdated treaty, as indeed it was. The American attitude was: 'The American people mean to have the Canal and they mean to control it. . . . England does not care enough about it to go to war . . . and it would be ruinous (for her) if she did make war on us.' There was to be an 'American canal on American soil for the American people'. The Canadians had wanted to make the Isthmus one side of a bargain which would also deal with the Alaskan boundary; but London was constrained to compound on the Canal question in isolation, leaving Alaska aside. A first treaty, too favourable to Great Britain, raised a violent outcry in the United States and was amended by the Senate, whereupon Great Britain declined to ratify. In the second and final treaty, ratified by the Senate in February, 1902, Great Britain conceded every major American demand and gained nothing concrete in return. In the circumstances, the price was probably worth paying. Great Britain needed United States friendship and could no longer contest United States predominance in the Caribbean as Palmerston had done. After the ratification of the Hay–Pauncefote Treaty, Great Britain withdrew naval forces from the West Indies.

In the case of the Alaskan boundary, which came next, the price paid was, in Canadian eyes, immoderately high. The Canadians felt that it was they who were bearing the burden of the good relations with Washington which were so necessary to London. What was in dispute in the Alaskan case was the landward boundary of the long strip of Alaskan territory stretching southwards down the seaboard towards British Columbia and cutting off the Canadian territory of the Yukon and northern British Columbia from the Pacific. The boundary between Alaska and Canada had been imprecisely described in the Anglo-Russian Treaty of 1825. The Canadians now claimed that this boundary should cross the fjord-like inlets so as to give them access to the sea, and not run round the heads of the inlets and well inland, as the Americans maintained. The main United States interest was Skagway, the port of entry to the Klondyke goldfields. The Canadian claim was weak, but it was thought that something might be secured from an arbitration. President Theodore Roosevelt used 'the big stick' and did anything but 'speak softly'. As he told Hay, he was going 'to be ugly'.[20] He would not allow a genuine arbitration, but insisted on a joint tribunal of jurists, three from each side, to act by a majority. The justices of the United States Supreme Court understandably declined to serve. Roosevelt, in addition to the Secretary of State, Elihu Root, appointed as arbitrators two senators who had little or no claim to be jurists and could not be called impartial. The British arbitrators were the Lord Chief Justice, Lord Alverstone, and two Canadian jurists of repute. Roosevelt made it plain that he expected a political and not a juridical decision. If the tribunal failed to agree he would 'request Congress to make an appropriation which will enable me to run the boundary on my own hook . . . without any further regard to the attitude of England and Canada.' Lord Alverstone after an initial deadlock took the American side, in what was held at the time to be a political not a juridical award. The award was rendered in October 1903. The two Canadian Commissioners refused to sign it on the ground that it lacked proper juridical character. Roosevelt had won a diplomatic triumph, based upon a strong case, mercilessly pursued. The Canadian claim may have been ill-founded (a distinguished United States historian has called it 'preposterous'), but the episode was an un-

[20] It would be fair to apply to Uncle Sam in this period the words used about John Bull in an earlier period by Edward Everett, one-time United States minister in London: 'In his foreign politics he is selfish and grasping, and when he dares, insolent.' The international manners of the United States in her high period of imperialism left much to be desired.

edifying one which reflected no credit on the United States. Canada had paid, though Canadian historians can now look on the affair more objectively than was possible at the time. Canada would have had nothing to gain from war, or from armed intervention on the part of the United States. The long frontier was now complete. From that day to this, as she came to conduct her own foreign policy, the cost to her of that frontier (now to be unarmed, as it had not always been in the past) would be no more than an unremitting alertness to withstand the embraces of the great republic, her friendly but over-powering and economically ruthless neighbour, as an independent member of the Commonwealth in allegiance to her own sovereign and as a state 'strongly monarchical in sentiment and as strongly republican in practice.'[21]

If further evidence is needed to show the value attached by Great Britain to her relations with the United States, it can be furnished by the Anglo-German attempt to enforce by naval action, including blockade and bombardment, the payment of claims for damage and interest on debt by Venezuela in 1902. The British claims were substantial, the German claims small. It was unfortunate that we were tied up with the Germans, whose relations with the Americans were bad (the Americans suspected the Germans, not without reason, of aiming to break down the Monroe Doctrine); and there was strong distaste in England for this connection. Under pressure from public opinion, the Government extricated themselves. In the end, the claims were referred to arbitration at The Hague. So great was the importance attached in London to the maintenance of American friendship that no more than a hint of danger to good relations with Washington was enough to halt our efforts to recover our just debts from a defaulting state.

Rising above political and economic embarrassments of which the people at large may not have been deeply conscious, England celebrated the Golden and Diamond Jubilees of Queen Victoria in 1887 and 1897. They were both festivals of Empire, followed by colonial conferences, as well as being demonstrations of personal loyalty and devotion to the sovereign. In 1887, the personal element was uppermost: in 1897, the imperialism was more self-conscious than before. In 1887, naval weakness and recent embarrassments in the foreign field did not mar the exuberance and overwhelming

[21] A. R. M. Lower, *Colony to Nation, A History of Canada*, Longmans, London, 1953, p. 120.

self-confidence of a nation-wide manifestation. In 1897, naval supremacy[22] could not wholly dispel a sense of uneasiness. Foreign monarchs and colonial prime ministers and rulers might congregate as before. The people might still be cocksure and the popular Press as much given to national swagger. But domestic political life had long been gravely racked by the Irish question, and inquiring minds would also ask themselves whether the basis of British greatness was as sound and enduring as it had been; whether, with the rising challenge to our commercial and industrial supremacy, the liberal principles of *laissez-faire*, free trade and free enterprise, were the best means to ensure the greatest happiness of the greatest number; or whether the new imperialism was as worthy a cause as it had seemed to be. Schoolboys a few years later, on the newly established Empire Day, would be marched up to salute the flag and would be required to write essays on the Empire: but they would also be taught to sing Kipling's 'Recessional', with its grim admonition to pause and reflect with due humility after the imperial self-congratulatory pomp of the Diamond Jubilee.

If one were to seek the highest achievement of that age, it might perhaps be on the human plane that one might find it, in Gladstone's administrative reforms and Disraeli's social reforms, but above all in the devoted work of our colonial administrators and especially in the work of the Indian Civil Service. We continued to send to India the best men we had, and began, as time went on, to train the best that India could supply. We gave India political unity, a uniform system of education based on a common language, a mature system of law, a civil administration of now legendary efficiency and integrity (if perhaps of old-fashioned ways and limited vision), sound finances, a superb army recruited from favoured communities, roads, railways and irrigation. The Indian Empire under its own government, subordinate though it might be to London, became an entity in its own right, with an impact upon British foreign policy and its own sphere of influence over neighbouring territories. This was achieved on the strength of the restored and again unquestioned

[22] In March 1898 we had twenty-nine battleships not more than fifteen years old. France had seventeen, Germany thirteen, Russia eleven, the United States five and Japan one. Gladstone had made his last protest against increases in the naval estimates when he finally retired from the government in 1894. 'The notion of establishing dominant . . . naval power in Europe' was, he said, militarism, which he had 'uniformly opposed'.

prestige of a small body of civilian officials and a moderate force of British troops. As one of the elder statesmen of India once remarked to the present writer, the British had given great gifts to India; equality before the law, the heritage of a great literature, the freedom of the individual and an instinct for liberal democracy. Some of these things may survive in the new, evolving India. Gifts these and other benefits may have been, but they were not free benefits. For all that was done in India, the Indian taxpayer paid, and paid heavily. Part of the interest on British investment in India in the last quarter of the century went to finance enterprises in other parts of the world. And the critic might suggest that there had been too much emphasis on law, order and justice and not enough creative imagination, initiative or sympathetic contact with or care for the life of the people, whether in agriculture and industry or in the field of human relations.

If the state of the Empire were the test, there need have been little cause for misgiving. The colonies of European settlement, though increasingly independent in outlook, were firmly attached to the Mother Country. The native dependencies were, it was held, enjoying the undoubted benefits of imperial rule. The Empire had become a part of the national consciousness. If there was pride in it, there was also a widespread sense of humanitarian mission. As Professor Nicholas Mansergh has justly observed: 'The sordid lure of easy wealth, the struggle for power, the lust for domination are motive forces well understood today, but the faith, the idealism, the passionate zeal to bring justice and civilization to the darker corners of Africa, whose wretched inhabitants were the victims of Arab slavery, of pest and disease, are things of which little is now understood.'[23] It was from these scourges that backward peoples were rescued by the so-called colonialism of the European powers. If today western governments, whether from self-interest or from a sense of human duty, are affording assistance to the under-developed peoples of Africa and Asia in their present plight of chronic under-nourishment, it is pertinent to remember that if, in part, their over-population is due to measures of health and hygiene introduced by the colonial powers, the backward peoples have in no small measure,

[23] *The Coming of the First World War*, Longmans, London, 1949, p. 42. The latest analyst of Empire, John Strachey, writing from a left-wing standpoint but in no unsympathetic spirit, concedes that '. . . of all the great imperialisms the British contained the greatest proportion of constructive elements.' (*The End of Empire*, p. 12.)

by their philoprogenitiveness, brought their troubles upon themselves.

'British Africa,' wrote Lord Lugard, 'was acquired not by groups of financiers, nor yet by the efforts of her statesmen, but in spite of them. It was the instinct of the British democracy which compelled us to take our share. When Mr. Gladstone's Cabinet in 1893 had decided to evacuate Uganda, he was told by his Scottish agent that if he did so he would have to evacuate Downing Street too.'[24] The wider public, enfranchised by the legislation of 1867 and 1884, had personal links with the settled colonies, thanks to the flow of emigration and to the newly developed postal communications. They also followed the exploits of a missionary-explorer like Livingstone in the journeys he undertook between 1851 and 1873, or of travellers like Speke and Stanley. For the world of finance, commerce and industry, the newly explored regions were fresh sources of raw materials and openings for trade and investment; and, under the impulse of steam-transport and of medical science and sanitation, their value in this respect became all the greater. In the 1880s, without encouragement from home, British interests in Africa were developed by the three great chartered companies—Goldie's Royal Niger Company (1886), Mackinnon's British East Africa Company (1888) and Rhodes's British South Africa Company (1889). At first against their will—since they thought that we already had enough territory in Africa—but later less reluctantly, the British Government were drawn in, and were led to annex or to declare protectorates, either in the interest of good government (brilliantly promoted by such administrators as Kirk in Zanzibar, Lugard in West Africa and Johnston in East Africa), or to protect the natives against private exploitation, or in order to keep other European governments out. Expansion in Africa and elsewhere had now become a factor in European politics, an outward projection of European rivalries which it was too dangerous for the powers to prosecute in Europe itself. The overseas ambitions of continental governments caused misgivings among British colonists which gained expression at the colonial conference of 1881. But the humanitarian motive, the imperative call to spread the benefits of civilization, was never far beneath the surface. 'If Great Britain yielded to [the new imperialism], she did so on compulsion, with a memory of past lessons, with a constant readiness to forgo advantages and co-operate with rivals, and without relinquishing for an instant that obligation of trusteeship to weaker races

[24] *The Dual Mandate in British Tropical Africa*, Edinburgh, 1926, p. 616.

which had been the glory of the humanitarians.'[25] The scramble for monopoly rights in colonial territories in Africa was little to the British taste. The British were still attached to free trade and the open door and, with the Portuguese, were alone in admitting all comers to equal rights in trade in their dependencies.

In the new scramble for Africa, the British had not been first in the field. King Leopold of the Belgians, by a personal initiative, had promoted an International Association of the Congo in 1879 which in 1884 gave place to a Congo Free State, recognized by the other powers. In 1881, the French occupied Tunis and raised the flag at Brazzaville on the Congo. In 1884 Bismarck, as a factor in his European policies, started to stake out claims and to acquire territories in South-west, East and West Central Africa. Continental European governments were much more directly concerned in these colonial moves than were the British Government, who were only roused to action when they saw their newly recognized objectives being threatened by foreign encroachments. The French went into Africa, with Bismarck's encouragement, with the deliberate and strongly pressed policy of reasserting their status as a great power after the defeat of 1870. The Germans went in at first in order to promote their objectives in Europe, and later in the mistaken belief that their territories in Africa (South-west Africa, German East Africa and the Cameroons) would supply an outlet for an emigrant German population.

A first allocation of 'spheres of influence'—a phrase now used for the first time—was made at the Berlin conference in 1884—a manifestation of the concert of Europe applied to Africa. According to this, the Congo basin became an ostensibly international Free State under the sovereignty of the King of the Belgians. Germany obtained the Cameroons and Togoland. France was allotted the belt lying north and west of the great Congo bend, while Great Britain secured the lower basin of the Niger. But this did not carry matters very far. The real scramble only began after the conference had closed, and continued for several years.

By three treaties signed in 1890, which have been described as the most positive achievements of Salisbury's foreign policy, and by later arrangements, Great Britain established her position in agreement with Portugal, Germany and France. It was in great measure thanks to Salisbury's initiative, diplomatic skill and reputation for

[25] Williamson, *A Short History of British Expansion,* ii. 166.

fair dealing, that the partition of Africa was carried out in a peaceful way on an enduring basis without a serious quarrel among the great powers. With Portugal, after an ultimatum, Great Britain successfully asserted her authority along a north–south axis in Mashonaland and Nyasaland as against the Portuguese aspiration for an east–west axis connecting the Portuguese colonies of Angola and Mozambique. With Germany, she succeeded in circumscribing German territory in German East Africa (now Tanganyika) and in erecting a barrier between German territory and the Nile Valley by consolidating her position in British East Africa (now Kenya) and Uganda. Since the British Government attached greater importance to colonial interests than to the claims of strategy in Europe, and did not yet foresee naval rivalry with Germany, Heligoland was ceded in return for a settlement in East Africa. With France, the potential conflict was more serious in that France was the most aggressively and deliberately expansive of the European colonizing powers. We faced two dangers from her. The first was the encirclement and infiltration of our West African possessions—Nigeria, Gold Coast and the rest. The second was the establishment of a French east–west sea-to-sea axis a few degrees north of the Equator, cutting across the upper Nile Valley in the Sudan. The first danger was peacefully warded off by Lugard's West African Frontier Force, and the position was stabilized by a convention concluded in 1898. The second was only averted, after Kitchener's courteous encounter with Marchand at Fashoda in 1898, at the cost of a crisis which seemed to have brought Great Britain and France close to war. In two other areas, difficulties with France were surmounted. The French annexation of Madagascar was recognized in return for French recognition of our position in Zanzibar. In South-east Asia, too, an accommodation was reached. Upper Burma was annexed in 1886 in the face of threatened French encroachment from Indo-China (Tongking, Annam and Cochin-China), and Siam was confirmed as an independent buffer state and a further barrier against French expansion.

If China did not suffer the fate of Africa and escaped partition, if not penetration, in spite of the disintegration of governmental authority, this was due first to the fact of a teeming population, not easily to be mastered, whose temper was to be shown by the violent anti-foreign Boxer rebellion of 1899–1900. It was attributable secondly to the fact that international rivalries in the Far East were more complex and more immediate than in Africa. Russia, the

United States and Japan were involved as well as the Western European powers. In a region so remote, the Western European powers would nibble: they would occupy key points and peg out spheres of influence and extort concessions, but they would not partition. Russia alone pressed forward, when the Japanese had been forced to disgorge their gains after the war with China in 1895. She seized Port Arthur and drove a spur of the newly completed Trans-Siberian railway to it across the Chinese province of Manchuria, and designed to take possession of Korea. The result was a collision with Japan, big with significance for the relations between Asia and Europe, in which, once again, as had occurred at Adowa a few years earlier, a European power was overcome in arms by a non-European power.

The last twenty years of the nineteenth century saw the development of what has been called economic imperialism. Its *modus operandi* was open Government support, if necessary by force, for the interests of private investors in foreign enterprises, leading to conquest or subjugation followed by permanent control or, at the very least, to the establishment of a measure of supervision over some aspects of internal life of the debtor country. In Canning's day there had been a clear rule that 'assistance would in no case extend to the claiming as from Government to Government the discharge of a debt due by a Foreign Government to an individual British subject.' By 1848, after a debate in the House of Commons, this doctrine was relaxed to the extent of saying that intervention in such cases was a right to be exercised with discretion. In 1867, Stanley declined to intervene on behalf of British bondholders in Venezuela. As late as 1873, the Corporation of Foreign Bondholders still took a cautious line; investors who went out for a high rate of interest took a risk with their eyes open, and the Government could not be expected to act on their behalf with its full weight. But by the middle 1870s there was a great change, precipitated by the failure of Egypt and Turkey to meet the charges on the heavy loans contracted by them on unfavourable terms and at high rates of interest, often through local intermediaries, with western money markets. European governments were now moved not only by the pressures which powerful financial houses could bring to bear upon them but also by the fear of internal chaos in such politically sensitive areas as those of the Straits and the Suez Canal. It was the advent of the loan to foreign governments, the appearance of the international financier, and the tendency of governments of creditor countries to use external investment as an instrument of foreign policy that made it now plausible to argue that one of the roots of imperialism lay in the export of capital. In Turkey, an international control was established over the foreign debt. In Egypt, a joint Anglo-French financial control was supplemented later by a six-power body and, as we have seen, Great Britain was led by a variety of motives to take over, in effect, the administration of the country itself. In all this, the influence of financial circles upon national policy cannot be denied, though it was far from being the sole determining factor. Of a different type was the action taken in order to secure openings for pioneers, as when, for example, in 1898, following upon similar action by other European governments, the Chinese Government was constrained by ultimatum to yield concessions to British concerns for the construction of railways in ten provinces, and to undertake not to allow other concessionaires into the Yangtse Valley.

The same kind of motive was to be discerned in the events which led to the Boer War in 1899, and there have been bitter controversy and conflicting judgments upon them. One of these judgments may be quoted: 'Here,' wrote Herbert Feis, 'the British Government, after long contemplation and doubt, undertook the direct support of an organized British group, controlling a vast investment, against a small republic which was moved by hatred and fear of losing its supremacy.'[26] This may have been so. The decisive impulse may have been the influence which the magnates of the Rand could bring to bear upon the Government, through the High Commissioner, Milner, and the Colonial Secretary, Chamberlain. But the Government in London was certainly reluctant. 'I see before us,' wrote the Prime Minister, Lord Salisbury, to Lord Lansdowne in August 1899, when war was impending, 'the necessity for considerable military effort—and all for people whom we despise, and for territory which will bring no profit and no power to England.' But there were influences both in London and in South Africa working for a forward policy. After the near hysteria of the Diamond Jubilee, there had been intense excitement over Omdurman and Fashoda. 'The taste of empire,' said the *Washington Post* in 1898, 'is in the mouth of the people even as the taste of blood in the jungle.' The British public, in one of its recurrent bellicose moods, was, as Grey afterwards noted, 'spoiling for a fight'. British subjects were being oppressed and should be protected. The colonies of European settlement were

[26] *Europe the World's Banker*, p. 111.

of like mind and sent substantial military contingents in support.

But another view is possible. It could be argued that the Boers were, in form and perhaps also in substance, the aggressors. The war was launched by an ultimatum from President Kruger. The Boer invasion of British territory was conveniently timed to catch the British at a military disadvantage and to give the Boers ample fodder for the mobile mounted forces in which their strength lay. It could be held to have been a well-matured act of aggression which only failed through faulty strategy to sweep the British out of the whole country.[27] The fundamental issue would thus be, not gold or diamonds, or the status of the foreign magnates, managers and mineworkers (the *Uitlanders*) who were, in Milner's phrase, being 'treated like helots' by an enriched, well-armed, tyrannical and anachronistic régime,[28] but the question who was to rule South Africa, the British or the Dutch, and whose system of government was to be applied to the native population. The answer to that question belongs to later history. The solution devised after the war—the grant in 1906 of colonial self-government to the Transvaal and Orange River territories, followed in 1910 by the establishment, on local initiative, of a unitary, not a federal, form of government of the four provinces with dominion status—was loudly acclaimed as a triumph of liberalism. Even Balfour, the leader of the Conservative opposition, said in August 1909: 'I do not believe the world shows anything like it in its whole history.' These acts of reconciliation, so liberal in intention, have confounded the expectations of their authors. Already by 1908, the Government was, as Milner said, in the hands of the Boer commandos. In the name of the principle of self-government and in face of protests from the radicals, the natives were handed over to the Boers without safeguards, illusory as such safeguards, however deeply entrenched, would, as experience has since shown, most probably have proved to be. Asquith's argument was that the whole scheme of union in South Africa would be wrecked if there

[27] Shortly before the issue of Kruger's ultimatum in September 1899, a prominent Orange Free Stater wrote: '. . . The only thing we are afraid of now is that Chamberlain, with his admitted fitfulness of temper, will cheat us out of the war, and consequently the opportunity of annexing the Cape Colony and Natal, and forming the Republican United States of South Africa.' (Quoted in a letter from Sir Evelyn Wrench in *The Times* of April 4th 1960.)

[28] The *Uitlanders* in the Transvaal outnumbered the Boers quite substantially. They paid more than nine-tenths of the taxes. They were disfranchised.

were to be any interference from London in native affairs. We can now see the full consequences. It is the Dutch, not the British, who rule South Africa, and among the Dutch it is the spirit of Kruger, not of Botha, that prevails. For the natives, the policy is white domination and *apartheid*. What would Campbell-Bannerman and Asquith think of their handiwork today?[29]

From the upsurge of imperialism in the late nineteenth century, and from episodes like the Boer War in particular, a whole influential theory of economic imperialism has been evolved, which attributes these developments solely to economic causes, and in particular to one manifestation of economic activity, namely foreign investment. Already in 1896, Sir William Harcourt, the Liberal leader, had talked about 'stock-jobbing imperialism'. In propounding this theory in 1902, J. A. Hobson, like Lenin and others who followed him, based himself less on full statistical evidence, which would not, in fact, have been available, than upon a process almost of divination. It may well be true that in the then existing structure of society, excessive capital accumulations, arising from under-consumption and over-saving, flowed into investment abroad where a higher rate of interest was to be earned than could be obtained at home. But in point of fact the statistical evidence suggests that foreign investment is not necessarily to be identified with the new burst of imperialism or to be set down as the determining cause of it. Nor is the correlation between the two established by specific historical evidence. The last twenty years of the nineteenth century, the heyday of European imperialism, were not, as it happened, a time of bounding foreign investment. They were, on the contrary, for the United Kingdom, a period when foreign investment was flagging. Strangely enough, it was in the years between 1850 and 1875, a period of anti-imperialism, that foreign investment was at its maximum for the century. As has already been noted above, the annual average long-term British investment abroad was substantially higher in the years 1870–74 than at any time thereafter until 1904–1909. It is difficult to see why, if investment was held to have given rise to imperialist expansion in the 1880s and after, it had not done so in the earlier years, when its volume was much greater. Nor was British investment in the later or imperialist period directed rather to the British Empire than to foreign countries—on the contrary; and both in the Empire and in

[29] It could be argued that, without the liberal concessions, we should have been faced with a most dangerous situation in the two world wars.

foreign countries it went chiefly to the more advanced lands of European settlement and not to colonial or other backward terri-tories which the theory would indicate as the prime target for an-nexation or control and as the victims of exploitation by interna-tional finance.[30]

For these and many other reasons, the validity of Hobson's theory is not accepted by modern economists, except perhaps by those of Marxist persuasion or residual colour.[31] But the deep misgivings about 'the seamy side of imperialism' which had provoked its for-mulation have left their mark on the public mind, and have induced a tender conscience about the Empire which has facilitated its trans-formation into Commonwealth.

The effect upon both creditor and debtor countries, and upon international relations, of these movements of private capital over international frontiers has been long debated. Would the British people have been better off if less capital had gone abroad? Would the undeveloped regions of the world have been better off if they had remained unchanged by British enterprise and British capital? Were the international movements of capital and the activities of international financiers a determining cause of war or did they, on the contrary, contribute to the maintenance of peace? Those who have studied these questions most deeply are usually the most cautious in giving their replies. The answer is sometimes in one sense and sometimes in another. There are cases where the calcula-tions and activities of profit-seeking groups have kept antagonism alive and, in their search for congenial conditions of operation, have been able to recruit the political and military power of their govern-ments in their support. There are also cases where the influence of the great financial houses of Europe has been exerted on the side of peaceful statesmanship. On these debatable issues it is safer to sus-pend judgment.

Meanwhile, one of the aspects of international economic relations came to exercise the conscience of governments. In consequence of an initiative by Luis M. Drago, the Argentine Foreign Minister, the Hague conference of 1907 formulated by agreement, as an element of positive international law, the doctrine that states would not 'have

---

[30] These conclusions emerge from the figures given in Feis, *Europe the World's Banker*, p. 23.

[31] John Strachey in *The End of Empire* argues in its favour, though with substantial qualifications.

recourse to armed force for the recovery of contract debts claimed from the government of one country by the government of another country as being due to its nationals.' This would, however, not apply if the debtor state refused arbitration, or failed to submit to an arbitral award.

As for the question of how best to afford assistance to less advanced countries, whether from governmental or from private sources, and in particular whether such assistance should or could be given with or without 'strings', political, economic or military, this is a problem with which the world is now once again concerning itself. In advanced countries, there is a recognition of the duty to help and there are now once again surpluses available for this purpose. What the less advanced countries need is a 'starter', sufficient initial financial and technical assistance to enable them to take off upon the road to industrialization. Failing such help from outside, they would have to squeeze the necessary capital from their agricultural population, and in most cases this would be beyond their powers, and almost certainly so in the absence of a totalitarian system of government.

The Colonial Conferences of 1887 and 1897 settled, in a negative sense, one of the characteristic constitutional principles which would govern the Commonwealth as it would emerge in the next century, and as it exists today. Disraeli, speaking in 1872, had advocated 'some representative council in the metropolis which would have brought the colonies into constant and continuous relations with the home government.' Sir J. R. Seeley, in the lectures delivered at Cambridge in 1881 and published in *The Expansion of England* (1883), looked forward to the integration, based on complete national identity, of all the English-speaking subjects of the Crown, whether at home or overseas, in one comprehensive federation like the United States of America. He felt that only by so combining could the British peoples save themselves from being overshadowed by the rising might of the United States and Russia. Like Dilke, he was opposed to the acquisition of dependent, native territories; and he foresaw the time when India must break away. The conception of imperial federation had some considerable vogue for a time, but when the Colonial Conference met in 1887, it was seen to have no future. The colonial representatives showed no enthusiasm for it, and it was not included among the subjects for discussion. At the Colonial Conference of 1897, Chamberlain, in his opening speech, suggested a council of the Empire which might develop into a Federal Council; but his suggestion was not seriously examined; it was clearly not a live issue. Thus early, the course was set for a family association of independent units, a fraternity of democracies. Canadians, Australians and New Zealanders would be subjects of the sovereign: but they would be Canadians, Australians and New Zealanders first. There could be some measure of co-operation in imperial defence, and even in arrangements for imperial preference or other arrangements in line with Chamberlain's abandonment of the policy of *laissez faire* in regard to colonial development. But, in spite of later efforts by Milner and others in favour of an organic empire, there would be no formal imperial political link other than the monarch, whether by virtue of allegiance or symbolically, through mere headship of the Commonwealth. The formulation of this conception lay in the future; but the basis for it was already laid.

When Queen Victoria died early in 1901, after a reign of sixty-four years, the peoples of the United Kingdom and of the Empire might feel with foreboding that one of the fixed points in their lives had been removed, and that, with the opening of a new century, they must face an ominously unknown future in a changing world. Foreign monarchs, so many of them related to the Queen, and foreign statesmen, might think that the British realm had lost one of its most pervasive sources of moral influence in the world. But as for governing circles at home, devoted as they might be to their august sovereign, there might not have been absent from their minds a feeling of relief at the passing of this once forceful personality, so strong in common sense and right feeling, yet so fixed in old-fashioned ways, and following for so long the precepts of the Prince Consort, now forty years dead. Lord Salisbury had once said that the Queen was more of a burden to him than either the Prime Ministership or the Foreign Office. Her successor would be more open-minded, less bound by family and dynastic loyalties, which were coming to mean less and less in the world of the twentieth century. It was well that these bonds should be somewhat loosened, since the time was now come when Great Britain could, in the interest of the security not merely of the Empire but of the metro-polis itself, no longer delay to embark upon a new course in her foreign policy. There must be a re-awakening and a re-adjustment to meet the problems of a new age. Not once only but repeatedly in the coming century we were fated (as the Victorians, for all their anxieties, never were) to face the possibility of national ruin.

Part III

REAWAKENING AND READJUSTMENT: ANGLO-JAPANESE ALLIANCE TO NORTH ATLANTIC TREATY

CHAPTER XII

Return from Isolation

In a memorandum dated May 29th 1901 addressed to Lord Lansdowne, his successor as Foreign Secretary, Lord Salisbury set down some thoughts on British foreign policy which were of significance as a judgment on the past and as a precept for the present and future. They were of significance also in the response which they prompted from the new Foreign Secretary. The question at issue was whether Great Britain should accept a German overture that she should join the Triple Alliance. As to this, Salisbury wrote: 'Except during [Napoleon I's reign] we have never even been in danger, and, therefore it is impossible for us to judge whether the "isolation" under which we are supposed to suffer, does or does not contain in it any element of peril. It would hardly be wise to incur novel and most onerous obligations, in order to guard against a danger in whose existence we have no historical reason for believing.'

It was probably true to say that, thanks to the Navy, we had in fact not been in danger in the homeland since 1815. It would not have been true to say that no responsible British statesman since that time had had any sense of peril. Salisbury himself could be quoted to the contrary. The possibility of a continental league of France, Russia and Germany against Great Britain was a familiar thought to Salisbury, Chamberlain and Lansdowne. Our overseas interests had certainly been felt to be in jeopardy. It was apprehension of the designs of Russia and France that had led to fruitless approaches to Germany by Salisbury's own government for a direct understanding, the price of which we were, however, unwilling to pay. Lansdowne's answer, dated November 1901, said in effect: 'I think . . . that we may push too far the argument that, because we have in the past survived in spite of our isolation, we need have no misgivings as to the effect of that isolation in the future. In approaching the Japanese we have, indeed, virtually admitted that we do not wish to continue to stand alone.'

This revolutionary turn in our foreign policy, marked by the conclusion of the Anglo-Japanese Alliance of 1902, was not prompted by fear of Germany. We still hoped for friendly relations with her and, in spite of later naval rivalry, we were to continue to pursue this objective almost down to the outbreak of war in 1914. The Anglo-Japanese Alliance, the Entente Cordiale of 1904 and the Anglo-Russian Convention of 1907 were primarily intended to relieve ourselves of anxiety for our interests in overseas countries—in the Far East, in Egypt and in Persia—where we were at odds, not with Germany, but with Russia and France. The Franco-Russian Alliance had always had an anti-British aspect. In 1901, France had agreed to finance a railway in Central Asia designed to threaten India, and the two governments had drafted an agreement for joint military action against Great Britain. In the mind of Delcassé, the French Foreign Minister, there may have been little more than tactics in this, a means of putting the screw on Great Britain to give way to France in Morocco in return for neutrality in the Far East. But in the light of this, and since a satisfactory agreement with Germany covering Manchuria was unattainable in the absence of a sufficient common interest, Japanese approaches for an understanding received a favourable response. Here were two countries with a common objective, namely, to halt the Russian threat to their interests in the Far East, and with a willingness to pay the price which each would require of the other—the two indispensable conditions for any firm alliance.

The treaty covered British interests in China and Korea (it was extended in 1905 to cover India and East Asia generally); and it provided for mutual aid if either party were attacked in the Far East by two other powers (the renewed treaty of 1905 provided for assistance in the case of attack by one power).[1] What Great Britain was, in effect, undertaking to do was to keep France out of any future Russo-Japanese war; and this she could readily do now that the Navy was freed from the involvement of the Boer War.[2] In

[1] i.e. by Russia, if she should rebuild her fleet and seek revenge. Our calculation was that the prospect of meeting the Royal Navy would discourage her from rebuilding her fleet.

[2] In April 1902 we had thirty-three battleships not more than fifteen years old. Germany had seventeen, Russia fifteen, France thirteen, the United States ten and Japan six.

making the treaty of alliance, Great Britain was sacrificing three things. By agreeing to recognize Korea as a Japanese sphere of interest, she was sacrificing the principle of the maintenance of the *status quo* in the Far East to which she had been attached. By withdrawing naval forces from the Far East she was admitting that she would no longer undertake the defence of her interests everywhere in the world by her own hand alone. But, more important, she was now at last engaging in advance to take military action in circumstances which could not be foreseen. This was a signal reversal of a policy which had been enunciated by a whole line of British statesmen from Castlereagh and Canning to Salisbury. Defending the alliance against criticism in the House of Lords, Lansdowne gave what was, in effect, a further answer to Salisbury's doubts as to the need to depart from the policy of isolation. After pointing to the growing scale of armaments and to the suddenness with which war might now break out, he said: 'When we consider these features of the international situation we must surely feel that a country would indeed be endowed with an extraordinary amount of self-sufficiency which took upon itself to say that it would accept without question, without reservation, the doctrine that all foreign alliances were to be avoided as necessarily embarrassing and objectionable. Therefore I would entreat you . . . to look at the matter strictly on its merits and not to allow your judgment to be swayed by musty formulae and old-fashioned superstitions as to the desirability of pursuing a policy of isolation for this country . . . *Prima facie* if there be no countervailing objections, the country which has the good fortune to possess allies is more to be envied than the country which is without them.'

The alliance was welcomed in Germany. 'At last,' said the Kaiser, 'the noodles have had a lucid interval.' It served Germany in Europe because it tended to estrange Great Britain and Russia. It served Great Britain in Europe because it made her less dependent on German support in the Far East, and it was thus likely to make Anglo-German relations easier. By weakening France's position in relation to Russia and threatening her with a tragic dilemma in the event of war in the Far East, it contributed to the Anglo-French Entente. It also enabled us to stand aloof for a few more years from the balance of power in Europe. In the Far East, it ensured that the approaching Russo-Japanese conflict would be confined to them alone. When unexpectedly to Japan herself, Russia, fighting alone, was decisively defeated in the war of 1904–1905, both the more immediate and the more distant consequences of the Anglo-Japanese Alliance were to be momentous. Russian ambitions would be diverted from the Far East back to the Balkans, where her rivalry with Austria would be one of the causes of a world war. The triumph of an Asian country over a European empire would serve, in course of time, to undermine Asian acceptance of white predominance and to impair the prestige by which, in great measure, British rule in India was sustained. Japan's successful embarkation upon the course of empire would, within forty years, lead her to seek to drive us out of the Far East and South-east Asia, and to challenge the United States itself. Korea, the cockpit of the Far East, for which Japan had gone to war with China in 1895, and the control of which was one of the main issues in the Russo-Japanese War, would again emerge to bedevil the relations of the great powers in the Far East. Such would be the revolution in affairs that Korea would, in the middle of the twentieth century, in a conflict instigated by Russia, involve a revived China in hostilities with the United States and with other members of an international organization.

It is impossible for statesmen to foresee all the future consequences of their acts, and it is futile for them to try to take very long views in foreign policy. They can only decide to do what, in all the circumstances, seems to them best to do at the time. A Foreign Secretary who takes his decisions on the best information he can get, on the best judgment he can reach on a short-term view, is less likely to make a major mistake than one who decides upon a too confident long-term forecast, or upon grounds of political or ideological doctrine, or upon a plan which is too closely defined. For one thing, his policy will have flexibility and can profit by trial and error. In politics there is much to be said for what is contemptuously called 'muddling through'.

Was it worth making an alliance with Japan for the sake of our interests in China? The answer can only be, first, that our position in China, both political and commercial, in the competitive imperialist conditions of the time, had acquired a possibly exaggerated importance for us and had to be safeguarded; and secondly that, China or no China, we felt that we needed an ally of some kind. Our imperial interests stood in the way of our finding an ally in Europe, and this for two reasons. The first was the fear on the part of, for example, Germany that an alliance with us might involve her in overseas conflicts where she would be serving our interests rather than her own. The second was the obvious fact that the other two European powers chiefly in question, France and Russia, were themselves imperial powers with whom we were ourselves in acute rivalry in many parts of the world. Japan was the obvious choice. Once we had strengthened our international position by allying ourselves with her, we were better placed to strengthen our position still further by coming to an accommodation with our chief imperial rivals. There was still no obvious single enemy, but the world was becoming increasingly dangerous. We had sensed this as far back as 1889, when we took the first steps to build up a navy strong enough to meet almost any conceivable challenge.

To ask oneself whether it would not have been better for us to ally ourselves with Germany at this time is like asking whether it would not have been better for us to agree with Russia to partition the Turkish Empire in the middle of the nineteenth century, or for Great Britain and France to conclude an alliance with Russia against Germany in 1939. It might or might not have been better: we cannot say. But in each case the answer is probably the same, namely, that in the circumstances of the time none of these things was possible. The prospective allies, or some of them, were not willing to pay the necessary price. In retrospect, with the advantage of hindsight, it may be counted a fortunate chance that we did not become the ally of Germany in the early 1900s. Certainly, this is what some of our statesmen wanted. Chamberlain, Rosebery and Lansdowne thought that Germany was our 'natural ally'. Almost certainly, it would have been to Germany's advantage to ally herself with us. This was Pribram's view: 'By their rigid insistence upon the principle of "all or nothing", the German statesmen missed the opportunity to enter into a union which would have proved of advantage to Germany'; and he adds, 'and perhaps beneficial to the entire world', which is much more doubtful.[3]

William II and Bülow thought otherwise. The 'free hand', they believed, was the right course for Germany. It was, in their view, completely out of the question that Great Britain and Russia could ever come together. Germany could safely let them quarrel, and stand uncommitted between them. If the need ever arose, Germany could have the alliance of either Russia or Great Britain for the asking. In fact, Germany's leaders, with incredible folly, estranged both

[3] *England and the International Policy of the European Great Powers*, p. 90.

Great Britain and Russia at the same time, and set out upon a world-policy without first making sure of Europe or even of the stable political future of their ally, Austria-Hungary. If Germany had paid the price of an alliance with Great Britain, namely the risk of overseas complications, she could probably have obtained the mastery of Europe.

When one contemplates the incalculable and unforeseeable history of the Far East in the fifty years that followed the Anglo-Japanese Alliance, the course of which was, in some measure, determined by it, the imagination boggles at the problem of plotting the train of events had there been an alliance between Great Britain and Germany in the first years of the century. But it is clear enough that for Great Britain to have allied herself with the strongest power in Europe, an expansionist power which was to develop aggressive world ambitions, would sooner or later have landed her in acute political embarrassment. Hermann Rauschning was not speaking for his own time alone when he said in 1939 that 'the liberalism of the English mind' was 'the essential and almost insuperable obstacle to an alliance between England and Germany.' So to act would also have contravened the first principle of the balance of power. That events should have directed our statesmen's minds in another direction was a lucky escape. After 1900 it began to be clear to the Admiralty that the short-range German fleet was designed for war against Great Britain and that, in the event of war with France and Russia, it would be dangerous to us. The Government decided to put the Navy on a 'three-power' standard.[4] Steps were taken to build up a fleet in the North Sea, based on a new station at Rosyth. As a result of agreements with the United States and Japan we were enabled to withdraw naval forces from the West Indies and the Far East and to concentrate them in European waters. Dreams of the 'natural alliance' with Germany began to fade: the desire for her friendship remained.

Lansdowne's next great step in foreign policy after the Japanese Alliance was the conclusion of the Entente Cordiale with France in 1904. This, unlike the treaty with Japan, was nothing in the nature of an alliance. It was what its name implied, a cordial understanding, not a commitment to act. It did nothing to tie us contractually more closely to continental Europe. It was the kind of arrangement that

[4] In March 1905, the figures were: Great Britain forty-four, Germany sixteen, France twelve, Russia eleven, United States twelve, Japan five.

could have been reached by almost any British Foreign Secretary in the nineteenth century.[5] It was not in itself a move away from isolation. Its significance lay not in the character of its terms, but in the power with whom it was concluded, in the moment at which it was signed, and in the development in Great Britain's relationship to continental Europe which followed it. Its conclusion was possible because both Great Britain and France had seen a strong common interest in a broad accommodation between them in the colonial field, and were both willing to make their contribution to a bargain.

Since 1882, Great Britain had been embarrassed in her administration of Egypt by the diplomatic opposition of France and her associates, and had been constrained, much against her will, to rely on German support. In 1898, she had re-conquered the Sudan for herself and for Egypt, and had at Fashoda barred the advance of France across the upper Nile. Her treaty with Japan in 1902 had weakened France's position in relation to Russia, and had lessened her own need of German support. She saw a chance to free her hand in Egypt from past embarrassments. For his part, Delcassé, the French Foreign Minister, even at the time of Fashoda, had said that an alliance with Great Britain was his ultimate aim. In 1902, the year of the renewal of the Triple Alliance, he had made an agreement with Italy which in some measure cut across that alliance. Under stress of the rising crisis in the Far East, where France might be caught between Russia and Japan, the allies respectively of herself and of Great Britain, he was all the more ready to reduce colonial friction with Great Britain, and even if driven to it, to liquidate the Egyptian difficulty. For this, Lansdowne would have to pay the price, and it would be a big one. Delcassé would have a strongly anti-British public opinion in France to pacify. Lansdowne, as it proved, was in the end willing to pay, and to pay in Morocco where the Anglo-French difference was now at its most acute.

The first approach was made by Chamberlain to the French ambassador, Paul Cambon, early in 1902. Later in the year, Cambon approached Lansdowne himself. The intense hostility of French public opinion, fanned both by Fashoda and by the Boer War, was much allayed by the great success of King Edward's visit to Paris in May 1903. Cromer pressed hard for the agreement in the interest of

[5] E.g. such other colonial agreements as the Heligoland Treaty with Germany of 1890, Rosebery's Pamirs agreement with Russia of 1895 or the Hay–Pauncefote Treaty of 1901 with the United States.

his financial schemes in Egypt. It was signed in April 1904, two months after the outbreak of the Russo-Japanese War. It covered Newfoundland, West Africa, Siam, Madagascar and the New Hebrides as well as the two major issues of Egypt and Morocco. France at last gave Great Britain a free hand in Egypt in return for Great Britain's recognition of a free hand for France in Morocco, a state which, like Turkey and China before it, was held to be on the eve of disintegration. Each government gave the other a promise of diplomatic support. What Lansdowne gave up in Morocco was an out-dated aspiration to run the country as a kind of British puppet state with the adventurer, Kaid Maclean, as a kind of Cromer. The Admiralty had much disliked the prospect of seeing the southern shore of the Strait of Gibraltar in the hands of a great power. To meet this, the French were persuaded to agree that a northern strip should be reserved to meet the historic claims of Spain, and that there should be a provision for its non-fortification.

To Lansdowne, the Anglo-French agreement seems to have been a means of relaxing embarrassing tensions in many parts of the world, and particularly in Egypt.[6] It had for him no relation to the balance of power in Europe and was not directed against Germany; but though Germany had in 1902 disclaimed any interest there, the bargain about Morocco was later to bring France and Germany into a grave conflict of interest which was to imperil the peace of Europe. For Delcassé, on the other hand, it was something more than a colonial agreement. It was a first step towards a wider understanding with Great Britain which would engage her with France in Europe and which might, however great the difficulties, lead on to a *rapprochement* between Great Britain and Russia. He seems already to have had a Triple Entente in mind. 'This liquidation [of colonial grievances] should lead us,' he said early in 1904, 'and I desire that it shall lead us, to a political alliance with England . . . Now I can believe I am near my goal.' 'It would be difficult,' he admitted, 'to combine with the Russian Alliance. But each day has its task.'

The Anglo-Japanese Alliance and the Russo-Japanese War had

[6] Apart from its importance for Anglo-French relations and for European politics, the Entente, in so far as it bartered Egyptian interests over the heads of the Egyptians, takes its place with Napoleon's invasion and the British occupation, and with other later events, as a stimulus to Egyptian nationalism and as a factor in the development of the Egyptian attitude towards Europe.

strengthened Great Britain's international position, and had enabled her to conclude a bargain with France which was perhaps more immediately advantageous to herself than it was to France. The Entente still further strengthened her position. Great Britain had awakened to her predicament and had once again asserted herself to good purpose in the international field.[7] With France friendly, with Russia weakened by defeat and revolution, with Germany not yet seen as an immediate menace and her support not now needed, with an ally in the Far East and a friendly power across the Atlantic, and with unassailable naval supremacy and some revival in prosperity, she could in late 1904 feel more secure at home and overseas and more surely master of her fate than at any time since the days of Palmerston's Foreign Secretaryship between 1830 and 1841. She could continue to feel that the affairs of Europe need not call for her intervention.

Germany had at first taken the Anglo-French Entente calmly: she confidently expected that the two powers would soon quarrel about Morocco or about something else. She had great hopes that the war in the Far East would embroil Great Britain with Russia. However, towards the end of 1904, she tried, by offering an alliance to Russia, to place France before the choice, on the one hand, of coming into a continental league against Great Britain and breaking the Entente or, on the other, of holding to the Entente and breaking her alliance with Russia. The attempt was renewed during the fantastic episode at Björkö in July 1905, after the destruction of the Russian fleet at Tshushima in May, when Nicholas II, meeting William II alone at sea, was persuaded to sign the treaty. This treaty was soon rendered inoperative by the course of events and allowed to fall to the ground in the face of the horrified opposition, assumed or genuine, of the advisers of the two potentates. German hopes and expectations were deceived. Great Britain and France did not quarrel. France skilfully evaded the choice. Anglo-Russian relations, tested by the Dogger Bank incident of October 1904,[8] proved to be less fragile than had been supposed. The prospect of an Anglo-Russian

[7] Grey, at that time in opposition, has recorded the profound relief with which he welcomed the conclusion of the Anglo-French agreement. By contrast, that other Liberal imperialist, Rosebery, thought that it would lead 'straight to war'. His sympathies were with Germany rather than with France.

[8] The firing by Russian warships, outward bound for the Far East, upon English fishing vessels in the North Sea.

conflict, whether over the Near East or over Central Asia or over the Far East, which had been one of the standing assumptions of European diplomacy for two generations or more, now seemed to have receded. The Anglo-Russian Convention of 1907 was to give formal warrant for this belief. But before it had been concluded, Great Britain's short-lived complacency about the state of Europe had been shattered and she was again deep in continental affairs.

William II had tried to separate Russia from France. Bülow, by intervening without any clear objective in the Moroccan question, hoped somehow to separate France from Great Britain. His ground was the assertion of a German interest, which he had at an earlier period disclaimed. His method was to make a display of German power. The main events in this revealing and decisive episode—the first hint that a European war was a possibility that must be taken into practical account—were the flamboyant visit of the Kaiser to Tangier in March 1905 in order to assert Germany's interest in the future disposition of the Moroccan state; the attempt to appease Germany by the forced resignation of Delcassé; Bülow's successful insistence on the holding of an international conference about Morocco, thus establishing, against the French thesis, that Morocco was of European and not merely of French concern; the diplomatic support given to France by Great Britain, according to the agreement, under her new Foreign Secretary, Sir Edward Grey,[9] at the conference of Algeciras (January–March 1906); the weakening of Germany's, and the strengthening of France's position and the consolidation of the Anglo-French Entente after this first deliberate attempt by Germany to disrupt it and to make France of no account in Europe; the Kaiser's exultant congratulations to the Austro-Hungarian Foreign Minister for his services as 'the brilliant second'; and President Theodore Roosevelt's strangely naïve message to the Kaiser congratulating him on 'his epoch-making success' and on a policy which had been 'masterly from beginning to end'.

It was in the light of this trial of forces that the British and Russians came to terms. Like the Anglo-Japanese Alliance and the Anglo-French Entente, the Anglo-Russian Convention was entered into by Great Britain for the safeguarding of overseas interests. Like the

[9] When Grey became Foreign Secretary at the end of 1905, there was some doubt whether he could combine his departmental duties with his parliamentary duties as a member of the House of Commons. Since the end of 1851, except for periods amounting to about four and a half years, the Foreign Secretary had sat in the House of Lords.

Entente, the Convention was concluded, in the main, for the sake of India. The Entente gave us a free hand in Egypt and effective control in the Suez Canal Zone. The Convention, by the sub-division of Persia into a large Russian sphere of influence in the north (including Tehran) and a smaller British sphere of influence in the south-east, with a neutral zone of equal opportunity (including the shore of the Persian Gulf) lying between them, kept Russia's exclusive ambitions away from the Gulf. India's position was further safeguarded by Russia's recognition that Afghanistan was outside her sphere of influence, by her agreement to conduct her political relations with Kabul through the British authorities, and by joint self-denying ordinances in regard to Tibet, which was recognized to be under the suzerainty of China. The long-standing fear of Russian invasion of India, exaggerated though it had probably always been, was now laid. Like the Entente, the Convention was in no sense an alliance, even a disguised alliance. It composed differences, but made no commitments to give either diplomatic or military support. It was not, in Grey's mind, designed to encircle Germany. Germany had shown herself to be a troublemaker; but the period of intense naval rivalry was still to come. Both Great Britain and Russia desired still to be on good terms with Germany. As Grey himself afterwards said, he had had India primarily in mind.

Nevertheless the agreement was of prime significance for British policy. A Liberal government, against strong opposition, had concluded an agreement with the despotic government of a police state, and, with it, had resorted to the reactionary device of apportioning spheres of influence in an under-developed country without that country's consent. In the wider international sphere, though the Germans again took it calmly (having been informed of it by Izvolski, the Russian Foreign Minister, before he signed it), it had important effects. It helped to free Russia from subservience to Germany. It provided the first link, however tenuous, between France, Great Britain and Russia, and it laid the foundation of the Triple Entente. It drove Germany closer to Austria and increased the chances of her involvement, in the wake of Austria, in the Balkans, on which Russia was now concentrating her attention. It also implied that, for Great Britain, Russian expansion in the Balkans was a lesser evil than expansion there by the Central Powers. Like the Anglo-Japanese Alliance, it had consequences which have continued to determine the course of international affairs down to our own day.

Reawakening and Readjustment

In the ten years before 1914, as in the 1930s, Germany had only to bide her time and to use her potential military power and her economic resources in support of a skilful diplomacy in order to win the mastery of continental Europe without war. She failed to guard against the complications that would be sure to arise if, under nationalist pressure, Austria-Hungary broke up after the death of Francis Joseph. And she would not keep quiet. By her patent and restless ambitions, she turned the tenuous Triple Entente into something more like a reality. Her attitude was made manifest in two European crises, the Bosnian crisis of 1908 and the Agadir crisis of 1911, of which the first was more pregnant for the future than the second.

The main events in the Bosnian affair were: an unwritten agreement in September 1908 between Izvolski and the Austrian Foreign Minister, Aerenthal, for the transformation of the Austrian occupation of Bosnia-Hercegovina into annexation in violation of the Berlin Treaty of 1878, and the opening of the Straits by Russia in violation of the Paris Treaty of 1856; the double-crossing of Izvolski by the sudden annexation of Bosnia by Austria in October 1908; the strong opposition by Grey to treaty violation by either party, and the reluctance of France to become involved in Russia's Balkan quarrels; Germany's unreserved support ('in shining armour', in the Kaiser's characteristically imprudent phrase) of her ally's anti-Slav *Drang nach Osten*; Izvolski's failure to secure compensation for Serbia; and the capitulation of Russia in March 1909 to a diplomatic ultimatum from Germany, demanding Russian acknowledgment of the annexation. Russia was forced to submit to foreign dictation and was unforgivably humiliated, as some of the wiser Germans perceived. Never again would this be allowed to happen, as would be seen in 1914.

In the Bosnian crisis, Great Britain played little effective part. She did not regard the Anglo-Russian Convention as involving her in the affairs of Europe. In the Agadir crisis, a much more immediately serious affair where her own interests were in question, she was to intervene with striking effect. Here the main events were: the relief by French forces in May 1911 of the city of Fez against local insurgents at the request of the Sultan of Morocco; a German demand for compensation, discussed at informal Franco-German conversations; the despatch in July of the German gunboat *Panther* to Agadir by the adventurously inclined Foreign Minister, Kiderlen-

Wächter, ostensibly to protect non-existent commercial firms but in fact to constrain France to meet inflated claims for territorial compensation in French Africa; British alarm, not in fact well founded, at the possibility of the establishment of a German naval station on the Atlantic coast of North Africa, or of a French bargain with Germany over Morocco at the expense of Great Britain and Spain; a speech of strong warning at the Mansion House in July 1911 by the reputedly pro-German and pacific Chancellor of the Exchequer, Lloyd George; preparations in Great Britain for possible war with Germany; and, after long-drawn-out negotiations, in which Great Britain firmly supported France, the conclusion of a compromise settlement, Germany recognizing a French protectorate over Morocco and France yielding some territory in the French Congo.

Lloyd George's words are noteworthy: 'Britain should at all hazards maintain her place and prestige among the Great Powers, and if a situation were to be forced upon us in which peace could only be preserved by the sacrifice of the great and beneficent position that Britain has won by centuries of heroism and achievement—then I say emphatically that peace at such a price would be a humiliation intolerable for a great country like ours to endure.' Not since Palmerston's day had such strong words been so effectively spoken. Great Britain had regained her position of authority in Europe. The warning could have been addressed to France as well as to Germany. We had given France a free hand in Morocco; but this did not entitle her to make agreements with other powers, as the French Prime Minister had been bent on doing, to the detriment of our interests under the Act of Algeciras. This had already been made clear to her in 1905, when there was a fear in London that France might buy Germany off with a port on the Atlantic coast of Morocco.[10] From the point of view of public opinion, the importance of the Agadir crisis was that it brought home to the British people for the first time that there was a real danger of a European war in which they would most probably be involved. Having estranged Russia over Bosnia, Germany had now further estranged Great Britain, already much disturbed by the German naval programme. Only an agreement to limit naval armaments could reassure British public opinion.

[10] There was a hint of this again in a speech by Asquith in the House of Commons, a few days after Lloyd George had spoken, when the Prime Minister made it clear that if the current Franco-German negotiations broke down, Great Britain might have a right and a duty to intervene actively in the situation in defence of British interests.

Reawakening and Readjustment

While the Boer War had made Great Britain disagreeably conscious of her isolation, it had brought home to the German authorities that—as Grand Admiral Tirpitz had already urged—without a fleet Germany could not use her power outside Europe. Both powers had started to repair the defects in their situation.

Great Britain had already begun to build up the Royal Navy in 1889 after a period of neglect and on the strength of a naval scare. For her security in an increasingly dangerous world, she established a two-power standard—France and Russia. The German Navy Laws of 1898 and 1900 caused no particular alarm in London. But by 1902, German naval strength began to be taken more seriously into account. By 1903–1904 a three-power standard was achieved— France, Russia, Germany. The German calculation had been that it was necessary for Germany to possess a fleet which, in the event of war, could do such damage to the British fleet as to render it inferior to the combined French and Russian fleets. This should carry Germany through the period of risk when her own fleet was still much inferior to the British. It was not a very sensible calculation. The Anglo-French Entente and the Anglo-Russian Convention, by their political implications rather than by their content, undermined the basic German assumption of British hostility to France and Russia. The Russian fleet had been destroyed. Great Britain had been able to draw naval reinforcements from the Caribbean and the Far East. The laying down of the *Dreadnought* in 1905, the all-big-gun ship that could fight beyond the extreme range of torpedoes, was to create a new naval situation. The race for naval superiority had now to be conducted on a new basis. Meanwhile, as a measure of precaution, a powerful Home Fleet was assembled late in 1906, based on the Nore. For her part, Germany would now have to widen the Kiel Canal to take her *Dreadnoughts*—this was not complete before the summer of 1914. If the British Government had not, as a futile gesture, curtailed their building programme in 1907, Germany would not have been given a chance to catch up, and Great Britain would have had an overwhelming superiority in the new great ships after that date.

What was clear by 1906 to Eyre Crowe, that able but still junior official in the Foreign Office, and even to Grey himself, namely that Germany was forcing the pace in armaments and bidding for the domination of Europe, became evident to the Government in London by 1908, after the evidence of the first Morocco crisis and the

262

Bosnian affair. The agile and slippery Chancellor, Bülow, and his ineffective successor, Bethmann-Hollweg, as well as Moltke, the Chief of the General Staff, had misgivings about the policy of challenging British sea-power and of declining all suggestion of limitation; but the Kaiser and Tirpitz were too strong for them. In the crucial years, 1908–1909, the inexorable race was on. Tirpitz thought he could overtake Great Britain in from ten to twelve years. An unheralded acceleration of the German programme by Tirpitz in 1908 was the last straw. By early 1909, the British public, as well as the Government, were roused to the German danger ('we want eight, and we won't wait'). Never since the anti-Russian storms of 1854 and 1878 had the people been so deeply moved. There was, indeed, a dissenting minority of what Grey called 'pan-Germans' and 'pacifists'. As in the 1930s, and again in the 1950s, there were those who scoffed at the warning that the enemy was at the gate: either he was not an enemy; or if he was, he was not at the gate; and, anyhow, he could be appeased and bought off. But the general public were strongly behind the Government in determining not to be outbuilt. As Grey saw it, there was no half-way house in naval affairs between complete security and absolute ruin. However strong the Royal Navy, we could not reach Berlin; but with a superior fleet, the German Army could conquer England. It was clear after the Agadir affair that, unless there could be some agreed limitation in naval building, there could be no easing of Anglo-German tension. The Haldane mission in 1912 brought nothing more from Bethmann-Hollweg than the German requirement, already put forward by Kiderlen-Wächter in 1909, that the *sine qua non* was British neutrality in the event of a German war with France and Russia. Great Britain was to keep out of Europe. This was an undertaking which Grey steadily declined to give. As he had said in 1909: 'If we sacrifice the other Powers to Germany we shall eventually be attacked.' The competition in Dreadnoughts went on until the end, and in the end superiority over Germany was maintained. In 1910 the figures were 5 to 2; in 1911, 8 to 4; in 1912, 12 to 7; in 1913, 15 to 10. In January 1914 the figures were: Great Britain 18, Germany 13, France 8, United States 8, Japan 4.[11]

The formation of the Triple Entente, a term which Grey himself disliked, did not mean that the parties acted diplomatically in unison.

[11] These and earlier figures given are from E. L. Woodward, *Great Britain and the German Navy*, Oxford, 1935, Appendix I.

Of the three, Great Britain was probably the most faithful to the spirit of the understandings which linked the three powers. She was in what appeared to her to be a more dangerous situation than the other two. Neither France nor Russia could stand up to Germany on land singlehanded; but they could hope that if they could hold together under the Dual Alliance, with Great Britain in the background, Germany would hesitate to launch a direct attack. It was no new situation to them in their history to have to look to the defence of their frontiers. To Great Britain, her position was new and disturbing and one which she had not known within living memory, the homeland threatened by the strongest military power in Europe backed by a navy that might, by ill chance, open the way to invasion. She could not count on the support of France and Russia. The Entente of 1904 and the convention of 1907 had not meant the laying aside of French and Russian ambitions or projects in Morocco and in Persia detrimental to British interests and contrary to the agreements. France and Russia disliked the acute Anglo-German naval rivalry with its menace to peace and with the possibility of their own unwelcome involvement in a conflict. Nor were they averse to taking diplomatic advantage of it. No more than Great Britain had they aggressive designs against Germany, and, like her, they were anxious to relax tension with Germany. If they could do this with advantage to both Germany and to themselves, at the expense of Great Britain, they would not be deterred from this course by the restraints of their agreements with the latter. As late as 1911, France was contemplating letting Germany into Morocco ahead of Great Britain. Great Britain herself did her best to relax tension with Germany. Relations became less acute when it was clear that we could outbuild Germany at sea, and when in 1912, under Poincaré, French strength and confidence began to revive. Attempts were continued to improve Anglo-German relations by seeking agreements almost down to the outbreak of war. Anything less like the encirclement of Germany it is difficult to imagine.

There is one further thread running through Great Britain's relations with France and Russia which remains to be noticed, namely the successive steps which she took, cautious though they were, towards the possibility of British participation in land operations on the Continent, as well as at sea, in the event of war. These were not provided for or even implied by the terms of the Anglo-French Entente or the Anglo-Russian Convention, nor were they the direct consequence of the Anglo-German naval rivalry, which was itself the consequence rather than the cause of Anglo-German tension. They grew progressively, at need, along with the march of events, out of the evolving situation which had brought those agreements into existence. They were the marks of a reversion by Great Britain to the policy of the balance of power.

This process may be said to have begun with a suggestion made by Lansdowne to Delcassé during the Moroccan crisis in the spring of 1905, shortly before the latter's fall. What Lansdowne said was that the two governments 'should discuss any contingencies by which they might in the course of events find themselves confronted'. This cautious statement was inexplicably interpreted by the French, then and later, and so described by them to the Russians, as a promise of military co-operation, and even as holding out the prospect of an alliance. In January 1906 on the eve of the Algeciras Conference, Grey, the new Foreign Secretary, while promising unreserved diplomatic support to France over Morocco under the agreement of 1904, could do no more than tell the French ambassador, Paul Cambon, in reply to an urgent and pointed question, that in his personal opinion, in the event of a German attack on France in consequence of an agreement with Britain, public opinion 'would be strongly moved in favour of France'. But he agreed to non-committal unofficial conversations between the two war offices. His argument was that we 'must be free to go to the help of France as well as to stand aside.' If no plans were made beforehand, though we would be free to stand aside, 'we should in effect not have preserved our freedom to help France.'

To use this argument, and to authorize military talks, however inconclusive, is to establish a moral, if not a contractual, obligation of no little force. For the first time since 1878, Great Britain had faced the possibility of military operations on the Continent. Lloyd George's Mansion House statement in 1911 has already been noted. In 1912, Grey would not go beyond the assurance that 'although we cannot bind ourselves under all circumstances to go to war with France against Germany, we shall also certainly not bind ourselves to Germany not to assist France.' He would warn Germany without committing himself to France, as Neville Chamberlain would do in the summer and autumn of 1938. In March 1912, the bulk of the Mediterranean fleet was ordered to withdraw from Malta to home waters, and the rest to concentrate at Gibraltar. Later in the year the

French fleet was moved to Toulon. There was no formal agreement: but the implication was a concerted geographical allocation of defensive roles. The French tried again for a firm commitment, but the British would not surrender their freedom of action. It was agreed in November 1912, when the military conversations were placed on an agreed basis with cabinet approval, that discussion was to be on the point 'whether both governments would act together to prevent aggression and to preserve peace, and if so, what measures they would be prepared to take in common.' Nevertheless, the French told the Russians that there was 'a verbal agreement, by virtue of which England has declared herself ready to aid France with her military and naval forces in case of an attack by Germany.' This was, in form, not so; but, in effect, Great Britain would have found it hard not to act accordingly, had the case arisen. Grey's personal view was that if Germany attacked France, Great Britain should support France in arms; but this he could not say.

His problem was to maintain the Entente, and yet at the same time to establish good relations with the German Chancellor and Foreign Minister, for what that might be worth in view of the predominant influence of the ruling military and naval clique. In this he can be said to have been successful. He and Cambon worked together in complete confidence, while as late as June 1914 von Jagow, the Prussian Foreign Minister, spoke of the 'pleasant cordiality' of Anglo-German relations. In the two or three years immediately preceding the outbreak of war, Grey worked unceasingly not only to ease relations with Germany, but to reconcile the two opposing groups of powers and to maintain the peace of Europe.

His action during the Balkan Wars of 1912–13 illustrates the purposes of his policy and the standing which Great Britain had achieved under his guidance. The first Balkan war left Bulgaria, Greece and Serbia victorious over Turkey. The second Balkan war of the summer of 1913 left Serbia, Greece and Roumania victorious over Bulgaria, with Turkey once again master of Adrianople. There was grave danger of conflict among the Great Powers, particularly between Austria and Russia. They were agreed that Turkey should retain Constantinople and that none of the Balkan States should be allowed to seize it. But about the future of Albania, where Serbia, Montenegro and Greece had made conquests of territory, they were at odds, Austria opposing the Slav claims and Russia favouring them, though neither was ready to go to extremes. Grey proposed a conference. He suggested Paris as the meeting place, but London was chosen: Grey was preferable to Poincaré as chairman. The other members of the conference were his good friends the ambassadors of France, Russia, Germany, Austria and Italy. The conference met informally and intermittently from December 1912 to August 1913, while the wars were proceeding. The virtue of the conference was that it remained in being, and that the participants were people who were not only knowledgeable and skilled negotiators, but also people who had complete confidence in each other. They did not reach any final agreement, but they disposed of difficulties as they arose. As Grey himself said afterwards: 'When we ceased to meet, the present danger to the peace of Europe was over; the things that we did not settle were not threatening that peace; the things that had threatened the relations between the Great Powers in 1912–13 we had deprived of their dangerous features.'[12] If the conference was to this extent successful, this was because at the time none of the participating powers was bent on local war or ready to face general war. Russia, Germany and Austria all showed a spirit of conciliation and compromise. That being so, the method was a good one. In other circumstances, the conference might have proved fruitless, even if it could have met at all. It is a tribute to Grey's own impartiality in the conduct of the proceedings that Cambon seems to have thought that he did not sufficiently espouse the Russian thesis, though the Russian ambassador, Benckendorff, himself made no complaint about this.

It was no part of Grey's policy to stand in the way of Germany's projects, provided that these were not inimical or dangerous to British interests, or to exacerbate relations between Germany and other members of the Entente. In the case of the German military command in Constantinople, for example, he records that he did his best to ensure its being discussed between Germany and Russia direct and not made the subject of formal representations in Constantinople by the Entente powers. In June 1914, he reached agreement with Germany about the Baghdad railway, as the French had done a few months earlier. The Germans could have their railway as far south as Basra, provided that the British position in the Persian Gulf was secured; and here the potential threat was from Russia as

[21] *Twenty-five Years, 1892–1916,* Hodder and Stoughton, London, 1925, i. 272.

well as from Germany. The Convention of 1907 had not put an end to Anglo-Russian rivalry in Asia. Grey recalls that even after the agreement Persia tried his patience more than any other subject. Finally, there was the 'cynical business' (as Sir Arthur Nicolson called it) of the Portuguese colonies. In 1898, Salisbury and Balfour had made an agreement with Germany by which, in the event of the Portuguese Empire collapsing, Angola and Mozambique, the Portuguese colonies in southern Africa, would be partitioned between the two countries. The partition plan was revised in Germany's favour in 1913 by Harcourt, the Colonial Secretary, who thought that Germany should have 'a place in the sun'. The amended agreement was initialled but never concluded. Grey declined to sign it unless it could be published, together with the assurance given by Great Britain to Portugal that the Anglo-Portuguese Alliance, which guaranteed Portugal's possessions, was regarded as still in force. He wished it to be known that Portugal would not be deprived of her colonies against her will. The Germans at first held back and only assented later when war was in sight. The revised agreement remained a dead letter. But the fact that it had ever been contemplated in London was a pointer to the British desire for an easing of relations. Like Salisbury, Grey was ready to make 'graceful concessions' to Germany for this purpose. In modern parlance, it might be called a policy of appeasement.

In the character and attainments of their statesmen, a clear advantage lay with the democratic against the autocratic powers. When one assesses William II, Bülow, Kiderlen-Wächter and Bethmann-Hollweg; Francis Joseph, Aerenthal and Berchtold; Nicholas II, Lamsdorff, Izvolski and Sazonov; there is not one of them who can stand up not merely against the great figures of the mid- and later nineteenth century—Palmerston, Cavour, Bismarck and Salisbury—but even against the clear-sightedness, tenacity of purpose and diplomatic skill of Delcassé, the massive strength of Poincaré or the patent sincerity, even the touch of grandeur, of Edward Grey. The levity with which some of them, particularly the Kaiser, played with the gravest issue of peace and war reads nauseatingly today. Typical is his greeting of Delcassé's fall with 'Hurrah! for dry powder and well-sharpened swords', and his reception of Nicholas II's rejection of his suggestion that he should declare war on Japan: 'The Emperor Nicholas's attitude was still a poor-spirited one; he seemed not to want to fight.' Edward VII, unlike his brother monarchs, did not interfere actively in foreign policy,[13] but placed his royal prestige at the service of his ministers. Here, in the mediocrity or lack of scruple of their statesmen and in the meddling of their sovereigns, may be found one of the elements of weakness in the three European empires and one of the contributory causes of their defeat in the First World War.

Grey's handling of affairs in this anxious period of our history is a model of how these things should be done. It has been made a reproach to him that he had little personal acquaintance with foreign countries and was therefore ill-fitted for his office. There is little in this point. It can be a clear advantage for a Foreign Minister to have a wide knowledge of foreign personalities and the foreign scene. It can also be a disadvantage, if it leads him to harbour strong personal preferences or antipathies, or to suppose that he has nothing to learn. It need be no disadvantage for a Foreign Minister to have small experience of foreign travel, provided that in his own person he has the qualities requisite for his office. He must—now that the volume of work has become overwhelming—be able to use his official staff to the best public advantage, both in the Foreign Office and in the missions abroad. However much he knows, he will have to rely on his officials for information and advice, and these he must be able to test. He must have a ready grasp of the problems that come before him, and of the background to them that may determine how they should be handled. He must be able to treat foreign problems in a broad but accurate way, whether in conversations with ambassadors, or in submission to the Cabinet, or in speeches in Parliament. Above all, he must inspire confidence in his dealings with foreign governments, for upon this his influence will rest. Grey had it in him to satisfy all these tests, and few, if any, of our Foreign Secretaries have satisfied them better.

The maxims which he throws out here and there both reveal the man and explain the strength and dignity of his diplomacy and the regard in which Great Britain was held in his time. Foreign Ministers, he holds, are best guided by the immediate interest of the country rather than by elaborate calculations for the future, or large conceptions or great schemes. To calculate far ahead, and calculate

[13] As A. J. Balfour wrote to Lord Lansdowne on January 11th 1915: 'Now, so far as I can remember, during the years you and I were his Ministers, he never made an important suggestion of any sort on large questions of policy.' Quoted in Newton, *Lord Lansdowne, A Biography*, Macmillan, London, 1929, p. 293. Grey's evidence is to the same effect, though he thought the King to be 'a real asset of national stability'.

wrongly, is to court disaster. It is seldom possible to see much beyond direct consequences. Ministers should seek peace and stability, and not make mischief or stir up strife or create expectations which they cannot fulfil, or try to pull off momentary diplomatic scores. In diplomacy, confidence has very shallow roots. A policy which rules out all moral purpose except national interest is unlikely to achieve enduring success. To indulge hatred is to spoil wise policy and sound statecraft. In negotiation, an atmosphere of reticence, even to the point of dullness, is favourable, provided there is good faith and a desire to keep the peace. All in all, Grey was the kind of chief whom any official would most wish to serve.

He was happy, too, in his relationship with his Prime Minister, Asquith. It has been our good fortune, again and again, to find our Foreign Secretaries and Prime Ministers working together in concord and mutual support. Liverpool and Castlereagh, Grey and Palmerston, Churchill and Eden, Attlee and Bevin are cases where this relationship existed. But there have been none, perhaps, who steered a course in dangerous times and in difficult domestic circumstances with greater intimate sense of common purpose than Asquith and Edward Grey. How much we lose when there is lack of common purpose is clear when we think of Disraeli and Derby, of Lloyd George and Curzon or of Neville Chamberlain and Eden.

It is a frequent reproach of historians and political commentators that statesmen so seldom see the way the world is going or adapt their policies today to the undercurrents in affairs which will dominate the situation tomorrow. But the recorded prognostications of such publicists are not markedly enlightening or perspicacious. Norman Angell, in *The Great Illusion* (1910), thought, like many another, that France was more militarist than Germany. He argued that war could not pay, that military and political power gave a nation no commercial advantage, and that it was an economic impossibility for one nation to seize or destroy the wealth of another. But against this, it is fair to note that Napoleon I had shown, and that Hitler was to show, that war could indeed be made to pay, at any rate so long as one was winning. And the world of 1910 was not the world of Napoleon or of Hitler. It was, as Angell saw it, a world of economically civilized nations, bound indissolubly together in interdependence by a complex, delicate and all-pervading credit and banking system. The day was gone when conquered peoples could be enslaved by the conqueror or when tangible booty could be the fruit of conquest. No nation would be tempted to breach the secure laws of economic liberalism upon which the welfare of all depended. On these assumptions, there was a good deal to be said for Norman Angell's thesis. What he did not foresee (why should he?) was that the prevailing integrated world economy was doomed to be widely superseded by economic nationalism with its concept of self-sufficiency, and that before mid-century totalitarian régimes of the new mould would ruthlessly apply the methods of the old colonial system at its worst even to civilized European communities. One is reminded of the man who said in the late 1930s: 'It is all one to me whether the Nazis come and take us over or not. I've got my pension: they can't touch that.'

Even the European territorial *status quo* was held to be secure and untouchable in those halcyon days, when the only menaces to peace visible to radical eyes were the machinations of secret diplomacy, the rapacity of armament manufacturers or the sinister operations of international financiers. H. N. Brailsford wrote in 1914: 'the dangers which forced our ancestors into European coalitions and Continental wars have gone never to return . . . In Europe the epoch of conquest is over . . . My own belief is that there will be no more wars among the six Great Powers.'[14] Jean Jaurès, the French socialist leader, had said in 1904, eight years before the Balkan war: 'the great upheavals, either the passionate efforts of nationalities which wished to establish themselves, or the attempts at repression which crushed them, have ended . . , No nation has now a vital interest in altering the map of Europe.'[15] Brailsford thought that the Poles were so bound to Russia by considerations of trade and finance that, though they might demand autonomy, they 'would regard separation as an economic disaster' and would 'reject independence as a free gift.'[16]

In spite of the example of Jacobin rule in France in the 1790s and of the Paris Commune of 1871, it was not sufficiently realized that the ideas enunciated by Rousseau and the Enlightenment in the eighteenth century, and by Hegel and Marx in the nineteenth, might, if given practical application, establish totalitarian dictatorships in liberal Europe. It was not only Acton who held (in 1895, in

[14] *The War of Steel and Gold*, Bell, London, 1914, pp. 30, 35.
[15] Quoted in D. W. Brogan, *The Development of Modern France (1870–1939)*, Hamish Hamilton, London, 1940, p. 397.
[16] *The War of Steel and Gold*, p. 35.

his Inaugural Lecture on the Study of History): 'This constancy of progress, of progress in the direction of organized and assured freedom, is the characteristic fact of Modern History, and its tribute to the theory of Providence.' It was not realized that the new nationalism, which had given due warning of its explosive power in the nineteenth century, would in the twentieth, of its own motion, and in reaction to the conservative resistance to it, disrupt the established political order in Europe, and release forces which would open up to new political ambitions the prospect of mastery in Europe and, maybe, in the world. Already, before the end of the nineteenth century, the attack on the rational basis of European thought had begun. The dethronement of reason in favour of intuition and the inner drive would lead to a cult and practice of violence which would afflict Europe in the new century.

Comparing the doctrines of dissenting publicists like Brailsford and Hobson with the work of sober historians who base their labours upon a study of the voluminous original documents now available, one would think that they were not writing about the same world. When all is said, it could be argued that Lansdowne and Grey, however limited their vision and however improvised their policies might be, did, as practical statesmen, see the immediate realities of the European situation in clearer perspective than did their radical doctrinaire critics. By the successive conclusion of the Anglo-Japanese Alliance, the Entente Cordiale and the Anglo-Russian Convention, Lansdowne and Grey took concrete steps which, in the event, when the war came, placed Great Britain in a diplomatic and military position thanks to which she was able, with her European allies and later with indispensable American assistance, to save herself, and to help to save Europe, from German domination. They had a clearer perception of the coming needs of the twentieth century than had Brailsford, when he wrote in 1914: 'We play with the legendary inheritance of the Balance of Power, until we persuade ourselves that our homes are in danger, and our faiths and liberties at stake. These are the terms of an older world, as insubstantial today as the ghosts of Marlborough and Wellington . . . A clearsighted generation will scan the horizon and find no enemy. It will drop its armour, and walk the world's highways safe.'[17] Brailsford was as far wrong about Imperial Germany as the Webbs were to be later about Soviet Russia, and Neville Chamberlain about Hitler.

[17] *The War of Steel and Gold*, pp. 315, 317.

Return from Isolation

The improvement in Anglo-American relations at and after the turn of the century has been judged by an American historian to be one of the decisive events of modern history'. British opinion, both governmental and popular, was sympathetic to the new United States imperialism.[18] United States governmental opinion (though not, to the same degree, popular opinion) had a better understanding than in the past of British overseas problems. The United States representative was the only foreign diplomatist at the official banquet to Lord Kitchener at the Mansion House in November 1898. Great Britain, first of the European powers, recognized the growing strength of the United States and welcomed her accession to the ranks of the world powers. Great Britain's growing feeling of insecurity made her determined to seek American good-will. Henry Adams, speaking of 1898, recalled that 'the sudden appearance of Germany as the grizzly terror which in twenty years effected what Adamses had tried for two hundred in vain—frightened England into America's arms—seemed as melodramatic as any plot of Napoleon the Great.'[19]

But the United States herself was not free from alarm at the rise of Germany. Relations had been bad during the Spanish-American War of 1898. The conclusion of the Anglo-Japanese Alliance was approved by the United States. The building up of the United States Navy from 1906 onwards had Germany directly in view. The General Board of the United States Navy reported in 1906: 'The welfare of the United States and its immunity from entanglements with other powers is greatly strengthened by strong ties of friendship and by unanimity of action with Great Britain.' 'We have got,' wrote Henry Adams in 1906, 'to support France against Germany, and fortify the Atlantic system beyond attack; for if Germany breaks down England and France, she becomes the centre of a military world, and we are lost.'[20] The writings of Admiral Mahan had shown how close the two countries were linked by the interests of sea-power. But while there could be a friendly understanding, there could be no alliance. Washington was no more willing to commit itself to London than was London to commit itself to Paris.

The friendly understanding with the United States enabled the

[18] Kipling's poem about the 'white man's burden' was written as a tribute to the United States civil administrators in the Philippines.
[19] *The Education of Henry Adams*, Constable, London, 1918, pp. 362–63.
[20] Quoted in Allen, *Great Britain and the United States*, pp. 608, 621.

Admiralty to withdraw naval forces from the Caribbean, as the alliance with Japan and the Entente with France had allowed us to do in the Far East and the Mediterranean, in order to concentrate a great force in and near home waters. On the other hand, the Alaskan dispute had shown that the United States would press Great Britain hard to gain an advantage over her; and from time to time an old ghost would walk. In the debate on the reciprocity agreement with Canada in 1911, Champ Clark, the Speaker of the House of Representatives, said that he supported the measure 'because I hope to see the day when the American flag will float over every square foot of British North American possessions clear to the North Pole.'

The development of German policy which had brought Great Britain into agreement with France and Russia and into close understanding with the United States also tightened the bonds of empire. There were by now two new Dominions: New Zealand (1907) and the Union of South Africa (1910). Two further suggestions for the creation of imperial institutions, one by the Colonial Secretary, Alfred Lyttelton, in 1905 and one by Sir Joseph Ward, the Prime Minister of New Zealand, in 1911, were noted but not pursued at colonial or imperial conferences. The principle of inter-imperial relationship remained that of intimate consultation and imperial unity based upon decentralization and local autonomy. At the imperial conference of 1911, it was decided that whenever possible the Dominions should be informed of any proposed transactions by the United Kingdom government with foreign countries in the sphere of commercial relations before they should be concluded. But the most striking advance was made in the realm of defence. The Dominions increased their naval forces, whether these were organized as local forces or as contributions to the Royal Navy. One battle-cruiser each was contributed by Australia, New Zealand and Malaya. Canada, under the influence of the Liberal opposition, led by Sir Wilfrid Laurier, was not able to do likewise. At the special imperial conference on defence held in the crucial year 1909, the Dominion representatives heard a statement on British foreign policy by Sir Edward Grey. They agreed that in time of war, when the Dominion naval contingents, in whole or in part, had been placed under the control of the imperial government, the ships were 'to form an integral part of the British fleet, and remain under the control of the British Admiralty.' It was also agreed that Dominion representatives should attend meetings of the Committee of Imperial

274

Defence when questions affecting them were under discussion. German opinion had confidently expected that the colonies and Dominions would break away from the United Kingdom if the latter went to war in Europe. This is only one of the many cases where German political judgment in the pre-war years was widely at fault.

The first few years of the twentieth century have seemed to deserve special attention for two reasons. They marked a decisive turn in British foreign policy, a reversion to the recognition and practice of the balance of power. Great Britain was once more operating actively as a great power among great powers, *primus inter pares*. There was a renewed alertness, an awakening to the grim realities of the international situation. Secondly, during these brief years, Great Britain was, for the last time, able to base her foreign policy upon the expectation of the complete security of the metropolis behind the shield of the Navy, provided that its strength could be duly maintained. The day was not far off when the submarine would bring us near to starvation, and when we should have a foretaste of the effect of air-power that could stride over the intervening seas. As to the maintenance of naval supremacy, there was, in spite of strongly argued dissent on the part of radical opinion, which at one time included both Lloyd George and Churchill, no hesitation on the part of the Government or of the public at large. The need was recognized and it was fully met, without undue strain on the economy. Great Britain still had the financial and industrial strength to pursue effectively both a European and a world policy. She could counter the threat with adequate defence. She was willing to negotiate, and could do so from strength. It is a mark of the Edwardian era, seldom remarked upon, that, whether under a Conservative or a Liberal government, whether with Lansdowne or with Grey as Foreign Secretary, Great Britain was perhaps at this time able to exercise her influence in international affairs more freely than she had been able to do since the reigns of George IV, William IV and early Victoria, when her foreign policy was in the strong and skilful hands of Castlereagh, Canning and Palmerston. Great Britain was still a world-power, but not now in her own strength alone. Forced once again to meet a threat from Europe, she had felt the need of links of alliance or of association with other powers.

The Edwardian age is thought of as lush and raffish, and so, in certain circles, it was. But this was the froth and not the substance of national life. It was a time of economic stagnation; of industrial and commercial lethargy which provoked the future George V to the admonition, 'Wake up, England!'; of perhaps excessive search for easy money in investment overseas. And yet it was a time of renewed energy, political, social and intellectual, which too often expressed itself in extreme and violent courses. R. C. K. Ensor has spoken of 'the seething and teeming of this pre-war period, its immense ferment and its restless fertility.'[21] As G. K. Chesterton had noted, a cloud had been lifted from the mind of man.

A fresh current of new ideas revivified the Navy and the Army. The turbulent genius of Sir John Fisher, the 'dark angel' of the Navy, gave us the all-big-gun ship, the *Dreadnought*, and if he had had his way, would have ensured an overwhelming superiority over Germany, though in some spheres of equipment and training—gunnery, range-finding, high explosive, mines and scouting aircraft—the Germans were ahead of us. Unlike the Germans, too, we still had no adequate general staff of the Navy. The intellectual grasp and administrative skill of Haldane, building upon the work of Lansdowne and Wolseley, gave us a quickly mobilizable, well balanced and well equipped expeditionary force with adequate reserves, the like of which we had never possessed before. But it was, compared with the continental conscript armies, as the Kaiser is reputed to have said, 'contemptibly small'.

The Government of Asquith had, with an efficiency hitherto unexampled in our history, perfected in advance the administrative arrangements which it would be necessary to bring into operation if war were to break out. It was not merely that a general staff had been created and that the expeditionary force would be smoothly transported overseas. Through the Committee of Imperial Defence, future military problems were exhaustively studied and common action with Dominion governments was foreshadowed. Plans were made for such things as blockade, trading with the enemy, the treatment of neutral and enemy ships, censorship and the treatment of aliens. All these arrangements were embodied in a War Book; and the necessary draft Orders in Council accompanied the King wherever he went so as to be ready in case of emergency. But the perfecting of administrative arrangements, however laudable, is no substitute for the laying of concrete plans, political, strategic and economic, and in the realm of supply, in preparation for war. Here our arrangements were either defective or non-existent.

[21] *England, 1870–1914*, p. 557.

Return from Isolation

In the history of our diplomacy also these years mark a new era. Like many of his predecessors, Salisbury had done a good deal of his most important work himself, with the help of his private secretary and a small junior staff. Lansdowne and Grey, on the contrary, consulted fully with their senior advisers in the Foreign Office. None the less, the Secretary of State was master in his own house. 'I did not,' said Grey, 'regard anything except my own letters and official papers as deciding policy.' The professional staff of the Foreign Office, now substantially increased in numbers, were no longer so heavily charged with menial tasks but were expected to give advice on action and policy. It was a sign of the times that a junior official, as Eyre Crowe was then, should have composed and submitted so grave a state paper as his famous memorandum on Germany of January 1st 1907. So also in the field of diplomacy. We had had eminent ambassadors in the nineteenth century—Stratford, Cowley, Odo Russell, Lyons, Lytton, Dufferin, Pauncefote, to name no others. But ministers would sometimes complain of their wilfulness or idiosyncrasy. With the new century, there is a growing coherence between the home and foreign branches of the service which will later be given institutional form. After the complaints of Clarendon and Disraeli, it is refreshing to read the tribute paid by Asquith to H.M. Ambassadors for their services in the pre-war crisis: 'We were singularly fortunate in these critical days in having as our representatives at Berlin, Vienna and St. Petersburg three diplomatists so qualified to handle a situation of almost unexampled difficulty, by long experience, trained insight, and complete understanding both of the aims and methods of British policy, as Sir E. Goschen, Sir M. de Bunsen and Sir G. Buchanan.'[22]

Opinion had been deeply divided, majority against minority, about the Boer War. It was violently and more equally divided about Ireland. It had been at odds, majority against minority, about Germany. Even the Cabinet itself was more in the nature of a coalition between Liberal imperialists and pro-German or non-interventionist radicals than a single party body. It says much for the prudence of Asquith and Grey in not prematurely posing the question of European commitment that the Cabinet was held together until German action in Belgium removed doubts from almost all minds. When Germany brought war to Europe, national unity on the gravest issues, which had so often been the source of British

[22] *The Genesis of the War*, Cassell, London, 1923, p. 202.

strength and influence in the world, was again manifested with only minor dissent. Great Britain was again to be tested, as she had not been tested for a century. Her statesmen, Conservative and Liberal, with the help of her diplomatists, sailors and soldiers, had ensured that she was well prepared for the test.

It has been suggested that Grey might have done more to educate parliament and the public about the state of affairs in Europe. But to have talked more about it, to have posed questions of policy too clearly, might well have increased tension abroad and fomented disunity at home, inside and outside the Government. In the end the Germans themselves, by their open disregard of their international obligations in the case of Belgium, made the British decision easier. By being enabled to go into the war on behalf of Belgium, instead of upon the more controversial issue of support for France, we ensured national unity: the military conversations with France did not, as they might have done, determine the issue; they merely ensured that the expeditionary force could be established smoothly and expeditiously beside the French. By going into the war at all, we almost certainly saved ourselves from having to stand alone later against a Germany supreme in Europe. Upon such a narrow margin of fortune or of choice does the fate of nations sometimes depend.

Could Great Britain, by a more vigorous and resolute exercise of her influence in Europe, have averted the conflict? The answer, almost certainly, is that she could not. Germany, Russia and Austria showed no such spirit of accommodation as they had done during the Balkan wars and the London Conference. There were currents in European opinion and policy which it was not within the capacity of one power to divert: South Slav nationalism, with its deliberate aim to follow up the disruption of the Turkish Empire in Europe by that of the Austro-Hungarian Empire; Austria's desperate determination to avert this calamity, preferably by force; Russia's absolute refusal to contemplate a repetition of the humiliation of 1909; Germany's unwillingness to respond to the conciliatory tenders of both France and Great Britain whose governments included strong pro-Germans, early exemplars of policies of appeasement; and her readiness to see a European war break out, for the sake of what she could get out of it, and first of all in the Near East. Nothing that Grey could have said would have deterred Austria from launching her ultimatum or embarking on her war against Serbia, relying as she could, upon repeated assurances of unconditional support from

Return from Isolation

Germany. In October 1913, the Kaiser told Berchtold, the Austrian Foreign Minister: 'Whatever comes from the Vienna Foreign Office is a command for me.' 'I am ready to draw the sword whenever your action requires.' Before the ultimatum, Bethmann-Hollweg assured Berchtold that, whatever Austria's decision, Germany would stand behind her as an ally; and, after the ultimatum, Germany, it was said, would support Austria 'whatever the risk'. Germany brought the war on, not perhaps of deliberate purpose—her policy was subject to no firm central direction—but driven rather by inner anarchic necessity, the necessity that knows no law.

What Grey could do, he did. He offered to mediate between Serbia and Austria-Hungary. On July 26th, after the Serbian reply to the Austrian ultimatum, he proposed a conference on the lines of the Balkan conference of 1912–13. It seemed to him that, if such a conference met, it might be possible to agree that there should be no mobilization so long as the conference was in being. Germany declined the proposal: Europe was ripe for war. Austria declared war on Serbia on July 28th. By now diplomacy was in fact powerless. Diplomacy requires time, and no time was to be given. Effective authority in countries with great conscript armies passed, in time of war crisis, to those who were concerned with assembling and setting these armies in motion, and in Germany the last word, here as elsewhere, lay with the Kaiser. The dominating thought in the minds of those charged with these duties was the problem of mobilization. No one could afford to allow a possible adversary to steal a march on him. And since German mobilization was rapid and Russian mobilization was slow, and since Germany thought immediate action was necessary for her security, Germany would not forgo the advantage which this gave her. The march of the military machine over-ran the conference table. Wisely had King Frederick William IV of Prussia said in 1854: 'The green table of the Conference Room is the sheet anchor of the world.'

Could Great Britain, by making alliances with France and Russia and thus making clear her intention to go to war if the case arose, have deterred Germany from exacerbating the conflict or have prevailed upon her to help to halt the war? There are several answers to this. The first is that it was, for internal reasons, not possible for Great Britain to enter into such alliances. Sir Arthur Nicolson, when he was ambassador at St Petersburg, pressed for the convention to be turned into an alliance; and when he was Permanent

279

Under-Secretary at the Foreign Office, he and Eyre Crowe urged Grey to conclude an alliance with France. Grey maintained that neither the Cabinet nor public opinion would accept this. But even had this been possible, the effect on Germany would probably not have been very great. British intervention had already been accepted as almost a certainty. In September 1912, the Kaiser declared that the Entente meant 'only one thing for Germany's enemies: they fight and arm together against us.' Later in the same year, he said: 'From envy and hatred of Germany England intends absolutely to stand by France and Russia against us.' The general staff had made their calculations on the assumption that the invasion of Belgium would bring Great Britain in. They discounted the value of British intervention to such a point that they made no attempt to hinder the transport of the British Expeditionary Force.

Those who would claim that Germany did not bear the primary responsibility for precipitating a European war have some simple and formidable facts to explain away: Germany's evident appetite for war, noted with consternation by Colonel House on a visit in May and June 1914; Germany's unconditional support of Austria both before and after the ultimatum to Serbia; her declarations of war against Russia and France; and her invasion of Belgium, whose neutrality she had guaranteed. This last was an act admitted by Bethmann-Hollweg to be a violation of international law; it was also the key to the whole long-matured German military plan in the west. It may well be that, given time, Russia would have declared war against Austria, that Germany would then have gone to war with Russia under her treaty with Austria, and France with Germany under her treaty with Russia. None of this happened. Germany, though under no threat to her security, launched a preventive war. Indeed, the only country which entered the war in fulfilment of a treaty was Great Britain herself.[23]

[23] In the early years of the twentieth century, as again in the 1930s, Germany could have achieved a good measure of mastery in Europe, as a step towards world power, by peaceful means. She had only to use her political, economic and military potential with skill and resource, and the prize could have been hers.

There were Germans who thought they saw how this could be done. The objective, it was said, would be to displace Great Britain from her un-deserved pre-eminence as a world power. The purpose of intensive econo-mic development and the expansion of naval armaments would be to establish a position of strength in face of which the British might be peace-fully persuaded to yield up their position of naval supremacy. The osten-

Return from Isolation

Could Great Britain have kept out of the war and have remained neutral? The answer is that, in view of her staff conversations with France from 1906 onwards, the concordant if not formally concerted dispositions of the British and French Navies, and the naval conversations with Russia agreed upon in 1914, she could not in honour have done so. As Sir Eyre Crowe wrote on July 30th 1914: 'The argument that there is no written bond binding us to France is correct. There is no contractual obligation. But the Entente has been made, strengthened, put to the test and celebrated in a manner

sible objective would be to replace a European balance of power on land resting on predominant British sea-power by a wider world-balance of sea-power based on German predominance in Europe. The minor powers would thus be released from the stranglehold of the Royal Navy. Germany would be waging what the historian, Hans Delbrück, called a 'dry war' against Great Britain in terms of what we should now call 'peaceful co-existence'. If Great Britain yielded, well and good. Germany, a peaceful power, would have secured a peaceful change. If Great Britain did not yield, the 'dry war' would go on until she was goaded into making war in order to extricate herself from the mounting pressure. In that event, she would be the aggressor, and would make war in conditions materially and morally unfavourable to herself. (Dehio, *Germany and World Politics*, passim.)

It is possible that if war had not broken out in 1914 in the way it did, some such Anglo-German collision might have occurred. But Germany had neither the wisdom nor the patience to play her part in this kind of drama to its due conclusion. Nor perhaps had she the material resources to go on building both navy and army. By 1913–14 she was feeling the strain much more than was Great Britain. The British paid for their arms from the proceeds of taxation. The Germans armed themselves chiefly on credit and, to recoup themselves, needed a short, successful war, with vast indemnities. Then again, with a few more years of peace, Russia might have become increasingly formidable. (The massive industrialization of Russia was not started by the Bolsheviks: it had been going on for twenty years before 1914.) Like Napoleon and Hitler, Imperial Germany would have to try to dispose of Russia first. In the event, war, when it occurred, was not a war between Great Britain and Germany based on imperial rivalry. There was no concrete issue between them which was remotely worth a war. War between them occurred because Germany could not refrain from involving herself in an eastern European conflict, and, by a fatal development of her own involvement, bringing Great Britain in. Her lack of European statesmanship landed her in a position where she could not face the consequences of an Austro-Hungarian collapse, and the advantage which Russia would seek to draw from them; and the stupidity of Austro-Hungarian policy made that collapse certain. Great Britain did indeed declare war on Germany. But she did not go to war under provocation, as a last desperate resort, alone, in defence of her own world position, as Germany's presumed plan would have required. She went to war freely, in fulfilment of an obligation, when Germany, by her own act, had already arrayed Russia and France against herself.

justifying a belief that a moral bond was being forged. The whole policy of the Entente can have no meaning if it does not signify that in a just quarrel England will stand by her friends.' When Grey still hesitated to declare himself in the first days of August, Paul Cambon bitterly remarked to Nicolson: 'I am wondering whether the word "honour" is to be erased from the English language.'

To pursue the question whether Great Britain could have remained neutral, we have to go further back. If her military talks and naval dispositions morally bound her, was she right to enter upon them? Could she not have rested upon her agreements with France and Russia which bound her by way of contract to no action beyond diplomatic support? The only answer one can give is that those who were charged with our affairs came to the conclusion that it was no longer possible for us to continue to stand alone, or almost alone, in the world. The argument was conducted, at the crucial moment of decision in 1901, between a Conservative Prime Minister and his successor as Foreign Secretary, and it was Lansdowne's policy that prevailed. Of that policy, Grey's policy was a natural extension. Here, if anywhere, the error occurred, if error there was. To the present writer it is clear beyond question that the right decision was made.

When Grey delivered his historic speech in the House of Commons on August 3rd 1914, his task was made easier by the news, not yet fully confirmed, of Germany's ultimatum to Belgium and her violation of the Belgian frontier. In making his plea, he did not rely upon Belgium alone. He based the case for supporting France both upon obligations of honour and upon considerations of expediency. 'If France is beaten, if Belgium fell under the same dominating influence . . . consider what would be at stake from the point of view of British interests . . . I do not believe, for a moment, that at the end of this war, even if we stood aside and remained aside, we should be in a position, a material position, to use our force decisively to undo what had happened in the course of the war, to prevent the whole of the west of Europe opposite us—if that had been the result of the war—from falling under the domination of a single power.'

To the need to meet an obligation of honour, and to uphold the public law of Europe, was added the age-old argument, the need to prevent western Europe from being dominated by a single power. Great Britain was once again contemplating armed intervention by land forces on the continent of Europe; and she was doing so for the only reason which had in the past justified such a course, the need to see to her own security. The wheel had come full circle. The difference was that, since 1870, what had to be safeguarded was not only the integrity of the Low Countries but the independence of France herself.

The primary objective of British foreign policy was still linked with the practice of the balance of power even in its newest manifestation, that is to say, the building up of two opposing groups, ill-assorted though they might be, each working for its own predominance and against the predominance of the other. One group was defensive, the other offensive. One of them hoped that the balance, shifting though it might be, would preserve peace; both hoped that if peace were broken, the advantage would rest with itself. In the event, the balance proved to be so nearly even, and military techniques so favourable to the defence, that a war of attrition followed, with the Germans getting the upper hand. The intervention of the United States, provoked by the last of a long line of Imperial German follies, turned the scale. Europe could no longer look after herself. The German question, which for three hundred years had nourished the rivalry of Valois, Bourbon and Habsburg, next became the concern of the peripheral powers, Russia and Great Britain. Now the United States had been drawn in. Today, the German question lies at the heart of the conflict between the United States and Russia.

There are still those who think that the sacrifices of the war were in vain, and that it would have been better if Germany had been allowed to prevail. Earl Russell said in March 1959: 'I thought, as a politician, and I still think, that it would have been very much better for the world if Britain had remained neutral and the Germans had won a quick victory. We should not have had either the Nazis or the Communists if that had happened, because they were both products of the First World War.'[24]

Against this confident discernment of a hypothetical event by a great logician, one may set not only the emphatic opinion of the practical statesman, Edward Grey, that to have stayed out of the war would have left us 'nothing but a miserable and ignoble future', but also the ripe historian's judgment of Sir Llewellyn Woodward: 'Though Europe should not and need not have come to such a pass, between 1914 and 1918 I thought that the war which we were then

[24] *The Listener*, March 19th 1959, p. 504.

283

fighting was worth its cost. I think so today . . . If, in the circumstances as they were, it had not been fought, if, once undertaken, it had not been prolonged to the defeat of Germany, the damage to civilized society would have been immensely great . . . I would say that my own experience of living, enlarged by this reading about the experience of others, has led me to accept more readily the importance of active resistance to evil things although we can never know how our least action will reverberate through history.'[25]

[25] 'Some Reflections on British Policy, 1939–45', Stevenson Memorial Lecture, 1955, *International Affairs*, vol. XXXI, no. 3, July 1955, p. 289.

CHAPTER XIII

War and Inter-War

During the years between 1900 and 1914, Great Britain had moved step by step towards a revolution in her foreign policy, the result of which was her involvement in a European war. With her entry into that war, she faced, to her own surprise and to the surprise of the rest of the world, a sudden, inescapable and even more momentous revolution in her military history.

The need to go to war in 1914 was willingly accepted, though with little realization by the public of what war would involve, either in military operations or in its impact upon the life and economy of the participating nations. Large bodies of men had been engaged in the Russo-Japanese War of 1904–05 and in the Balkan wars of 1912–13. Battles had, apart from the four-day Battle of Mukden, been short and sharp and all of them had had a clear result. What most people had in mind was a six-months' war, with little dislocation of national life. Some members of the Government knew better. Both Grey and Asquith spoke in the grimmest terms. Kitchener, who had become Secretary of State for War, prepared at once for a long war. But the slogan was 'business as usual'. The Germans expected to be in Paris in six weeks. What moved the ordinary man to face this new experience so readily was the simple feeling that Germany was being an intolerable and dangerous nuisance, upsetting the world for her own aggrandizement and striking down small and peaceful nations. Serbia might have given provocation, but Belgium certainly had not. Economic rivalry had little or nothing to do with it—bankers, manufacturers and merchants were men of peace; in 1914, Germany was our second-best customer and we ourselves were one of her best; we were both profiting from the industrialization of Europe and from the growth of world trade. Nor was the war, at the outset, as it afterwards became for us, a war for survival as a great power.

Reawakening and Readjustment

Few things in our history have been finer than the nation-wide flow of volunteers into the forces between August 1914 and January 1916 when at last compulsory enlistment was introduced. It was not merely the spontaneous act of enlistment, but also the zeal with which the training was undertaken, the requirements of military discipline accepted, and the terrible ordeals of active service endured. An eminent commander in the Second World War was to say that, in the First World War, battles had been won by the rank-and-file, whereas in the Second they were won by the officers. The men of Kitchener's armies fought from the heart, with a strength drawn from a rebirth of national energy which, in some curious way, had come in with the new century. This was true of others besides the British. The Third Republic, which served France well for nearly seventy years, was now living through its greatest days. Profoundly pacific, France was roused to proud, passionate and heroic defence. The French Army, by a paradoxical development, had since the defeat of 1870–71 become the symbol and the agent of national revival, an element of continuity in the body politic. In England, the reverse process was seen. Here, the strength of national unity flowed into the new army and gave it form and substance. The endurance of the ill-led and ill-equipped Russian conscript armies, until they broke under the strain, contributed in no small measure to the final Allied victory. Of the German people, too, it must be said that they showed a skill and fortitude in the furnace of war not inferior to those of their adversaries.

When, at the first turning point in the war in September 1914, the German advance was halted on the Marne, short of Paris, the war of movement gave place to a war of open and continuous entrenched positions. Here, along a line between Switzerland and the Narrow Seas, four million western Europeans settled down to slaughter each other by mounting futile attacks upon field fortifications where barbed wire, artillery and machine-guns gave the defenders a marked advantage which military science had not yet found a way to overcome, and which it was not to find until the last year of the war. The small British Expeditionary Force had been swiftly transported across the Channel and placed in the line side by side with the French and Belgians. In time, the Expeditionary Force was to be built up until, in numbers, it could bear comparison with the armies of France. Both French and Germans had mobilized great armies before. For the British, it was an experience unique in their history.

They had become a great land power as well as a power holding supremacy at sea.

It is a matter for astonishment how these amateur soldiers were able to sustain the crippling losses which trench warfare inflicted upon them. At Verdun in 1916, where Falkenhayn had set out to bleed the French Army to death, the French lost 350,000 men and the Germans some 330,000. In the Somme campaign in the summer and autumn of the same year, the British losses were 400,000 against France's 200,000 and Germany's 500,000. In the battles in the Ypres Salient in the late summer and autumn of 1917 associated with the name of Passchendaele, the British losses were again 400,000. Both campaigns were mounted and inexorably pursued by Haig in order to relieve pressure on the French, at the urgent request first of Joffre and then of Pétain.

What were these men fighting for? On what strength did they draw? One answer to this question has been suggested by an American novelist in the words of one of his characters, looking down after the war upon Beaumont-Hamel, the key point in the Somme battle in which, on the opening day, July 1st 1916, the British Army lost 50,000 men: 'This Western front business couldn't be done again, not for a long time. The young men think they could do it, but they couldn't. They could fight the first Marne again, but not this. This took religion and years of plenty and tremendous sureties and the exact relation that existed between the classes . . . You had to have a whole-souled sentimental equipment going back further than you could remember. You had to remember Christmas, and postcards of the Crown Prince and his fiancée, and little cafés in Valence and beer gardens in Unter den Linden and weddings at the *mairie*, and going to the Derby, and your grandfather's whiskers.'[1]

The twentieth century was drawing on moral capital accumulated in the nineteenth. The blood of older times was summoned up. That other American, William Faulkner, looking back upon the England of 1914, saw '. . . that peaceful land where in green petrification the old splendid bloody deeds, the spirits of the blundering courageous men, slumbered in every stone and tree.'[2]

[1] F. Scott Fitzgerald, *Tender is the Night*, Penguin Books, Harmondsworth, 1955, p. 125.
[2] *Dr. Martino and Other Stories*, Chatto and Windus, London, 1958, p. 306.

Reawakening and Readjustment

In this war of attrition, the British were, as the war proceeded, to play a major part by land as well as by sea. Ludendorff's final all-out offensive at the junction of the British and French forces on the western front in the spring of 1918, designed to knock out France and Great Britain before the American forces could be built up, and before the strangle-hold of the blockade could be decisive, was successfully countered. At home the crisis was met by Lloyd George with an unflinching fortitude to which Winston Churchill has paid a discerning tribute.[3] In the field the Allies were saved from rout by the superb genius of Marshal Foch, now in command of all the Allied Forces on the Western Front. But once the front was stabilized, Haig and the new, finely tempered British and Dominion armies under his command shouldered the main burden of planning and executing the attack upon the now shaken German forces. Under their powerful thrusts the Germans gave ground and were driven in retreat until they could fight no longer. The French had prepared the way for the final advance, and the American forces under General Pershing, though inferior in numbers and in military experience, seemed by their presence and promise to turn the scale both materially and morally. The ten mature and virile Dominion divisions had played their part beside their younger British comrades. 'It was, nevertheless, mainly a British victory. Britain put far more proportionately into the pool than her partners, including more than the lion's share of the air forces, now the finest in the world and queen of the skies . . . This was a wonderful feat of arms, proof of fathomless spirit.'[4] Since the end of the battle for Verdun in 1916, the British had borne the major burden on the Western front. In the end, Haig was master of the field. The west was the decisive theatre; but, in more characteristic British fashion, there were interventions in more distant theatres—on Gallipoli, at Salonica and in Mesopotamia, where the Indian Army added its strength to the imperial power. Less than twenty years after the British Army had taken nearly three years to subjugate a small agricultural community in South Africa, it had successfully conducted far-flung campaigns

[3] 'One of the great qualities in Mr. Lloyd George was his power of obliterating the past and concentrating his whole being upon meeting the new situation. . . . The resolution of the Prime Minister was unshaken under his truly awful responsibilities.' *The World Crisis, 1916–1918*, Thornton Butterworth, London, 1927, pp. 423–24.

[4] Cyril Falls, 'Reflections on Armistice Day', *The Times*, November 10th 1958.

as well as matching itself victoriously with European armies of continental scale.

The German submarine war upon merchant ships came very near to bringing Great Britain to defeat. In April 1917, 870,000 tons were lost and we were left with food for no more than six weeks. The submarine menace was in the end defeated by new devices like the hydroplane, the depth charge and the spotter aircraft and by the old and tried but too-long neglected operation of the armed convoy. In this, the United States naval forces under Admiral Sims, a warm advocate of Anglo-American co-operation, gave whole-hearted aid. Side by side with our anti-submarine measures came our own distant blockade founded upon bureaucratic devices like the navicert and the black list, to which the neutrals submitted with more or less good grace. Before the end of the war, the blockade had cut off almost all imports into Germany. Germany's economic life was paralysed, and this more than anything else was the cause of her breakdown.

If in the days before the outbreak of war diplomatic action among the great European powers was over-ridden by the plans and requirements of the high commands, during the war itself the ability of diplomacy to determine the course of events was even more directly dependent on material power than in time of peace. It was closely proportional to the achievement or to the prospect of success in the field. One exception to this rule was the conduct of relations with the United States, who, as the great neutral, could stand aloof from the conflict and could settle her own policies in her own interest. The war-time diplomacy of the Allied belligerents would have a double objective. They must keep the allies they had, and try to attract new ones. They must also govern their conduct of the blockade so as not to drive the neutrals over to the enemy. As a result of these operations, Russia was kept in the war until after the Bolshevik revolution. Italy and Roumania were brought in as allies, though to no great advantage. Turkey and Bulgaria resisted all appeals and entered the war on Germany's side. But the great achievement of Allied diplomacy, and in particular of British diplomacy, was the skill with which the maximum possible scale of blockade was maintained without provoking a rupture with the United States. The risks to be run were that the United States would institute an armed convoy system to pierce the blockade or place an embargo upon supplies to the Allies, though it is fair to note that, in view of the great volume of Allied war-orders, there was strong domestic opposition in the

U

United States to any embargo. Credit must go to Grey for reconciling divergent views among his colleagues and for resisting popular clamour for more stringent measures than he thought prudent; and jointly to Grey and Walter Hines Page, the United States ambassador, for smoothing the flow of communications between the two capitals. Problems which had caused a war in 1812 were safely surmounted until the United States, becoming a belligerent herself, adopted the belligerent in contrast to the neutral view of contraband and blockade, though she refrained from infringing many, but not all, of the neutral rights which she had sought to defend before 1917. She usually left to us the work of interception and search, and the unpopularity that went with it. Unlike the Germans, we avoided the supreme folly of driving the Americans into action against us.

Those responsible for concluding the secret treaties by which Russia was kept in the war and Italy brought into it have been the target of much undeserved obloquy. In the main, the territories offered as a bribe or *douceur* were parts of the Turkish and Austrian empires which were plainly due for dissolution if the Allies won the war. It was reasonable to plan their disposition in advance. Such transactions in the interest of survival in the course of a war were surely no more morally reprehensible than war itself. What irked Grey about them, curiously enough, was not their content but their secrecy. As diplomatic operations, they were more than usually unedifying. The treaty with Russia, by which Russia was promised Constantinople and the Straits, was the direct consequence of the British-inspired Gallipoli expedition. The Russians, with memories of the nineteenth century, were afraid that if we got to Constantinople, we would stay there, and that we might even bring the Greeks in. We had to do something for them, not being able to send them munitions or to relieve pressure on them by winning victories in the west. In fact, having established ourselves in Egypt, we were now less interested in the Straits, and we were to further our own ends by bringing the neutral zone of Persia into our sphere of interest as our share of the deal. The French saw things differently. They had been negotiated out of Egypt in 1904, and they still maintained their interest in the Straits. By a chain reaction, to appease them, we then concluded in January 1916 the Sykes–Picot Agreement, by which there was to be a comprehensive partition of Asiatic Turkey, Syria being in the French sphere and Mesopotamia in the British, the Russians later getting their share in Armenia and Kurdistan. It was a cause of great future trouble that this agreement was in conflict with promises already made to the Arabs

If Great Britain promoted the treaty with Russia, the treaty with Italy was promoted by France. The Italians opened their mouths very wide, but they somewhat moderated their demands when they saw that Austria might after all be defeated without their help. The Tyrol would be acquired at the expense of the German Austrians; but Istria and Dalmatia were Slav in population and their allocation to Italy was repugnant to Serbia and would be the seed of future trouble. There were also vague promises about Asia Minor and about Colonies.

At the opening of the war, the Allied war-aims were of the most general description, other than the aim to achieve victory. A few days after the declaration of war, Asquith said that we were fighting to fulfil an international obligation and to vindicate the principle that small nationalities were not to be crushed in defiance of international good faith. In November 1914, he spoke of the recovery of Belgium, the security of France, the rights of small nations and the destruction of Prussian military domination. In December, Grey, in a letter to Theodore Roosevelt, said that we were fighting also to save the British Empire. Not until October 1917 was the recovery by France of Alsace-Lorraine made an essential British war-aim. It was not until President Wilson challenged the Allies to state their aims that these were, early in 1917, formulated even in rudimentary form.

There was little or nothing in the policy of the United States in the twenty years before her entry into the First World War—including the period of open United States imperialism—which justified the attitude of moral superiority which then and later she adopted towards the Allied powers who were at mortal grip with Germany. In point of political morality, the Spanish-American War and the Boer War had been on a par, and the Americans whom Mr Dooley mocked at supported both of them. The one episode that stood out like a beacon of right-dealing was Wilson's successful pressure for the repeal of the unjustly discriminatory clause of the Panama Tolls Act of 1912. Having been forced at last into war with Germany in her own direct interest—war trade with the Allies had raised the United States out of a depression and the resumed unrestricted submarine campaign was threatening the whole United States economy with collapse—the United States had claimed to be moved by moral and idealistic motives.[5] She was, as President Wilson said, fighting to make the world 'safe for democracy' and for the universal dominion of right in international affairs. For a century, the British Navy had stood between her and Europe when she was vulnerable. For two and a half years, the three major allies had been locked in conflict with a Germany who, if victorious, would—as American statesmen had recognized—be ready to challenge the United States herself. Colonel House, on his first enthusiastic, untutored, roving mission to Europe, reported from Germany early in 1916: 'If victory is theirs, the war lords will reign supreme and democratic governments will be imperilled throughout the world.' As Wilson himself once admitted: 'England is fighting our fight.' Germany, indeed, now seemed to be on the edge of victory. Every consideration of self-interest would call on the United States to intervene. But it has been rightly remarked that democracies will not so willingly fight wars for self-interest as for some moral cause; and there is little doubt that President Wilson was conforming not merely to his own deeply held conviction but also to his judgment of his own people and their legislature when he cast a moral cloak upon an operation of power-politics. Instead of allying himself with his associates, he would—mindful of the traditional policy of the Fathers—do no more than associate himself with those who were in very truth his allies. 'He is not,' said H.M. Ambassador, Sir Cecil Spring-Rice, 'a belligerent among other belligerents, but something apart.'

There was the same combination of idealism and straight politics in the peace terms which Wilson put forward during the war, and in the settlement which he secured during the negotiations at the peace conference in Paris. As Clemenceau once put it, he had a way of talking like Our Lord and of behaving like Lloyd George. There were three main elements in the Fourteen Points which he enunciated in an Address to Congress in January 1918. First there was a series of general propositions designed to eliminate what were imagined to be the basic causes of war. These propositions related to 'open covenants of peace openly arrived at, after which diplomacy would proceed always . . . in the public view'; 'absolute freedom of navigation upon the seas, alike in peace and in war'; 'equality of trade

---

[5] Had the first Russian revolution of 1917 occurred two months earlier, Germany might not have needed to resume unrestricted submarine warfare. The American entry into the war might then have been, from our point of view, disastrously, even fatally, delayed.

conditions among the nations'; a guaranteed reduction of armaments; and 'impartial adjustment of all colonial claims'. Most of these propositions fell by the wayside as the peace negotiations proceeded. Secondly, a specific programme of territorial settlement based on restoration of conquests and self-determination[6] of peoples. Thirdly, 'a general association of nations', with 'mutual guarantees of political independence and territorial integrity to great and small states alike.' What the Allies found chiefly lacking in the Fourteen Points was any provision for compensation or reparation from Germany, a point upon which Allied opinion in Europe felt very strongly indeed. What they found chiefly objectionable was the provision for the Freedom of the Seas. On this, Lloyd George was emphatic: 'This point we cannot accept under any conditions, it means the power of blockade goes; Germany has been broken almost as much by the blockade as by military methods. Therefore my view is that I should like to see this League of Nations established first before I let this power go.'

Wilson did not create nationalism in Europe or invent the conception of self-determination. As early as the revolutionary times of 1848, there had been abortive projects by the Liberal government of Prussia to partition Posnania on national German-Polish lines, on a basis that became progressively less favourable to the Poles. The growth of nationalism had been deplored by John Stuart Mill in 1849 when he reflected upon the feelings which made men indifferent to the rights and interests 'of any portion of the human species, save that which is called by the same name and speaks the same language as themselves. These feelings are characteristic of barbarians.' Such a judgment would not seem to be harsh when it was recalled that Kossuth, the admired champion of Hungarian independence, had planned the complete extermination of the Serb population of southern Hungary.

The new European nations were not called into existence by the Fourteen Points. With the crumbling of the Austrian, German and Russian empires, the captive peoples liberated themselves and

[6] The word 'self-determination' was not itself used in the Fourteen Points or in the supplementary and additional points. The phrases used in the Fourteen Points were 'autonomous development' and 'clearly recognizable lines of nationality'. In the supplementary points it is said that peoples and provinces 'are not to be bartered about', and that territorial settlements are to be 'upon the basis of the free acceptance . . . by the people immediately concerned.'

declared their own independence or their new allegiance. What Wilson did was to erect the principle of self-determination into what he believed to be a sure basis of peace for the future. If peoples could be governed by governments of their own choice, much of the tension would be removed from international affairs. Here, rather than in the bartering of territories by way of compensation under the mechanism of the balance of power, was the best hope for peace and security in war-ridden Europe.

The peace settlement concluded after the First World War between 1919 and 1923 has been compared unfavourably with that which followed the Napoleonic Wars in 1815. And it is true that exasperated and resentful public opinions would not tolerate in regard to Germany the forbearance which far-sighted governments had shown to France. Yet the later settlement was a comprehensive and statesmanlike conception. The reparations clauses imposed on Germany in the Treaty of Versailles may be justly criticized. They were drafted in their severe form against the better judgment of, at any rate, the British Government, under pressure from public and parliamentary opinion. 'Heaven only knows,' said Lloyd George on arrival in Paris, 'what I would have had to promise them if the campaign had lasted a week longer.'[7] 'Statesmen,' Wilson had once prophetically declared, 'must follow the clarified common thought or be broken.' The peoples, having suffered the effects of total war for which they held Germany responsible, would insist on exacting large retribution. The clauses themselves were, as a matter of fact, in their terms open to a more merciful and less far-reaching application than statesmen, and particularly French statesmen, tried to secure for them. In this sense, they proved to be unenforceable. Before many years had passed this was recognized. Meanwhile the effort to enforce them bedevilled political and economic life and played some part, though not a major part, in the onset of the economic storm which struck Europe in 1931. But the remainder of the provisions of the peace settlement, had they been maintained, might well have established a long period of peace in Europe. The main defect of the Treaty of Versailles was that it was not enforced. The peace treaties and the Covenant of the League of Nations formed an inseparable whole. Together, they provided in the main for three things. There was first, a territorial settlement, weighed indeed in

---

[7] Castlereagh, by contrast, had been able to resist the popular clamour for revenge against France in 1815.

places against the vanquished, particularly in favour of Poland and against Hungary, but based generally on the principle of self-determination with provisions for the protection of minorities—Germany was not to rule over Poles or Czechs or even over Germans in the Greater Germany of Pan-German dreams. Secondly, there was to be a world-wide international organization which laid down rules of conduct and made provision for procedures of conciliation in the event of international disputes and (in the eyes of many, this was its main purpose) for the possibility of common measures of coercion against a covenant-breaker or, in other words, any attempt to upset the peace-settlement by force. Thirdly, there was some admittedly vague provision for the possibility of peaceful change, the reconsideration of treaties which had become inapplicable and of international conditions dangerous to peace. The compulsory disarmament of Germany would be followed in due course by a general convention for disarmament applicable to all. As a special measure of security, a guarantee of assistance would be given by Great Britain and the United States to France against unprovoked aggression by Germany.[8]

Regarded on its merits, this bold and imaginative project would seem to have been no less well designed than was the Vienna settlement of 1815 to usher in an era of peace. The difference lay in the fact that it could not be, and was not, adequately carried into effect and maintained. In 1815 there had been one power, Great Britain, strong enough and wise and skilful enough both to promote a just and moderate settlement and to lead the concert of Europe in the interest of European peace in the years that followed. In 1919 there was no power able or willing to play a similar part. The territorial settlement of Vienna had been based on considerations of power and had paid little regard to the claims of nationality. When it was modified, on the basis of nationality, whether over Belgium in and after 1830 or over Italy in and after 1859, regard was still paid to considerations of power. It was not until Bismarck started upon his

[8] An American historian has observed that Wilson probably knew and Clemenceau must have suspected that the Senate would refuse to consider this 'permanent alliance', which was not to come into force until ratified by all three parties. He suggests that its conclusion was a device to bring France into line at a difficult point in the peace negotiations. 'It was a way the diplomatists had to get around a difficult corner.' (Samuel F. Bemis, *A Diplomatic History of the United States*, Henry Holt, New York, 1955, pp. 636–37.) The excuse is thin, and the manoeuvre, if manoeuvre it was, unworthy of Wilson.

course of expansion in 1864, again on the basis of nationality, that the balance of power was disrupted and a good part of the Vienna settlement was torn up. By contrast, the territorial settlement in Europe after the First World War, being based substantially on nationality and not substantially on considerations of power, proved to have no such long-lasting stability. The victors had not the will to maintain it. The League of Nations could not take the place of the concert of Europe acting through a balance of power as an agent of cohesion. Within a little over twenty years, at the touch of power from a resurgent Germany, the territorial settlement had collapsed, and it required a second world war to restore it.

Great Britain, France and Russia had exerted all their strength and had been unable by themselves to subdue Germany. Russia had been struck down, and, in contrast with her position in 1815, could play no positive part in the post-war European concert. Austria, too, had been eliminated as a force in the peace settlement. The United States had come into the war to redress the balance which Europe herself had been no longer able to maintain. The balance had, indeed, become a world balance, of which the United States was an essential part; but the United States had withdrawn.[9] Left to themselves, and seriously weakened as they were by the exertions of war, Great Britain and France proved incapable of preserving the security and tranquillity of Europe against the resurgence of vanquished Germany, now for the first time conscious of her terrible latent strength, or against the incalculable menace of revolutionary Russia. The belt of smaller states in central and eastern Europe which had been brought into existence or augmented upon the collapse of the pre-war empires, were, since the League could not save them, open to domination or absorption when Germany and Russia revived their strength and ambitions. Only the United States, who had won the war (she had two million men in France in October 1918), and who had made the peace, could have been expected to lend the League the requisite strength and authority. The United States defected and left Europe to its fate. The Senate rejected both the Treaty of Versailles and the Covenant of the League of Nations. At one stroke the possible effectiveness of the League and the guarantee to France were destroyed. The League, given the terms of the Covenant, might still

[9] In and after 1919, the United States alone of the powers could have played the beneficent part which Great Britain played in and after 1815. In and after 1945, she did not withdraw, and Russia remained present.

have been ineffective even had the United States been a member, but without the United States it was doomed to failure from the start.

Some American historians have explained this revulsion from Europe on the part of the United States as having had a positive and not merely a negative basis. It was a deliberate withdrawal on high moral grounds from the contamination of a hated Europe which would smirch the high destiny and sacred mission of the American people, the chosen of God. Hence also there was worked up, in justification, the legend that the United States had entered the war not in her own interest but as a result of a joint conspiracy by native financiers and armament manufacturers and by foreign, chiefly British, propagandists.

Even so, the tragic ineptitude of Wilson's handling of his own people is hard to credit. His party having been defeated in the mid-term Congressional elections in late 1918—the Republicans gained control of both the House and the Senate—he could still make the astonishing assertion on his way across the Atlantic to the peace conference that the men whom he was about to deal with 'did not represent their own people'. On the contrary, both Lloyd George and Clemenceau had seen to it that they had the widest public support. Wilson made no attempt to associate the victorious Republicans with his proceedings at the conference. And, at the end, he refused all compromise with the Senate, declining to accept a reservation that would have satisfied the Europeans and would still have saved the substance of the Covenant for him, believing wrongly that he could carry the integral text when it came to the vote. He was decisively defeated. This was a tragedy for Europe and for the world. Truly, there are times when intellectual intolerance and moral assurance, arrogantly maintained, can work great evil.

One would have thought that, in this situation, Great Britain and France would have drawn together and have acted in close concert to lead the post-war world into ways of stability and order. But in the early post-war years their rivalry and dissensions were more in evidence than their co-operation. In Europe, there was an honest difference of outlook. Outside Europe, particularly in the Middle East, there was a conflict of imperialist ambitions of the traditional kind ending in the confirmation of Great Britain's position in Egypt and a partition of the Arab world into spheres of influence, the mandates for Iraq, Palestine and Transjordan going to Great Britain and those for Syria and the Lebanon going to France. The menace to their common security having been for the time being removed, they reverted to their late nineteenth-century bickerings. Their behaviour in the early post-war years does neither government much credit. Lord Curzon and M. Poincaré were hardly made to understand each other.

In Europe, France was insistent upon getting the maximum of reparation deliveries from Germany, and upon retarding the revival of German political and economic strength. Having been denied in the treaty the full measure of security in the Rhineland which she held to be requisite, and having lost the United States guarantee and American presence in the League, she set about building up alliances to reinforce her security, similar to those which she had erected against Austria in earlier centuries—alliances with Poland against Germany, and with the succession states of the Little Entente (Czechoslovakia, Jugoslavia and Roumania) in support of the central European settlement. At the same time she promoted schemes to supplement the military effectiveness of the League as an organ of international security. At a later stage, in 1935, she was to make a treaty with the Soviet Union.

On the other hand, Great Britain, as a world-trading power, would wish to see the earliest possible revival of international commerce and, as a contribution to this, a revival of the German economy. Feeling herself secure in Europe now that the German Navy had been destroyed, she felt no need of compensating alliances. She tended to regard French policy as designed to establish a French hegemony in Europe which would be out of place in the post-war world, and France under Poincaré was indeed again at the height of her power and influence in the earlier post-war years. Great Britain did offer France a treaty of guarantee in 1922, but Poincaré who, like Wilson, was apt to insist on all or nothing, declined to accept it unless it could be accompanied by a specific military convention. In retrospect, it is impossible not to sympathize with the French in the situation in which they were placed. Denied the security which they needed, they were intransigent on every issue that arose. It would have been better if London could have placed a more favourable interpretation upon their acts and policies than was in fact forthcoming. The interminable series of international conferences[10] which kept heads of governments moving here and there in western

[10] There were twenty-three such conferences in the three years 1920, 1921 and 1922.

Europe from 1919 onwards might not have had a better result, but the atmosphere would have been calmer and less charged with empty acrimony. The problem was not an easy one. Germany was set upon evading by every possible subterfuge the disarmament and reparations clauses in the settlement and had in the end linked up with Soviet Russia, the other pariah in Europe, for political co-operation and for the secret rearmament of Germany. Not until 1925, when there was a British Foreign Secretary favourable to France (Austen Chamberlain), a French minister with a liberal European policy (Briand) and a German minister (Stresemann) adhering ostensibly at any rate to the policy of fulfilment, was it possible to achieve a *détente* in Europe in the Treaty of Locarno. If any one event contributed to this, it was the French occupation of the Ruhr in 1923. This called a halt, temporarily at any rate, to the German campaign of evasion, brought home to the Germans that they had indeed lost the war, and drove them to a policy of fulfilment. The strong trend of sympathy for Germany in British opinion which had opposed Grey's policies before the war and would in the 1930s lend support to those of Neville Chamberlain, now led Great Britain most unfortunately to lean towards Germany and against France at this most crucial testing time.

The twenty years' crisis between 1919 and 1939 is bisected by the year 1929, when the economic blizzard struck the United States with progressively deepening effects, and after that spread to most of the rest of the world, and when the climate of affairs in Europe and elsewhere, and with it the position of Great Britain, underwent a decisive change. In the first half of the period there are three events by which we may test the position of Great Britain: the Locarno Treaty of December 1925; the American debt settlement of February 1923; and the Washington treaties of 1921–22.

In entering upon the Treaty of Locarno in December 1925, Great Britain was acting as a European power, in equal association with France, the other main prop of European security, and with Belgium and Italy as well, in an attempt to solve a European problem: the problem, namely, of how to bring Germany, the main ex-enemy, into harmonious relations with her western neighbours and to place European security upon a permanent basis. The League of Nations had been designed for precisely this kind of purpose: but the League, though of service in minor ways, was failing to establish general security. It was not merely that the absence of the United States had robbed it of its main substance. Its members were at odds as to the application to be given to its security provisions. There were those, like Canada and the European neutrals and a good part of Conservative opinion in Great Britain, who thought that, in the first flush of Utopian enthusiasm, and in a passionate determination to prevent another war, its British and American framers—the original draft of the Covenant was as much British as American—had gone too far in providing a general obligation for all members to preserve as against external aggression the territorial integrity and political independence of all other members. It was too much to think that governments and peoples would be willing to face the incalculable hazards of war for something less than their own vital interests. On the other hand, there were those, like the French, Belgians and European succession states, and (with some reservations) the British Labour Governments of 1924 and 1929, who held that the Covenant, as drafted, did not provide for sufficiently explicit measures against a covenant-breaker, and that it still left loopholes for war to be made without breach of the law.

In their search for more perfect security, the French and those who thought like them made various attempts to make good these defects in the Covenant. One of these was the draft treaty of Mutual Assistance of September 1923, which would have allowed for the formation of regional agreements but, going beyond the Covenant, would have provided for automatic and obligatory military sanctions against an aggressor within the areas covered by those agreements. Another was the Geneva Protocol of 1924 which was based upon the opposite principle of universality. A test of aggression would be provided, the gaps in the Covenant would be closed and the whole field of international disputes, legal or otherwise, would be covered by a system of compulsory arbitration. As Arthur Henderson claimed in the House of Commons in March 1925, on behalf of the Labour Opposition, it would provide a system of 'pooled security, whereby the might of nations would become the servant of international justice.' There was a saving clause that each state would co-operate 'in the degree which its geographical position and its particular situation as regards armaments allow.' Neither of these projects found sufficient favour with the members of the League to be brought into force. In opposing the acceptance of the Geneva Protocol in February 1925—an attitude which was shared by the Chiefs of

Staff and by the Dominions—Austen Chamberlain (Foreign Secretary since October 1924) had said that it provided 'a form of guarantee which is so general . . . that it . . . gives no sense of security to those who are concerned in our action.' When informing the League Council in March 1925 of the British Government's decision not to accept it, he had made it clear that Great Britain was not retreating into isolation, but would be willing 'to supplement the Covenant by making special arrangements in order to meet special ends.' It was out of this statement, itself building on suggestions made by the Germans and others, that the Locarno Treaty eventually grew.

It was a strictly limited regional arrangement. Great Britain (and Italy) agreed to protect Germany's western frontier against attack from either side, from either Germany or France, and the inviolability of the demilitarized Rhineland zone. But Great Britain declined to give any corresponding undertaking in regard to Germany's frontiers in the east with Poland and Czechoslovakia. All that could be secured here were arbitration treaties between Germany on the one hand and France's allies, Poland and Czechoslovakia, on the other. Germany, who would now enter the League, received the assurance that each member of the League was only bound to resist aggression 'to an extent which is compatible with its military situation and takes its geographical position into account.' It was expressly provided that the treaty imposed no obligation upon any of the British dominions, except upon their formal acceptance.

From the British point of view, this was an obligation of the traditional pattern and a departure from the general obligation of the kind laid down in the Covenant and from the full security which the League purported to provide. The Leader of the Opposition, Mr Attlee, was to point out later (on March 26th 1936) that Locarno had been 'an attempt to evade the main League position and to limit liability.' The League, he held, was not concerned with national defence or alliances or the balance of power. 'The real League position does not . . . say that this country is more interested in the frontiers of Holland and Belgium, because of the historic position, than in the frontiers of Czechoslovakia or the frontiers of Poland. The League position is that we are out to defend the rule of law and not particular territories.' This pure milk of the doctrine was accompanied by an attitude on the part of the Labour Opposition which would deny the Government the arms requisite for national defence unless it would subscribe to the integral principle of collective security, intervention in arms for all against all.

The Locarno Treaty kept Europe quiet in the period before the great economic crisis. It is one of the ironies of history that when Hitler violated the terms of the Locarno Treaty by marching into the Rhineland in 1936, neither France nor Great Britain lifted a finger to eject him; and that when, in September 1939, he invaded Poland, it was Great Britain who, even more resolutely than France, went to war in defence of a country whose frontiers she had in earlier years firmly declined to guarantee, and indeed in defence of the Polish Corridor for which, as Austen Chamberlain had said in 1925, 'no British Government ever will or ever can risk the bones of a British grenadier.'

The agreement for the settlement of the British war-debt to the United States concluded by Stanley Baldwin in January 1923 has several kinds of significance for the standing of Great Britain and of Europe in the world and for the outlook of the United States on world affairs at this period. Great Britain and France had not been able to subdue Germany without massive financial support from across the Atlantic; Europe was no longer self-sufficient; as Lord Northcliffe had reported from Washington: 'If loans stop, war stops.' Secondly, Europe was faced with the stiff economic orthodoxy and the complacent isolationism of the United States. These might be typified by two famous *dicta* attributed, perhaps wrongly, to President Calvin Coolidge, when he said of war-debts: 'They hired the money, didn't they?' and when he claimed, in regard to the international position of the United States: 'We are so snug here, nothing they can do can touch us.'[11] Speaking in retrospect on May 30th 1942, that steadfast Wilsonian, the United States Under-Secretary of State, Sumner Welles, declared: 'In 1920 and in the succeeding years, we as a nation not only plumbed the depths of material selfishness, but we were unbelievably blind.' So much for the 'normalcy' proclaimed by the Republican President Warren G. Harding. Thirdly, the settlement showed how extremely high a price Great Britain,

---

[11] A remark to be matched by the assertion broadcast by Colonel Charles Lindbergh on May 19th 1940, a year and a half before Pearl Harbour: 'Nobody wishes to attack us, and nobody is in a position to do so.' Lindbergh however had some excuse. As late as October 1941 General MacArthur said at Manila that Japan needed a long period of recuperation before she could undertake another major war.

even in her weakened economic position, was willing to pay for the maintenance of good relations with the United States and for the safeguarding of her reputation for financial integrity upon which she conceived her world position to depend.

The first thing to note is that the finance provided by the United States was by way of loan and not of subsidy. Repayment, so Congress decided in February 1922, was to be complete by 1947, interest being at 4¼ per cent. The situation after 1919 was thus very different from what it had been after 1815. Between 1793 and 1816, Great Britain had provided subsidies to her allies to the amount of over £50 million, without expectation of repayment, and of the rest, amounting to about £10 million, she had been repaid only about £2½ million. From a sentiment of solidarity and a recognition of common interest with her allies, she had wiped the slate clean. To the United States, the Europeans were not allies in a common cause but debtors.

Then there was the complication of inter-Allied debts. Besides borrowing from the United States, the European governments had lent to each other. Great Britain owed the United States about four and a quarter billion dollars borrowed on her own behalf or on behalf of her allies, but had lent to her allies outside the Empire the equivalent of nearly ten and a half billion. France had borrowed seven billion and loaned three and a half. A second complication was the difficulty of securing reparation payments from Germany upon which European governments relied to find means to repay their American debt. A third complication was the extreme protectionist policy of the United States which made it impossible for the European debtors to earn dollars by exports to meet the debt.

In August 1922, Great Britain tried to cut the Gordian knot. She pointed out in a note to her debtors that she was owed by her allies more than twice as much as she owed to the United States; that she was willing to remit all debts due to her by the Allies in respect of loans, and by Germany in respect of reparations, if this formed part of a general international settlement; but that, as the United States insisted on repayment, she would ask from her allies, not the whole debt but only so much as would suffice to pay her creditors. This would have left the United Kingdom, on balance, with a heavy deficit, but it would have been a price worth paying in order to relieve the world economy of the incubus of debt and reparation payments. The Allies did not like the proposal. The French held, for example, that war debts represented a material contribution to the common cause to which France had contributed otherwise, that is to say, in flesh and blood, and that they might well in fairness be waived, whereas reparations were compensation for damage actually done and suffered.

Stanley Baldwin, Chancellor of the Exchequer, and Montagu Norman, Governor of the Bank of England, who represented Great Britain at the negotiations in Washington, felt that they had no alternative but to make definite arrangements to repay the American debt, however difficult this might be. The debt, including interest, was fixed at 4,600 million dollars, repayable over sixty-two years instead of by 1947, and at an average rate of interest of $3\frac{1}{3}$ per cent instead of $4\frac{1}{4}$ per cent. The Americans calculated that this represented a cancellation of 30 per cent of the debt. These terms were only accepted with the gravest of misgivings by the Government in London. Baldwin had closed with the Americans without authority from the Cabinet, and the Prime Minister, Bonar Law, had serious thoughts of resigning. Many people, including J. M. Keynes, thought that it would have done no harm if we had dug our toes in and relied upon the natural strength of a debtor's position; and that (as we were later to prove over Abadan) it is usually better to make no agreement than to make a bad one. The Americans subsequently made debt settlements with other European governments on much less onerous terms. Up to 1931, Great Britain repaid nearly 2,000 million dollars, or three-quarters of all the payments made to the United States.

In the end, events were stronger than men. Neither reparation nor war debts were fully paid. Reparations from Germany, which had in 1921 been fixed by the Reparations Commission at 33 billion dollars, were in effect extinguished in the early 'thirties. By then, Germany had paid about $4\frac{1}{2}$ billion dollars, and had borrowed about $2\frac{1}{2}$ billion dollars in the United States in order to do so. In the years before the slump, Europe had subsisted, and indeed prospered, on lavish American loans. When the flow ceased and money was called in, Europe collapsed. All debtor states except Finland defaulted on the war debt in June 1933. These unrealistic and unrealizable financial transactions were engulfed in the economic storm of which they had been one of the contributory causes.[12]

[12] It has been suggested that the most deep-seated cause of the economic crisis was the rapid mechanization of agriculture after the First World War; the build-up of surplus stocks of wheat, coffee, sugar and rubber;

At Locarno, Great Britain contracted for a limited liability in Europe. On war-debts, she submitted to the United States. In the three Washington treaties of 1921–22 (five-power, four-power and nine-power), she abdicated her position of naval supremacy and, in common with the United States, opened the way for future Japanese predominance in the Far East. At the end of the war, the Royal Navy was still superior in strength to the United States Navy. Naval opinion on both sides was still bent on competitive building. Even Lloyd George, at the height of the controversy with President Wilson about the freedom of the seas, could say: 'Great Britain would spend her last guinea to keep a navy superior to that of the United States or any other Power.' But financial considerations, reinforced by a recognition of the special character of Anglo-American relations, prevailed. By March 1920, British official opinion was reconciled to the acceptance of a one-power standard and therefore to the acceptance of parity with the United States. The days of the two- and three-power standard had gone, never to return. This made it possible for Arthur Balfour, at the Washington Conference, to accept the proposal by the United States Secretary of State, Charles Evans Hughes, that the ratio of the five chief naval powers (Great Britain, the United States, Japan, France and Italy) should be 5–5–3–1·7–1·7, and that there should be some scrapping, and a naval holiday in capital ships. This agreement related to capital ships alone. There were differences about cruisers and submarines which were tackled but not finally solved at later conferences. The truce in naval competition did not endure. By 1936, Japan had almost reached parity with the United States. Great Britain started a great new naval programme, and 'in 1935 and 1936 the American Congress voted the largest naval appropriations in the peacetime history of any nation.'[13]

The four-power treaty (Great Britain, United States, France, Japan) marked a retreat from the Far East by Great Britain and, in some measure, by the United States. The Anglo-Japanese Alliance of 1902 had allowed Great Britain to lighten her naval forces in the Far East and to concentrate increased forces in home waters. The Alliance had enabled Japan to secure handsome pickings from Germany during the war. She had pursued an expansionist policy

the break in the market, followed by panic measures of self-protection on a basis of self-sufficiency by both primary producing and manufacturing countries. See E. Lipson, *Reflections on Britain and the United States*, Pall Mall Press, London, 1959, pp. 54–59.

[13] Morison and Commager, *The Growth of the American Republic*, ii. 499.

in China, and had entrenched herself in Shantung, Manchuria, Mongolia and Eastern Siberia. The continued existence of the Anglo-Japanese Alliance was unwelcome to some of the Dominions, in particular to Canada, as well as to the United States. It was somewhat embarrassing to Great Britain herself to be allied to a potentially aggressive power, and one which might come into conflict before long with the United States. For the present, Japan, under a liberal régime, was relatively quiescent. Nevertheless it was thought better to terminate the alliance, which, in the event of a conflict between the United States and Japan, would be an acute embarrassment and which was also not easily reconcilable with the League Covenant.

This was done by substituting for it a wider and looser arrangement among the four powers. Under this agreement they undertook mutually to 'respect their rights in relation to their insular possessions in the region of the Pacific Ocean' and to settle controversies by joint conference. There was no guarantee here; merely a promise not to attack. The benefit of this to Japan, the power on the spot, was reinforced by a provision in the five-power naval treaty which prohibited the building or extension of fortifications in Hong Kong and of American and other British insular possessions in the Pacific. Japan's home territory and her communications with China, Manchuria and Korea could be made safe against attack. The British settlements in Hong Kong and on the China coast could not. Until the base at Singapore was established, the Royal Navy had no berth east of Malta capable of refitting a capital ship. And even when the base had been built, Great Britain had not the power to defend it against Japan, as events were to show. She could no longer hold her position in the Far East, and only the United States could re-establish her.

Japan did indeed withdraw from Shantung and Siberia and give up some of her demands on China; and the nine-power treaty (the five powers, plus Holland, Belgium, Portugal and China) did profess to do something to protect China from further foreign exploitation. The traditional United States policy of maintaining the 'Open Door' and the political and territorial integrity of China was now submerged in a wider international agreement having the same ostensible purposes. Unless China could learn to protect herself, opportunity would lie with Japan as soon as there was again an expansionist Japanese régime. The Washington treaties secured for Japan a position of paramount military and naval power in the Far East;

and China's last state was likely to be worse than her first. The period of Japanese expansion opened in 1931. Japanese exports had fallen by nearly a half between 1929 and 1931; China was attacking the Japanese treaty position; the Chinese boycott continued; Manchuria was coming within the Chinese nationalist sphere; something drastic had to be done. Japan struck in Manchuria. As for Great Britain, try as she might, she would have to retreat in the Far East and she would have no one to help her. One way or the other, Chinese nationalism and Japanese ambition would be too strong for her and for European interests as a whole, of which she was the chief representative. Even for the United States, the Washington treaties represented a retreat, an isolationist evasion of responsibility. Again and again, during and after the war, the United States, in pursuance of her policy of the 'Open Door', had made unavailing efforts to set limits to Japanese action against China. By the Washington treaties, she gave up her individual efforts and merged them in an ineffective arrangement for common international action. The consequences of this were made plain in the Manchurian crisis of 1931–32, when neither the United States nor Great Britain was in a position to halt Japanese aggression.[14]

It is curious to recall that the occasion of the conclusion of the Washington treaties was hailed by *The Times* as 'a great day for all time in the history of the world'. A recent American historian has described this kind of reception of the results of the Washington Conference as marking a 'silly season in diplomacy' and has roundly condemned the results of the Conference, except for the naval provisions, as 'a shabby farce, a parade of hollow pretence'.[15]

If, after the First World War, Great Britain did not hold the position of international authority which she attained and kept for many years after the Napoleonic Wars a century before, the reason is not far to seek. She had played the part, in a long war of attrition, both of a great naval and of a great land power. She had lost nearly a million of her young men.[16] She had supported her own great war

---

[14] The story, still current, that the United States would have imposed sanctions on Japan if Great Britain had not refused to join is another of the common errors in history.

[15] Nathaniel Peffer, *The Far East: A Modern History*, Mayflower, London, 1959, pp. 264–65.

[16] Russia lost more than 2 million, Germany nearly 2 million, France nearly 1½ million, Austria-Hungary 1¼ million. The American losses in killed and wounded were about 130,000.

efforts from her own resources, thanks to the possession of a flexible and resourceful economic system and of reserves of financial and economic strength. In addition she had made loans to her allies, first direct and, after the United States had entered the war, as the intermediary of the United States. The result of this, as we have seen, was that after the war she owed over 4,500 million dollars to the U.S.A. and was herself owed very much greater sums by her allies. The United States, from being a debtor country, had become the world's greatest creditor and now exercised undoubted economic and financial predominance in the world. The British national debt increased nearly twelvefold in the four years of war. Like the rest of Europe, Great Britain would have to make good the effects of war-dislocation; rebuild her economy; repair her finances; reconstitute her foreign investments, nearly a quarter of which had been lost; re-equip her merchant fleet; and restore her overseas trade, into which both the United States and Japan had made serious inroads. United States exports had trebled in value during the war. The predominance of financial and economic power had moved across the Atlantic, and with it political and military primacy, if the United States were minded to develop them. As A. J. Balfour said early in the war: 'The world will more and more turn on the Great Republic as on a pivot.' Walter Hines Page, United States Ambassador in London, declared: 'The great economic tide of the century flows our way. We shall have the big world questions to decide presently. Then we shall need world policies.' As early as 1911, Theodore Roosevelt had said: 'We are ourselves becoming, owing to our strength and geographical situation, more and more the balance of power of the whole globe.'

After the immediate post-war boom, which gave delusive hopes of restored prosperity, the essential weakness of the European economies, and particularly of the British, became apparent. There was chronic unemployment between 1921 and the late 1930s, the figure reaching nearly three million in 1933. The various steps taken by British governments were palliatives or forced short-term remedies rather than curative measures determined on a settled plan. There was the over-optimistic and premature return to the gold standard in April 1925; the abandonment of the gold standard and the adoption of deflationary measures in the financial crisis of 1931; the perhaps too long-delayed institution of a general tariff after 1931,[17] and the, on the whole, beneficial arrangements for imperial preference

[17] Baldwin's tariff policy had been rejected by the electorate in 1923.

under the Ottawa agreements of 1932. But the ills from which the British economy was suffering were deep-seated. Not only did the growing fear of war and the increase in expenditure on armaments in the later 1930s adversely affect international trade as a whole, and therefore bear with especial severity on Great Britain. Primary producers, our best customers, were themselves becoming manufacturers also. There was still too wide a reliance upon coal, cotton textiles and steam engineering products as the staple of our export trade. The export of textiles, which had been until 1914 one of the mainstays of our overseas trade, had slumped in the post-war years[18] and our markets for heavy industrial products were threatened. It would not be until, after the stimulus of the emergencies of the Second World War, we turned to the more highly skilled manufacture for export of electrical, electronic and synthetic products, motor vehicles and aircraft, atomic products and the like, that we again became competitive with the industries of the United States and western Europe. Thanks to a renaissance of the British inventive genius during and after the war of 1939–45, and to a revival of our famous skill in industrial craftsmanship, we moved again to the front rank among industrial powers and placed our export trade upon a sound technical and commercial basis. The years of energy before the First World War had been a passing phase. The inter-war years were years of withdrawal, of negation, of reluctance to face present facts or future probabilities, of hesitant leadership and sterile controversy. They may also have been years of quiet recuperation. Certainly, when the Second World War came, Great Britain could again live some of her finest hours.

There were three other things (among others) which made the early post-war international scene, and Great Britain's place in it, different in character and quality from what it had been before the war. The first was the existence of the Soviet power. The second was the existence of the League of Nations. The third was the development of the British Commonwealth.

It had been foreseen by many people in the nineteenth century— by de Tocqueville, Napoleon III and Henry Adams in particular— that the predominant powers of the twentieth century would be the United States and Russia. The character of a Russian revolutionary

---

[18] In 1912, 85 per cent of Lancashire cotton piece-goods were exported. By 1938, the percentage was 50 and it later fell to 25. We could no longer live by selling cheap machine-made cotton textiles to backward countries.

government had been predicted by the British ambassador, Sir Arthur Nicolson, as far back as 1907 (though he had the social revolutionaries rather than the Communists in mind), when he said: 'The revolutionaries care nothing for constitutions or Dumas or reforms. Their sole aim is by a course of ruthless terrorism to render all government impossible and to pave the way for a socialist republic of the most advanced type.' What had not been foreseen, though the French revolutionary government had given a foretaste, was that it would be a government which would attack other governments behind their backs, addressing itself to their home populations and to the populations in their dependent territories. This set the Soviet Government in a class apart from other governments. The Soviet Union had indeed been recognized by most of the other chief powers, except the United States, by 1927; but it was not until the 1930s that, in face of the growing menace from Germany, she came to be treated as a more or less normal member of the international community, joining the League of Nations in 1934 and remaining until expelled in 1940. In the early post-war years, with Russia ostracized, Germany subject to servitudes under the peace settlement, and the United States in rigid isolation, the normal play of diplomacy was frustrated. Great Britain and France were faced with a burden which was to prove to be heavier than they could bear. And though Soviet Russia was not yet a military menace, she was able in the early years of her existence to exercise a powerful influence in eastern countries which for a time seriously weakened the position of western governments there. To Afghanistan, Persia and Turkey, Russia was now no longer, as in the past, an object of dread, the chief enemy to be feared. From her declarations, she now appeared as a friend; and the eastern governments no longer needed to reinsure with Great Britain, who now took the place of Russia as the country chiefly to be distrusted, if not feared. They all in their turn made treaties with Moscow and for a time turned their backs on the British connection. They felt it safe to flout Great Britain, for two reasons.

The first was the largely, but not fully, accurate perception that, although Great Britain might seem to be at the plenitude of victorious power, the British post-war public was in an anti-imperialist mood, with no will to find either men or money for armed action in remote parts of the world. The consequent uncertainties and hesitations in British policy impaired the prestige upon which our influence had been founded. This suspicion of the impotence of Great

Britain was for a time shattered early in 1923 when Lord Curzon,[91] by a diplomatic *tour de force* at the Lausanne conference comparable to that of Disraeli at the Congress of Berlin and, like it, a flash in the pan, won a single-handed victory over Turkey, secured a promise that she would join the League of Nations and thus drove a wedge between Turkey and Soviet Russia.

In the second place, it was the existence of the League of Nations itself which gave these eastern governments a new feeling of confidence that they could now safely disregard the admonitions and threats of the western powers. Were not all nations, great and small, now equal? And were not conciliation and international litigation to take the place of force in the relations of states, whether strong or weak? Would the imperialist powers now dare to outrage world public opinion by persisting in their old courses?

It might indeed have been expected that the international fabric would be strengthened by the formation of the League of Nations. But owing to a basic contradiction in the estimation in which the League was held by public and governmental opinion, the contrary happened. The League had been born of a determination to avoid the catastrophe of war. In the public mind, it was readily assumed that by the very existence of the League this objective had been achieved. Security was now collective. There was no need for vast expenditure on armaments. The force of public opinion would inhibit the aggressor. As Lord Robert Cecil had stated in the House of

---

[19] Curzon (Foreign Secretary, 1919–24) was a man of splendid attainments who just missed being a great statesman. He is an example of a Foreign Secretary who knew too much about one part of the world and not enough about the rest. He had great knowledge of, and a passionate interest in, Asia. This had a double disadvantage. He did not realize that his knowledge had become out of date and that his diagnosis of new situations could be faulty. Secondly, he saw the world not as a whole but through Asian spectacles, with small regard for larger interests. He had condemned the Anglo-Russian Convention of 1907 as being a sacrifice of an Asiatic tradition to the needs of European diplomacy. He would now sometimes propose British policies for Asia which were inconsistent with British interests in Europe. The fact that he was a bad European lay at the root of some of his disagreements with Lloyd George. And with this, there went a lack of sense of proportion, exemplified by his declaration: 'I would be as strong in small things as in big.' His eye for detail missed the larger perspectives and his academic approach inhibited the creative imagination.

He was a sore burden to his officials. For his own convenience, he superimposed upon the well-tried office mechanism for the submission of papers, a time-wasting and staff-consuming duplicate system of his own.

Commons when commending the League Covenant in July 1919: 'What we rely upon is public opinion . . . and if we are wrong about it, then the whole thing is wrong.'[20] Cecil himself was to recognize that this conception had been false. A great many people agreed with him. In the Peace Ballot of 1934, out of 11½ million people who answered the questionnaire, 6¾ million considered that if a nation insisted on attacking another, the other nations should combine to compel it to stop by military measures, if necessary. But here again there was the belief that the threat of military measures would be enough. There would be, could be, no question of war; otherwise, again, the whole thing would be wrong. It would be ridiculous if the only way to prevent war would be to make war universal. Governments, who would have to take the decision to act or not to act, to plan their military operations, to move and engage naval and military and air forces in action, to place their countries on a war footing with all that this would involve for the national life, could not take so light-hearted a view. The peoples hoped and believed that the League would be effective. The governments, who knew better, did not dare to try to disillusion them. The whole international structure rested upon an equivocation. The experience of the 1930s was to drive this lesson home. Members of the League may or may not have lacked adequate power to maintain the postwar settlement: but collectively they certainly lacked the will to do so. And there were those who thought the conduct of governments could be changed by putting a few extra words into the Covenant.

International disputes which had been handled in the past with reasonable discretion by the normal methods of diplomacy either by the parties alone or by a concert of powers, and had been settled or left unsettled, were now to be brought in public to the forum of the League. Every dispute would now be a world dispute. The public would expect a settlement, either by conciliation or by coercion. If there were no settlement, the main responsibility would be ascribed to those League members wielding the greatest influence and pos-

[20] Cecil was here a Tory proponent of an old radical thesis. Hume had said in 1832 that he was 'decidedly convinced that the expression of a strong opinion by the Powers of Europe would preclude the necessity of going to war' to protect the Poles against the Tsar. Gladstone, in an exposition of his views on foreign policy at Edinburgh in November 1879, during his Midlothian campaign, said: '. . . we always contended that in the case where the united authority of Europe was brought into action there was no fear of having to proceed to actual coercion.'

sessing, or judged as possessing, the most powerful available means of coercion. This in the public estimation, would mean Great Britain more than any other power. What to the Utopian League enthusiast could be made to appear as 'enforcement action under the Covenant' would to the Government, in simple terms, mean 'war'. Whatever else they might want, the bulk of the British public, in the inter-war period, did not want war. They could not believe that anyone in the world could want war after the experiences of 1914–18. They had in mind the perils of air warfare. Mr Baldwin had said that the bomber would always get through. Many thought that Germany had been badly used, that she had justified grievances, and—until the occupation of Prague in 1939—that no quarrel with her was worth a war. In the bye-election at East Fulham in October 1933, there may have been important local issues as well as the national issues of peace and disarmament. But the swing from a Government majority of about 14,000 to a pacifist Opposition majority of about 5,000, in the face of Germany's defiant withdrawal from the League of Nations and from the disarmament conference, was a monument of political irresponsibility.

The paradox would be that many people who would want to stay out of war at almost any cost would still light-heartedly advocate bellicose policies of 'fighting against Fascism' or 'resisting aggression' and at the same time seek to deny the Government the arms which such policies would require. Families were divided on the alternative policies of what was called 'appeasement' or of 'standing up to Hitler and Mussolini'. It seemed to some to be a wicked thing that, now that the future rules of the game had been newly framed in their own favour by those who had profited by a new world settlement of their own making, those rules should be questioned and the settlement challenged by those who had lost the game or had failed in the past to satisfy their ambitions. Yet why, it might also be asked, was the deadline of national expansion to be fixed at 1919?

Not for the first time, a civil war in Spain induced a kind of fever, and led young men to go out and take part in the killing on one side or the other in order to assuage their political passions with a good conscience. The story of the Spanish Civil War has moved into the realm of myth. It was, as Salvador de Madariaga said, an 'essentially Spanish' war which, 'by somewhat shallow parallelisms' was linked by men, by institutions and even by governments outside Spain with the contemporary ideological conflict in Europe. In truth, those foreigners who imagined that, by taking part in it, they were in some way fighting for democracy against Fascism were entertaining a pathetic delusion. The 'democratically elected' government of Spain soon became democratic in façade only, and in its later stages was hardly even that. Effective power came into the hands of revolutionary workers' organizations, anarchist, syndicalist or communist of various kinds, some of whom were at times fighting against others as well as against the insurgents. The war was between two sets of indigenous factions, moved for the most part by what Dr Toynbee has called a 'suicidal frenzy' or 'satanic passion', each of which was able to attract the support of about half the population of Spain. What were normally sober-minded Englishmen doing in this hell's kitchen?

In face of policies of intervention by Italy, Germany and Russia, all morally reprehensible, the Anglo-French policy of non-intervention was not an heroic one. It was designed to avoid the outbreak of a wider conflict in Europe, and this is what most of the people in both countries wanted. In the summer of 1937, Eden, the Foreign Secretary, who cannot be accused of sympathy with Fascism, confessed that the policy was 'peace at almost any price'. About the same time, Léon Blum, the Socialist prime minister of a French popular front government, declared: 'Thanks to the lie of non-intervention, peace has been preserved.' There were limits to Anglo-French tolerance. Italy was warned at the outset against any breach of the territorial integrity of Spain, and against any threat to vital British interests in the Mediterranean. The attacks by Italian submarines upon British and other merchant ships in the Mediterranean were abruptly halted after the measures agreed upon at the Nyon conference.

For Italy, intervention was a serious enterprise. For Germany, it was an unimportant side-show: Hitler had little use for it, except as a means of distracting French and British attention from his larger designs. The fears, so loudly proclaimed by the British interventionists, that Italy and Germany would dominate Spain to our strategic detriment if Franco was not crushed, were wide of the mark. The British Government, here as so often more far-sighted than their critics, held, rightly as it proved, that Spanish national pride would stand in the way of this.

When war came in 1939, the popular front heresy was exploded. The imagined community of interest between radicals, socialists and communists, based on that most illusory of political slogans, *pas d'ennemi à gauche*, was dissolved. Franco Spain and Communist Russia were both formally non-belligerent, though both leaning to the side of the Nazis and Fascists against the democracies. Franco kept the Germans out of Spain. He was forced by his need of wheat and oil, which only the Allies could deliver, to supply wolfram for steel manufacture to the Allies and to curtail deliveries of it to Germany. The Allies were able to use Gibraltar for the North African landings undisturbed. What the French and the Germans would have done after the defeat of France in 1940 if there had been a popular front government in Spain, or a revolutionary syndicalist or Stalinist or Trotskyist régime, we cannot tell. One may suspect that Spain would have stayed neutral anyhow. It is conceivable that we were better off with a neutral Franco, whom Hitler (wrongly, as Goering thought) preferred to leave undisturbed, than with a régime of the left, whom Hitler might have attacked.

Co-operation with the Communists in Europe was temporarily restored in 1941, not on the basis of ideology but by the operation of power, not by the attack of Nazism upon Communism but by the predatory attack of German upon Russian power. When the war was over, the Communists, as soon as they could, turned upon the fellow-travelling socialists and devoured them: there were, after all, enemies on the left.

The passions of the time were real enough, and passion is of the stuff of life. Tension is a necessary part of the international fabric. We may feel that by committing our hearts to this cause or to that we may help to bring about the triumph of right, as we see it. But for all our travail, hopes may be deceived and fears prove exaggerated or groundless. Need one allow oneself to be so deeply moved by international controversies? Events are unpredictable. It would seem that 'the Nature of Things abhors a drawn line and loves a hodge-podge, resists consistency and despises drama.'[21] The mills of God grind slowly. The stone that the builder rejects may become the head of the corner. We cannot tell what will come of it all. Franco won the civil war, but his victory did not, as so many feared, bring lasting benefit to Germany and Italy. After the Labour victory in 1945, the *New Statesman* (August 18th 1945) declared: 'Franco must now realize that the days of his dictatorship are numbered': fifteen years later Franco still survived. Mussolini had his barren triumph in

[21] J. G. Cozzens, *Guard of Honour*, Longmans, London, 1949, p. 572.

Ethiopia. In the event, would it have mattered so much whether the Hoare–Laval agreement was accepted or not? Ethiopia is again independent today, still under Hailé Selassié. The Japanese erected their Greater East Asia Co-Prosperity Sphere, but they could not stand against the United States, roused to unmatched resolution and energy at last. The fact that we did not go to war against Hitler in 1938 but preferred to accept the humiliation of Munich did not prevent us from winning the war into which we entered in 1939. The British public, which rejoiced that peace had been saved in 1938, even at the expense of Czechoslovakia, a year later threw its weight in favour of a decision to go to war for Poland. We did not succeed in making an alliance with the Soviet Union in 1939, but Hitler himself made this possible for us in 1941. Czechoslovakia, sacrificed to Hitler in 1938, was in 1945 liberated from Hitler and restored, only to become in 1948 a satellite in bondage to the Soviet Union, whom we were, and still are, blamed for not calling to her assistance in 1938. We went to war for Poland in 1939; she was liberated from Germany but is now subject to the Soviet Union, to whom we were urged by some to abandon her in the Moscow negotiations of 1939. No one was more active than Edward Beneš, the Foreign Minister of Czechoslovakia, in getting the Soviet Union into the League of Nations in 1934; he was as confident that he could deal with Stalin as Neville Chamberlain was that he could deal with Hitler. As President of the Republic in 1948, he proved not to have taken a long enough spoon.

In one respect the post-war outlook was more cheerful. In 1919, the British Dominions became separate members of the League of Nations and so established their status as independent members of the British Commonwealth. This followed an already well-established trend of evolution. Asquith had declared at the Imperial Conference of 1911: 'We each of us are, and we each of us intend to remain, masters in our own house.' Many years before, at Adelaide in January 1883, Rosebery had declared, with singular prescience: 'The Empire is a Commonwealth of Nations.' The post-war status was defined in declaratory form at the Imperial Conference of 1926 and given legal substance by the Statute of Westminster in 1931. This was an institution unique in the world's history: a free association or fraternity of sovereign independent states, neither a federation nor a confederation nor an alliance nor a contractual association, bound together by a shared sense of obligation, of values and of ideals and owning a common political heritage. It could be disputed how far the possession of a colonial empire had reinforced the strength or fallen as a burden upon Great Britain in the past. But there could be little doubt that the emergence and happy development of these new independent states in family association with Great Britain, far from detracting from her prestige, enhanced her standing and increased her influence in the world. Her material strength might be in relative decline compared with others, but her political genius had never shone so brightly. The Dominions would influence her policies—they were cautious about international commitments under the League or otherwise; some of them sought the termination of the Anglo-Japanese Alliance; they were to approve the attempts made in the 1930s to come to terms with the dictators. They would not always vote with Great Britain in the League Assembly. But more often than not their line in foreign policy would be the same as hers; and when war came they were to be a comfort in adversity and a very present help in time of trouble.

Conversely, Great Britain's position as a European power and as a world power preserved her primacy in the Commonwealth. Even today, the Commonwealth fabric is still composed rather of bilateral links between Great Britain and each of the other members than of links among the others, though special relationships are growing up, like those between Canada and India and between Australia and the Malay Federation.

British policy and the position of Great Britain in the world in the 1930s are not to be understood without reference to the economic crisis which opened in the United States in 1929, reached a climax in 1933, and struck the European countries in varying degrees in 1931. It was not simply that we were forced off the gold standard, which had been prematurely re-introduced in 1925, or even that this occurred about the same time as the so-called naval mutiny at Invergordon, an event which had serious political effects at home and abroad but was in fact a minor outbreak of discontent about paycuts. Behind the immediate crisis lay a change for the worse in our trading position. We began to be conscious of deficits in our balance of payments. In the years 1933–35 there was no income available for investment overseas. Indeed there was an average annual adverse balance of £60 million, whereas in 1911–13 we had had an average surplus of over £200 million available for this purpose each year. Our exports in 1929 were below the level of 1913, and in 1937 they were below the level of 1924. Our customers in primary producing countries had not only been forced to cut their purchases: they were now increasingly becoming industrial producers also. Lancashire, which before 1914 had largely earned the foreign exchange for our foreign investment, had lost her predominant position in eastern and far eastern markets.

An economic crisis, massive unemployment and a downward trend in economic activity do not make for confidence in the conduct of foreign policy: nor do they allow a government to face with equanimity the need to rebuild the national armaments. But following upon the economic crisis, there came a growing need for rearmament. Before 1931, France and Great Britain had a decisive predominance in military power in Europe, and their interests were not immediately threatened elsewhere. During the 'thirties, first Japan, then Italy and then Germany challenged the existing order. Japan moved to prevent the unification and industrialization of China except under her own control. Italy sought an empire in Ethiopia. Germany set to work to reverse the territorial settlement and disarmament provisions imposed on her in Europe by the peace treaties, with, as a prospective objective, the grain, coal, iron and oil of the Ukraine and the Caucasus. Mussolini spoke in October 1938 of changing the map of the world. The Tripartite Pact of September 1940 looked forward to a 'new order of things'. In Germany in particular, the National Socialist revolution brought a great surge of national energy which was to enable Germany to overtop the power of Great Britain and France, and which would, under Hitler's leadership, for a time make Germany the architect of a barbarous new order in Europe. Through negligence or lack of spirit, Great Britain and France had allowed Germany to overhaul them. Unlike Germany, they had failed to develop their latent strength into an effective instrument of power. Even if they had made this effort, it might not have availed them. The experience of the war was to suggest that, exert themselves as they might, they were no equal match for Germany.

The course of events in the 1930s was to be set by the opening of the Japanese campaign in Manchuria in September 1931, and by Hitler's advent to power in Germany in January 1933. Bülow had remarked, after a visit to London in 1899, that it was difficult for the English to think that other countries had really bad intentions, and that they were incapable of believing that things could really ever go badly either at home or abroad. Colonel House had noted with surprise, when he visited London in the early summer of 1914, how calm the atmosphere was in comparison with the air of crisis which he had found in Berlin. So now again the Government in London was slow to recognize the full gravity of the new situation in Europe and the need for action, though, so far as Germany was concerned, the position had been put to them plainly enough by two successive ambassadors, Sir Horace Rumbold and Sir Eric Phipps.

They would have to meet a double challenge. The first was the increasingly clamant nationalist aspirations in Asia—in India for self-government and independence and in China for release from the 'unequal treaties'. Here the policy was a retreat in as good order as could be maintained. In India, it ended with independence and partition in 1947. In China, beginning with the yielding up of the Hankow concession in 1927, it led, under the impact of attack by both Chinese and Japanese, to the surrender of extra-territorial rights, the return of all concessions and settlements, the liquidation of investments and the curtailment of trade. This affected the other Europeans and the Americans as well as ourselves. Since the defeat of Japan and the success of the Chinese Communist revolution it has affected the Japanese also. Of the vast complex of British interests built up in China since the 1840s, for the sake of which, as a defence against Russian expansion, the Anglo-Japanese Alliance was concluded, there remains today only the prosperous island city of Hong Kong, with Kowloon and the leased territory on the mainland.

In face of the second challenge, that of the unsatisfied states, the policy was again the policy of retreat in as good order as possible. There was a determination not to go to war for anything but a clearly vital interest, and to keep our forces in being and to wait. If war once started, we might have to meet Germany, Italy and Japan all at once. Therefore do nothing to provoke a war and be prepared to pay a price to avoid one. This, at bottom, was the root of the so-called policy of appeasement of the 1930s. It was not possible to build up a diplomatic and military combination, even a tenuous one as had been done in the years before 1914. For different reasons, the United States and Russia could not be brought into the balance. Without one or other of them Great Britain and France were outweighted, or deemed themselves to be so.[22] They used the mechanism

[22] In 1939, the combined naval strength of Great Britain and France was only slightly greater than that of Japan, Germany and Italy: and

of the League of Nations, ineffective as it inevitably was, over Manchuria, over Ethiopia and over the Rhineland. They did their best, outside the League, to come to a general settlement with the unsatisfied powers. In the end they made an unavailing attempt to ally themselves with the Soviet Union.

Winston Churchill said of the Munich agreement of September 1938 that we had sustained 'a total and unmitigated defeat' and that it had been 'a disaster of the first magnitude' for Great Britain and France.

This judgment is just. The best that can be said for the Munich agreement is that it was a tragic necessity forced upon us by an international situation which we had neglectfully allowed to develop to our peril. Great Britain and France had fallen very low in the world. Had we been defeated in the war that followed, the framers of the policy of appeasement would have been held responsible. But since we were not defeated, the last word about Munich has not yet been said. It is doubtful whether history will think it as important, or as much a matter of passionate controversy, as it seemed to be at the time. By the war that began in 1939, Europe was liberated from Hitler's rule and was freed from the infection of Nazism. This result might have been achieved if war had come earlier: but it might not. The issue would turn on the question whether it would have been better to risk a general conflict over Czechoslovakia in 1938. That is a question which no one can answer with certainty. The war of 1939–45 was won, and victory covers a multitude of political and strategic errors. It would almost certainly have been no more possible to secure Russian action against Germany in 1938 than it proved to be in 1939. The difficulty about the transit of Russian forces through Poland would have stood in the way then no less than it did in 1939. But all the same it might have been better to make the attempt.

Going further back, it has been urged, fairly enough, that we ought to have rearmed earlier and halted Hitler at the very outset of his career of expansion. But this begs an important question. Given the prevailing non-interventionist climate of public opinion in the 1930s, akin in some ways to that of the 1860s and early 1870s,[23] was it

against Japan they were at a great strategic disadvantage. In 1939, Germany alone had more first-line military aircraft than Great Britain and France together: Germany and Italy together had nearly twice as many.

[32] The difference was that in the earlier period we were prosperous and

certain that any government with any hope of retaining office could have carried a really intensive rearmament or a resolute policy of armed intervention in Europe? Be that as it may, the Baldwin and Chamberlain governments, many of them members of the 'second eleven' which had first come to power in 1922 in reaction against Lloyd George's active foreign policy,[24] were themselves also infected with an almost Cobdenite non-interventionism, and made no serious attempt to meet the challenge. They preferred peace at almost any price.

It can fairly be said of Neville Chamberlain that he was not well versed in foreign affairs, that he had no touch for a diplomatic situation, that he did not fully realize what it was he was doing, and that his naïve confidence in his own judgment and powers of persuasion and achievement was misplaced.[25] But the words which he used to explain and defend his policy, if they are now re-read with a cool mind, compel one's respect. He may not have had the true vision of a leader, but, unlike so many of his opponents and detractors, he cherished no Utopian dreams, except perhaps his own belief that he could come to useful agreements with the dictators and that promises made by them to him personally would be kept. There is something refreshing in his dry and caustic realism, his stripping away of pretence and self-delusion. His attitude was at any rate as respectable as that of those of his political opponents who had advocated courses that might lead to war and yet, upon the excuse of a proclaimed divergence of policy, had until lately wished to deny the

reasonably secure. In the 1930s we were neither. And Palmerston, while he left Denmark to her fate in 1864, at least did not help Bismarck to despoil her.

[24] Much as Gladstone rode to power in 1880 in reaction against Disraeli's adventurous policy.

[25] As Prime Minister, Chamberlain took the conduct of the more crucial aspects of foreign policy increasingly into his own hands. He certainly consulted the Foreign Policy Committee of the Cabinet at this time and, in particular, an inner group of ministers consisting of the Foreign Secretary, Lord Halifax, and two former Foreign Secretaries, Sir John Simon and Sir Samuel Hoare. The policy was Chamberlain's, and he was strong enough to make it prevail; but it certainly had the general assent of Lord Halifax, if not of the latter's senior official advisers. An unusual feature of the period after Eden's resignation in 1938 was the extent to which Halifax acquiesced in the Prime Minister's conduct of important business that was proper to the Foreign Office through channels outside the Foreign Office. One cannot imagine Grey allowing Asquith to use someone like Sir Horace Wilson, as Chamberlain did, on Foreign Office business of first importance.

Government the arms which they would need if war came, and continued to oppose compulsory national service.

When he said in a broadcast speech on September 27th 1938: 'However much we may sympathize with a small nation confronted by a big and powerful neighbour, we cannot in all circumstances undertake to involve the whole British Empire in war simply on her account', he was echoing what had been said by Bright, Cobden and Stanley in advocacy of a policy of non-intervention, the refusal to embark on crusades for the right against the wrong (even if the distinction between them could be established) or for the defence of the weak against the strong. He was discountenancing what Gladstone had called 'knight-errantry': individual states had no moral responsibility to act, except as part of the general concert of Europe. But Chamberlain did more than refrain from helping Czechoslovakia. He agreed to an application of the Wilsonian principle of self-determination for the Sudeten Germans which could not fail to disrupt Czechoslovak national existence and thus to contravene the other Wilsonian principle of the rights of small nations. He then constrained the Czechs to accept this solution and to refrain from a resort to arms which would most probably have involved first France and then Great Britain, and thus have precipitated the general conflict which he was determined to avoid at almost any price.

When he went on to observe on the same occasion: 'If I were convinced that any nation had made up its mind to dominate the world by fear of its force, I should feel that it must be resisted,' he was saying what might have been said by any Prime Minister or Foreign Secretary for centuries past. Where he differed from some of his critics was that, unlike them, he did not recognize that the emergency which he had in mind had for some years past already been upon us. But when he said, as he did in the House of Commons on October 6th 1938, in a speech defending the agreement of Munich and his policy of appeasement,[26] that the policy of making, in time of peace,

[26] 'Appeasement', now a 'dirty' word, was once quite respectable. General Smuts in 1923 commended Great Britain as an adherent of 'the great cause of appeasement and conciliation among the nations'. Winston Churchill drew a valid distinction when he said in the House of Commons on December 14th 1950: 'Appeasement in itself may be good or bad according to circumstances. Appeasement from weakness and fear is alike futile and fatal. Appeasement from strength is magnanimous and noble and might be the surest and perhaps the only path to world peace.'

'military alliances with any other powers whom we can get to work with us', a policy involving 'entangling alliances, balance of power and power politics', was one which he rejected as being 'a policy of utter despair', he was casting aside the policy by which Great Britain and Europe had been saved by William III at the turn of the seventeenth and eighteenth centuries and by Lansdowne and Grey, though they would not have so described their policy, in the early years of the twentieth century. With what we may hope will be happy results, the policy which Chamberlain repudiated in the 1930s, was unreservedly embraced by Ernest Bevin and Anthony Eden in mid-twentieth century on a basis which linked the two sides of the Atlantic in a common system of security.

When Sir Samuel Hoare, speaking as Foreign Secretary at the Assembly of the League of Nations on September 11th 1935, said: 'In conformity with its precise and explicit obligations, the League stands, and my country stands with it, for the collective maintenance of the Covenant in its entirety, and particularly for steady and collective resistance to all acts of unprovoked aggression', the unspoken proviso was, as later events were clearly to show, 'provided that it is genuinely collective and does not land us single-handed in war.'[27] It was to be left to Neville Chamberlain to strip the veil and reveal the truth when he said in the House of Commons on February 22nd 1938: 'The League, as constituted today, is unable to provide collective security for anybody.' The most it could do was to act 'as a moral force to focus public opinion throughout the world'—a view which Lord Robert Cecil had expressed nearly twenty years before.

In the determination of our policy in these years, the state of public opinion was, as suggested above, a powerful factor. On July 20th 1936, Mr Churchill spoke in the House of Commons of 'a public whose opinion is more bewildered and more expressionless than anything I can recall in my life.' A few months before, on March 25th, Miss Eleanor Rathbone, M.P. had at a meeting in London remarked: 'The country is giving way to a wave of what may crudely

[27] This was a respectable proviso. The League of Nations Union stated in *Headway* in December 1937 that it 'advocates sanctions only in cases where the number and resources of the governments co-operating on the League's behalf make it reasonably certain that the would-be aggressor will abandon his intention so that war will not break out at all.' Quoted in E. H. Carr, *The Twenty Years' Crisis, 1919–1939*, Macmillan, London, 1939, pp. 201–02.

be described as sentimental pro-Germanism . . . The motives are sympathy with the under-dog, whom they strangely imagine to be Germany, and a horror of war.' It is doubtful whether any leadership could have brought the public round to accept the steps which Mr Churchill thought necessary and to depart from what he called (March 4th 1937), 'the present comfortable manner without any decisive impingement upon private trade or profit-making or demanding any temporary sacrifice of comfort and changes in our way of living in order that we may preserve ourselves in freedom.' Baldwin had no doubts about this. Speaking on November 12th 1936, some months after his retirement from the premiership, he said: 'Supposing I had gone to the country and said that Germany was rearming and that we must rearm, does anybody think that this pacific democracy would have rallied to that cry at that moment?'[28] Mr Churchill saw the past, present and future in a true light when he said in the House of Commons on February 22nd 1938: 'It is because we have lost these opportunities of standing firm, of having strong, united forces, a good heart, and a resolute desire to defend the right and afterwards to do generously as a result of strength, that when our resources are less and the dangers greater, we have been brought to this pass. I predict that the day will come when at some point or other, on some issue or other, you will have to make a stand, and I pray God that when that day comes we may not find that through an unwise policy we are left to make that stand alone.'

When at length Chamberlain took us into the war in 1939, we went in with a united country[29] and a united Commonwealth, as we could not have done in 1938. The Dominions supported now the resort to war,[30] as they had all, other than New Zealand, supported

---

[28] Compare also Ernest Bevin's remark in the House of Commons on July 29th 1941: 'If anyone asks me who was responsible for the British policy leading up to the war, I will, as a Labour man myself, make a confession and say, "All of us." We refused absolutely to face the facts. When the issue came of arming or rearming millions of people in this country, people who have an inherent love of peace, we refused to face the real issue at a critical moment. But what is the use of blaming anybody?'

[29] The country was perhaps united against Hitler rather than in favour of Poland. The public were moved rather by hatred of the tyrant than by sympathy for the victim. When Chamberlain spoke on September 27th 1938 of 'a quarrel in a far-away country between people of whom we know nothing', he was perhaps not so far astray from public sentiment about Czechoslovakia as we are now apt to think.

[30] Eire remained neutral: but Eire, though externally associated with the Commonwealth, was not, in her own conception, a dominion.

the policy of appeasement in 1938. We had done our best not to have to stand alone. We and the French had tried to make an alliance with the Soviet Union in 1939. A. J. P. Taylor has said that our failure to do so 'was the greatest set-back for British diplomacy in the twentieth century'.[31] Winston Churchill, for his part, has held that, by a bolder approach, we and the French should have 'proclaimed the Triple Alliance' with the Soviet Union, leaving military details to be adjusted later if war came. The present writer, who sat through the negotiations in Moscow in June and July 1939, can only state his opinion that it was an inevitable set-back, and recall the fact that the Russians would not make a treaty at all unless the military details were written into it.[32] It was on the proposed military convention that the negotiations foundered.

The fact that it was with Germany that the Russians eventually made their treaty in August 1939 has raised the question in many minds whether the Russians had ever genuinely desired to come to an agreement with the British and the French. There is little doubt that they thought it would be in their interest to do so, and that the negotiations were seriously intended. But they required certain conditions to be satisfied. If they were attacked by Germany, they wished to ensure that they would not be left to bear the burden alone. The treaty of mutual assistance would therefore have to be accompanied by a military convention making precise provision as regards the extent and forms of military assistance to be afforded. Secondly, they wished to be assured of assistance against what they called indirect aggression. If, for example, Germany acquired a predominant position in the Baltic States destructive of their independence or neutrality, and if, as a reaction to this, the Soviet Union found herself at war with Germany, she wanted the western powers to be under an obligation to come to her assistance. Thirdly, if the Soviet Union were at war with Germany under the treaty, she would require to have the right to send her forces into and through Poland.

It was on this third point that the negotiations broke down. The Poles declined to give their assent. Naturally enough: if the Russians ever entered upon the wide non-Polish areas acquired by Poland from Russia at the time of Russia's weakness under the Treaty of Riga in 1921, would they ever go out again? The political treaty had

[31] *Englishmen and Others*, Hamish Hamilton, London, 1956, p. 157.
[32] He has given an account of these negotiations in *Home and Abroad*, André Deutsch, London, 1956, Chapter V.

been successfully negotiated, except for one or two outstanding points which could probably have been settled. The military convention was not, and could not have been, concluded. The break in fact occurred over Poland, but it might equally well have occurred over a whole range of other points in the proposed military convention.

It was clear all along to the British and French Governments that if their negotiations for a treaty with the Soviet Union failed, the Russians had the alternative course, in keeping with the traditions of both countries and notwithstanding ideological differences, of reaching an accommodation with the Germans, by which in the event of war the Soviet Union would be neutral or might even be on the German side. It was known that the Russians and Germans were in contact, indeed the Russians made no secret of it. What was not known was the extent and timing of the conversations. From documents since published, it appears that it was the Germans rather than the Russians who made the running; and that it was not until about the end of July 1939 that the offers held out by the Germans became too tempting to be disregarded. Unlike Great Britain and France, Germany needed to ask Russia for no more than neutrality, and could offer a share of the territorial spoils of Poland and the Baltic States. Nevertheless, the Russian decision to close with the Germans was not precipitately taken and seems not to have been made final until about August 20th, only a few days before the Soviet-German Treaty was actually signed. The Russians saw their interest in territorial aggrandisement at the expense of the hated Poles, and in a breathing space during which, if war came, Germany and the western powers might be expected to exhaust each other. This proved to be a miscalculation.

The Soviet-German Treaty of August 1939 did not deter Great Britain from concluding her negotiations with Poland for a treaty of mutual assistance confirming the reciprocal undertakings given in the preceding spring. The Anglo-Polish Treaty was signed two days after the Hitler–Stalin Pact. The Moscow Treaty made war certain. Hitler now saw his way clear to what he supposed would be a quick and easy victory. He also miscalculated. As for Great Britain and France, they now had to face the war alone, a war which, though they might not recognize this, they were almost certainly not strong enough to win single-handed. There are times when, however uncertain the prospect, it is necessary to take up arms and fight; when there is a threat to security so imminent that there is no longer any real freedom of choice between peace and war. It is above all else the task of diplomacy to avoid being placed in such a predicament. This, as much as anything, was and is the *raison d'être* of the balance of power.

CHAPTER XIV

War and Early Post-War

In the Napoleonic Wars, Great Britain was able to carry the financial burden of the successive continental coalitions upon her own shoulders. In the First World War, she had enough resources to finance her own war-effort; but she could not bear more than a part of the additional burden of financing her European allies. The balance had to be made up by loans from the United States. In the Second World War she could not even finance her own war-effort. By the end of 1940, our realizable dollar resources were nearing exhaustion. Mr Churchill told President Roosevelt on December 8th that 'the moment approaches when we shall no longer be able to pay cash for shipping and other supplies.' Had it not been for the imaginative device of lend-lease assistance from the United States, made constitutionally possible (it was found) under an old Act of 1892, and now supplied under 'An Act Further to Promote the Defence of the United States' introduced in January 1941, Great Britain would have been within sight of having to abandon the struggle. Great Britain would now, as Roosevelt said on March 15th after the Act had been passed, receive 'unqualified, immediate, all-out aid' which would be 'increased—and yet again increased—until total victory has been won.' Roosevelt had side-stepped not only the Neutrality Acts but the whole problem of war debts. The United States was to be 'the great arsenal of democracy'.[1]

President Roosevelt had brought about a double revolution in United States policy, one internal and one external. At home, by the New Deal, in the economic crisis of the 1930s, he extended the

[1] Without decrying the generosity of lend-lease, it is fair to observe that, so long as we still had dollars, the policy of the United States was unimaginative and grasping; that lend-lease was reciprocal to an extent not always realized; and that its abrupt termination after the war had disastrous effects upon our post-war position.

scope of Federal concern in the sphere of economic and social legislation and administrative action, and in the course of these remedial measures, as Harry Hopkins remarked, 'the British Statute Book was raided on a wholesale scale.' In international affairs, he had with great skill carried the Congress and people of the United States away from the isolationism of the inter-war years. He had seen, and said, as early as January 1939 that the safety of the Rhine frontier was a vital interest of the United States as well as of France and Great Britain. Once more the United States would come to play her part as a world power, even more effectively than she had done in the time of Woodrow Wilson. Her portentous strength, long masked by the policy of neutrality, would at last be made manifest. Though not yet in the war, the United States was firmly committed to the democratic cause. In the Atlantic Charter in August 1941, Roosevelt, still non-belligerent, had joined with Churchill to speak publicly of the 'final destruction of Nazi Germany'. Indeed Harry Hopkins had assured Churchill in January 1941: 'The President is determined that we shall win the war together . . . At all costs and by all means he will carry you through.' Whether Roosevelt would have been able to bring the United States thus far if Great Britain and France had gone precipitately to war with Germany in 1938 in order to deny self-determination to the Sudeten Germans, instead of first passing through the humiliation of Munich for the sake of peace, can only be a matter of speculation. But a doubt must remain.

It was the mark of our own changed position in the world that in both World Wars we had to exert ourselves to the point of exhaustion in order to survive. We had to become a great land and air power as well as a great sea power. In neither struggle should we have come through without fundamental hurt had we not been able to draw upon the financial and military support of the United States, which may have been marginally decisive in the First World War but was absolutely indispensable in the Second. Nor indeed should we have been likely to hold out long enough to profit by full United States military support if the Germans had not, in the First World War, had to overcome the Imperial Russian armies and, in the Second World War, to break their strength against the armies of the Soviet Union. In neither war could western Europe save itself without calling on Russia and the United States. It still cannot save itself without calling on the United States.

It is doubtful whether, when Hitler provoked the outbreak of the

Second World War in September 1939, he expected that a general war would really occur, or if it did, that it would last very long. His experience of British and French pliability, and the fact of his Russian treaty, would suggest to him that neither Great Britain nor France would support Poland. Confident that he would not have to fight a long war against a combination of Great Powers but could reach successive limited objectives by threat or by short, sudden campaigns, he decided, against the advice of the General Staff, to arm in width rather than in depth. He entered the war with an economy that was still not sufficiently mobilized for a long-sustained large-scale conflict, and with inadequate stocks of equipment. To that extent, the war, as it developed, had not been planned. It was only after 1942 that Speer was able to gather the economy together for purposes of total war. Even then, mobilization was less complete than it became in the United Kingdom. Hitler had thought in 1939 that he could get by in time with a navy that was inadequate and an air force that was approaching obsolescence.

When Great Britain and France went to war in 1939, they could not hope for an early victory. In 1938, the military expenditure of Greater Germany had been double that of Great Britain and France combined. In London it was assumed that the war would have to last at least three years, and that, as in the First World War, our main, continuing and, it was too optimistically hoped, decisive weapon would be the blockade. The Germans, by a military master-stroke, upset these calculations. They also, by opening a threat to American military security, turned the course of United States history.

Our own 'finest hour' in 1940 was born of inner strength[2] triumphing over material weakness. Winston Churchill's speeches, like that of Queen Elizabeth I at the time of the Armada, still ring in our ears. They drew upon, as well as contributed to, that inner strength. 'Oh, I was very fortunate,' he said to Lord Woolton in October 1943. 'I did nothing more than give expression to the opinion of the people of this country, and I was fortunate in being able to put their sentiments into words.'[3] Never was a people more nobly mirrored to itself.

The German break-through in France in the summer of 1940

---

[2] At the very heart of the crisis, Parliament could pause and assert its faith in the future by passing a Development and Welfare Act for the benefit of the colonial empire.

[3] The Earl of Woolton, *Memoirs*, Cassell, London, 1959, pp. 261–62.

was a clear defeat for the well-led but inadequately equipped forces of Great Britain as well as for those of France, which, unlike our own, proved to be uncharacteristically lacking both in competent leadership and in fighting spirit. In British eyes, the defeat was given the colour of a deliverance by the safe withdrawal at the end of May and in early June of nearly 340,000 men, somewhat less than half of them French and Belgian, over the beaches at Dunkirk. Our men left behind them all the arms and equipment which they could not carry with them, including 2,300 guns, 7,000 tons of ammunition and 82,000 vehicles. This so-called 'miracle', which so powerfully if incongruously raised our spirits, was the result of a skilful retreat and delaying operation by Lord Gort in the presence of the enemy; and of the successful conduct by Admiral Sir Bertram Ramsay of 'Operation Dynamo', the despatch of over three hundred naval and passenger vessels, and the organized and controlled use—not, as we are apt to think, the spontaneous *levée en masse*—of close on six hundred small craft of all kinds to bring the men away, in spite of all that the German air force could do. It was achieved, not least, by the political impulse given by the Prime Minister.

Of the Battle of Britain, the second 'crowning mercy' of 1940, it should be said that just as Hawkins gave Howard and Drake the ships to beat the Armada and Barham gave Jervis and Nelson the ships for the French wars, so Air Chief Marshal Sir Hugh (later Lord) Dowding and his band of brothers, British, Dominion, French, Polish and Czechoslovak, had in hand in August and September 1940, just in time, the Hurricanes and Spitfires, the new-model, fast and hard-hitting fighter aircraft which blunted and turned aside the attack of Goering's great bomber force. For this, the name of Sir Philip Cunliffe-Lister, later Earl of Swinton, Secretary of State for Air, 1935–38, who ordered the Hurricane and the Spitfire, the latter straight from the drawing-board, and who was responsible for the inception of radar (which proved in 1940 to be an instrument of victory) and of the 'shadow' aircraft factories, should be honourably remembered. It may be true that Fighter Command did not bring down quite so many bombers as, to our joy, was reported at the time. It is possible that if the Germans had not, towards the end, switched the attack from our air-fields to militarily less rewarding targets, the result might have been more nearly what Goering later maintained that it had been, a draw. The fact remains that, in its effects, immediate and long-term, it was one of the decisive battles of the world, one of the supreme achievements in our history. Had we, after the withdrawal from Dunkirk, thrown our reserves of fighter aircraft into the Battle of France, as the French Government implored us to do, the Battle of Britain would have been lost. It was rightly judged in London that nothing that we could do could stem the German advance on land and that the only hope for ourselves, and ultimately for France, was to await the assault behind our own shores. What seemed at the time to be a desertion, even a betrayal, proved in the end to be the saving of France.

Once again, we were to be saved from invasion. In the absence of air-superiority, the German Navy could not clear the way for the Army and 'Operation Sea-Lion' was abandoned. Once again the Channel, rightly used, had enabled us to bar the way to an invader. A few years later, rightly used, it would enable us once again to make a landing on the Continent. It is useless to speculate what would have happened if it had not been there. If the land-bridge with the Continent had never been submerged in pre-historic times, our whole history would have been entirely different.

Here, in our situation in late 1940, was a divorce between power and influence. Our effective military power, apart from the Navy, was small. We were on the verge of financial collapse. But we stood as an inspiration to men of free mind throughout the world. The exiled governments of Europe were established among us. The voice of London, broadcast day by day, gave encouragement to resistance and hope of victory. The Commonwealth sustained us. 'It was the presence of Canadian forces in the United Kingdom, of Australian, New Zealand, South African, and Indian forces in the Middle East, comprising as they did so large a proportion of the trained forces at the disposal of the British Commonwealth after the evacuation from Dunkirk, that ensured survival.'[4] Little by little at first, and then by leaps and bounds as American assistance flowed in, our military strength was to grow.[5] We continued to maintain the blockade of the

[4] Professor Nicholas Mansergh, *Survey of British Commonwealth Affairs, 1939–1952*, Royal Institute of International Affairs, Oxford University Press, 1958, p. 127.
In 1945 the total strength in manpower of the armed forces of Canada, Australia, New Zealand and South Africa, as compared with those of the United Kingdom, was approximately: Navy, one-sixth; Army, equal; Air Force, treble. Ibid. p. 189.
[5] In 1944, 61·2 per cent of the materials and munitions supplied to British and other non-American Allied forces were produced in the United

enemy. As soon as we could, and at considerable risk to our safety at home, we sent reinforcements to Egypt. We began again to fight battles overseas, we and the Dominions alone, or together with the forces of our occupied European allies, or with the Americans—in North Africa, in Italy, and at last, under General Eisenhower's happily governed Supreme Command, in the final assault on the German positions across the Channel and in the advance across Germany to meet the Russians beyond the Elbe. Farther afield, we drove the Japanese back out of Burma and Malaya and received the Japanese surrenders in French Indo-China and in the Dutch East Indies. We sent a naval contingent to contribute to the unexampled and superbly conducted American operations against the Japanese in the Pacific under Admiral Nimitz and General MacArthur.

These were very considerable military operations, never so large either in numbers engaged or in losses sustained as in the First World War, but marked, on the whole, by a political direction and a military organization and leadership much superior to the record which the First World War could show. We made more effective and more economical use of our men and material. It is true that we were far surpassed in military strength by the United States and the Soviet Union, and that we were entirely dependent upon the United States for means to continue the war. But, so long as hostilities lasted, the influence, both political and military, which we were able to exercise upon the conduct of the war was out of proportion to the effective power which we could deploy. Our relative weakness was cloaked by the range and variety of our indispensable contribution to every aspect of the common effort.

There were good reasons for the continuing strength of our voice in the Allied councils. The chief of these was the personality and the qualities of the Prime Minister himself. It was a fortunate chance that, by family background and political education, he had acquired a just understanding of United States policies and institutions and, at this crisis in our history, could establish with the American President a political and personal friendship of such momentous consequence for the two countries. Thanks to this, the American and British war-efforts could be married so as to achieve what General George C. Marshall, the Chief of Staff of the United States Army, could call 'the most complete unification of military effort

Kingdom, and 28·7 per cent in the United States. But of course British production was liberally financed from the United States.

ever achieved by two allied nations', of which General Marshall's own affectionate relationship with Field-Marshal Sir John Dill, his British colleague on the Combined Chiefs of Staff Committee in Washington, was a shining example. Thanks also to this relationship between President and Prime Minister—however intimate it was, the proper distance between a head of government and a head of state was never overstepped by Mr Churchill—political misunderstandings which might arise from the President's deep-seated misapprehensions about British imperial and European policies and about Russian designs could to some extent be mitigated.

Mr Churchill's position was also strengthened in two other ways: first, by the circumstance that the British political and military machine was both more flexible and more closely knit than the American; and secondly, by his capacity, which Lloyd George had not possessed, to establish and maintain—in spite of all controversies—relations of confidence with Chiefs of Staff and commanders in the field and afloat. The fact that the President was Commander-in-Chief of the forces of the United States would place the American Chiefs of Staff individually and as a body in a position of greater weight in Washington than their colleagues could attain in London, where the Prime Minister was not Commander-in-Chief but Minister of Defence and where the mechanism of Cabinet, Cabinet Committees and Cabinet Secretariat would ensure the co-ordination of political and military policies and the supremacy of civilian control. And whereas President Roosevelt, so it has been recorded, would only confer with his Secretary of State, Cordell Hull, at not very frequent intervals, Churchill would not only meet the Foreign Secretary, Anthony Eden, at every Cabinet, but would, between meetings, carry on an unceasing—and it must be confessed, time-consuming—exchange of arguments on paper interspersed with personal consultations. The benefit to domestic administration, to the organization of the war effort, to the conduct of military operations and to the promotion of British influence abroad, of the mechanism of ministerial and official committees and secretariat created and perfected before and during the war to serve the purposes of cabinet government can hardly be over-estimated. It helped ministers and officials all to speak with one voice and to concert their efforts to the same ends. General de Gaulle, in his account of his years in London during the war, has remarked, with wry humour, upon what it felt like to be at the receiving end of a concerted assault by the serried ranks of Mr Churchill's administration: 'For to resist the British machine, when it set itself in motion to impose something, was a severe test. Without having experienced it oneself, it is impossible to imagine what a concentration of effort, what a variety of procedures, what insistence, by turns gracious, pressing and threatening, the English were capable of deploying in order to obtain satisfaction. . . . Everyone around us got to work on it, in all ways, at all levels. There were official conversations or informal ones, in which those in the most diverse positions invoked friendship, interest or fear, according to the occasion.'[6]

In the field of grand strategy, Churchill had many a hard battle, which happily, and these the most important, he sometimes won. The most far-reaching and, for him, most welcome decision of all, though it was one which was received with dismay in Australia, was the decision to give the war against Germany priority over the war against Japan. The conclusion that 'Germany is . . . the prime enemy and her defeat is the key to victory' was, however, not one of those which Churchill had to fight for. As early as March 1941, long before Pearl Harbour, the American and British planners, in informal talks, had reached the conclusion that this was the right policy, if the war were to spread to the Pacific, and it was maintained when war came. The Prime Minister's most hard-won successes were the decision to make the Anglo-American landings in North Africa, so as to free the Mediterranean rather than to launch a premature and almost certainly disastrous assault upon the Channel coast; and the decision to defer the cross-Channel operation itself until the early summer of 1944, when it could have a good chance of success. On this latter issue, Churchill had to withstand Stalin as well as Roosevelt. The Americans were wedded to their characteristic confident strategy of going straight for the main objective with concentrated force and were misled by an imperfect appreciation of the hazards of a cross-Channel operation. If the assault failed, they were strong enough and confident enough to try again. The British, having already been so long in the war and having suffered so much, probably could not. Therefore the British view was: let us take a little more time and make sure. We would rather lose time than lose men. The Russians were naturally anxious that an attempt should be made to draw off German forces from the eastern front, but the

[6] Charles de Gaulle, *War Memoirs. The Call of Honour, 1940–1942*, Collins, London, pp. 167–68.

grim implications for Great Britain and, in a lesser degree, for the United States if a grand seaborne assault should fail, would leave them unconcerned: if the western powers should exhaust themselves as well as the Germans, so much the better for the Soviet Union.

One other matter on which the Prime Minister had his way on an issue of direct British interest was the allocation of the zones of occupation in Germany. The President pressed hard for the allocation to the United States instead of to Great Britain of the industrialized and maritime north-west zone which had been so closely linked to us in our history, rather than the more remote southwestern zone. After a prolonged engagement, the President was induced to give way.

In the field of normal diplomacy also, and away from what is now called the 'summit', there is evidence that the weakened material position of Great Britain did not impair her bargaining power. Between January 1944 and the summer of 1945, the European Advisory Commission, on which Great Britain, the United States, the Soviet Union, and later France, were ambassadorially represented, held over a hundred meetings in London at which it successfully negotiated agreements to settle the terms of surrender, occupation and control of Germany and the occupation and control of Austria. The British representative on the Commission can testify that, during the whole of these transactions, he was at no time conscious of representing a country inferior in power to the United States or the Soviet Union. The representatives of these countries negotiated on equal terms, and it cannot be said that one of them more than another dominated the proceedings. Indeed, there is evidence that President Roosevelt himself disliked the Commission, since its location in London and the excellence of the British administrative machine gave the representative of the United Kingdom an opportunity to seize initiatives and, as he saw it, to threaten American leadership.[7]

At the conference in Moscow in the late autumn of 1943, between Eden, Cordell Hull and Molotov, a conference, the 'prodigious results' of which, as Churchill called them, represented the highwater mark of three-power wartime agreement, Eden's influence

[7] The present writer has given some account of the proceedings of the European Advisory Commission in *Home and Abroad*, Chapter VI, André Deutsch, London, 1956.

was in no way inferior to that of his two colleagues: indeed, the part which he played was, if anything, the most effective of the three.

At his meetings with Roosevelt and Stalin, whether separately, or *à trois* as at Tehran in December 1943 and at Yalta in February 1945, Churchill was not overshadowed by his two great contemporaries. Some American participants in these conferences have in their memoirs represented him as having been a poor third in these colloquies. This is not the view of Mr Herbert Feis, the recent American historian of these transactions.[8] For him, it is Churchill who most pervades the scene, a 'vital spirit' reacting with 'his usual resiliency', pursuing his purposes 'in a spirit of adventure' with a 'supple and bold initiative'. He was 'unhappy but unwearied' when rebuffed, 'boyishly pleased' when successful. He met Roosevelt's appeals with 'his usual generous response' and put a rein upon his natural vivacity in face of deliberate rudeness by Stalin. 'No man of greatness ever placed his temper at the service of a good cause more admirably than Churchill.'

Stalin, from beginning to end, never lost sight of the Soviet political objective. At Russia's darkest hour, in December 1941, he could still, in his talks with Eden in Moscow, stake out the full measure of Soviet post-war claims in Europe. Roosevelt, so magnificent as a war leader and so brilliant and zestful a politician, was unwilling or unable to look ahead in order to relate the operations of war in specific terms to the looming problems of peace. His judgments, too often marked by levity or superficiality, rested upon too tenuous a foundation of fact and of reflection.[9] He was insufficiently informed himself, and drew insufficiently upon the resources of the State Department, to reach a just diagnosis of the policies of his two chief allies or a realistic conception of the shape of the world after the war. Like most Americans in positions of authority, he failed to recognize the stature of General de Gaulle, already seen by many in London to be one of the great men of our time. He was certain that Stalin was no imperialist, and he was confident that, by his personal touch, he could handle him successfully. If, he said,

[8] *Churchill, Roosevelt, Stalin*, Oxford University Press, London, 1957.
[9] 'Roosevelt was no thinker; he collected ideas as readily as postage stamps and discarded them as readily as paper towels.' H. G. Nicholas, in review of *What Roosevelt Thought*, *International Affairs*, Oxford University Press, January 1960, p. 144.

Stalin were generously treated, he could be counted on to respond—
it would be a case of *noblesse oblige*. He held, and rightly so, though
in a sense which he could little suspect, that China would be one of
the post-war great powers; but, as Eden presciently remarked to him
in Washington in the spring of 1943, China would probably have to
go through a revolution first. For Churchill, on the other hand,
there was no divorce between war and policy. He was always alert
to make strategy serve the ends of policy and policy subserve the
operations of war. Hardly can any statesman ever have been so
ludicrously misjudged as Churchill was in May 1945 by President
Truman's emissary, the notorious Mr Joseph Davies, who said of
him: 'As I had heard him inveigh so violently against the threat of
Soviet domination and the spread of Communism in Europe, and
disclose such a lack of confidence in the professions of good faith in
Soviet leadership, I had wondered whether he . . . was now willing
to declare to the world that he and Britain had made a mistake in not
supporting Hitler.'

By the time of the meeting with Truman and Stalin at Potsdam in
July 1945, the situation had somewhat changed. The war against
Germany, in which Great Britain had played an indispensable part,
was over. In the war against Japan, our part was very much smaller,
and it was Soviet participation that the United States now wanted.
Even though the use of the atomic bomb was imminent, its success
could not be assured. Truman looked upon Stalin as the person
with whom he would settle affairs: 'I felt hopeful,' he said later, 'that
we could reach an agreement that would be satisfactory to the world
and to ourselves.' Great Britain was economically dependent on the
United States and would have to conform. Churchill no longer had
quite the same status as before. This, in fact, mattered the less in
that Anglo-American differences were narrower and Anglo-American
agreement wider at Potsdam than they had been at Yalta. American
eyes were being slowly opened to Russian designs. When, in the
course of the conference, with the change of government, he and
Mr Eden gave place to Mr Attlee and Mr Bevin, the fact of our de-
clension became rather more evident than before. It is to the enduring credit of the Labour Government, and of the Foreign Secretary,
Ernest Bevin, in particular, that, by-passing party doctrines, they
framed policies which were suited to strategic realities and to the
national interest, as traditionally understood, and which were well
devised to take account of the change in our place in the world and

to enable us, even in the altered circumstances, to play a continuing worthy part on the international stage.[10]

It is sometimes said—though less often by historians than by military men and political commentators—that we won the war but lost the peace. This sweeping judgment is based upon the undoubted but unfortunate fact that after the end of the war, central and eastern Europe and most of the Balkan peninsula came under Soviet control and that, except for Jugoslavia and the Soviet Zone of Austria, this is still the situation at the time of writing. It is less easy to see how, as a matter of practical politics, this result could have been avoided. Theoretically speaking, it would have been possible for us to make peace with Hitler instead of offering all assistance to the Soviet Union as Churchill did immediately upon the German attack on Russia in June 1941. Had we done so, Hitler would probably have subdued the Soviet Union, and we ourselves might have preserved the Empire and perhaps secured the liberation of Norway, Denmark, the Netherlands and Belgium, if we had been willing to leave the French to save their empire if they could. Whether we should have been safer so, and what would then have happened in the Far East, it is impossible to say: but this was not a solution which Winston Churchill or the British people could have brought themselves to contemplate. Theoretically, again, it would have been possible for the United States and Great Britain to insist in 1945, if necessary to the point of war, upon the fulfilment by Stalin of the agreements of Yalta and Potsdam about the liberties of Poland and Roumania and the unity of Germany. But here again, at a time when it was the essence of Western policy to draw the Soviet Union into the United Nations, neither Roosevelt nor Truman nor Churchill could have contemplated such a course for a moment, nor would the British and American peoples have willingly turned their arms against their ally, however unco-operative and unfriendly the latter

---

[10] In 1934, Attlee, when in opposition, could say: 'We have absolutely abandoned every idea of nationalist loyalty. We are deliberately putting a world order before our loyalty towards our own country.'

In 1948, Bevin, as a member of the Labour Government, said: 'The safety of our respective countries must be the first claim upon responsible statesmen.'

This contrast has been ably treated by a young American scholar, C. R. Rose, in a thesis for the degree of D.Phil. in the University of Oxford entitled: 'The Relation of Socialist Principles to British Labour Foreign Policy, 1945–51', from which the foregoing quotations and some others in this chapter have been drawn.

might be. To save the peace, if by this is meant keeping the Russians out of central and eastern Europe, would have called for either an early compromise peace with Hitler or a war with the Soviet Union.

But in truth the causes of Russian domination in the belt between the Baltic and the Black Sea lie further back. Palácky, the Czech patriot and historian, said in mid-nineteenth century that without the unity of the Austrian imperial state 'the peoples of different race and language bordering the Russian frontier could not hope to stand against the overwhelming power of Russia.' With the collapse first of the Ottoman Empire and then of the Austro-Hungarian Empire the new states established on the basis of nationality could hardly hope to survive alone in face of any revival of ambitions on the part of reinvigorated neighbouring great powers. Once it was clear, in the period between the wars, that the League of Nations was impotent and that France and Great Britain could not defend them, they were brought within the German sphere; and later, with the defeat of Germany, the heritage passed to Russia. Those who thought it good policy in the nineteenth century to prop up the Ottoman Empire and to sustain the Austrian Empire as long as possible were not as blind as we are now apt to suppose. What can be said is that the march of history was against them. Those who thought that we had backed the wrong horse, if their reason was that independent national states in the Balkans would be a better barrier against Russia than a decrepit Ottoman Empire, were perhaps mistaken. The tragedy was that the two empires could not possibly survive; and that, though they could not know it, the peoples who were liberating themselves on the basis of the principle of self-determination were sooner or later to exchange one tyranny for another, a tyranny which they may, not unnaturally, think preferable to that from which they originally escaped, in that, though they are captive, they still retain their cherished nationality.

When hostilities with Japan ended in August 1945, there were two questions upon the answers to which the future of the world would depend. Would the United States now revert to the isolationism of the inter-war years, or would she rise to the international responsibilities which her power was laying upon her? And would the Soviet Union exercise with moderation and in a spirit of international co-operation the power which she also had achieved through her herculean exertions during the war? The answers were not slow in coming. The Soviet Union broke the Yalta agreement about free elections in eastern European countries and the Potsdam agreement about the economic unity and progressive political unification of Germany. Having stripped the Soviet Zone of industrial equipment for the benefit of her own economy, she proceeded to build it into her Communist satellite system. It became increasingly plain, and clear beyond question from the end of 1947, that the Soviet government would not prolong even the precarious and uneasy co-operation of war-time into the post-war years, and that they would revert to the policies of an expansionist great power and supplement these, where appropriate, by the subversive practices of a proselytizing revolutionary creed. Attempts by Great Britain and the United States to base their policy on co-operation with the Soviet Union came to nothing.

The United States, after an initial movement of disengagement—rapid demobilization of forces and abrupt termination of lend-lease —awoke to the Soviet menace and recognized that, for the defence of the United States, it would be necessary to buttress the economies and build up the military potential of western European countries, and to enter upon political and military commitments unprecedented in her history in peace time. Like Great Britain at the turn of the century, she now became acutely conscious of her isolation. For the first time in her history she was menaced by an implacably hostile great power against whom she must protect herself in depth across both her encompassing oceans.[11] In President Truman she found a leader who matched the imperative needs of the hour.

Side by side with these two political upheavals, there were two developing processes in other parts of the world which would create grave problems for statesmen. The first was the tremendous scientific and technological dynamism of the United States and of capitalist and Communist Europe which increasingly widened the gap between their standard of living and that of the less-advanced peoples of Asia and Africa. The second was the irresistible movement among the dependent and backward peoples of Asia and Africa down the paths of independence and industrialization. With this, there was before long to be the portentous appearance of a strong military power in Communist China.

[11] The move of the United States away from isolation was reinforced by the growing dependence of her rapidly expanding economy upon imports of raw materials, particularly non-ferrous and alloy metals. Her economy was no longer virtually self-supporting, as before, on coal, steel, cotton and wool.

The problem which faced Ernest Bevin and his colleagues was to frame a foreign policy for Great Britain in conditions of grave economic weakness and of seriously diminished political and military power. With the cessation of lend-lease in the autumn of 1945, it was plain that, without substantial new aid from the United States, Great Britain would be virtually bankrupt. Our foreign trade had been disrupted. In 1946, we had a trading deficit of £450 million. In addition to war-time commitments which could not be immediately liquidated, we had a new obligation to help to sustain the economy of our zone of occupation in Germany.[12] Loans from the United States were made available, but they were inadequate for their purposes. The United States government had at first much underestimated the economic plight of western Europe, just as later they were to over-estimate the measure in which western European countries could themselves finance their contribution to the common defence. Not until the inception in 1948 of the brilliantly successful European Recovery Programme (the Marshall Plan), a blend of American assistance and European self-help, would a solution be found.

The foreign policy devised by Attlee's government in this new situation was marked by three main elements.

First, it was necessary, as an early measure, to disengage ourselves from commitments which we could no longer sustain. Spain and Holland and France had all, in the past, suffered from trying to play a part in the world which had outrun the resources at their disposal. Thus, early in 1947, Bevin told the United States government that we could no longer continue to afford aid to Greece and Turkey, and the Americans, under the new 'Truman doctrine', assumed the responsibility in our place. Bevin's attempt in 1946 to negotiate a withdrawal from Egypt was frustrated by a difference of opinion with Egypt about the future of the Sudan. In 1947–48 he declined to enforce single-handed against Arabs and Jews a United Nations' settlement for Palestine and withdrew our forces and terminated the mandate.

The second and third elements in post-war British policy were of longer range. One of them was the conception of the western community. The other was what has been called 'the liberal experiment', one aspect of which was 'the promotion throughout the world of the

[12] In 1946 we had to spend £80 million, much of it in dollars, in order to feed the population of the British Zone.

institutions of self-government as the only means by which societies may learn political responsibility' (Sir Llewellyn Woodward).

In the sphere of national security, it was clear to Bevin that past policies would no longer serve. Naval predominance was not to be attained. The mechanism of the balance of power in the old sense was made inoperative by the great world cleavage. Isolation was out of the question, and separate alliances could serve no purpose. In her relatively weakened position, Great Britain could not stand alone, and the other states of western Europe were in like case. The Commonwealth could not be self-sufficient in this field. The United Nations, like the League of Nations, could not guarantee security. This was not, as before, because the United States was not a member, but because, although the United States and the Soviet Union were both in it, they were deeply divided. As Mr St Laurent, the Canadian Secretary for External Affairs, remarked in September 1947, the United Nations Security Council was 'frozen in futility and divided by dissension'. Security must be sought by supplementing the United Nations but in a manner in harmony with its principles. Great Britain, departing from previous policies, now took the decision to join a regional community, accepting the fact of American power, entering into continuous intimate economic relations with like-minded states, merging her available military forces with those of other powers and undertaking definite military commitments, yet aiming at an association which, as Bevin said in January 1948, would be 'more of a brotherhood and less of a rigid system'.

Progressive steps were taken along this path by successive British governments, and often under their leadership. There was the Dunkirk Treaty with France; the Brussels Treaty with France and the Low Countries; the wider community of the Organization for European Economic Co-operation, which grew out of the Marshall Plan so promptly embraced by Bevin (he called Marshall's Harvard speech 'one of the greatest speeches made in world history') and which was the door by which the German Federal Republic was first drawn into the community; the North Atlantic Treaty of 1949, again promoted upon an initiative by Bevin, which brought commitments to and from both the United States and Canada as well as to and from a number of European states, again in due course including Western Germany; Western European Union, extending the Brussels treaty commitments to Italy and Western Germany, which was brought into being in place of the abortive European Defence

Community thanks to a bold initiative by Anthony Eden; and with all this, growing intimacy of military co-operation under an American Supreme Commander, and growing precision in the promises given for the disposition and use of the British armed forces. Truly, a revolution in our policy no less than in that of the United States and of Canada. Canada's part in this should not be overlooked. Mr St Laurent had seen as early as September 1947 the need for an association linking Canada and the United States with the United Kingdom and western Europe for purposes of common defence.

Of all our Foreign Secretaries, in spite of the obvious and profound differences between the two men, none perhaps worked more consistently than Bevin along the lines marked out by Castlereagh, though Bevin followed that path for purposes of which Castlereagh would have had little conception. The two were similar in temper, in their belief that fair dealing and a frank and realistic approach should be the basis of diplomacy, in their sense of positive and constructive purpose, in their conviction that meetings in conference of persons in high authority with something definite to talk about were the best means of dissipating misunderstandings and creating confidence, in their vision of a Europe bound together by a common purpose (they both spoke of a 'European Commonwealth'), and above all, in their faith that in the building up of an association of powers bound together by shared responsibility for peace and by a procedure for consultation lay the best hope of security for Great Britain and for Europe. Unlike Castlereagh, Bevin had the advantage that in his policies he was not rowing against the current of national opinion. He could almost always count on the steady support of the Conservative opposition. Like Castlereagh, Bevin died in office, broken down by the strain, but, unlike Castlereagh, unshaken to the end. Like Castlereagh again, Bevin gained the affection and regard of those who served him. It is difficult to think of a Foreign Secretary who inspired more whole-hearted devotion in the members of the Foreign Service at home and abroad than, by his qualities as a man and a statesman, this member of the unskilled working-class and trade union leader was able to do.[13]

[13] Bevin carried out the comprehensive service reforms introduced by Eden in 1943. After 1919, the diplomatic staffs of the Foreign Office and Diplomatic Service were amalgamated and the property qualification was abolished. Now, the Diplomatic, Consular, and Commercial Diplomatic Services have been fused into a single Foreign Service. Financial conditions have been improved and the field of recruitment widened.

War and Early Post-War

The pursuit of the 'liberal experiment' has been most signally marked by the emergence as new independent states, either inside or outside the Commonwealth, of territories formerly under British rule.[14] The older colonies of European settlement, that is to say, the Dominions, which had long been self-governing and independent in almost every practical respect, had their full and separate sovereign status recognized after the First World War. As time went on, they developed interests of their own and framed their policies accordingly. Their decisions to enter the Second World War were independently taken. The unity of the Commonwealth was unbroken under the fierce stress of war, and it proved itself in Mr St Laurent's phrase, to be 'stronger than any alliance in history'. It was, as General Smuts said in November 1943, 'a system that has stood the greatest stress to which any nations could be subjected'. A German naval officer had warned Hitler in 1940 that 'owing to the peculiar innate force of the political objectives embodied in the conception of the Commonwealth of Nations', the British Empire would endure.

Canada came to see herself as a bridge between London and Washington. While maintaining intimate relations with the United Kingdom in all fields and while joining the North Atlantic Treaty, she made separate defence arrangements with the United States. These were called for because, globally northwards, she is directly interposed between the United States and the Soviet Union. Her membership of the Commonwealth acquired increasing importance in her eyes. It enhanced her standing with the United States and opened up a special relationship with the new nations of the Commonwealth. Australia and New Zealand, perhaps more closely linked in sentiment to the United Kingdom, were also made conscious during the Second World War of their dependence upon the United States in spheres of defence. While joining with Great Britain in the South-east Asia Treaty Organization and in the Colombo Plan, they had also made a special defence arrangement (ANZUS) with the United States to which the United Kingdom was not a party. It is noteworthy that the commander of the Commonwealth forces

[14] In its world-wide aspect, some of the possible consequences of the 'liberal experiment' have aroused deep misgivings in some liberal minds. Norman Angell has suggested that the proliferation of new, ultra-nationalistic states may portend 'the suicide of the west'. Gilbert Murray in his last years thought that the irresponsible voting-power of these backward new states in the United Nations marked an advancing 'shadow of barbarism'.

of occupation in Japan was an Australian and that the Commonwealth member of the Allied post-hostilities organization in Japan
was supplied by Australia and not by the United Kingdom. The
value to the United Kingdom of the Commonwealth connection is
powerfully demonstrated by the facilities for air training afforded
by Canada in the dark days of the Second World War, and by the
facilities for the testing of missile weapons since afforded by Australia at the range at Woomera.

The achievement of independence within the Commonwealth by
India and Pakistan in 1947, followed by that of Ceylon within, and
by Burma outside, the Commonwealth, marks a decisive new and
unique development in the history of an already unique institution.
Membership of the Commonwealth was not now confined to countries of European settlement but was opened to countries of alien
race and ancient non-European civilization. Even more surprisingly,
they could remain members of the Commonwealth while no longer,
as republics, remaining in allegiance to the sovereign, and merely
recognizing her role as Head of the Commonwealth. India moved
into independence equipped with the English common law, a parliamentary system drawing its inspiration from London, a civil service
trained on British principles and an army imbued with the best military traditions. But India remained herself. As an eminent Indian
lawyer has recently said: 'The influence of the English in India was
never that of an alien conqueror. They came to trade and stayed to
administer, but they never took over the Indian peoples: their aim
erred rather in over-emphasizing the autonomy and incorrigibility
of Indian custom. They made it abundantly clear that they wanted
India to be Indian. And so it is.'[15] Her emancipation was probably too
long delayed.

Under the enlightened and masterful guidance of her Kashmiri
Brahmin Prime Minister, Pandit Jawaharlal Nehru, alumnus of an
English school and of an English university, India has so far maintained internal political stability under a parliamentary régime,
though her unsolved and perhaps insoluble economic and social
problems—over-population, chronic poverty, under-employment,
meagre rate of production—must render her political future uncertain. While following a neutralist foreign policy of her own, she
has remained in fraternal association with Great Britain and with

[15] J. Chinna Durai, 'Indian Democracy and Mr. Nehru', *The Listener*,
August 27th 1959, p. 306.

other members of the Commonwealth. The relationship between the governments and peoples of the two countries, political, economic and social, being now developed in freedom, has gained in depth and equability.[16] In point of power, Great Britain has lost the use of the Indian Army, which served with high distinction in both World Wars, and which was so valuable to her for employment in emergency in the Persian Gulf and elsewhere in Asia and in Africa. In point of international standing, both countries have been the gainers from the new association. In Asia, India stands against China as still being an exponent of the parliamentary as contrasted with the totalitarian system of government. India, once the 'brightest jewel in the Crown', has become the pioneer and prime exemplar in the latest development of the liberal experiment upon which Great Britain has deliberately embarked as a central feature of her external policy. The experiment is an experiment still. Its outcome lies in the future.

It was not long after the cessation of hostilities in August 1945 that the shape of the post-war world began to emerge. The turning-point may be set in the years 1947–49. By 1948, the cleavage between the Communist and anti-Communist parts of the world, with polarization of power in Moscow and Washington, had become unmistakably clear. In 1947–48 occurred the Russian veto upon the participation of the satellites in the Marshall Plan, the Communist *coup d'état* in Czechoslovakia and the Soviet blockade of Berlin. The United States Economic Co-operation Act and the Convention for European Economic Co-operation of April 1948, together with the series of Economic Co-operation Agreements concluded severally a few months later between the United States and the European beneficiaries, laid the foundation for the economic recovery of the countries of western Europe and enabled them in course of time to give evidence of a remarkable resiliency which is one of the most significant and encouraging developments of the post-war years. The 'Congress of Europe' at The Hague in May 1948 marked the beginning of a decisive move towards unity in western Europe on the basis of common policies and institutions. The conclusion of the North Atlantic Treaty in April 1949 and the establishment of the

---

[16] Thus, for example, it is estimated that British investment in India has more than doubled in the twelve years since independence and now amounts to nearly 81 per cent of the total foreign investment. (*The Times*, December 22nd 1959.)

standing political and military machinery of the North Atlantic Treaty Organization linked western Europe and North America in common defence against the Soviet power, with the forces entrusted to a Supreme Commander and with arrangements for intimate political and military consultations. The acquisition of independence by India and Pakistan in 1947, their acquisition later of a special status as republics within the Commonwealth, and the success of the Communist revolution in China in 1949 brought South and East Asia to the front of the world stage, and the change in China faced both the Soviet Union and the western powers with problems of great moment. After an era of subordination to western Europe, the harbinger of which was the arrival of the Portuguese navigator, Vasco da Gama, in his heavily-armed ocean-going ships at Calicut in 1498, South and East Asia were again taking an independent place in the world hierarchy. The establishment of the state of Israel in 1948, remote consequence of the fateful Balfour Declaration of 1917, intensified the already violent ferment in the Arab world, with untoward consequences for the western powers with interests in that region, and not least for Great Britain, still established in Egypt and deeply concerned both politically and economically in the area round the Persian Gulf and in Iraq. Great Britain was the less able to set her course in these troubled waters in that she was still dependent on the United States for financial assistance, and usually at odds with the United States on policy.

If the major tragedy of the early post-war period was the rift between east and west which the character of the Soviet government made inevitable, there was nevertheless much to be set on the credit side. In the earlier years after the end of the First World War there had been nothing to compare with the positive and concerted programme of political and economic reconstruction which was set on foot by the western powers after the close of the Second World War. The economic prosperity of western Europe was restored by the European Recovery Programme. The security of the western powers was reinforced by the North Atlantic Treaty. The total occupation of Germany, while it split Germany in two and delivered the eastern zone into Communist hands, enabled the western occupying powers, by an enlightened, generous and humane occupation policy, to save western Germany from the political and economic ordeals of the 1920s, to ensure for her a steady political and economic development, and to give the Federal Republic an opportunity of joining the community of western European peoples on a basis of equality. And looking beyond Europe, the specialized agencies of the United Nations have worked on a regional or a world-wide scale for the benefit of mankind, in the economic and social sphere, in food and agriculture, in health, in labour questions, in education and science, for a wide range of humanitarian objectives. The western powers in particular have come to a realization that, in their own interest no less than as a human duty, it is incumbent on them to look to the welfare of the backward and undeveloped peoples of the world, numbering more than half the human race, and most of them suffering from chronic malnutrition. The problem of food is seen to be no less pressing than the problem of peace. Whether these problems are to be solved, the future will show. Will the most economically fruitful impulse come from the Communist or from the non-Communist world? Will democratic methods serve as well as Communist methods to overcome the tremendous initial obstacles that lie in the path of industrialization in primitive communities? We cannot tell. But at least men do appear to have learnt something from experience, and to be making a deliberate effort, by the adoption of concrete measures taken in common, and by a practical application of the new conception of inter-dependence among nations, to shape their future in security and prosperity.

Part IV
THE LATEST PHASE

CHAPTER XV

The Last Ten Years: 1949–1959

The ten years between 1949 and 1959 were marked, for Great Britain, by political stability at home; by relative peace in industry—less than two hours per worker per annum on an average were lost through industrial disputes, a quarter of the figure for Belgium and one-seventh of that for the United States; by economic recovery[1]—after recurrent crises the period closed, per-

[1] The economic recovery of the United Kingdom in the post-war years has been notable. In the war, we lost a quarter of our pre-war wealth. We were left with an overseas debit of £3,000 million for war-time supplies of goods and services at inflated prices which is being repaid over the years by 'unrequited' exports. Production has increased by over 60 per cent and exports by over 100 per cent in volume since 1938. Our export effort has been re-shaped. Coal and textiles, once the major items in our export trade, now take a very minor place as compared with metals and engineering products, including electrical goods, road vehicles and aircraft. We are even exporting automobiles and aircraft to the United States. Whereas between 1929 and 1938 we had a serious cumulative deficit in current balance of payments, we had between 1949 and 1957 an average annual surplus of £100 million. We are once again, per head of population, the largest overseas investor in the world. It is fair to say that, except perhaps for two or three years before the First World War, the British economy was, in the few years before 1960, more flourishing than it had been at any time since 1873. Precariously poised though it must be from the fact that the pound sterling carries nearly half the world's trade and payments on less than 4 per cent of the world's exchange reserves, and thus vulnerable to the fluctuating judgments of the foreign money market, it had perhaps not been more healthily constituted or more broadly based at any time since the industrial revolution. It no longer thrives, as it once did, on monopoly, but in competition; and the national wealth is increasingly widely spread among the population as a whole. When the Prime Minister, Harold Macmillan, said that the British people 'had never had it so good', he was putting into colloquial terms what scholars have expressed more cautiously in more solemn language: 'Despite inflation it is probable that even in real terms the mass of the population in the 1950s have a higher material standard of living than ever before.' (David C. Marsh, *The Changing Social Structure of England and Wales*, Routledge, London,

haps precariously, with a strong pound, a substantial surplus on overseas account, flourishing high-grade exports, a stable price level and low unemployment; by a revived agriculture—we were now growing half our foodstuffs as against a third before the war; by progressive disengagement from untenable commitments abroad, including a negotiated withdrawal of British forces from the Suez Canal Zone; by unwearied pursuit of the liberal experiment resulting in new accessions of ex-colonies of non-European stock to the Commonwealth; by steady co-operation in the Atlantic and other regional associations, involving the location of United States air forces on British soil and precise commitments for the stationing of British forces on the Continent; by accession to the rank of a nuclear power—the Labour government provided the atomic bomb and the Conservative government made provision for the hydrogen bomb; by the development of nuclear energy for peaceful purposes; by uncertainty as to how best to organize and equip our now comparatively modest armed forces[2] to carry out their multifarious duties, national and collective, in the nuclear age; and by one aberration from traditional policy—the Anglo-French operation at Port Said in November 1956.

It has become fashionable among some political commentators to pretend that we have lost our influence in the world and that we now count for little in the councils of the nations. This is far from the truth, as will be evident if recent events are looked at with some regard for historical perspective. It is true that we cannot rival the United States or the Soviet Union in power or resources. We could not now, as we did in the Napoleonic Wars, and as the United States did during and after the Second World War, carry a great coalition

1958, p. 226.) The same is, of course, true of other economically advanced countries. If economic progress has been more rapid and more extensive in the United States and in some other western European countries than in the United Kingdom, this is in the main because the British economy cannot safely out-run the export basis on which it rests, and because British trade unions, unlike, for example, those of the United States, tend to cling to deceptive short-term security at the expense of technological development. This 'good time' in the western world may well be precarious. It has not yet been proved that the trade cycle, the alternation of periods of activity and quiescence, of boom and of slump, has been overcome, though its most serious effects may be mitigated.

[2] For example, in the Navy we had in 1959 one aircraft carrier for about every five of the United States; one cruiser for every six American and every three Russian; one destroyer for six and three; one submarine for four and ten.

on our shoulders. It is true also that, being dependent on United States assistance, we were, particularly in the early part of the decade, subject from time to time to strong pressure from the United States government on matters of foreign policy, a form of pressure which Bevin, for one, found extremely irksome. He longed to be able to conduct something more nearly approaching an independent foreign policy. It is true again that we could not, as the Soviet Union did in Hungary in 1956, proceed upon our own courses undeterred by world public opinion. But material power, indispensable as it may be, is not the sole basis of international influence. Though our power has declined, we have certainly left our mark on international history in the years since the end of the Second World War.

The record is impressive. It was the initiative of Bevin, as Foreign Secretary, that gave the first impulse to the working out of the Marshall Plan, that most successful and beneficent of all the post-war international enterprises. He was a fervent promoter of the Colombo Plan, first sponsored by Percy Spender, the Australian Minister for External Affairs. Bevin, again, was one of the first, if not the first, to see the need for a North Atlantic Treaty as the basis for our post-war security, and one of the first to work actively for it. It was Eden who, as Foreign Secretary, brought decisive restraining influence to bear upon the United States during the grave Indo-Chinese crisis before and at the Geneva Conference in the summer of 1954, and did most to make an agreement possible. It was he again who, by an imaginative initiative in the autumn of the same year, salvaged Western European Union from the wreck of the European Defence Community. It was Eden's comprehensive plan for the reunification of Germany by free elections and for the preparation of a peace-treaty, that engaged the attention of the conference of western Foreign Ministers at Berlin in 1954. It was this same plan that formed the basis of the proposals put forward jointly by the heads of the western governments at the so-called Summit Conference with the Soviet representatives, Khrushchev and Bulganin, at Geneva in 1955. It was the same plan again, modified to meet the new circumstances, which was jointly submitted by the western Foreign Ministers at the Geneva Conference with the Soviet Foreign Minister, Gromyko, in May 1959. It was largely owing to British initiative that the Summit Conference of 1955 was held; that the Geneva Conference on Nuclear Tests and the Geneva Conference of Foreign Ministers of 1959 were convened for negotiations with the Russians; and that direct contacts between Khrushchev and the heads of western governments were established.

In one sphere of international organization, however, Great Britain hesitated and held aloof. The movement for union among continental western European states on the basis of some measure of integrated authority took its rise from consciousness of post-war weakness; from the need for heroic measures of reconstruction; from the advance of the new technology calling for operation on a continental scale; from recognition of inferiority in the face of the United States and the Soviet Union; from fear of the Soviet threat; from an aspiration to reconcile France and Germany and to bring the late enemy into the western European fold; from a desire to acquire strength and stability by united action drawing inspiration from common traditions; and, in some minds, from an ambition to create a so-called 'third force' to stand as a unit beside the two great concentrations of power.

The first essay on this theme, the supra-national European Coal and Steel Community embracing six states, was cautiously received by Mr Attlee's government and Great Britain could do no more than associate herself externally with it. The abortive European Defence Community, and the European Economic Community created by the Treaty of Rome, were not arrangements which Great Britain could contemplate joining. One reason was that, since British policy is based upon special relations with the United States and with the Commonwealth as well as with western Europe, the creation of a constitutional link with Europe would hamper our liberty of action in other spheres, and would be out of harmony with the complete independence and absence of common institutions (other than the Crown) which marked inter-Commonwealth relations. Could Great Britain continue to play a leading role in the Commonwealth if she was tied hand and foot to Europe? If Great Britain could merge herself with western Europe, why not Canada with the United States? A second reason, which applied particularly to the Economic Community, was the existence of arrangements for imperial preference. But the fundamental reason was domestic.[3] In inter-governmental organizations like the O.E.E.C., where the assent of all is necessary, the consensus of colleagues' opinion can have a

---

[3] That the United Kingdom 'should join a federation on the continent of Europe . . . is something which we know, in our bones, we cannot do.' Mr Eden at Columbia University, New York, January 11th 1952.

powerful persuasive effect upon a dissentient; but since his acquiescence is required, his position is strong. In an integrated organization
where final decisions can be taken, as in the Coal and Steel Community, by an independent body, or, as in the case of the Economic
Community, by an inter-governmental body acting by a weighted
majority, the dissentient will have full opportunity to press his view,
but in the last resort, if the majority insists, the decision will be taken
against him, and his government must carry it out however distaste-
ful this may be. Our peculiar, insularly developed internal political
system, the steadily matured fruit of conflict and compromise, of
continuity in change, would be ill-mated with the historically less
stable régimes of France[4] and Germany. When one thinks how
jealous the House of Commons is of its powers, its privileges and its
pretensions, it is hard to expect that it would consent to remit a whole
range of future decisions intimately affecting the economic and
social life of Great Britain to be taken by a majority of continental
representatives against the British vote. In exceptional cases within
narrowly prescribed limits, as in Western European Union and in
the European Free Trade Association, we have accepted the operation of the majority vote: but not as a general principle of wide
application.

The six-power Western European Community has as its professed
objective to harmonize economic policies, to create common
political institutions and to act as a unit in world affairs. There
would be a substantial submergence of individual sovereignties.
The French statesman, Paul Reynaud, hardly exaggerated when he
said, in his mocking way: 'In Great Britain there is the House of
Commons, and above that, nothing, and then again nothing, and
then God.' It seems to the present writer that successive British
governments and British public opinion in general have been wise to
go to any possible length in inter-governmental co-operation, but to
hesitate to commit an economy so precariously poised, so subject
to the impact of world-wide forces as is the British economy, to the
hazards of inter-European decision.[5] Even the French, who have

---

[4] To take the case of France. '*Quinze régimes s'étaient succédé depuis
1789, chacun s'imposant à son tour par la révolte ou le coup d'État, aucun
ne réussissant à assurer l'équilibre, tous emportés par des catastrophes et
laissant après eux d'ineffaçables divisions.*' Charles de Gaulle, *Mémoires
de Guerre: Le Salut 1944–1946*, Plon, Paris, 1959, p. 236.
[5] That distinguished French political scientist and sociologist, Ray-
mond Aron, has recently drawn attention to an apposite observation of

been the most zealous promoters of the six-power community, and who, by the never-failing skill of their diplomacy, secured an advantageous position for themselves in the Economic Community under the Treaty of Rome, have had misgivings on this very point. The European Defence Community was rejected by the French parliament for a number of reasons, but one of them was that Frenchmen suddenly realized that, if the Defence Community came into being, France would no longer have an army of her own. And at a time of crisis in the European Coal and Steel Community in May 1959 about mounting coal stocks, the French Prime Minister, M. Debré, declared: 'It is difficult for governments to abandon to international authorities the power for which they are responsible before their nations.'[6] In a similar spirit, President de Gaulle in the same year withheld French naval and air forces from the N.A.T.O. command on the ground that the defence of France should be in French hands.[7] He made a noteworthy qualification, too, when he said on May 30th 1960, speaking of the six-power community: 'The nations which are becoming associated must not cease to be themselves, and the path to be followed must be that of organized co-operation between states, while waiting to achieve, perhaps, an imposing confederation.'

The formation of the six-power community was welcomed in Great Britain, and not least because it confirmed the attachment of Western Germany to western Europe and set a seal upon the *rapprochement* between France and western Germany. If there were misgivings, these arose from apprehensions lest the six powers should separate themselves politically or economically from the wider O.E.E.C. and N.A.T.O. groupings and thus split western Europe into two, or lest British trading interests should be adversely affected. This being so, the objective of British policy was to reconcile the existence of the six-power community with her own and with the wider international interest. Governments usually come to agreements on contentious issues when the external pressure upon them

Montesquieu: 'Jealous as a sovereign power of her own trade, England rarely binds herself by treaties and depends only on her laws. Other nations have subordinated commercial to political interests: England has always subordinated her political to her commercial interests.' (*The Times*, May 5th 1960.)

[6] *The Times*, May 29th 1959.

[7] Speaking to the French National War College in October 1959, he said: 'The system which has been called "integration" . . . has had its day. It is indispensable . . . that France defend herself by herself, for herself and in her own way.'

to do so becomes sufficiently great; when, in fact, the dangers of continuing disagreement are more to be feared than the sacrifices necessary for agreement. Great Britain would only be likely to overcome her reluctance to join the European Economic Community if it became plain that the disadvantages of staying out exceeded the disadvantages of going in. The question is: Would it be better to surrender sovereignty or to face competition from a western European economic league which might militate against continued intimate political and military co-operation? Can some reconciling compromise be found? What the final outcome will be cannot yet be foreseen.

The initiatives which we have taken since the war in international affairs have for the most part one common characteristic. They have in general been designed to promote international agreements. By helping to bring them about, we have served our own interests; but we have tried also to serve a general interest. The pursuit of this double objective, the attempt to serve both the national interest and the general interest, has long been a mark of our foreign policy. It has been imposed upon us as a maritime and trading community with vulnerable interests in all parts of the world. It has had the result that the characteristics of our foreign policy have usually been caution, compromise, patience and a long view. British foreign policy, for this reason, is essentially a liberal foreign policy. Our world-wide operations can only fully flourish if peace and good order are maintained, if international obligations are fulfilled and if international good faith is the rule. It should be the anxious concern of any British government to do all that it can to promote these conditions everywhere in the world, by precept and by example.

British foreign policy therefore normally partakes of what Sir Harold Nicolson has described as 'the civilian' or 'the commercial, the mercantile or the shopkeeper conception' of diplomacy, as opposed to what he called 'the warrior conception'. It is a policy that usually prefers compromise to victory; that seeks by mutual concession to reach durable understandings; that will prefer not to allow questions of prestige to interfere unduly with practical diplomacy for concrete ends; that will pay a price and take a risk for the sake of good order. It is a policy for which a heavy premium may sometimes have to be paid. It is opposed by those trends of opinion which prefer to use the rough word and the strong arm, and their influence sometimes prevails. But both ministers and officials learn by experience that long patience, steady firmness and unruffled forbearance are good investments in diplomacy.[8]

It is this conciliatory quality in British foreign policy which is often a cause of concern to foreign governments, and indeed of unjust suspicion. 'The British,' they are apt to complain, 'cannot be relied upon to stand firm. At a pinch, they will always give way. If you are associated with them, you have to watch them, in case they come to their own terms with the adversary.' Critics will rake up memories of the separate peace we worked for in the war of the Spanish Succession and in the Seven Years War. Nearer our own day, they will point to Neville Chamberlain's Anglo-German Naval Agreement and to his colloquies with Hitler at Berchtesgaden and at Godesberg in 1938. Malicious and unfounded whispers of separate British concessions to Germany during the Algeciras Conference in 1906 disturbed for a while the confidence between the French and British Governments, so recently associated in the Entente Cordiale. As Grey himself remarked, the complaint was that the British were 'always taking a hand and never taking a side'. In a similar way, Mr Macmillan's visit to Mr Khrushchev in Moscow in the spring of 1959 provoked murmurings in Paris, Bonn and Washington, lest he should be bent upon usurping the leadership of the western powers and upon surrendering points in the hitherto united and firmly held western position. There was no foundation for either supposition. But that such suspicions should be so readily aroused, makes it incumbent upon every British government to take deliberate pains to see that they do not arise. Grey was painfully aware of the abyss of suspicion that threatened the Entente in its early years when he wrote, in retrospect: 'One false step, one indiscreet or incautious word, one necessary word delayed or unspoken at the critical moment, and the result might have been fatal.' Yet those who distrust British resolution and good faith should recall that, twice in this century, Great Britain with united voice deliberately risked her world position and even perhaps her national existence by entering upon a war in fulfilment of a solemn obligation to another state, and did not withdraw from the conflict, however heavy the sacrifice, until the enemy had been subdued.

In nothing is the liberal outlook of the British government and

---

[8] General de Gaulle once said: '*L'avenir dure longtemps. Tout peut, un jour, arriver, même ceci qu'un acte conforme à l'honneur et à l'honnêteté appaaise, en fin de compte, comme un bon placement politique.*' Op. cit., p. 73.

people more evident than in their promotion of the institutions of self-government and independence both in British dependent territories and in the world at large. This policy can be looked at in two ways. It can be regarded as a retreat under duress, a yielding in face of the attack of anti-colonial nationalism, a reluctant adjustment to the new spirit of the times, a forced liquidation of the British Empire. There is some truth in this; and it forms the ground for such opposition as the policy has encountered in right-wing spheres of opinion. But there is much more in the policy than a capitulation. It is a policy which has for long been an essential part of the national make-up. It is a characteristic manifestation of national behaviour in the modern age, an act of faith, the expression of a deeply rooted moral idea. That moral idea was strongly in evidence in the early nineteenth century when the United Kingdom was near the height of her influence, and it took its rise even earlier. It survives and fructifies today, when British power and influence have relatively declined. Ever since Pitt's India Act of 1784, British imperialism has assumed an element of trusteeship, and the eventual attainment of complete self-rule has been regarded as the ultimate destiny of the dependent peoples. The process started seriously in India with the gradual indianization of the services from the 1870s, and it took shape in the talks about Indian home rule in the 1920s and 1930s. The most recent developments have merely hastened a process that had already been seen, for example, in the acquisition of dominion status by the colonies of European settlement and in the abandonment of the mandate in Iraq. It was widely recognized before 1939 that the change was coming and, when it came after 1945, the political parties, the Press and the public were ready for it and accepted it with hardly a serious word of protest. Although the rest of the world could not see it in this light, the sentiment in Great Britain was one of fulfilment rather than of loss or humiliation. What we have seen is, as Gilbert Murray saw, 'a privileged class giving up its privilege on grounds of conscience or humane principle.' Nowhere does the British achievement shine more brightly in the world than in the array of communities of many races and of many religions, some of them of mixed race and religion, which have been and are being introduced to independent statehood and endowed with the apparatus of a free society on the model evolved over the years by western European civilization. Since the Second World War over 500 million people in former British dependencies have become completely self-governing. This is a major event in world history. The assumption that has been made is that these new states will in course of time imbibe, together with free institutions, the moral content which, in spite of all imperfections, informs the working of these institutions in the states of the western world.

Yet it is hardly to be expected that backward communities in tropical climates will apply successfully or preserve unchanged an apparatus of government which is based on principles evolved over the centuries in temperate zones and which is exercised with no small political craftsmanship by mature western societies. It is not merely that these liberal constitutions may have been provided for peoples who are not yet ready for them. This difficulty need not be insuperable, if there is any validity in the liberal maxim that the best way to learn to be responsible is to have to bear responsibility. As Macaulay said: 'If men are to wait for liberty till they become wise and good in slavery, they may indeed wait for ever.' There is also the problem of adjusting western forms to indigenous institutions and traditions, since these latter are likely to retain their potency, and to contain in them elements which could be of as great value as the western prototypes in guiding the emergent community towards modern nationhood. Some of the new members of the Commonwealth face the grim prospect of fast-growing over-population. The minds of some of the new governors, faced with the need to carry a primitive agricultural community[9] through an industrial revolution, may also be turned to the now well-known techniques of one-man leadership and one-party government, to the emasculation or jettisoning of parliaments, or, in time of difficulty, to the refuge of military rule. Parliamentary régimes, unlike dictatorships, cannot function well without a good supply of well-qualified and public-spirited civil servants. In this respect India is more fortunate than other new states; and this will go to explain why it is in India alone among them that the parliamentary system would seem so far to have taken root. How all the new régimes will work out in practice no one can foresee. But certainly, the new states will need, and should not be denied, patient sympathy and forbearance.

To frame the requisite constitutions for these emergent territories, in the hope that they will be successfully operated, is a task calling

[9] For example, 83 per cent of India's population live in villages, and 70 per cent of them derive their means of subsistence wholly or mainly from the land.

for patience and ingenuity. Great Britain has turned some of her most lucid and capacious minds on to these exercises in political architecture. The problem has varied from territory to territory. In the two West African territories of Ghana and Nigeria, there were regional, tribal and religious differences calling for adjustments between central and local government. In Uganda, the difficulty has been that tribalism is stronger than nationalism. In the West Indian Federation, the problem has been to link a group of ten widely dispersed islands into a single system, a problem not made easier by disparities in natural wealth and in constitutional development and by the strong individual loyalties of the separate island communities. In the Malayan Federation not only were there nine separate Malay Sultanates and two British colonial settlements to be linked together in one system; there was also the problem of a plural society of Malays, Chinese, Indians and Pakistanis. In Cyprus the problem lay in the juxtaposition of Greek-speaking and Turkish-speaking populations, both infected with the prevalent nationalism; in a murderous campaign of terrorism; and in the reconciliation of an advance towards self-government and self-determination with strategic needs and firmly held international positions. The solution which was eventually framed after great travail, and which may be hoped, perhaps too optimistically, to bring peace at last to the island, reflected great credit upon the wisdom and courage of the Greek and Turkish governments. This was a case where, with lapse of time, the parties recoiled more from the growing exacerbation of their differences than from the sacrifices necessary for an agreement, and where (as in the earlier problem of Trieste between Italy and Jugoslavia) the traditional confidential processes of diplomacy were able to bring the negotiations to a successful conclusion.

There are, however, cases where special difficulties arise, namely in territories like Kenya and Southern Rhodesia, where there is a minority of European settlers established among a majority of indigenous inhabitants. Will it be possible to evolve in British territories the multi-racial community based on partnership, in accordance with the principle of British colonial policy, enunciated as early as 1923, that wherever the interests of natives and of European settlers appeared to conflict, those of the natives would not be subordinated to those of the Europeans? Here is one of the challenges of the future. As for the peculiar South African conception of white supremacy in a system of 'separate racial development' or *apartheid*, all that need be said is that it is one which is strongly repugnant to opinion almost everywhere outside the Union, and one which may well set up acute strains within the multi-racial Commonwealth.

The retreat from Asia and from the land-bridge with Africa affected other western European countries besides Great Britain. The French lost possession of Indo-China and much of their influence in the Levant. The Dutch yielded up authority in the East Indies. The British, as the chief imperial power, seemed to have suffered most in authority and prestige. India and other territories became independent members of the Commonwealth. Apart from Hong Kong, North Borneo, the Aden Colony and Protectorates and some scattered islands, the vast Asian Empire of Great Britain had gone. She no longer possessed, in the Indian Army, the most efficient land force on the mainland of Asia; and she could no longer maintain a naval force in the Far East adequate to defend imperial interests. In the Middle East, though she retained her protective treaty relationship with the small states of the Persian Gulf and South-east Arabia, she was constrained to end her military presence and to forfeit her special position of authority in Iraq, Jordan and Egypt. The Suez Canal itself passed into sole Egyptian hands, though still subject to the provisions of the Convention of 1888. The mantle of imperialism in Asia, so long worn by Europeans, was slipping from British, French and Dutch shoulders. The Russians never discarded it. It is now being resumed by China. While Great Britain and other members of the Commonwealth, under the Colombo Plan and other schemes of economic and technical assistance, were returning to Asia in a new constructive spirit of partnership, the Chinese intervened in arms in support of North Korean aggression and sustained with supplies the Communist-directed attack upon the French in Indo-China. The armed terroristic rising in Malaya was of Chinese Communist inspiration. The revival of Chinese imperialism, foreshadowed by Chiang Kai-shek in his published writings, was made manifest when Chinese Communist forces set themselves to suppress the liberties of Tibet, as Russia had smothered the cry for freedom in Hungary. Some of the illusions created in Asian minds by Chinese acceptance at the Bandung Conference of the famous 'five principles' of co-existence were progressively dissipated, and not least in India, where the Chinese threat to the northern frontier could no longer be ignored. The Bandung Conference was certainly of high significance. It foreshadowed the establishment or resumption of inter-Asian relationships on a pre-colonial basis, and the possible emergence of a third grouping of powers. It proclaimed the crying need for economic development. India and China stood out as the two predominant Asian powers. But the belief that at Bandung the voice of Asia had struck a new and resounding note in the world—which seemed questionable to some who attended the Conference itself— was increasingly seen to be largely illusory. On the one hand, the Afro-Asian states could not maintain a common line. On the other, the Communists were showing themselves in their true colours. Even Russian economic and technical assistance, so liberal and beneficent in appearance and indeed often in fact, was not seldom found to belie its promises, whether in quality, in timing, or in the conditions in which it was afforded and was to be reimbursed. Asia, apart from China and the Communist-dominated states in Korea and Indo-China, showed little sign of breaking its links with the western countries, and it would be the less likely to do so in that the political, social and economic ideas which governed the great Asian movement towards independence and industrialization had their roots in western thought and practice. To this, the British contribution had been outstanding.

Two episodes in the decade may be adduced for consideration as having significance both for the position of Great Britain and for the development of the United Nations. These are the Korean War, which began in the summer of 1950, and the Anglo-French operation at Port Said in October–November 1956.

Korea, the cock-pit of the Far East, where China, Russia and Japan have contended for mastery, is a country which, like Germany and Viet-Nam, is now cut in two by the frontier between the Communist and the anti-Communist world. In June 1950, the Communist North Koreans attacked across that frontier with modern arms supplied by the Russians. They were met by the South Koreans who had had economic assistance, but little in the way of military supplies, from the Americans. And now accident takes a decisive hand. The first accident was the temporary absence of the Soviet Union from the Security Council. This enabled the Council, unimpeded by a Soviet veto, to pass immediate resolutions calling for a cease fire and a withdrawal, and requesting members to furnish assistance to repel armed attack and to restore peace and security. The second accident was that a great power, the United States, had forces in the vicinity and had the will to use them. Even before the second United

Nations resolution had been passed, orders had been given to United States naval and air forces to provide cover and support for the South Koreans. There is little doubt that the Russians, who had almost certainly favoured if they had not inspired the North Korean attack, were much disconcerted by this prompt American reaction, particularly since from recent statements it appeared that the Americans had been inclined to relinquish their interest in Korea. From now onwards the Russians, unlike the Chinese, were to preserve an attitude of prudence towards the conflict. They clearly had no wish to see it spread, with all the risk of atomic warfare which this might involve.

The forces contributed by members of the United Nations, the great majority of them American, were assembled at the invitation of the Security Council. General MacArthur, who was in command, was, in form, a United Nations commander conducting a police operation under the United Nations flag and reporting to the Security Council. It is symptomatic of the weakened position of the British Commonwealth in the Far East that, in addition to air forces and a naval squadron which joined the U.S. fleet for action in Korean waters, they could furnish no more than a division to the land forces employed in the campaign.[10] India sent a medical unit. From the point of view of command, the position was unprecedented. In the field was the masterful MacArthur, little amenable to authority, and enjoying an unusual degree of autonomy. In Washington, the United States government were desirous as always to get their own way in Allied councils and, as experience in the war had shown, would sometimes take their own line. They also had an ungovernable public opinion to deal with. In New York were the Security Council and the General Assembly, responsible for the first time for a substantial police action launched under the authority of the Council.

For a commander in the field the conditions in which the campaign had to be conducted were frustrating in the extreme. Were the United Nations forces to cross the 38th parallel in pursuit of the North Koreans? There was a warning that this might bring the Chinese into action, as indeed might have been expected, since

[10] In 1951, the Commonwealth had about 12,000 troops in Korea and the United States between 160,000 and 200,000. Great Britain, besides her anxieties in Europe, had heavy commitments in the Middle East and in Malaya, where extensive guerrilla operations were going on against Communist insurgents.

The Last Ten Years: 1949–1959

Korea is to China something like what Belgium is to us. The answer was taken to mean 'yes', though the terms of the United Nations resolution were imprecise, being directed ostensibly 'to ensure conditions of stability throughout Korea', as a step towards unification. President Truman's view was that in crossing the line MacArthur had not exceeded his authority. Were the United Nations' forces then to advance to the Manchurian frontier? Though advised by the Joint Chiefs of Staff to hold his non-Korean forces back, MacArthur maintained that he had no orders not to continue his advance. The entry of Chinese forces into Korea in late October 1950, in a burst of revolutionary anti-American fervour, started what MacArthur called 'an entirely new war'. Were the United Nations' air forces now to bomb Chinese bases in Manchuria or to cross the frontier for up to two or three minutes' fighting-time in 'hot pursuit' of attacking enemy aircraft? The answer was 'no', though, as regards bombing, the British agreed later that there should be a slight relaxation in certain conditions. Manchuria became, as MacArthur said, a 'privileged sanctuary', and he was, he complained, subjected to a 'handicap without precedent in military history'. Were Nationalist Chinese forces from Formosa to be used in Korea? Again the answer was 'no'. Was the atomic bomb to be used? Stung by the retreat of MacArthur's forces in face of the Chinese onslaught, Truman had at the end of November 1950 incautiously spoken of authorizing MacArthur to use the bomb at his discretion if the United Nations were to authorize action against China. At the urgent request of other Commonwealth governments, the Prime Minister, Mr Attlee, at once flew to Washington to see him. Great Britain and the other members of the Commonwealth, like the majority of the United Nations, were opposed to any spread of the conflict. Attlee obtained a promise that the bomb would not be suddenly used or the war extended, and secured agreement to an effort to negotiate a cease-fire, which proved abortive. At a later stage, Great Britain, while agreeing reluctantly to have China declared an aggressor by the United Nations, constrained the United States to delete a clause in the resolution which would have provided for further measures against China. The bomb was never used.

Whether these answers were given by the United Nations or by the United States government itself, which was in these matters more moderate and prudent than much United States opinion, they were the subject of exhaustive debate, either in New York or through the diplomatic channel between governments. It can be said that in these councils the advice of Great Britain carried no little weight and that on one or two occasions it was perhaps decisive. But the relationship between the two governments was disturbed by British recognition and American non-recognition of the Peking régime. On the United Nations side, the campaign was conducted with caution, lest it should touch off a general war. Even as a war of conventional weapons, it was subject on both sides to considerable limitations. The Russians may not have altogether welcomed the massive Chinese intervention in an area where they had an interest of their own, and they did nothing to spread the conflict. In April 1951, after the Chinese had driven the United Nations' forces back over the 38th parallel, and had themselves again begun to retreat, MacArthur, without authority, delivered himself in public of his views on the way in which the war should be conducted. He was thereupon relieved by President Truman of all his positions and thus removed from the command of the United Nations' forces. It was an informal Russian initiative in June 1951 which opened the way for talk about an armistice which was to continue for over two years before terms could be agreed upon. The American losses were about 145,000[11] including 33,000 killed or missing, a small fraction of the total losses on both sides in a war that was extremely costly in human life, Korean and Chinese.

British participation in these United Nations' operations had the full approval of public opinion, and the Commonwealth contingent served with conspicuous distinction. By contrast, the Korean War was, it has been said, the most unpopular war in the history of the United States; and this was so because it was a limited war, frustrating in its limitations, and because it was thought of as the one war in her history which the United States had not carried to final victory. That this opinion should be held is not surprising. After the decisive, world-shaking victories over Germany and Japan it would be galling, and not a little humiliating, for United States forces to be for a time driven in retreat by Chinese armies, and Communists at that, and to be restrained by the injunctions of the United Nations, by the hesitant counsels of allies and by prudential political decisions by the Government in Washington from putting forth full strength and at a

[11] To preserve the scale, it may be noted that this figure is less than three times the British losses in the single opening day of the Battle of the Somme, July 1st 1916.

stroke liberating and uniting Korea and delivering what might be a decisive blow at the Chinese Communist aggressor.[12] Nothing shows more clearly that, in an international system where there is a genuinely accepted sharing of responsibility for peace with justice, not even the strongest of states can conduct a fully independent foreign policy or shape its conduct without regard for the views of others.

This is even more evident in the case of states of lesser strength. It is too early to pass confident judgment upon the Anglo-French expedition to Port Said in November 1956; but a few reflections may be hazarded. International lawyers are not of one mind on the question whether or not, and if so, how far, the nationalization of the Suez Canal Company by the government of Egypt in July 1956 was a breach of international law. It would not be an unduly cautious view to assume that the International Court could not be counted upon to declare that it was. It was naturally not in this cool and dispassionate light that Colonel Nasser's act was judged by politicians and peoples. Illegitimate or not, it struck at a vital interest in the most provocative possible way in circumstances of acute international anxiety. In Great Britain it aroused a deeply hostile reaction, as strong as it was widespread. It was seen as an affront to the British sense of what is proper in the conduct of world order. Nasser was not only striking at the interests of the British people at a sensitive point; he was also outraging their moral sense and riding roughshod over their deep predilection for good order in international affairs. His wanton blocking of the Canal at a later date aroused similar emotions, but by that time opinion had been deeply divided by the launching of the Anglo-French operation.

As to that operation, there will also be debate among jurists whether or not it could be brought within the ambit of the right of self-defence reserved to members of the United Nations under the Charter, given the condition of international affairs in which the Charter has now to be applied; or of the liberty of states to protect the lives of their citizens or vital international rights. Here the weight of the argument would probably be adverse to Great Britain and France. But here again, purely legal considerations would not be

[12] There was also concern in the United States about the poor showing of American prisoners of war in Communist hands. The British, better educated and less pampered, did better: the Turks, tough peasant types, did best of all.

the decisive factor in the formation of opinion. World public opinion, in so far as it deserves the name, as expressed by the representatives of the members of the United Nations in the General Assembly, was on political grounds—rights or wrongs apart—condemnatory of this attack by two great powers upon the territory of a small country.

That the operation was politically inopportune, however deep the provocation, could with difficulty be denied. Yet the case of the two governments was a sustainable one.[13] They remembered the consequences of failure of resolution in the period of appeasement in the 1930s and the success that had attended resistance at the time of the Berlin air-lift. They saw Nasser as the successor of Mussolini and Hitler. The question would be whether this was a valid parallel or not; and how far it is wise to frame courses of action upon analogies from history. The operation was one conducted, as they saw it, in the common interest for the maintenance of peace and security. It was justified in their eyes by the state of extreme emergency that had arisen in the Suez area—an attack by Israel against Egypt that threatened to spread the field of hostilities to the Canal and to send the whole Middle East up in flames. Any serious outbreak of hostilities in so explosive a region could not fail to be regarded by both governments with the utmost concern, since it might provide the spark which could set off a wider conflict. These international hazards were powerfully increased by the growing evidence of Soviet intervention in the Middle East to foment disorder. To meet this emergency, no international remedy under the United Nations Charter was in sight. The Security Council could not be expected to act effectively, as its nerveless handling of the Arab–Israel question in the past had conclusively and most disappointingly shown. The United States, on the eve of a presidential election, was impotent. Indeed, by lending countenance to disruptive forces in the Middle East, by supporting Musaddiq and Nasser upon doctrinaire considerations of anti-colonialism and pro-nationalism, which, as so often, they later recognized to be fallacious, and by helping to undermine British influence without putting anything effective in its place, the Americans had a heavy share of responsibility for the situation that had arisen. In these circumstances, the two governments felt inescapably compelled to act independently. And since, although Israel was the invader, the earlier provocations by Egypt

[13] It is argued at length by Sir Anthony Eden in his memoirs of the years 1951–57, *Full Circle*, Cassell, London, 1960.

had been so flagrant as to allow of no clear allocation of the respective responsibilities, the two governments addressed their summons to both sides; and upon its acceptance by one side and not by the other, they acted. To find a parallel for such an act of sudden violence, we have to go back to Canning's seizure of the Danish fleet at Copenhagen in 1807 and to Winston Churchill's attack upon the French fleet at Mers-el-Kebir in 1940. Both these acts were dictated by what was seen as an imperative need in time of war to remove a threat to the Royal Navy at a juncture when Europe was organized by a conqueror against us.

The French, whose collusion with the Israelis may be presumed, had been exasperated beyond measure by Egyptian interference in North Africa. The British, who may be cleared of collusion, though they may perhaps have had an inkling of what was afoot, had a domestic political difficulty to face. To the 'Suez Group' of the Conservative Party, the nationalization of the Canal had been the last straw. Eden himself was on record as far back as 1929 in holding that the Canal could not be committed to the good will of the people of Egypt; and so now he held that it could not be left to the unfettered control of a single power. It is a legitimate surmise that in deciding to embark on the operation as later events unfolded, the Prime Minister may in some measure have been swayed by the need to avoid what might have been a serious party crisis. The operation not only brought down upon the British government a weight of international reprobation unexampled since the Boer War; it divided the country as it had not been divided since the Civil War in Spain and the months following the Munich agreement. In this trend in right-wing opinion, we may discern the power of myth in national and international politics. In the minds of many, the conception of what Great Britain had been able to do in the past in the way of independent coercive action, and the assumption of what she would be able to do in present-day conditions, went well beyond the sober fact.

Certainly, the so-called 'gun-boat diplomacy' had had its successes in the past. But it had been the thesis of Lord Robert Cecil in the 1860s, in his blistering attacks upon the government of Palmerston and Russell, that their policy had been marked by brutal violence against the weak, and by soft words to those who could resist. Two later occasions on which light naval vessels had been in action in inland Chinese waters—the incident of the *Cockchafer* at Wanhsien in 1926 and the episode of the *Amethyst* in 1949, both on the Yangtse

—had shown that the method was obsolete.[14] Lightly armed and armoured vessels close in to land were seen to be 'paper tigers' and were treated as such.

Independent action by Great Britain on a larger scale was also now out of date. Secure in our naval strength, we had acted alone in bombarding the forts at Alexandria and in conducting military operations in Egypt in 1882. We had gone to war against the Boers in 1899, though not, in this latter case, without misgivings about our isolation as the war progressed. The Boer War was to be the last big military operation upon which we should embark single-handed. We should in future be inhibited from any such course, even if tempted to pursue it, both by respect for the rules of the international community laid down in the Covenant and the Charter and by consciousness of growing inability to play an independent role in the arbitrement of war, if it were to come. It was unwise for Great Britain and France to think that they could safely in 1956, relying on their own strength, embark upon independent military action even against a weak adversary, given that once military operations are started no one can say where they will end. They were engaged in an adventure possibly involving far-reaching and incalculable consequences which they no longer had the political, military or economic strength to bear. Their economies were in fact too vulnerable to be subjected to such strains. If, at a given point, they did call a halt to the operation and undertake to withdraw their forces on condition that the United Nations would take over the physical task of maintaining the peace, this need not be attributed to the threat of nuclear bombardment from Moscow—they could safely leave it to Washington to counter this. Nor need it be set down wholly to a virtuous compliance with a vote by the General Assembly of the United Nations, including the United States and some of our closest associates, though this was undoubtedly an element in the decision of the Government in London, impelled thereto by a strong element in their own public opinion.[15] A further factor was that, in the absence of support from

[14] The action of the British and United States naval forces in putting down an artillery barrage at Nanking in 1927 in order to secure the escape of their fellow nationals from danger of massacre may be quoted as a successful example to the contrary.

[15] A noteworthy part was played by Canada in the Assembly in promoting the proposal, first put forward by Eden himself, that a United Nations force should be immediately organized to take over security duties at the seat of the disturbance. It was this that facilitated the withdrawal of

the United States, which would certainly not be given unless the operation were called off, the pound sterling was in jeopardy and the British economy gravely prejudiced.[16]

In the parallel case of Hungary, no United Nations' vote made the slightest impression on the Soviet Union. Nothing but the threat of nuclear attack, if even that, would have forced the Russians off their chosen line. This is one measure of the difference, in the relative hierarchy of power, between the United States and the Soviet Union on the one hand and Great Britain and France on the other. The greater powers have the capacity (if they have the will) to face a major war on their own; the lesser powers have not. The stronger unscrupulous power can also over-ride the law and outface reprobation; the weaker law-abiding power will not.

But this is far from the whole story. The influence, standing and prestige of nations have never been strictly proportionate to immediately available material strength. It is one of the characteristics of the present age that the part played by material strength in determining the degree of influence exercised by a government in international affairs has tended to decrease rather than to increase. There are several reasons for this.

Even at the climax of our authority relative to others during the generation or so after 1815, we were not omnipotent. We were still less so in the latter part of the nineteenth century. We could safeguard the peace of the seas. We could keep the lesser states in order. We could usually, though not always, intervene effectively where the scene of action was within range of the Navy. In relation to other great powers, our influence was strongest where our adversaries in diplomacy were states, like France, which were the most vulnerable to naval action. We could do nothing to help the Poles against the Russians, or the Armenians against the Turks or the Danes against the Prussians and Austrians. In our disputes with the United States, even before she became a great power, we had as often as not the worse of the diplomatic exchanges. But the essential fact was that, so long as we maintained naval supremacy, we were secure in the homeland from attack from abroad, and this, together with our economic strength and our diplomatic skill, was the basis of our influence.

the Anglo-French forces and the closure of the main incident. This constructive and reconciling action by a member of the Commonwealth compared favourably with the rigid and sterile attitude of the United States.

[16] During November 1956 we lost 279 million dollars—nearly 15 per cent of our total gold and dollar reserves.

We were never able to dominate the world: what we could do was to dominate a good deal of the non-European world—but it was in Europe that the centre of power still lay. In Europe we could sometimes use effective influence, sometimes not.

Clearly, the situation is different today. We began to retreat from world-power when we lightened our naval forces in the Far East, the Caribbean and the Mediterranean on the strength of agreements with Japan, the United States and France in the early years of the present century. We did so because the homeland was threatened from Europe. Today we cannot make ourselves safe in the homeland. We have lost our old security. The mere pressing of a button somewhere in the Soviet Union could blow our cities to pieces. But what we have lost is something which no one else now possesses. We do not stand in jeopardy alone. Every state, even the most powerful, lies under a similar threat. So that if our situation has changed for the worse, the change does not lie merely in loss of security.

Then again, while we are today very greatly inferior to the United States and the Soviet Union in point of immediately available material strength, and perhaps still more in latent, developable strength, we are, as a possessor of nuclear weapons, more powerfully equipped than we have ever been in the past, and stronger relatively to other powers except the United States and the Soviet Union. Never in our history until recent times have we had it within our capacity, if we wished, to strike a devastating blow far in the interior of continents.

But in interpreting both our inferiority in point of material strength to the two greater powers and our superiority to the others, there is another consideration to take into account. It is not only the possession of power, or the measure of the power possessed, that counts: what matters also is the use which we and others are able or willing to make of it. There is, for example, the case of Iceland. Iceland in effect claimed to annex a belt of the high seas and to exclude our fishermen from it. We were entitled to regard this as a breach of international law. We certainly had the physical power to put an end to it, as in similar cases in former days we might well have done. Here was a field where the gunboat policy could easily be made effective. If we used gentler measures of protection, if we proposed judicial settlement by the International Court, this was in deference to other compulsions—to the fact that Iceland is an ally, and to the consideration that, by the rules of the international community established by the United Nations Charter (subject indeed to uncertainty of interpretation), we do not, except in individual or collective self-defence, resort to force of arms. In the operation at Port Said again—where we did resort to force of arms—it was not insufficiency of military power to achieve the immediate reoccupation of the Canal Zone from Port Said to Suez that stood in the way of completion: we had military strength enough for that. Whether we had forces enough and resolution enough to maintain the occupation against Egyptian guerrilla action and popular riot and boycott is another question. What counted most was economic weakness and the consciousness of vulnerability to enforcement action, even if only economic, which might be brought in to back up the expression of an adverse international public opinion, to which the two strongest powers had given their voice, acting upon two essentially law-abiding governments. In neither case could it help that we were a nuclear power.

So we may say that the possession of power today, no matter by whom possessed, is in theory limited in its effectiveness to the extent to which its use would be in harmony with the laws of the community, and, in practice, though this can be a very different thing, to the extent to which those laws are observed by those who possess the power. Observance will vary from state to state. In the absence of effective international sanction against the most common forms of delinquency, the unscrupulous state, even the small one, will have the advantage. Peace will often go before justice. Being, on the whole, a scrupulous, law-abiding state with a general interest in the observance of obligations by all, we should expect to find that this condition of affairs would work to our disadvantage. But, imperfect as the United Nations may be, its existence does tend in some measure to inhibit the arbitrary, independent use of power by sovereign states for their own ends.

Even compared with the two greater powers, our position should not be under-valued. To be a nuclear power, even on a much smaller scale than they, is a factor the value of which is not easily calculable. In a contest it is often the marginal that counts. Battles can be won as well as lost by exhausted troops. The last straw can be decisive. The 'thin red line' may hold. In 1914 'the contemptibly small' British Expeditionary Force, whose passage the Germans did not think it worth while to try to interrupt, may have given that margin which saved Paris from capture, and opened the way for that turning-point in the war, the victory of the Marne. And in a later day: 'Never in the field of human conflict was so much owed by so many to so few.' This is an element that may strengthen us in our transactions with our potential enemies.

But there is again a sense in which the present international system can strengthen us also in face of our friends. If it is true that we can no longer have a fully independent foreign policy, the same is true of our closest associates also, even of the United States. The more extensive the international obligations, whether world-wide or regional, whether under the Charter of the United Nations or under such instruments as the North Atlantic Treaty, the narrower the liberty of action of those who have assumed them. These obligations are nowadays very extensive, and they are tending to become more so. As a member of the United Nations, as a party to the North Atlantic Treaty and to other regional instruments, as a participant in various western European organizations, and, last but not least, as a member of the Commonwealth family, we should not find any very wide field where we were free to act without the obligation or duty to consult others. Others are subject to a similar obligation or duty. By close association, we not only reinforce each other's security: we tend to harmonize our policies, the stronger and the weaker together. In some contexts we are the weaker: in others the stronger. Membership of a community certainly limits freedom of independent action, but within those limits it opens up a field for useful initiative within the community. It gives an opportunity for the weaker as well as for the stronger members to have their say. It tends to reduce inequalities among members.

In a book published in 1954, that eminent American political scientist, Professor Hans J. Morgenthau, in an attempt to strike a rough balance of power, suggested that, while there might be a weight of seventy in the Russian scale, the weight in the American scale might be one hundred, of which America's strength would be seventy, Great Britain's ten and that of other actual or prospective allies twenty. He concluded that if the British weight were removed from the American scale,[17] the heavier weight would still be on the American side. His general argument was that, given the existing bi-polarity of power and the modern technology of war, neither

[17] In the first edition of the book (1948) he had added: 'and placed into the Russian'. These words are deleted in the later edition.

Great Britain nor any other third power could now hold the balance as in the past. Even as late as the Second World War, the alignment of Great Britain on one side or the other might have made for Germany and Japan the difference between victory or defeat; but in existing circumstances the attitude of Great Britain in an armed American-Russian conflict might well not decisively affect the outcome.[18]

Americans have often tended to under-estimate British strength,[19] and especially the strength of the Commonwealth. Great Britain was certainly very weak in 1948 (when Professor Morgenthau first made his assessment),[20] particularly in financial and economic resources. She would certainly be stronger as an ally of the United States, who could help to supply the sinews of peace and war, than of the Soviet Union, who would be less able and less willing to do so. Nevertheless, if Professor Morgenthau's equation meant that if *per impossibile* Great Britain had cut adrift from western Europe and, instead of becoming a party to the North Atlantic Treaty in 1949, had made an alliance with the Soviet Union, then the United States could in 1948 or in 1954 have regarded herself as still having a substantial preponderance, it is doubtful whether many Americans with a responsibility for the formulation of policy would have made the

[18] *Politics among Nations.* Alfred A. Knopf, second edition, New York, 1954, p. 328. Professor Morgenthau seems, however, to depart from his own thesis when he says later (ibid., p. 337): 'The superpower that could add India or a united Germany to its allies might well have gained a decisive victory in the struggle between East and West.'

J. M. Keynes had made a similar comparative evaluation between Great Britain and the United States for another purpose in 1919: 'The population of the United Kingdom is about one-half that of the United States, the income about one-third, and the accumulated wealth between one-half and one-third. The financial capacity of the United Kingdom may therefore be put at about two-fifths that of the United States. This figure enables us to make the following comparison: Excluding loans to allies in each case (as is right on the assumption that these loans are to be repaid), the war expenditure of the United Kingdom has been about three times that of the United States, or in proportion to capacity between seven and eight times.' (*The Economic Consequences of the Peace.* Macmillan, London, 1919, pp. 258–59.)

[19] Thus as late as 1956, a distinguished American historian, Professor Anatole G. Mazour, could write: 'Britain's economic power, her naval and political force that commanded the respect of the world is all of the past. Britain virtually lives on America's dole.' ('An Historian's Reflections', *World Affairs Quarterly*, University of Southern California, July 1956, p. 116.)

[20] Op. cit., first edition, 1948, p. 274.

calculation with quite such Olympian unconcern. They would be still less likely to do so in 1959. Since 1948, and even since 1954, the marginal weight of British power has, if anything, increased, even though it is no more than marginal. The more closely pressed the United States feels herself to be by the range and volume of Russian nuclear weapons and by Russian technological capacity and industrial potential (a feeling which has become increasingly acute since 1954), the greater, it would seem, should be her reliance upon the strategic facilities which her allies can afford and upon the military potential which they can contribute towards the buttressing of her own security. In parallel with this, the greater also should be the influence which her allies can exert upon her policies. In this situation, Great Britain has been apt to feel that she can do best for herself by being a co-operative ally. France has seemed at times to prefer to make good her position in an opposite way. In this, both nations have followed a traditional bent.

One conclusion from this would seem to be that, though it is true that we now take a lower place in the hierarchy of power than we used to do, this may not make quite so much difference as we might think. We could not now act alone in face of opposition so freely as we were once able to do. But by entering into obligations of collective defence, we have somewhat reinforced our own security. The consequent limitation of our freedom of action in international affairs may be a price worth paying. If we cannot now defend our interests abroad as effectively as we once could, this is not simply or even mainly due to lack of power, but to the way in which the world is organized and the way in which the world behaves. If we were a good deal more powerful than we now are, we should not be in a much better position in this respect unless we threw aside all scruple and took the law by force into our own hands, where our power was sufficient for the purpose. This is not a thing which we could easily do, because it has for long been, and still is, a British interest that in the world at large international law should be respected and international obligations observed. This must be so in especial degree for a country that depends for its existence upon overseas trade. The world is unfortunately not in a law-abiding mood, and that must be bad for us. The best that we can do is, by precept and example, to encourage the building up of a tradition of international conduct based upon tolerance and good faith among nations; and be on the alert to use our still powerful influence in our own and the general interest. It is one of the more comforting facts of international life today that states of lesser strength can on occasion exercise a measure of influence disproportionate to their material power in the interest of good understanding among nations. The voice of reason can still be heard, and it will sometimes command attention. We ourselves have much to offer. One of the great problems of the world today is how to gear together the tremendous scientific and technological development and the phenomenal expansion of productivity of the advanced countries which has marked the 1950s, and the urge for independence and industrialization of the countries which are politically, economically and socially backward and chronically under-nourished. As an ex-colonizing power and as the inaugurator of a new Commonwealth, we have a wealth of skill, experience and understanding to contribute. Herein should lie one of our main roles in the future.[21]

[21] The present chapter in places owes something to four articles on 'Britain's Foreign Policy' contributed by the author to *The Glasgow Herald* on October 6th–9th 1958.

CHAPTER XVI

Retrospect 1960

To say that there has been continuity in British foreign policy does not mean that the policy has remained unchanged through the years. This is manifestly not so. What it does mean is that there are certain permanent features in the position of Great Britain which Foreign Secretaries have consciously or unconsciously to take into account and which will, in some measure and sometimes decisively, determine their course of action in each succeeding situation. The continuing outlook of Great Britain upon the world has for centuries been that of a small island kingdom which is situated close to the north-west ocean shore of a turbulent sub-continent and which has established flourishing settlements of her own stock overseas and has developed maritime, trading and imperial interests of world-wide scope. The interests of this kind of community will not themselves be subject to very great change. But in pursuing and promoting those interests, any Foreign Secretary is likely to find himself constrained by the pressure of other considerations to modify the policies which, taken by themselves, those interests would require. He must be influenced, for example, by the distribution of power in the world and by the place of Great Britain in the hierarchy. He cannot disregard the existing state of international relations. He must, for instance, consider what weight must be given to the interests of those countries with which we may, for the time being, be in the closest relationship, and to the advantage which we may hope to secure over states whose policies may, for the time being, be in conflict with our own. He must always have in mind the interests of the other members of the Commonwealth. And he will not be blind to the measure in which his policies will serve the common interest, the promotion of which is also a British interest. He will pay heed to the understandings of international law and to the obligations

380

accepted in the Charter of the United Nations. These are not the only factors which a Foreign Secretary must weigh in reaching his decisions. Such factors are legion and are domestic as well as foreign in character:[1] he is a member of the Cabinet, a member of Parliament, a member of a party, and a citizen, as well as being Secretary of State for Foreign Affairs. He must take cognizance of, and must decide how far to respond to, the views of his cabinet colleagues, of the House of Commons, of his party organization and of the general public, as well as of pressure groups and of the promoters of good causes of various kinds. The international situation is in a constant state of flux. The kind of decision that was good yesterday may not be good today. Every new event must be examined with a fresh eye in the light of the attendant circumstances as they may have happened to develop at the particular moment. A Foreign Secretary may look ahead and think about the questions which may face him in the future, and he may try to prepare himself for them. But he will always be driven back to the imperative question what to do next, and as likely as not he will find that the preparations which he has made for it no longer meet the case. In his official life, a Foreign Secretary is faced with one predicament after another, and there will often be a degree of improvisation in the course which he adopts. He cannot contract out of his responsibilities. He must do something, even if that something is a decision to wait a while.

Looked at in retrospect, British foreign policy may seem to be characterized by alternation rather than by continuity. But the continuity lies in the objective while the alternation arises from the method.

Under Elizabeth I, England was a relatively weak state in a strong strategic position, forced to fight, chiefly by sea, for long years against Spain, first to avoid subjugation and then for security. Under the early Stuarts, England was more secure than before and could be in or out of war as she chose, and she kept out of the Thirty Years War. The Protectorate was secure, but aggressive and bent on expansion at Spain's expense; about this time, with the development of a new conception of mercantilism, there comes one of the turning points in our foreign policy. William III and Anne had to meet a great peril from France and did so successfully by promoting coalitions

---

[1] For a fuller treatment of this topic, see the author's article on 'The Formation and Control of Foreign Policy' in the *Durham University Journal*, vol. XLIX, No. 3, June 1957.

with European states having a common interest with ourselves in resisting domination; and, in addition to customary naval action, by engaging in land operations on the Continent. Under Walpole, as under James I and Charles I, there was a lull: England could again be in or out of war as she chose, and for the most part she kept out. Then comes the era of Chatham, when, as in the time of Cromwell, England, now a world power, was aggressively bent on further expansion overseas in the interest of trade. After this, a descent from the pinnacle of power and influence until the American War of Independence, when for perhaps the first and last time in her history, Great Britain had to face a great, hostile continental coalition, frustrated by a fortunate naval victory. Then later, another great peril from France under Napoleon, met, as before, by naval action and by the promotion and financing of coalitions and military operations on the Continent. After the Napoleonic Wars, a second turning-point in our foreign policy, a new temper and a new outlook associated with the name of Castlereagh, international consultation for the maintenance of peace, and concern for the general as well as for the national interest. There was an interlude under Canning and Palmerston when Great Britain could ride high upon the crest of power and prestige. After that she was to be secure from serious peril, though not always unperturbed, for most of the remainder of the century. She would have no need to form great coalitions or to undertake more than the minimum of military commitments. She could slip sometimes into non-intervention and sometimes into isolation, but still with an eye on the turbulent Continent. About mid-nineteenth century, a third turning-point in our foreign policy, the swing away from mercantilism to free trade. Then at the turn of the century, a fourth turning-point, the recognition of a new peril from Germany, a return from isolation, the sketching out of a Triple Entente. In the latter part of the period between the two World Wars, again a period of relaxation, a deceptive and dangerous lull, with more reliance than was prudent upon an ineffective system of collective security. Great Britain neglectfully allowed her own safety to be imperilled. The so-called policy of appeasement was defended on grounds, some of which might have been found in the speeches of Fox or Cobden or Bright, against participation in European wars. Great Britain was not now, as she had been at the time of the earlier Stuarts or at the time of Walpole or in the mid-Victorian era, free to go in or out of war as she chose. The decision lay with Germany.

Great Britain was forced, for the sake of her own security, to enter a war in company with France which they could have little prospect of winning single-handed. Then at mid-century, after the victory, a fifth turning-point, a new system to meet a new peril, Great Britain in company with like-minded states in western Europe stretching out hands across the Atlantic in a bond of mutual assistance for common security.

Again and again we have escaped from the edge of disaster, by prudence, by boldness, by endurance, by the mistakes of adversaries, by timely help or relief, by luck. Escape in 1545 from France, then in 1588 from Spain, then in 1690 again from France. Several times during the eighteenth century wars with France when invasion might have succeeded, or a hostile coalition might have crushed us; more dangerously still, in Napoleon's threat of invasion or of economic strangulation; in 1917, when we came near to starvation from the German submarine war upon our shipping; and more lately in 1940 and in 1941, until that night of December 7th, 1941, after the Japanese attack on Pearl Harbour, of which Winston Churchill has written: 'No American will think it wrong of me if I proclaim that to have the United States at our side was to me the greatest joy . . . We had won the war. England would live; Britain would live; the Commonwealth of Nations and the Empire would live . . . Being saturated and satiated with emotion and sensation, I went to bed and slept the sleep of the saved and thankful.'[2]

Ours has been a fortunate history. We have escaped most of the ordeals that have fallen upon continental peoples. We have endured nothing like the religious wars or peasant revolts of the sixteenth century or the devastation of Germany in the Thirty Years War in the seventeenth. Our own Civil War, grievous though it was, cannot stand comparison with these calamities. We have avoided revolutions like those of France and Russia. We have not since 1066 suffered under foreign domination as the Italians did under Austria or as the Irish did under ourselves. We have had no experience of the sufferings of the Balkan peoples under the Turkish yoke, or of the age-long oppression of the Poles by Russia and Germany culminating in the horrors perpetrated in the Second World War. Our country has not been heavily fought over from end to end. We have not languished under brutal occupation as so much of Europe did in the two World Wars. The worst that we have suffered is shortage of food

[2] *The Second World War*, Cassell, London, 1950, iii. 539–40.

in our three last great wars, and the air bombardment of the Second World War, an ordeal that was much less crushing than that sustained by the Germans and the Japanese.

It is usual to say that repeatedly in our history we have had to fight for survival, but perhaps survival is not in all cases the right word. If we had been subjugated and invaded by Philip II or by Louis XIV or Louis XV or by Napoleon or by William II, we should certainly have suffered intensely and the course of our history would have been diverted. But we do not know what the conqueror would or could have done: in each case his design was frustrated. A parallel or precedent is not easy to find. No whole foreign people, for example, was held for very long under the domination of Napoleon or of Imperial Germany. None of these potentates, if victorious, would have been as forbearing as the victors at Vienna; and the Treaties of Brest-Litovsk and of Bucharest suggest that the German impositions, if Germany had been victorious in 1918, would have far exceeded in severity the settlements imposed upon Germany after the two World Wars. Nevertheless, though we should most probably not have saved the Empire from France or Germany, our national life would almost certainly have been maintained.

What Hitler, that master of absolute evil, would have done with us, we cannot say. Machiavelli lived in a gentler age than ours when he could say: 'Victories are never so complete that the victor can disregard all considerations whatsoever, more especially considerations of justice.' Hitler might have tried to blot us out like another Carthage. He would at least have tried to keep us in subjection, as Napoleon or William II might have done. He might have given us relatively easy terms at first on condition that, under a subservient government, we acted as a subordinate ally in a war against the Soviet Union. Extermination would have been a possibility in Hitler's mind; and nuclear energy and bacteria have placed new instruments of mass slaughter in men's hands. But, short of extermination, peoples, unless they are small ones, do not allow themselves to be blotted out for ever, even if their spirits are temporarily broken. Nor is it an easy problem—indeed it requires unsleeping alertness and unblunted resolution—to keep a whole people permanently in subjection. Muscovites and Arabs lived through the Tartar conquests, though Iraq has only now begun to repair the irrigation system which was then destroyed. Jews and Armenians have survived as peoples, and Israel and Poland have rebuilt themselves as nations.

Recovery tends to follow upon each step towards liberation or towards release from servitudes. One of the most astonishing things in human history is the capacity of men, within the space of a few years, to reconstruct their political, economic and social life and to recover their national strength, once they are free to do so, after what might have been thought to be crippling disaster. Cases in point are the revival of France after 1763, 1815 and 1870, of Germany after 1918 and, in varying degrees, of the belligerent peoples, including the Russians, after the war of 1939–45. After all vicissitudes, the nations of western Europe, once again liberated, still retain their independence and now again live in freedom and prosperity. Germany, it is true, is still divided, but no one can doubt that, for good or ill, Germany will again sooner or later be reunited. The peoples of central and eastern Europe still remain under the domination of Russia, but here again it may be confidently hoped that, as events unfold, they will at some future time be able to reassert their own national life. They are held captive, but they are not being destroyed.

In the light of this recital, what, if any, are the permanent problems which British foreign policy has, since Tudor times, been called upon to solve? If the test is permanence, the answer must verge upon platitude, since change is more many-sided than is continuity. There seem to be three such problems. The problem, first, of ensuring the peace and security of the realm; secondly, of providing for the prosperity of the people through the development of overseas trade; and thirdly, of protecting our overseas interest and our lines of communication with them.

This enumeration might fit the cases of other countries also. The particularity of our own case will lie in the way, or in the various ways, in which we have gone about to solve these problems. There is no lack of variety in the methods which we have chosen in response to changing circumstances.

Thus, in providing for the peace and security of the realm, we have at one time kept a free hand, facing the risks of isolation on the strength of naval supremacy. At another—and this most recently— we have gone to the other extreme and have merged our forces in peace-time with those of a community of like-minded states. At still another, we have taken the intermediate course of temporary alliances or manœuvrings with the mechanism of the balance of power or the procedures of the concert of Europe. Whatever the theory of the balance of power may say, we have often taken the side of the stronger rather than of the weaker continental power—in the combination against France after 1815 and against Russia in 1853 and 1878, and with Germany rather than with France for a generation after 1870. We have done so because, having no continental ambitions and wishing only for security, we have seen the best hope of achieving this in association with the stronger power, if the stronger power is friendly. Only if the ambitions of the stronger power threaten our security do we look elsewhere for support and try to redress the balance. We have never, ourselves, had either the will or the power to develop Napoleonic, Bismarckian or Hitlerite ambitions: on the contrary we have, so long as this has been possible, pursued an empirical policy, involving only the minimum of intervention on the Continent necessary to maintain our security. In line with this, we have usually made it an object of our policy to prevent the domination of Europe, and particularly of the Low Countries, by a single hostile great power. We have for the most part most readily, and most wisely, intervened in force in Europe only when Europe has become acutely dangerous to our security. For most of our history we have been inferior in population to our continental rivals: we have had all the more need, therefore, for diplomatic skill.

Then again, in attending to our economic life and in particular to our overseas commerce, we have swung from mercantilism on the one hand to free trade on the other, from state intervention to *laissez-faire* and back again. We have at times resorted to tariffs, to quantitative restrictions, to exchange control; at other times, we have moved back towards liberalization. At other times again, we have looked towards the development of an international association in the economic, as well as in the political and military sphere.[3]

In shaping our diplomacy so as to protect our overseas interests and communications, we have sometimes relied on the threat or the reality of the ubiquitous impact of naval supremacy, and upon such military forces as we could bring to bear. This has meant, above all,

[3] The mutability of British economic policy since the First World War has been strongly criticized. Not only were the measures taken to meet the great depression self-contradictory. More generally 'Britain, which formerly led the world in economic thought and (more important still) in enlightened economic practices, has displayed in recent decades a remarkable avidity for absorbing the most fashionable economic nostrums.' E. Lipson, *Reflections on Britain and the United States*, pp. 64, 71–72.

at any rate down to the most recent times, the safeguarding of the road to India. Hence our long continued preoccupation with the Mediterranean, with the Straits, with Egypt, with the Persian Gulf and with central Asia, though in some of these areas, India has not been the sole interest: the road to India is also the road to the Far East and to Australia. At other times, and this most recently, we have had to rely on such measure of recognition of common interest and on such degree of respect for the law as we have been able, by precept and example, to inspire in the minds of foreign authorities and overseas clients.

The motives which have impelled the British and other people in modern times to create empire have been various. Trade—the establishment of trading posts for the exchange of goods, the accumulation of precious metals or the traffic in slaves; of naval stations for their protection, and later of coaling stations to serve merchant ships and warships. Military operations undertaken to safeguard trading posts against attack, pushed forward by expansionist soldiers for further security. Administrative control over expanding territories in the interest of security, of good government, of the propagation of humane western ideas, followed, often unwillingly, by the proclamation of protectorates or of annexation. Parallel with this, emigration and settlement, in order to escape from religious or political disabilities at home, or, under population pressure, to find more ample economic opportunity. Wider strategic objectives—to establish a secure frontier or, by military presence in key areas, to safeguard communications with distant parts of the world or the uninterrupted supply of vital commodities. The lure of adventure inspired by missionary-explorers like Livingstone; the sense of mission to bring true religion and civilized ways of life to suffering, primitive peoples; the urge to exploit the natural resources of the world and to spread the achievements of western industrial civilization; the search for markets, for raw materials, for outlets for the investment of surplus capital; the pursuit of national glory and the transfer of national rivalries to the field of colonial expansion. And now, in the end, the retreat from empire, under the impact of world wars, and under the pressures of internationalism among the advanced peoples and of nationalism among the less advanced, colonial peoples; and the advance into Commonwealth.

What has the Colonial Empire profited us? Shall we be better off in the future without it? What is the balance of debit and credit in the account of the colonial peoples themselves as a result of the incursion of western peoples into their lives? On these points, the wisest men still suspend judgment. Yet there is no good evidence to suggest that the loss of our colonial empire will, as used to be so generally feared, impair our domestic economic situation. Indeed the past and present prosperity of countries having no colonial possessions, and our own continued prosperity today with the Empire far gone in dissolution, would point to a contrary conclusion.

And as to our political standing in the world, there are pluses as well as minuses. The dissolution of the British Empire may have been inevitable. But what was by no means inevitable, indeed what could have been presaged as improbable, was that so world-shaking a transformation should be achieved on the whole without violence and with consent. Out of a dying empire there emerged an institution unique in history, a living and growing multi-racial Commonwealth. The British were ready for the change. It was for them in the logic of things. The outside world may have found this hard to believe but, as we have suggested above, the British had a sense of fulfilment rather than of loss.

The decision of India in 1949 to remain as an independent republic in a Commonwealth in which the monarch of the United Kingdom would be a symbol of the free association of its independent members and as such the Head of the Commonwealth, marked a turning point in post-war history. And so, for that matter, did the agreement of the older members of the Commonwealth to accept and recognize this new conception of the Commonwealth. We cannot yet tell how this multi-racial and variously linked Commonwealth will fare in face of the gathering influx of newly-independent states of non-European race. We may hope that shared experiences, unhappy though some of these may have been, the habit of dealing with each other, the possession in some measure of a common outlook on the conduct of government and on the administration of the law, a recognition of common interest and of the merits of inter-dependence, and the reassurance that may be gained by belonging to a community, will form an enduring bond. To have made this possible and to have played the major part in bringing it about is Great Britain's outstanding achievement in these latter years.[4] She has brought something without precedent and of bright promise into

[4] By aiming to transform the French Union into the French Community, France, under the Fifth Republic, has embarked upon a similar course.

the world. She may have made a virtue of necessity, but how shining the virtue, how deeply rooted in her history, and how unguciously achieved!

What of Great Britain herself today?

Hard things have been said of the English, many of them by themselves. Twelve hundred years and more ago, an unknown monastic scribe wrote some marginal notes on the character of the peoples he had known or read of. To the Greeks, he ascribed wisdom, to the Romans fortitude, and to the Franks, cruelty. To his own people, he ascribed folly: *Stultitia Saxonum vel Anglorum.* 'Alas,' wrote Sir Thomas Malory in *Le Morte Darthur* about the year 1470, 'this is a great default of all Englishmen, for there may no thing please them no term . . . they were better pleased with Sir Mordred than they were with King Arthur . . . the people were so newfangle.' 'I know,' wrote Queen Elizabeth I to the Scot, Maitland of Lethington, 'the inconstancy of the people of England, how they ever mislike the present government and have their eyes fixed upon that person that is next to succeed.' Louis XIV's minister, Torcy, as noted above (p. 57), charged the English with fickleness, instability of opinion and lack of serious purpose. More Prime Ministers than one might echo the words of Malory and Elizabeth as he watches the swing of the electoral pendulum; and foreigners for centuries have asked, with puzzled surmise, how a people so little given, as they would allege, to systematic application of mind and to sustained power of work can have brought off their unique achievements at home and abroad.[5]

It is sometimes said of the British in the present age that although, like most of the other western peoples, they have moved with the times in taking deliberate thought for the organization of their internal life, they lag behind some others in the dynamism which they apply to the solution of the problems of the modern world. Thus, it is observed that the rate of increase in industrial production, though superior to that attained in the later years of the nineteenth century and in the earlier part of the twentieth, falls below that now achieved, for example, by the United States, Western Germany and the Soviet Union. Governments, it is said, have not attended with

[5] Beatrice Webb remarked in March 1918: 'The British governing class, whether aristocratic or bourgeois, has no abiding faith in the concentrated and disinterested intellectual toil involved in the scientific method,' as applied to economics and politics. *Diaries, 1912–1924*, Longmans, London, 1952, p. 118.

sufficient boldness and vision to the renewal of the dying centres of our towns and cities, to the construction of a system of roads suited to modern traffic requirements, to the modernization of the railways, or to the building of hospitals. It is a standing reproach that so little is spent on the fostering of the arts. They have too long tolerated anomalies in the criminal law and confusion in the laws governing gambling, Sunday observance and the public consumption of alcohol; and they have not ventured to review the laws regulating the operations of trade unions, to curb abuses in the conduct of industrial disputes, or to re-examine the position of trade unions in the state. More generally, it is complained that too much of the time of Parliament is taken up by 'dreary little men moving dreary little amendments'.

Much could be quoted on the other side: the launching of a far-sighted programme for the production of electric power from nuclear energy; the creation of great new electronics and synthetics industries; a whole range of scientific inventions and discoveries from radar and jet propulsion to penicillin and revolutionary advances in chemistry and nuclear physics; the reshaping of our export industries; the building of new towns to draw off the excess population from the larger cities; an ambitious and comprehensive housing programme successfully launched—3,300,000 houses having been built since the war; a recasting of the education system and the liberal provision of new schools; wide reforms in national insurance for health and unemployment; a new code for the treatment of mental illness; and comprehensive, if still imperfect, measures for town and country planning, including the establishment of national parks.

Nevertheless, if the mark of the British way of life in its modern manifestation is caution and steadiness rather than dynamic adventure, there are a number of explanations for this, of which two, and these perhaps the most important, may be suggested. The first is our inescapable dependence upon our export trade. The second, which may be itself in part a product of the first, is the nature of the system of government which we have evolved to meet our special circumstances.

It has been noted that the cast of our foreign policy has been substantially determined in recent times by the range and vulnerability of our overseas commerce and other overseas interests. Similarly our domestic economic policy must today be conditioned by the vigour of our export trade, which is the foundation upon which the whole economy rests. We cannot safely expand our industrial production beyond the point at which it would call for imports greater than our exports can pay for; and exports cannot be planned—they have to be earned. No longer enjoying the advantages in overseas trade which we held for so long in the nineteenth century, we must keep an anxious watch on our balance of payments and on the state of our gold reserves, and must tread the narrow path between boom and slump, and especially so since sterling carries so high a proportion of the trade of the world.[6] We must do so, knowing that our future course may be determined as much by external events as by our own volition.

The health of the British economy depends in large measure upon foreign confidence in the stability of the pound sterling. No government can escape from this predicament, and no government has been unfailingly successful in meeting it. For the British, in the present phase of their history, to live is to live dangerously. There is no need to seek adventure in national policies: national life in itself is adventure enough. Hence we must again and again defer the execution of ambitious schemes of reconstruction which, however desirable, would outrun the capacity of our export trade to sustain their effects upon our foreign exchange position, and this is the more so in that so substantial a proportion of our resources is pre-empted for purposes of defence and for the fulfilment of overseas commitments.

In the domestic political sphere, too, our history has been marked by steadiness rather than by adventure, by evolution rather than by revolution. We have moved through a continuous process of regeneration and reform. Maintaining an integrated social structure, we have passed, on the whole sedately, from Elizabethan paternalism, through the major interludes of puritan regimentation and earlier nineteenth-century *laissez-faire*, to the paternalistic Welfare State. We have come through two world wars with the fabric of our institutions still intact. Punctuating this regular course, there have been spells of increased activity at intervals of about forty years, when reforms have been more rapid and have ranged more widely and more deeply than usual: the parliamentary reform of 1832; the political, administrative and social reforms round about the time of

[6] By contrast, during the nineteenth century there was a remarkable degree of equilibrium in the British balance of payments, with almost no need for governmental intervention in the gold mechanism. See Imlah, *Economic Elements in the Pax Britannica*, p. 11.

Gladstone's government of 1868–74; the social reforms of the Liberal government of 1906 and of the Coalition and Labour governments in the 1940s. This rhythm, if rhythm it is, was not disturbed even by the two world wars. The process is one of advance and consolidation; the method is by trial and error.

There have been real shifts in the location of authority, but these have tended to be masked by the preservation of old appearances. This is the classic procedure of liberal democracy. 'The liberal approach assumes politics to be a matter of trial and error, and regards political systems as pragmatic contrivances of human ingenuity and spontaneity.'[7]

It is in view of this that the gibe about 'dreary little men moving dreary little amendments' is completely misplaced. Rightly or wrongly, our governments do not normally bring in legislation until public opinion is ready for it, or is becoming ready for it. In the drafting of legislation which will affect the pocket or the health or the liberty of the citizen, care is taken to seek the opinion, and if possible, the assent of all organized interests or sections of opinion who may have views to express. In Parliament every clause is subjected to scrutiny by members of both Houses who between them will have a high measure of *expertise*, no matter what may be the subject of the bill. These are the 'dreary little men' who move amendments. They move them either to extract an explanation of policy or of intention from the government, or to have the points at issue thoroughly ventilated, or to secure a change in the draft if they can. They will want to make sure, so far as possible, that any change proposed will not be a change for the worse. Every 'dreary little amendment' will affect in some respect the daily life of some body of citizens, large or small. This is what government by discussion, what democracy in our sense of the word really means: the making sure, so far as this can be done, before a law is passed, exactly how it will affect the people who will become subject to it when it comes into force.

This care for the impact of the law upon the citizens individually and as a body, this opening of the debate to all shades of opinion, has its bearing also upon the spirit in which government is conducted. The House of Commons is omnicompetent. The House of Lords can impose no more than a short delay. The royal veto is dead.

[7] J. L. Talmon, *The Origins of Totalitarian Democracy*, Secker and Warburg, London, 1952, p. 2.

Retrospect 1960

There is in theory no limit to what a majority can do if it wishes, except such limit as might be set, within the normal constitutional procedures, by fear of electoral consequences, and, in a revolutionary context, by fear of widespread and resolute public revolt. A government, once securely in power, could abolish the monarchy or, by recasting the electoral law, ensure its own continuance in office. In the 1930s there was a question whether the Labour Party, if it came into power with a clear majority, would follow the procedures of a constitutional parliamentary party or would, as Henry VIII did, use the omnicompetence of the House of Commons for revolutionary purposes. Party theorists were talking of the need for a Labour government to pass emergency legislation immediately on taking office by which it would assume plenary powers, including the power to abrogate any effective opposition, much as the National Socialists did in Germany in 1933. It was even suggested that parliamentary government itself would only be allowed to continue to operate on the assurance that the opposition, if it subsequently came to power after an election, would not repeal the acts of its predecessor. There was, in fact, to be democracy on terms. There was even talk of appointing local satraps to govern the country as Cromwell's major-generals had done. When, in 1945, the Labour Party came to power with a large majority—its leading members having served an arduous and sobering apprenticeship in Churchill's wartime Coalition Government—none of these things happened. The Labour government carried through its comprehensive programme of reform with due regard to traditional constitutional forms, though with some curtailment of the delaying power of the House of Lords. Their legislation was not resisted beyond reasonable measure by their opponents inside and outside parliament, and it was not reversed, except marginally, by the conservative opposition when it was returned to power in 1951.

There has been on the whole, on the part of both our main political parties, what E. H. Carr once called that 'willingness not to insist on all the prerogatives of power' which he saw as the surest foothold which morality could establish in international, and perhaps also in national, politics.[8] The political realist might interject that, since the electorate is at present almost equally divided between the two main parties, and since the Conservatives cannot afford to lose their working-class vote nor the Labour Party their middle-class vote, the

[8] *The Twenty Years' Crisis*, p. 213.

393

disparity between the two party programmes would not be fundamental. Nevertheless, a sense of moderation does seem to be characteristic of our political life in the present phase. It is to be found also, though less markedly so, in the trade unions. With the increasing centralization of the production and distribution of power and other services, it would be possible for a small body of key men to bring whole industries or even the national economy almost to a standstill.[9] On the whole, the unions have used their strength with moderation, and with some regard for the national interest; though some shop stewards and militant groups of workers have often failed to show any such sense of responsibility. But here again the realist might observe that the unions must also have the interest of their own members in view, since if there were a standstill, none would suffer more than the main body of the workers themselves.

This steadiness in our internal political and industrial life, though it may verge on dullness, is something which, in the world at large, gives confidence in our stability, and thus maintains our influence.[10] But—perhaps even more important—it also asserts the continuing vitality and validity in a changing world of the democratic method of government as we understand and practise it: that is to say, in the framing of policy, consultation and discussion; in the execution of policy, liability to be called to account.

One further factor making for steadiness in our political life has been the monarchy. Though many of them have been in their persons mediocre or worse, our sovereigns have served as an element of continuity, a fixed point in the evolving political scene, a national symbol, a convenient piece of mechanism. Yet the monarchy has been subject to fluctuations in public esteem. Even Queen Victoria from time to time in her earlier and middle years was widely unpopular, and there was a strain of republicanism in the middle years of the nineteenth century. The monarchy again, for all its continuity, has also been subject to profound change in its functions: it has, except

[9] In February 1960, an official strike of fifty-five electricians threw out of work over 30,000 employees of the motor-car manufacturing industry.

[10] In the course of his address to the members of both Houses of Parliament in Westminster Hall on April 7th 1960, General de Gaulle said: 'Sure of yourselves, almost without seeming so, you put into practice in freedom a well-founded and stable political system. With you, in the political field, tradition, loyalty, and the rules of the game are so strong that your Government is quite naturally endowed with cohesion and endurance . . . in brief, it is in a sense in the nature of things that your executive and legislative powers are balanced and co-operative.'

in form, become decreasingly a political and increasingly a social
institution. Its irreducible formal functions remain. Its real life is in
the hearts of its peoples at home and overseas. Elizabeth I and the
Lord Protector Cromwell, like the President of the United States
today, were their own Prime Ministers. William III, our first constitutional monarch, though still his own Foreign Minister, was wise
enough to wait on the support of Parliament for his great policies.
Victoria was the last of our sovereigns to persist in exercising what
she held to be her prerogative in foreign affairs. Her attempts were
sometimes resisted, sometimes tolerated, by her ministers, and she
would in the last resort defer to their views. When she had her way,
this was because her strong common sense, her personal prestige
and her vast experience lent persuasive force to her arguments.
George V was the first of our sovereigns to serve as the sole constitutional link binding the Commonwealth together. If at home, in
their realm of the United Kingdon, he and his son George VI, in
Walter Bagehot's now classic formulation,[11] exercised their three
constitutional rights, the right to be consulted, the right to encourage
and the right to warn, their personal service extended well beyond
this. No reader of Sir Harold Nicolson's *King George V* or of Sir
John Wheeler-Bennett's *King George VI* can fail to recognize how
intimate and all-pervading was the public concern of these two
sovereigns, whose reigns covered the period of the First and Second
World Wars.

If one looks at the history of Great Britain in the twenty years
since 1939, the impression, so far as it is one of steadiness, reflects
the steadiness not of inertia but of the tight-rope walker. In the First
World War, Great Britain had lost the flower of her young manhood,
and in the Second her economy was crippled. Russia was now
massively industrialized and the United States moved out of isolation. Great Britain yielded her place in the hierarchy of power. She
was constrained to beat a strategic retreat and to think upon her
future in terms of survival.

The international environment also became increasingly inimical
to world-wide overseas empire and, in some parts of the world, less
favourable than before to the operations of international commerce.

---

[11] It was in truth a forecast of twentieth-century practice rather than an
accurate description of current Victorian practice. George V as a school-
boy made a deliberate study of Bagehot's exposition of the duties of a
constitutional monarch.

Russia and China had come under Communist rule, and were bent on undermining the stability of countries where free institutions still prevailed. The great and rapidly increasing populations of Asia and Africa were avid for independence. The foundations of British power in the Far East, in South Asia and in the Middle East were undermined. Nuclear weapons of terrifying destructive power and of fantastic cost became part of the armoury of any power that, given the necessary resources, would claim to contribute worthily to its own and the common defence.

In meeting this crisis in her fortunes, Great Britain has in some ways maintained the old and in others brought in or developed the new. There has been both continuity and change. She has kept intact her monarchy and her parliamentary institutions, her system of law and her machinery of local government, her tradition of free discussion, and the nation-wide complex of private, voluntarily organized bodies for instruction, argument, agitation or good works which enriches the life of her people. The city of London is becoming again the chief financial centre of the world, and the pound sterling once more carries a large part of the world's international exchange of goods.

On the side of change, she has carried out an ambitious programme of social reform. She has met the demand for security and sought a path to prosperity by accepting a system of intimate association with others in the military, political and economic spheres. This move towards the collectivization of international decisions seems likely, as a policy, to serve her as well as any other could do in view of the present state of the world and her position in it. A nation of 50 millions cannot now stand alone. She has found the resources, scientific, industrial and financial, to equip herself with the nuclear weapon, and to develop nuclear energy for peaceful purposes. She is meeting the demand for independence among her dependent territories by embarking upon a wide and imaginative process of constitution-making within a family association of nations, the like of which the world has never before seen. She has instituted a generous scheme of colonial development and is, in addition, playing her part with other western powers in the provision of economic and technical assistance for other backward countries.

This *tour de force* has ensured survival and has opened up the vista of a new era in our history. It was made possible in part by bountiful assistance furnished by the United States in the early post-war years. But it would not have been performed without the political good sense, strong social discipline, steady application, cheerful endurance, healthy scepticism and practical idealism which, preferable in the circumstances to other more dynamic qualities and accompanied indeed by attributes less worthy of esteem, have enabled the British people to provide for their growing needs with the minimum of strain and disturbance. Nor would it have been possible without the skill and prudence displayed (in spite of occasional lapses) by successive British governments in framing and executing domestic and foreign policies suited to the changed situation in which the country found itself. Great Britain has fallen in power, but her ancient virtues have not departed from her. Her influence, though it may be in some places temporarily in eclipse and in others diminished in immediacy and scope, has not decayed. It is no mark of complacency or of undue self-satisfaction to claim—as sagacious foreign observers have noted—that that influence has been founded upon her position as the centre of the Commonwealth, and, in spite of occasional aberrations, on her political maturity in home and foreign affairs, upon her realism and tolerance, and upon her reputation for fair dealing and for regard for the common interest.[12] To have fought the Second World War as she fought it, and to have refashioned her life as she has since done, is a political achievement of the first order. The last twenty years will hold comparison with any other like period in her history. Of this period it can be said as Palmerston said a century and more ago: 'This country has represented a spectacle honourable to the people of England, and worthy of the admiration of mankind.'

Nevertheless, when all this is said, a nagging doubt persists. So far, so good: but what of the future? Under the impact of two world wars we have carried out peacefully a social revolution chiefly at the expense of the well-to-do upper and upper middle classes (to use somewhat out-moded terms). Much that is good, much that has

[12] Here is the verdict of an American professor of history, but related by him to the past rather than to the present: 'Britain's record is a valuable source of political experience, of diplomatic skill and circumlocution, of administrative sagacity and all based on the principle of fair play. British technique can be best described as opportunist and pragmatic: it represented perhaps the most unsystematic system known to history. And yet it was the most practical world policy despite all its fallacies . . . we can learn much from British poise, tact and even from the style of diplomatic language with the admirable dignity it bears.' (Professor Anatole G. Mazour, op. cit., pp. 116–17.)

in the past contributed to our greatness and to the dignity of our national life, has been sacrificed for what has been rightly held to be the common good, namely the search for social justice and the broadening of the basis of domestic purchasing power. Our proletariat is being gradually eliminated. The percentage of the population of England and Wales over the age of 16, classed as poor, unskilled workers, fell from 10 per cent to 7 per cent between 1947 and 1955, while the percentage of skilled and semi-skilled workers rose from 55 per cent to 64 per cent. We are becoming a nation of which the predominant feature is an immense intermediate income-range of lower middle class and well-paid working class: the percentage rose from 75 per cent to 81 per cent between the same years. The well-to-do have decreased from 5 per cent to 4 per cent and the upper middle class from 10 per cent to 8 per cent.[13] The question which cannot as yet be answered is whether, in an environment of placid and cosy uniformity, where high taxation blunts the edge of enterprise and social security muffles the call to effort, there can be developed the driving force in politics, science, commerce and industry which are necessary for national advancement, or the leadership which can give a new turn to events. As far forward as we can see, we shall have to go on walking our tight-rope. We cannot afford not to make the best possible use of our human and material resources. We do not possess the necessary safe margin for social experiments which would set out deliberately to discourage the formation of an intellectual *élite*, as the Americans seem to be doing.[14] Will there be the necessary vigour and sense of mission among the members of the new, diffused and enlarged intermediate income-range, reared on the Welfare State, home-centred and open to the impact of mass media of communication? Will it develop a personality of its own, or will it be a mere concourse of individuals, sunk in what de Tocqueville, a century and more ago, called that 'honest materialism' which would almost imperceptibly loosen the springs of thought and

[13] These figures are drawn from David C. Marsh, *The Changing Social Structure of England and Wales*, p. 198.

[14] The Americans themselves have no such safe margin in their fateful encounter or, as an authoritative American spokesman has recently put it, their 'fierce and inescapable struggle' with the Soviet Union. See the devastating and most disturbing contrast between United States and Russian methods and achievement in general and technical education drawn by Vice-Admiral Hyman G. Rickover, the American 'father of nuclear propulsion', in his testimony before the Committee on Appropriations of the House of Representatives on August 18th 1959.

action? Was the liberal nationalist, Mazzini, right when he said that socialism, by its materialistic outlook, made men believe that a people can regenerate itself by getting fat? Will the rising tide of mediocrity, as John Stuart Mill feared, submerge all that is original and vital? The misgivings that weighed so heavily upon political philosophers a hundred years ago proved, on the whole, to be ill-founded. The free and aspiring human spirit has not been wholly stifled. But yet the same questions still press for an answer, and upon the answer to them much in our future will depend.

Through all vicissitudes of continuity and change, the power and influence of Great Britain, fluctuating as they have been, have depended in the last resort upon the fibre of the British people. At times our people have shown a temporary failure of resolve. In the 1930s, in face of a manifest peril, they declined to attend adequately to their own security. Having survived, thanks to a recovery of their prowess, rewarded by beneficence of fortune or miracle of Providence, they learnt their lesson. Wisely, in the late 1940s, they recognized a no less manifest peril and established their security upon a collective basis. They must not now, faint-heartedly reverting to the comfortable illusions of the 1930s, throw it away again in the 1960s.

Index

Index

Index

Index

Index

Index

Dual Alliance (France, Russia), 264

Dubois, Guillaume, Cardinal, 73

Dudley, John William, 1st Earl, 121

Dufferin, Henry Temple Blackwood, 1st Marquess of, 277

Dunbar, Battle of, 66 n.

Duncan, Adam, 1st Viscount, Admiral, 92

Dundas, Sir David, General, 95

Dunes, Battle of the, 44

Dunkirk: Cromwell secures from Spain, 44, 53, 55, 55 n.; pirates from blockade Thames, 45; Charles II sells to France, 55; War II retreat from, 330–31; Dunkirk, Treaty of, post-War II (Great Britain–France), 343

Dupleix, Joseph Frances, Marquis, 79

Dupuis, Charles, *Le Principe d'Équilibre et le Concert Européen*, 25 n., 73 n., 94, 94 n.

Duquesne, Marquis de, 84

Durai, J. Chinna, 'Indian Democracy and Mr Nehru', in *The Listener*, 346 n.

Durham, John George Lambton, 1st Earl of, 150

Durham University Journal, 381 n.

Dutch: wars, in East Indies, 40, 75, 99; 41 seqq.; sixteenth-century strength of, 43; obstacle to English expansion, 48; Cromwell challenges trade monopoly of, 53 seqq.; naval strength, mid-seventeenth century, 54; England's three wars with; 1st war, 53–56; 2nd, 58–59; 3rd, 59–60; William III strengthens position of, in Europe, 60, 61, 62; lack of domestic resources of, 62; in alliance with England against France, after 1688, 62; in Grand Alliance against France, 1701, 64; exhaustion of, at end of War of Spanish Succession, 68

East Africa, Bismarck and, 221

East India Company, 48, 49, 55, 147, 149

East Indies, 40, 59, 87, 115; *see* Amboyna, Dutch, Singapore

Economic co-operation, post-War II, 347; *see* European

Economist, qu., 138

Eden, Sir Anthony, 110, 270, 323, 372 n.; on non-intervention in Spain, 314; in 1943 Moscow talks, 336–37; 1938 resignation of, 321 n.; Foreign Service reforms of, 344 n.; work with Churchill, 334; Bevin succeeds, 338; and Western European Union, 343–44; and Indo-China crisis, 355; on federation of Europe, 356 n.; *Memoirs*, 370 n.; and Suez, 371

Edict of Nantes, 43, 63

Edinburgh, Treaty of, 32

Edward VII, 255, 268–69; Edwardian age, 275–76

Egypt: in Napoleonic wars, 92; financial crisis in, 159; Gladstone goes into, 207, 212 seqq.; in Mediterranean Agreements, 221–22; Salisbury foresees independence of, 217; and Sudan, 228; and foreign debts, 239, 240; and Entente Cordiale, 256; controls Suez Canal, 364

Ehrman, John, on Pitt, 81

Eire, in Second World War, 324 n.

Eisenhower, General Dwight D., 333

Electricians' strike, February 1960, 394 n.

Elgin, James Bruce, 8th Earl of, 150

Elizabeth I of England, 28 seqq., 60, 330, 381, 389, 395; and Spain, 30–40, 60; apocryphal story of Sully and, 30; achievements of, by 1603, 30–31; aids Henry IV of France against Catholic League, 41; aids Calvinists in France and Netherlands, 44; and Puritans, 30–33; trade and exploration in reign of, 47–48; and parliaments, 58

Ellenborough, Edward Law, 1st Earl of, 149

Emerson, Ralph Waldo, qu., 132

Emigration, early seventeenth century, 48

Empire, British, second, 147–51, 158; mid-Victorian anti-imperialism, 151, 171; self-government in, 172; late nineteenth-century imperialism, 233–38; imperialism, economic, 239–44; motives for creation of, 235–37, 387; *see* Commonwealth

Empire Day, 234

408

Index

Index

Index

Index

Muscovy, Elizabethan travels in, 48; Muscovy Chartered Company, 49

Mussolini, Benito, 313, 315-16, 318, 370

Mutual Assistance Draft Treaty, 1923, 300

Nanking: incident, 1927, 372 n.; Treaty of, 1842, 127

Napier, Francis, 10th Lord, 180-81

Naples, 168; and Sicily, 177-78

Napoleon I, Napoleonic Wars, 16, 32, 70, 79-80, 81, 85-96, 104, 118, 125, 130, 148, 195 n., 270, 328, 354, 382, 383, 384, 386; Louisiana purchase, 84; and European coalitions, 94; plans for subjugation of Great Britain, 93-94

Napoleon III, 130, 164, 172, 197, 309; and Tsar Nicholas I (Crimean War), 173-74; and Kingdom of Italy, 176-9; and Polish insurrection, 179-81; 'policy of pickings' of, 192; and Belgium, 1852, 1866, 193. *See also* Louis Napoleon

Narrow seas, struggle for (Dutch and English), 54 seqq.

Nasser, Gamal Abdel, Colonel, 369, 370

Natal, 148

National Socialism, 393; *see* Hitler

Nauman, Friedrich, qu., 226

Navarino, Battle of, 99

Navarre, 35

Navicerts, 289

Navigation Acts, 49, 54, 59, 84 n., 131, 152

Navy, under Commonwealth, 51, 52; under Charles II, 61; as main arm in maritime school of strategy, 64; as decisive arm against French, 66, 92, 158; in Seven Years War, 77; George III's neglect of, 78; Barham's work for, 85, 93; Napoleon checked by, 85, 86, 95; Pitt (the Younger) and, 85-86; strength of, until 1840, 99; and Palmerston, 152, 154; becomes antiquated by 1870s, 196; at end of nineteenth century, 200; Bismarck's policies lead to regeneration of, 221-22; and German Navy Laws of 1898 and 1900, 224, 225, 226, 261-63; at time of Vene-

zuela boundary dispute, 229; esti- and strengths in 1898, 1902, 1905, mates 1939, 1959, 234 n., 250 n., 254 n., 319 n., 320 n., 354 n.; at three-power standard after 1900, 254; under Sir John Fisher, 276; after War I, 305; as factor in British power and influence, 158, 373-74; 386-87; of U.S.A., after 1906, 273; Dominions' contributions to, 274-75

Neale, Lieut.-Colonel, on Kagosima, 185

Neale, Sir John, 'The Fame of Sir Edward Stafford', 34 n.

Nehru, Jawaharlal, Pandit, 210, 346

Nelson, Horatio, 1st Viscount, Admiral, 82, 92, 93, 331

Netherlands: Settlement (Palmerston), 118-19; in War II, 339

Neutrality Acts, lend-lease and, 328

Neutrality guarantees (Belgium, Switzerland), 118

New Amsterdam (later New York), 59

New Brunswick, 147; *see* Maine

New Deal (F. D. Roosevelt), 328-29

New England, 48-49, 58, 59

New Granada, 139

New Guinea, Bismarck and, 221

New Hebrides, in Entente Cordiale, 256

New South Wales, 147, 148

New Statesman qu., 315

New York Herald qu., 165

New Zealand, 148; responsible government, 1852, 172; as new dominion, 1907, 274; naval contribution, 274; opposes appeasement, 324-25; in and after War II, 332, 345-46

Newcastle, Thomas Pelham, 1st Duke of, 80

Newfoundland: England gains (with Nova Scotia) by Treaty of Utrecht, 67; in Entente Cordiale, 256

Newton, Thomas Wodehouse Legh, 2nd Lord, *Lord Lansdowne: A Biography*, 269 n.

Nicaragua, 139

Nice, France acquires, 130, 177

Nicholas I, Tsar, 120, 173

Nicholas II, Tsar, 257, 268

Nicholas, H. G., *What Roosevelt Thought*, 337 n.

417   CC

Index

cc*

Index

Index

Index

Index

Index